WHO'S WHO
IN GOLF

WHO'S WHO IN GOLF

AN A-Z GUIDE TO THE LEADING PROFESSIONAL GOLFERS

RAB MACWILLIAM

hamlyn

First published in Great Britain in 2001 by
Hamlyn, a division of Octopus Publishing Group Ltd
2–4 Heron Quays, London E14 4JP

ISBN 0 600 60397 0

A CIP catalogue record for this book is available
from the British Library

Printed and bound in Finland

10 9 8 7 6 5 4 3 2 1

contents

INTRODUCTION   6

A–Z of Golfers   10

Appendices: 264
   I CUPS   266
   II MAJORS   268
   III USPGA MEN'S TOUR   279
   IV EUROPEAN MEN'S TOUR 285
   V MISC MEN'S TOUR   289
   VI LADIES TOURS   290
   VII SENIORS TOURS   294

BIBLIOGRAPHY   298
INTERNET GOLF   300

ACKNOWLEDGEMENTS   301

Introduction

The unpredictability of professional golf is one of its greatest attractions. Although over the course of a season the best golfers invariably rise to the top of the money lists, individual tournaments can spring real surprises. Few could have predicted that the unknown Brian Watts would come off the Japanese Tour to reach a play-off against Mark O'Meara in the 1998 British Open, that 41-year-old journeyman Andrew Oldcorn would win the prestigious Volvo PGA in 2001, or that rookie Garrett Willis would triumph at the 2001 Tucson Open on his first event on the US Tour ('Ain't this a great country?', enthused a delighted and significantly wealthier Willis). However, these things happen and will continue to occur in a game where, on a good day and with the right combination of skill, luck and determination, the minnows can live with the giants.

Much has been written on the stellar names of international golf – Woods, Mickelson, Sorenstam, Montgomerie, Westwood et al – but there is not much information so easily available on the lesser lights of the sport. These are those players who possess the talent, consistency and temperament to succeed but who have not quite made it to the top of the golfing ladder. There are also those who have had their moments of glory but who continue to play the circuits, basking in their victories of yesteryear yet desperately striv-

ing for a return to the winner's circle. There are the journeymen who will, in all probability, never win a tournament but who manage, particularly on the US Tour, to make a more than decent living out of the game. There are the meteors who blaze briefly but who burn away to face a bleak future of qualifying school, sponsor invitations and missed cuts. And there are the brash, younger golfers constantly breaking through who are the stars of the future. The field at any given tournament is a mixture of the dominant and the wannabe, the confident and the cowed, and the arrogant and those grateful simply to be playing. Although many of these players rarely come under the continuing scrutiny of the viewer, they have all had differing backgrounds, career paths, successes and failures.

The purpose of this book, then, is to give biographical information on 600 of the world's top players, including not only the superstars but also the ex-champions, journeymen, rookies and nearly-men (and women). I do not claim that these players are definitively the best in the world. The statistical manipulations of the world rankings provides this information. However, the reader can find in the following pages a cross-section of outstanding golfers from Tours across the world who appear regularly on television and at tournaments.

The list has been selected on a somewhat arbitrary basis, but seems to me to be a sensible one. I picked the top-150 golfers from both the European Tour and the USPGA Tour, based on the 2000 money lists. I also included the players who graduated from the lesser tours – the Buy.Com Tour in the USA and the Challenge Tour in Europe – to the main tours, and those who qualified for a tour card via Qualifying School. For the women, I picked the top 90 on the 2000 LPGA Money List and the top-20 on the European Tour. As for the Seniors, the 2000 money lists again provided the criteria with the leading 75 on the US Senior Tour and the top-25 on the European Senior Tour. I also added the leading money winners from the Australasian, Japanese, South African and Asian Tours. In some cases, there are famous, still relatively active players well outside the money lists – eg Nancy Lopez and Arnold Palmer – whose exclusion would appear odd and even disrespectful, or tried-and-tested players with exemptions who played below their best or who were injured in 2000, eg Costantino Rocca and Scott Simpson. No doubt there will be objections to this selection, and accusations of US/European bias, but these attract more television coverage and are by some distance the largest tours (with the exception of Japan, which is shown infrequently, if at all, in the West).

So far as the individual entries are concerned, I have given the name, date and place of birth, country of nationality, main Tour played, tournaments won, Major victories or highest finish in Majors, international team competitions, Tour ranking in 2000, and a brief profile of the player concerned. I have described the players' achievements in their careers, as well as a section on their performances in the year 2000. If a golfer has been particularly notable or finished in the top-3 of a competition in the 2001 season, I have also included this information but, due to the constraints of book production and distribution, my cut-off date is end-May 2001.

A possible source of confusion, particularly on the USPGA Tour, is that the names of some of the tournaments have changed over the years, largely to suit the demands of sponsors. For instance, although the Kemper Open and the Bob Hope Chrysler Classic have more or less always been the Kemper Open and the Bob Hope Chrysler Classic, the 2000 Compaq Classic of New Orleans has been called variously the Entergy Classic, Freeport-McDermott Classic, Freeport-McMoran Classic and the USF&G Classic. And that was only in the 1990s. Likewise, the Buick Classic rejoiced under the title of Manufacturers Hanover Westchester Classic throughout the 1980s. I have generally followed the convention that

the book lists the tournament name in the year of the victory rather than what it may now be called, and this applies to all the other Tours. To mitigate any misunderstanding, in Appendix II I list the US Tour tournaments in 2000 alongside their previous names over the past 20 years.

As sure as the average hacker's slight fade inexorably turns into a wild slice, the first tournament to be played after this book's publication will be won by someone who does not feature in these pages. Although historical information is a useful aid to predictability, it is unfortunately far from 100 per cent accurate and there will almost certainly be players who will emerge from relative obscurity to international attention before they make an appearance in what I hope will be the next edition of this book. Conversely, there is equally little doubt that, by the end of the coming season, several of the golfers herein will have disappeared from the public gaze with the depressing finality of a misguided tee shot plopping into the nearest lake. Such is the reality of modern competitive golf.

Nevertheless, I believe that the comprehensiveness of this volume (and the many hours of research when I could have been out on the golf course) will furnish spectators with sufficient background information to discover more about the golfers they are viewing and provide them with a richer context in which to enjoy this most fascinating and hypnotically watchable sport.

ABOUT THE TOURS

USPGA TOUR

The PGA Tour was formally established in 1968 when the Tournament Players Division of the PGA split from the PGA of America. The Ben Hogan Tour, a developmental circuit, was formed in 1990 and it became the Nike Tour in 1994. In 2000 it was re-christened the Buy.Com Tour.

There are 34 classes of 'exemption' (the right to play on Tour for a given period) arranged in order of priority, i.e. those players in the top classes are guaranteed the opportunity to play in all tournaments while those in the lower categories generally have to wait until places become available. Class 1 includes winners of such events as the USPGA Championship and the US Open (who receive a five-year exemption) and the other classes include PGA Tour winners, sponsor exemptions (up to eight places in a field), past champions, the top-125 on the Money List, the top-15 on the Buy.Com Tour and the top qualifiers from Qualifying School (35 in 2000). The last three classes receive a one-year exemption. The size of the field on the average PGA tournament is 156, although this can vary upward (AT&T Pebble Beach National Pro-Am) or downward (Bay Hill Invitational) and, depending on the event's popularity and money on offer, lesser-ranked players can squeeze into the field. The 2001 season contains 46 official tournaments (excluding the four World Golf Championships), began with the Mercedes Championship and ends with the Tour Championship (a limited entry field for the top ranked players).

Qualifying ('Q') School is held each year at the end of November at La Quinta, California. This is a nerve-racking tournament where the leading 35 (plus ties) receive their Tour cards for the following season. There are 12 1st stage and six 2nd stage regional qualifiers before Qualifying School proper, where the hopeful golfers play six rounds without a cut. The lucky winning group enter the PGA Tour while the next 51 become fully exempt for the next season's Buy.Com Tour.

USPGA SENIORS TOUR

This was established in 1980 for golfers of 50 years and over (there is also the Georgia-Pacific Super Seniors Tour for golfers of 60 and over, which is played as a part of many Senior Tour events). The Tour has been described as one of the most commercially successful events initiated over the last 20 years in the world, as older players such as Hale Irwin, Jack Nicklaus, Arnold Palmer, Tom Watson and Lee Trevino have joined and added their charisma and popularity to the Tour. The exemption categories include the top-31 from the previous year's Money List, the top-31 on the all-time career Money List and the leading eight qualifiers from Qualifying School. The field is also made up from sponsors' invitations and Monday pre-qualifiers. A tournament normally lasts for three rounds, with the exception of the four Majors which are four rounds in length. The 2001 season comprises 39 official events, which began with the MasterCard Championship and ends with the Senior Tour Championship.

PGA EUROPEAN TOUR

The European Tour officially began in 1971 and the junior tour – the Satellite Tour – was formed in 1986. The latter Tour's name was changed in 1990 to the Challenge Tour. There are 13 exemption categories, ranging from the Open winner (ten year exemption) through to other Major and top European tournament winners and also including the top-115 and top-15 on the Order of Merit and Challenge Tour respectively (one year exemption). After several pre-qualifying rounds the Qualifying School is held at San Roque, Spain in late November where 168 contest the tournament in a six-round struggle (unlike the US Qualifying School, there is a cut after round four). In 2000, the top-35 received one year's exemption for the following season. Most fields on the European Tour are, like the US, 156 strong. The 45 (excluding World Golf Championship) events in 2001 began with the Johnnie Walker Classic and ends with the Volvo Masters.

EUROPEAN SENIORS TOUR

This began formally in 1992 and again there are various classes of exemption, the highest being the top-25 on the previous year's Order of Merit. The top-10 at Qualifying School gain one year's exemption for the following season. The 2001 season contains 23 tournaments, beginning with the Royal Westmoreland Barbados Open and ending with the Senior Tour Championship.

US LADIES TOUR
Founded in 1950, the LPGA has grown in stature and now offers prize money of around $36 million per season. The exemption priorities begin with the top-90 on the Money List and include the Hall of Famers, career winnings and sponsor invitations. The 2000 Qualifying School was held at Daytona Beach and 14 qualified with exempt status. The top-3 in the junior Tour, the SBC Futures, also qualified for the 2001 Tour. The YourLife Vitamins LPGA Classic kicked off the 2001 season of 37 official events, and the season ends with the LPGA Tour Championship

EUROPEAN LADIES TOUR
Formed in 1979, the European Ladies Tour is now formally known as the Evian Tour. There are 13 categories of exemption, starting with the top-80 on the previous year's Money List and also including tournament winners, career money winners, invitations etc, as well as the top-40 qualifiers from Qualifying School at Aroeira Golf Club in Portugal. The 2001 season comprises of 16 events, starting with the ANZ Ladies Masters and ending with the Ladies World Cup.

Rab MacWilliam

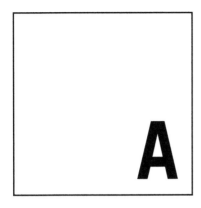

Tommy Aaron

Born 22 February 1937
Place of Birth Gainesville, Georgia, USA
Year turned Professional 1960
Tour Ranking 79th

TOUR VICTORIES
SENIOR TOUR: 1
1992 Kaanapali Classic

The greatest moment in Tommy Aaron's career was undoubtedly winning the 1973 Masters, at Augusta National, 13 years after turning professional. Five years earlier, at the very same tournament, he mistakenly recorded an incorrect score on Roberto De Vicenzo's card. Consequently, the Argentinian signed for a score of 71 when he actually shot 70. The Rules of Golf state that the higher score stands and De Vicenzo missed a place in the sudden-death play-off by one shot. Aaron's only win to date on the US Senior Tour came in 1992 when he beat Dave Stockton on the last hole in the Kaanapali Classic.
2000 SEASON. Aaron played once again in the Masters and became the oldest player in history to make the cut. He made four top-20s on the Senior Tour; his best finish, T11, coming in the SBC Senior Open. He also finished 12th in the over-60 Super Seniors Money List.

Jim Ahern
US Seniors Tour

Born 26 February 1949
Place of Birth Duluth, Minnesota, USA
Year turned Professional 1972
Tour Ranking 35th

TOUR VICTORIES
SENIOR TOUR: 1
1999 AT&T Air Canada Senior Open

Ahern played on the USPGA Tour for four years in the 1970s, finishing no higher than T9. He joined the US Seniors Tour in 1999 and won a tournament as a Monday qualifier – the AT&T Air Canada Senior Open – in his rookie year, beating Hale Irwin in a play-off.
2000 SEASON. Although Ahern was forced to miss a month with a back injury, he had his best finish – 2 – at the Comfort Classic. He is a long hitter and is regularly in the top-10 of the driving distance statistics.
2001 STOP PRESS. Ahern finished second at the Farmer's Charity Classic.

Kristi Albers
US Ladies Tour

Born 7 December 1963
Place of Birth El Paso, Texas, USA
Year turned Professional 1986
Tour Ranking 38th

TOUR VICTORIES
US: 1
1993 Sprint Classic

Albers joined the LPGA Tour after a prominent amateur career. Her best year was in 1993 when she won her only title – the Sprint Classic – and produced seven other top-20 placings.
2000 SEASON. She was runner-up in the Michelob Light Classic and had eight finishes in the top-20.

Jim Albus
US Seniors Tour

Born 18 June 1940
Place of Birth Staten Island, New York, USA
Year turned Professional 1968
Tour Ranking 43rd

MAJORS VICTORIES
SENIOR PLAYERS CHAMPIONSHIP 1991

TOUR VICTORIES
SENIOR TOUR: 5
- **1993** GTE Suncoast Classic
- **1994** Bank of Boston Senior Classic, Vantage at the Dominion
- **1995** Dominion Seniors
- **1998** GTE Classic

Albus is one of the relatively few Senior Tour players who did not compete previously on any of the main regular PGA Tours. A long-time Long Island club professional in New York, he qualified for the Senior Tour in 1991 and immediately shocked the golf world by claiming the prestigious and lucrative Senior Tour Players Championship in only his sixth start on Tour. He has since won five further events, his last victory coming at the GTE Classic in 1998.

2000 SEASON. Albus passed the $5 million mark in Tour career earnings and posted four top-10s, his highest being T5 at the State Farm Senior Classic.

Amy Alcott
US Ladies Tour

Born 22 February 1956
Place of Birth Kansas City, Missouri, USA
Year turned Professional 1974
Tour Ranking 149th

MAJORS VICTORIES
US OPEN 1980
DINAH SHORE 1983, 1988, 1991
PETER JACKSON CLASSIC (NOW DINAH SHORE) 1979

TOUR VICTORIES
US: 24
- **1975** Orange Blossom Classic
- **1976** Colgate Far East Open, LPGA Classic
- **1977** Houston Classic
- **1978** American Defender Classic
- **1979** Elizabeth Arden Classic, Mizuno Japanese Classic, United Virginia Bank Classic
- **1980** American Defender Classic, Inamori Classic, Mayflower Classic
- **1981** Bent Tree Ladies Classic, Lady Michelob
- **1982** Kemper Open
- **1984** Lady Keystone Open, Portland Ping Championship, San Jose Classic, United Virginia Bank Classic
- **1985** Circle K Tucson Open, Moss Creek Women's Invitational, Nestlé World Championship of Women's Golf
- **1986** LPGA National Pro-Am, Mazda Hall of Fame Championship
- **1989** Boston Five Classic

With 29 victories to her name, Alcott was one of the leading players on the US Ladies Tour during the 1970s and 1980s. She won her very first tournament in 1975 – the Orange Blossom Classic – on only her third start on Tour and by 1980 had won a further 12 events, including two Major Championships – the US Open and the Dinah Shore (then called the Peter Jackson Classic). At the latter tournament she started her now traditional way of celebrating victory in the event by diving into a lake beside the 18th green. She repeated the feat – and the celebration – in 1988 and 1991. She was *Golf Magazine's* Player of the Year in 1980, and in 1983 she passed the $1 million mark in career earnings. In 1984 she won four tournaments in one season for the third time. She was elected to the World Golf Hall of Fame in 1999.

2000 SEASON. Alcott's best finish was T17 at the Giant Eagle Classic.

Helen Alfredsson
US Ladies Tour

Born 9 April 1965
Place of Birth Gothenburg, Sweden
Year turned Professional 1989
Tour Ranking 72nd

MAJORS VICTORIES
DINAH SHORE 1993

TOUR VICTORIES
US: 3
1994 Ping Welch's Championship
1998 The Office Depot, Welch's Circle K Championship
EUROPEAN: 9
1990 Women's British Open
1991 Hennessy Cup, Trophee Coconut Skol
1992 Hennessy Cup, IBM Open
1994 Evian Masters
1996 Hennessy Cup
1997 McDonald's WPGA Championship of Europe
1998 Evian Masters
AUSTRALASIAN: 1
1991 Queensland Open
OTHER: 2
1992 Itoki Classic
1997 Itoen Tournament

SOLHEIM CUP 1990, 1992, 1994, 1996, 1998, 2000

A tall Swede with a powerful, attacking swing, Alfredsson was six times Swedish Amateur Champion in the 1980s before joining the European Tour in 1989, after a spell as a fashion model in Paris. She was Rookie of the Year that season and won her first title – the British Open – in 1990, finishing top of the Order of Merit. She joined the US Tour in 1992 and was Rookie of the Year again. The following year she won the Nabisco Dinah Shore, and in 1994 she won the Ping Welch's Championship in the US and the Evian Masters in Europe. She was sidelined with a hamstring injury in 1995, but came back to win twice in America in 1998 and also pick up three further European titles. She ended 1998 top of the European Order of Merit, having been second on five separate occasions. She has played in every Solheim Cup to date.

2000 SEASON. Her best US finish was T7 at the Giant Eagle LPGA Classic.

Stephen Allan
European Tour

Born 18 October 1973
Place of Birth Melbourne, Australia
Year turned Professional 1996
Tour Ranking 61st

BEST FINISH IN MAJORS
Tied 42nd US OPEN 1999

TOUR VICTORIES
EUROPEAN: 1
1998 German Open

A llan was born in Australia to Scottish immigrant parents. He joined the European Tour in 1997 immediately after turning pro and in his first year, he finished second in the Dubai Desert Classic behind Jose Maria Olázàbal and then won the German Open in Berlin. He finished 16th in the Order of Merit. In 1999 he made the cut in both The Open and the US Open.

2000 SEASON. Allan finished T4 at the Loch Lomond, his highest finish of the season. At the 2000 USPGA Qualifying School, he won the tournament and received his Tour card for season 2001.

Fulton Allem
US Tour

Born 15 September 1957
Place of Birth Kroonstad, South Africa
Year turned Professional 1976
Tour Ranking 187th

BEST FINISH IN MAJORS
Tied 31st USPGA 1993

TOUR VICTORIES
US: 3
  1991 Independent Insurance Agent Open
  1993 NEC World Series of Golf,
      Southwestern Bell Colonial
SOUTH AFRICA: 14
  1985 Palaborwa Classic, Sun City Million
      Dollar Challenge
  1986 Minolta Match Play Championship,
      Palaborwa Classic,
      South African PGA Championship
  1987 Palaborwa Classic,
      South African PGA Championship
  1988 Palaborwa Classic,
      Sun City Million Dollar Challenge
  1989 Minolta Match Play Championship
  1990 Goodyear Classic,
      Lexington PGA Championship,
      Twee Zongezellen Masters
  1991 ICL International

DUNHILL CUP 1993
PRESIDENTS CUP 1994

Courtesy of his victory in the prestigious NEC World Series of Golf in 1993, which earned him a cool $360,000, the stockily-built Allem has a valuable exempt status on the US Tour until 2003. Holder of no less than 14 South African titles, he has played regularly on Tour since 1988, his best season coming in 1993 when he also won the Southwestern Bell Colonial and finished the season 9th on the Money List. Since that year he has not won another tournament and his best finish was T4 at the 1996 Doral-Ryder Open, although he has recently showed signs of regaining his form, finishing T11 in the Honda Classic in 2001. Like many of his compatriots, Allem is often near the top of the sand save statistics rankings.

2000 SEASON. Allem made only one top-25 finish, T21 at the Buick Invitational.

Robert Allenby
US Tour

Born 12 July 1971
Place of Birth Melbourne, Australia
Year turned Professional 1991
Tour Ranking 16th

BEST FINISH IN MAJORS
Tied 10th BRITISH OPEN 1997

TOUR VICTORIES
US: 3
  2000 Advil Western Open,
      Shell Houston Open
  2001 Nissan Open
EUROPEAN: 4
  1994 Honda Open
  1996 Alamo English Open, One2One
      British Masters, Peugeot Open
AUSTRALASIAN: 6
  1992 Johnnie Walker Classic, Perak Masters
  1993 Optus Players Championship
  1994 Heineken Australian Open
  1995 Heineken Classic
  2000 Australian PGA Championship

DUNHILL CUP 1993
PRESIDENTS CUP 1994, 1996, 2000
WORLD CUP 1993, 1995

Allenby, whose parents emigrated to Australia from Leeds, was the great young hope of Australian golf. As a 19-year-old amateur he finished second in the Australian Open. In 1992, his first year on Tour, he won the Johnnie Walker Classic and became the first rookie to top the Australasian Order of Merit. A fine driver of the ball and a fantastic putter, Allenby played on the European Tour winning three tournaments in 1996 and finished 3rd on the Volvo Order of Merit. He came through Qualifying School in 1998 to join the USPGA Tour.

2000 SEASON. His first Tour victory came at the Houston Open, beating Craig Stadler with a 10-foot putt on the fourth play-off hole, and he tied with Rocco Mediate for second place, one shot behind Tom Lehman, in the Phoenix Open. He claimed his second Tour victory at the Advil Western Open when he beat Nick Price on the first play-off hole. Interestingly, his four European PGA victories were also in sudden-death play-offs. He also claimed three other top-10 places and rounded off a highly successful season by winning the Australian PGA on home soil.

2001 STOP PRESS. Allenby won again on the US Tour, inevitably after yet another play-off. He hit a superb 3-wood to within five feet of the pin, which set up a birdie on the first extra hole of the Nissan Open, in California.

Stephen Ames
US Tour

Born 28 April 1964
Place of Birth San Fernando, Trinidad
Year turned Professional 1987
Tour Ranking 63rd

BEST FINISH IN MAJORS
Tied 5th **BRITISH OPEN 1997**

TOUR VICTORIES
EUROPEAN: 2
1994 Open V33
1996 Benson & Hedges International Open

OTHER: 1
1989 Trinidad & Tobago Open

The son of an English father and a Portugese mother, Ames was born in Trinidad and is the only Trinidad and Tobago player on the USPGA Tour. Recurring visa problems throughout the 1990s meant that he missed a number of tournaments in the USA, so between 1993 and 1997 he played most of his golf on the European Tour, where he has won twice. His second victory – the Benson & Hedges International Open at the Oxfordshire – was notable for the way in which he held his game together in appalling weather. Regarded as one of the more affable players on Tour, Ames qualified for the US Tour in 1997 and was Rookie of the Year in the 1998 season, when he posted three top-10 finishes. He now lives in Calgary and is hoping to secure Canadian citizenship.

2000 SEASON. Ames' best finish was T4 at the Compaq Classic. He was tied third after the fourth round at the Bob Hope Classic but had to withdraw due to a shoulder injury.

Danielle Ammaccapane
US Ladies Tour

Born 27 November 1965
Place of Birth Babylon, New York, USA
Year turned Professional 1987
Tour Ranking 127th

TOUR VICTORIES
US: 7
1991 Standard Register Ping
1992 Centel Classic, Edina Realty Classic, Lady Keystone Open
1997 Edina Realty Classic
1998 Safeway LPGA Golf Championship, Titleholders Championship

SOLHEIM CUP 1994, 1998

The 1985 Public Links Champion, Ammaccapane joined the LPGA Tour in 1987. She has won seven tournaments, the last two being in 1998 when she beat her sister Dina and Emilee Klein by three strokes at the Safeway Golf Championship and then when she defeated Michelle Estill by one shot at the Titleholders. She represented the US in the 1986 Curtis Cup and the 1992 Solheim Cup.

2000 SEASON. She played a limited number of tournaments as she gave birth to her first child in February.

Dina Ammaccapane
US Ladies Tour

Born 21 July 1968
Place of Birth Bayside, New York, USA
Year turned Professional 1990
Tour Ranking 49th

Danielle's younger sister, Dina played on both the European and Asian Tours before qualifying for the LPGA Tour in 1992. To date, she is still awaiting her first victory.

2000 SEASON. Dina achieved her highest-ever finish when she tied for second place at the State Farm Rail Classic. She also had two other top-10s to end the season in the top-50 on the Money List.

Jeremy Anderson
US Tour

Born 11 May 1978
Place of Birth Louisville, Kentucky, USA
Year turned Professional 2000
Tour Ranking Tied 11th (Qualifying School)

Without any Buy.Com experience and with only one previous US Tour tournament under his belt, the 23-year-old Anderson qualified for his US Tour card at his first attempt with a T11 finish. However, he missed the cut in ten of the first 13 events he entered during the 2001 season.

Billy Andrade
US Tour

Born 25 January 1964
Place of Birth Bristol, Rhode Island, USA
Year turned Professional 1987
Tour Ranking 45th

BEST FINISH IN MAJORS
Tied 12th USPGA 1992

TOUR VICTORIES
US: 4
   1991 Buick Classic, Kemper Open
   1998 Canadian Open
   2000 Invensys Classic of Las Vegas

Known as 'Chachi' on the US Tour because of his resemblance to the TV series *Happy Days* character, Andrade was the first golfer in 12 years to win successive tournaments on the US Tour. In 1991 he beat Jeff Sluman in a play-off to secure the Kemper Open and the next week he defeated Brad Bryant by one stroke to capture the Buick Classic. In 1998 he won his third tournament, scoring four rounds in the 60s to beat Bob Friend by one stroke and lift the Canadian Open title.

With his old friend Brad Faxon, he founded the Billy Andrade/Brad Faxon Charities for Children organization in 1991. He was once famously turned down by Tiger Woods when he asked him to autograph a golf ball for charity.

2000 SEASON. Andrade finished at 28 under par – one shot clear of Phil Mickelson – to win the Invensys Classic of Las Vegas and moved from a disappointing 159th to 43rd in the Money List. He finished the season in 45th place on the Money List.

2001 STOP PRESS. Andrade secured fourth place in the Sony Open early in the season.

Donna Andrews
_____ US Ladies Tour

Born 12 April 1967
Place of Birth Lynchburg, Virginia, USA
Year turned Professional 1990
Tour Ranking 69th

MAJORS VICTORIES
DINAH SHORE 1994

TOUR VICTORIES
US: 5
1993 Ping-Cellular One LPGA
1994 Ping Welch's Championship,
ShopRite Classic,
Welch's Circle K Championship
1998 Long Drugs Challenge

SOLHEIM CUP 1994, 1998

A keen horsewoman, Andrews has won five LPGA Tour titles, her last, the Longs Drug Challenge, in 1998. She also had four runner-up spots that year.

2000 SEASON. Her top finish was T11 at the New Albany Golf Classic.

Isao Aoki
_____ US Seniors Tour

Born 31 August 1942
Place of Birth Chiba, Japan
Year turned Professional 1964
Tour Ranking 51st

TOUR VICTORIES
SENIOR TOUR: 8
1992 Nationwide Challenge
1994 Bank One Classic, Brickyard Crossing Championship
1995 Bank of Boston Senior Classic
1996 BellSouth Senior Classic, Kroger Senior Classic
1997 Emerald Coast Classic
1998 BellSouth Senior Classic

Six foot tall, Aoki was nicknamed 'Tower', after Tokyo Tower, by the Japanese press. He is one of Japan's finest-ever golfers, even though his ungainly-looking swing and his wristy and unorthodox putting stroke, holding his hands very low at address and pushing the toe of the putter into the air, would perhaps suggest otherwise. He won his only tournament on the USPGA Tour in dramatic fashion by holing a chip shot on the last hole of the 1983 Hawaiian Open and remains the only Japanese golfer to win a USPGA Tour title. He is also remembered for his battle with, but ultimate defeat by, Jack Nicklaus in the 1980 US Open at Baltusrol.

Aoki joined the US Senior Tour in 1992 and won the Nationwide Challenge in his rookie year, becoming the first Japanese player to win on both the PGA and Senior Tours. Since then he has collected seven other titles, his last being the BellSouth Senior Classic in 1998 when he shot 18 under par. He had back problems in 1999 and finished outside the top-30. He has accumulated nearly 70 victories worldwide.

2000 SEASON. Aoki made a limited number of appearances, his best effort coming at the State Farm Classic when he lost a sudden-death play-off at the second hole to Leonard Thompson. Well placed heading into the last round of the US Seniors Open, he shot a closing 83 to slip well down the leaderboard.

2001 STOP PRESS. Aoki finished in second place at the Royal Caribbean Classic, in Florida, one point behind multiple-winner Larry Nelson in the modified stableford event.

Stuart Appleby

US Tour

Born 1 May 1971
Place of Birth Cohuna, Australia
Year turned Professional 1992
Tour Ranking 24th

BEST FINISH IN MAJORS

Tied 4th **USPGA 2000**

TOUR VICTORIES

US: 3

1997 Honda Classic
1998 Kemper Open
1999 Shell Houston Open

AUSTRALASIAN: 1

1998 Coolum Classic

DUNHILL CUP 1997, 1998, 1999
PRESIDENTS CUP 1998, 2000

An Ex-Australian Rules footballer Appleby played on the Australasian Tour before joining the US Tour in 1997. In his rookie year on Tour he became the first Qualifying School graduate to earn more than $1 million in his first season, claiming the Honda Classic title and five top-10 finishes. His wife, Renay, was tragically killed in a road accident outside Waterloo Station in London in 1998, but he came back from this tragedy to win the Shell Houston Open the following year, shooting 9 under par to beat Hal Sutton and John Cook by one stroke. In doing so, he became the seventh foreign-born player to win on the US Tour in 1999. Although not always the most accurate of drivers, he is very long off the tee and has a neat and compact golf swing.

2000 SEASON. His best finishes were second at the Sony Open and third at the International. He also finished T4 at the USPGA Championship at Valhalla behind Tiger Woods, Bob May and Denmark's Thomas Björn. Although he missed the cut at both the Masters and the US Open, he finished T11 in The Open Championship at St Andrews.

George Archer

US Seniors Tour

Born 1 October 1939
Place of Birth San Francisco, California, USA
Year turned Professional 1964
Tour Ranking 29th

TOUR VICTORIES

SENIOR TOUR: 19

1989 Gatlin Brothers Southwest Classic
1990 Gold Rush, GTE Northwest Classic, MONY Senior Tournament of Champions, Northville Long Island Classic
1991 GTE Northwest Classic, Northville Long Island Classic, Raley's Senior Gold Rush
1992 Bruno's Memorial Classic, Murata Reunion Pro-Am, Northville Long Island Classic
1993 Ameritech Senior Open, First of America Classic, Kaanapali Classic, Raley's Senior Gold Rush
1995 Cadillac NFL Golf Classic, Toshiba Senior Classic
1998 First of America Classic
2000 MasterCard Championship

At 6 feet 6 inches the tallest player on the US Senior Tour, Archer joined the Seniors in 1989 after a USPGA Tour career crowned by 12 victories including the 1969 Masters, when he beat Billy Caspar by one stroke. 14 days after his 50th birthday he won his first tournament – the Gatlin Brothers Southwest Classic – and by 1999 he had collected a further 17 wins. He has earned over $7 million in his Seniors career. He is an excellent, if ungainly, putter with an unusual grip well down the shaft, and he held the PGA Tour record for the lowest number of putts in a tournament, 94, at the 1980 Heritage Classic.

2000 SEASON. Archer beat Trevino, Quigley, Irwin and Marsh in the MasterCard Championship to record his first win since 1998 with a 3 under par 69 in the final round. He also had four other top-10 places.

Tommy Armour III

US Tour

Born 8 October 1959
Place of Birth Denver, Colorado, USA
Year turned Professional 1981
Tour Ranking 122nd

BEST FINISH IN MAJORS
Tied 24th USPGA 1989

TOUR VICTORIES
US: 1
  1990 Phoenix Open
OTHER: 1
  1993 Mexican Open

Grandson of the famed three-times Major winner, Armour III was the first player to win consecutive tournaments on the Nike Tour in 1994. He gained his only tournament win on the main Tour in 1990, collecting the Phoenix Open, in Arizona, by a margin of five strokes over Jim Thorpe, and in 1999 he reached the play-off at the Tucson Open, only to lose to Gabriel Hjerstedt by two strokes.

2000 SEASON. His best finish was T5 at the Nissan Open in California, but he also missed the cut in more than half the tournaments he entered and was in danger of losing his Tour card.

Woody Austin

US Tour

Born 27 January 1964
Place of Birth Tampa, Florida, USA
Year turned Professional 1986
Tour Ranking 100th

BEST FINISH IN MAJORS
Tied 23rd US OPEN 1995
Tied 23rd USPGA 1996

TOUR VICTORIES
US: 1
  1995 Buick Open

Ex-bank clerk Austin joined the US Tour as winner of the 1994 Qualifying Tournament. By the end of 1995 he had won the Buick Open in a play-off and had played in the Tour Championship where he finished T4. Although rookie David Duval finished the 1995 season higher on the Money List, Austin was voted Rookie of the Year by virtue of having won a tournament and rose to 24th on the Money List. Three years after his triumphant opening season, however, Austin's form slipped and he found himself back on the Nike Tour, but he rejoined the main tour the following year.

2000 SEASON Austin squeezed back into the top-100 thanks to a T4 at the Buick Open and two other top-10 finishes.

Paul Azinger

US Tour

Born 6 January 1960
Place of Birth Holyoke, Maine, USA
Year turned Professional 1981
Tour Ranking 27th

MAJORS VICTORIES
  USPGA 1993

TOUR VICTORIES
US: 11
  1987 Canon Sammy Davis Jr Greater Hartford Open, Panasonic Las Vegas Invitational, Phoenix Open
  1988 Hertz Bay Hill Classic
  1989 Canon Greater Hartford Open
  1990 MONY Tournament of Champions
  1991 AT&T Pebble Beach National Pro-Am
  1992 TOUR Championship
  1993 Memorial Tournament New England Classic
  2000 Sony Open in Hawaii
EUROPEAN: 2
  1990 BMW International Open
  1992 BMW International Open

RYDER CUP 1989, 1991, 1993
PRESIDENTS CUP 1994, 2000
WORLD CUP 1989

One of the world's most dominant players during the late 1980s and early 1990s, the rangy Azinger ('Zinger') won ten titles between 1987 and 1993. In 1987, when he was voted Player of the Year, he finished second behind Nick Faldo in The Open Championship at Muirfield, in Scotland, losing by just one shot when his 30-foot par putt slipped by the hole on the final green. In 1993 he won his first, and to date, only Major – the USPGA – beating Greg Norman in a play-off at Inverness CC. That season he also won the Memorial Tournament by one shot, holing out from a bunker at the last hole to beat Corey Pavin, and the New England Classic.

Then his world fell apart when he was diagnosed as having Hodgkin's Disease, a form of cancer of the lymph glands. However, he displayed strength of character and iron determination to conquer the disease and was back playing again in 1995. He is a committed and competitive golfer, particularly renowned for his accurate short game and putting touch.

2000 SEASON. In 2000 Azinger had his best season since 1993 and was right back to his peak form. He won the Sony Open – his first victory since beating cancer – in emphatic style, going wire to wire and by a margin of seven strokes over Stuart Appleby in the first full event of the year. The popular Azinger's first win for seven years was warmly welcomed by fellow professionals on Tour. He finished the British Open tied for seventh place, and had six other top-10 finishes. He ended the season in 27th place on the Money List, his highest placing since 1993. He also represented the US in their Presidents Cup victory.

2001 STOP PRESS. Always a man for the big occasion, Azinger performed well in the lucrative Players Championship, where he finished seventh, and second in the Jack Nicklaus' Memorial Tournament in Columbus, Ohio.

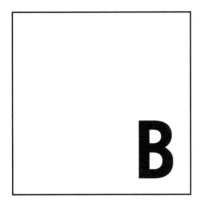

Aaron Baddeley
Australasian Tour

Born 17 March 1981
Place of Birth Lebanon, New Hampshire, USA
Year turned Professional 2000
Tour Ranking 1st

TOUR VICTORIES
AUSTRALASIAN: 3
1999 Australian Open
2000 Australian Open
2001 Greg Norman Holden International

Australian prodigy Baddeley won the 1999 Australian Open as an amateur and won it again in 2000 as a professional. He was the youngest player, at the age of 19, ever to have won the Australasian Order of Merit.

2001 STOP PRESS. Baddeley beat Spain's Sergio Garcia with a birdie putt on the first hole of a play-off to win the Greg Norman Holden International. He also played in the Masters, but failed to make the cut.

Hugh Baiocchi
US Seniors Tour

Born 17 August 1946
Place of Birth Johannesburg, South Africa
Year turned Professional 1971
Tour Ranking 37th

TOUR VICTORIES
SENIOR TOUR: 3
1997 Pittsburgh Senior Classic
1998 Comfort Classic, Kroger Senior Classic

South African Baiocchi played on the European, Asian and South African Tours before qualifying tenth at the 1996 US Seniors Qualifying School for a partial exemption in 1997. In his rookie year he won the Pittsburgh Senior Classic, beating Bob Duval in a play-off, carded 14 top-10s and earned just under $1 million. He won back-to-back tournaments in 1998 and moved into the top-10 on the Money List. Having struggled with his putting, he recently adopted the "cross-handed" method.

2000 SEASON. Baiocchi ended outside the top-31 – in 37th place – for the first time. However, his four top-10 finishes helped him break the $4 million mark in career earnings.

Briny Baird
US Tour

Born 11 May 1972
Place of Birth Miami Beach, Florida, USA
Year turned Professional 1995
Tour Ranking 4th (Buy.Com Tour)

BEST FINISH IN MAJORS
Tied 40th **US OPEN 2001**

Baird joined the US Tour from Qualifying School in 1999 and ended the season in 186th place on the Money List. He played the Buy.Com Tour in 2000, gaining one victory and nine top-10 finishes to claim fourth place and qualify for the 2001 US Tour.

Peter Baker
European Tour

Born 7 October 1967
Place of Birth Wolverhampton, England
Year turned Professional 1986
Tour Ranking 57th

BEST FINISH IN MAJORS
Tied 14th **BRITISH OPEN 1998**

TOUR VICTORIES
EUROPEAN: 3
  1988 Benson & Hedges Open
  1993 Dunhill British Masters,
       Scandinavian Masters

RYDER CUP 1993
DUNHILL CUP 1993
WORLD CUP 1999

A Walker Cup amateur, Baker joined the European Tour in 1986. He won his first tournament two years later, in 1988, by scoring two eagles on the 18th hole at the Benson & Hedges International on the last day to grasp the title from the then reigning Open Champion, Nick Faldo. Despite a scare over the health of his new-born daughter, on the eve of the competition Baker was also a hero for Europe in the 1993 Ryder Cup at The Belfry, winning three of his four matches and, crucially, claiming the scalp of Corey Pavin in the the final day singles with a fantastic putting performance.

2000 SEASON. Baker's best finishes were T3 at the Spanish Open and T5 at the Italian Open.

Craig Barlow
                                        US Tour

Born 23 July 1972
Place of Birth Henderson, Nevada, USA
Year turned Professional 1995
Tour Ranking Tied 21 (Qualifying School)

B arlow played in the 1994 US Open as an amateur and joined the US Tour at Oakmont as a professional in 1998. He went to Qualifying School and gained his card for 1999, when his best career finish of T3 at the Buick Challenge helped him to retain his card for 2000. Barlow worked in Pizza Hut for five years before playing on Tour.

2000 SEASON. Barlow's highest placing was T10 at the Tampa Bay Classic and he returned to Qualifying School securing his place for the 2001 season by finishing in the T21 spot.

Brian Barnes
                                    US Seniors Tour

Born 3 June 1945
Place of Birth Addington, Surrey
Year turned Professional 1964
Tour Ranking 81st

TOUR VICTORIES
SENIOR TOUR: 3
  1995 Senior British Open
  1996 Senior British Open
  1998 AT&T Canada Senior Open

A n ebullient, long-hitting player, Barnes won ten times on the European Tour. Two months after his 50th birthday he won the Senior British Open and repeated his success in 1996. He then joined the US Senior Tour and won his only title, the AT&T Canada Senior Open, in 1998. He played in six Ryder Cups, his most memorable moment coming when he beat the great Jack Nicklaus twice in one day. A recovering alcoholic, Barnes famously once marked his ball on the green with a beer bottle, but he stopped drinking in his late 40s.

2000 SEASON. Health problems plagued his season and his highest finish was T11 at the State Farm Senior Classic.

Tina Barrett
                                    US Ladies Tour

Born 5 June 1966
Place of Birth Baltimore, Maryland, USA
Year turned Professional 1988
Tour Ranking 45th

TOUR VICTORIES
US: 1
  1989 Mitsubishi Motors Ocean State Open

arrett won a tournament – the Mitsubishi Motors Ocean State Open – wire-to-wire in her rookie year of 1989. Since then she has been winless but has claimed the runner-up position on seven occasions. She passed the $2 million career earnings mark in 1999.

2000 SEASON. Barrett was T3 at the Subaru Memorial of Naples and had two other top-10 finishes.

Doug Barron
US Tour

Born 24 July 1969
Place of Birth Memphis, Tennessee, USA
Year turned Professional 1992
Tour Ranking 108th

BEST FINISH IN MAJORS
Made Cut **US OPEN 1999**

arron played on the Nike Tour in 1995 and 1996 and entered the US Tour by finishing third in Qualifying School in 1996. He made the cut 21 times in 31 tournaments in his rookie year and finished 116th on the Money List. He has remained on Tour since but has never cracked the top-100.

2000 SEASON. Barron had his best-ever career finish when he ended T4 at the Air Canada. He also had a T5 at the Greater Hartford Open.

Jean Bartholomew
US Ladies Tour

Born 26 May 1967
Place of Birth Queens, New York, USA
Year turned Professional 1990
Tour Ranking 58th

nown as one of the longer hitters on the LPGA Tour, Bartholomew spent most of the 1990s playing on the European and Japanese Tours. She qualified for the US Tour in 1997, but had to return to Qualifying School in 1998.

2000 SEASON. Her best finish was T2 at the First Union Betsy King Classic. She posted two other top-10s and was 3rd for driving distance.

Ben Bates
US Tour

Born 12 June 1961
Place of Birth Quincy, Florida, USA
Year turned Professional 1984
Tour Ranking 149th

ates played on the Nike Tour from 1990 until 1997 and joined the US Tour in 1998, via Qualifying School. He was subjected to the same fate in 1999, however, and finished the tournament tied for second place. His highest finish on Tour is T8 at the 1998 Buick Challenge.

2000 SEASON. His highest placing was T9 at the Westlin Texas Open.

Cameron Beckman
US Tour

Born 15 February 1970
Place of Birth Minneapolis, Minnesota, USA
Year turned Professional 1993
Tour Ranking 7 (Qualifying School)

eckman has qualified for the US Tour via Qualifying School a record three times in succession. His best finish before 2001 was T13 at the Buick Challenge.

2000 SEASON. Beckman posted six top-25 finishes, his best being two T14s.

2001 STOP PRESS. Beckman had his first ever finish in the top-10 at the Buick Invitational.

Rich Beem
US Tour

Born 24 August 1970
Place of Birth Phoenix, Arizona, USA
Year turned Professional 1994
Tour Ranking 146th

BEST FINISH IN MAJORS
Tied 70th **USPGA 1999**

TOUR VICTORIES
US: 1
    1999 Kemper Open

Unusually for a US Tour player, Rich Beem has no previous experience on any of the other feeder tours. He qualified for the Tour via 1998 Qualifying School, finishing ninth, and had an unexpected, but deserved, victory at the hot and humid Kemper Open in 1999. As *Golf World* magazine headlined 'Who in the World is Rich Beem?'. Prior to his one stroke win over Bill Glasson and Bradley Hughes in the tournament, he had been placed no higher than T45 in 11 tournaments. Beem was nominated for Rookie of the Year that season but was edged out by Carlos Franco. His colourful life story, and in particular his relationship with caddie Steve Duplantis, is entertainingly described in Alan Shipnuck's book *Bud, Sweat and Tees: A Walk on the Wild Side of the PGA Tour.*

2000 SEASON. Beem found it impossible to replicate his successful 1999 season and could only finish 146th on the Money List, his highest placing being T12 at the Bob Hope.

Notah Begay III

                                  US Tour

Born 14 September 1972
Place of Birth Albuquerque, New Mexico, USA
Year turned Professional 1995
Tour Ranking 20th

BEST FINISH IN MAJORS
8th **USPGA 2000**

TOUR VICTORIES
US: 4
    1999 Michelob Championship,
            Reno-Tahoe Open
    2000 FedEx St Jude Classic,
            Greater Hartford Open

PRESIDENTS CUP 2000

Half Navajo and half Pueblo, Begay III is the only native American currently playing on the USPGA Tour. A contemporary and playing partner of Tiger Woods at Stanford University, he became the first player to shoot 59 on the Nike Tour – at the Dominion Open – and finished tenth on the Nike Tour in 1998. In 1999, he won his first tournament by beating Chris Perry and David Toms at the Reno-Tahoe Open where he shot a course record 63. He then beat Tom Byrum at the second hole sudden death play-off at Kingsmill to collect the Michelob Championship trophy. A month later, he finished T15 at the Tour Championship.

2000 SEASON. Despite spending seven days in prison for drunk-driving in March, Begay continued his winning ways with back-to-back victories in June 2000. He picked up the Fedex St Jude Classic by a one-shot margin over Chris DiMarco and Bob May and the following week he won the Greater Hartford Open when his 25-foot birdie putt on the last hole beat Mark Calcavecchia by a stroke. He played in the Presidents Cup partnering Tiger Woods.

Although he has an unorthodox swing and alternates between putting left and right handed, he seems set for more successes on Tour. A folk hero to many native Americans, he works with Indian youth teaching them golf.

Maurice Bembridge
European Senior Tour

Born 21 February 1945
Place of Birth Worksop, England
Year turned Professional 1960
Tour Ranking 14th

TOUR VICTORIES
SENIOR TOUR: 2
 1996 Hippo Jersey Open
 1998 Swedish Seniors

Bembridge collected nine European Tour victories between 1967 and 1979 and has won several other international events, including the Kenya Open three times. He co-holds the record for the lowest score for a round at the Masters – 64 – which he shot in 1974 when he finished T9 at the competition. He joined the Senior Tour in 1995 and has two victories to his name. He is actively involved on the European Senior Tour Committee.

2000 SEASON. He tied with Ross Metherell for second place behind Denis O'Sullivan at the Dan Technology Senior Tournament of Champions, and he finished the season in 14th place on the Order of Merit.

Jorge Berendt
European Tour

Born 19 July 1964
Place of Birth Formosa, Argentina
Year turned Professional 1982
Tour Ranking 31 (Qualifying School)

An ex-caddie in his native Argentina, Berendt joined the European Challenge Tour in 1989 and the full European Tour the following year. He finished 220th on the Tour in 1994 and dropped back into the Challenge, from which he returned to the main Tour in 1999. He has won nine tournaments in South America. Berendt narrowly lost his card at the end of the 2000 season, finishing 118th on the Order of Merit, but qualified for the

2001 European Tour with 31st place in Qualifying School. His best finish on the European Tour was second after a play-off at the 1993 Portuguese Open.

David Berganio
US Tour

Born 14 January 1969
Place of Birth Los Angeles, California, USA
Year turned Professional 1993
Tour Ranking 11th (Buy.Com Tour)

BEST FINISH IN MAJORS
Tied 28th **US OPEN 1999**

A 'muni' golfer who learnt his golf on the public courses of Los Angeles, Berganio won the 1991 and 1993 US Amateur Public Links Championships and turned professional after his second victory in the event. He played the US Tour in 1997, finishing T9 at the Buick Challenge, and the Nike Tour from 1998 to 2000. In 2000 he won one tournament and had three other top-10 finishes, enabling him to take 11th place on the Money List and procure a card for the 2001 US Tour.

2001 STOP PRESS. Berganio was surprise first round leader at the AT&T Pebble Beach Pro-Am, carding a course record 64 on Spyglass. He ended the tournament T9.

Marco Bernardini
European Tour

Born 6 May 1978
Place of Birth Rome, Italy
Year turned Professional 1999
Tour Ranking 15th (Challenge Tour)

Bernardini, whose father Roberto played on the European Senior Tour, won the Italian PGA Championship in 1999. He qualified for the 2001 European Tour by squeezing into 15th place on the 2000 Challenge

Tour. In spite of a bad start to the season, he won the BMW Russian Open and had a ninth place finish at the Rolex Trophy.

John Bickerton

European Tour

Born 23 December 1969
Place of Birth Droitwich, England
Year turned Professional 1991
Tour Ranking 62nd

BEST FINISH IN MAJORS
Missed Cut BRITISH OPEN 1996

Bickerton graduated from the Challenge Tour in 1994 and has remained on the European Tour ever since. After several years languishing in the lower echelons of the Order of Merit, he finished the 1999 season strongly, leaping up to 20th position with two second-place and three fourth-place finishes. Bickerton has been hit twice by lightening on the golf course as an amateur, but thankfully escaped injury both times.

2000 SEASON. His best finish was at the Madeira Open where he finished T5.

2001 STOP PRESS. Bickerton finished in second place to Irishman Des Smyth at the Madeira Island Open. He also tied for tenth place at the French Open and the Deutsche Bank SAP Open.

Thomas Björn

European Tour

Born 18 February 1969
Place of Birth Silkeborg, Denmark
Year turned Professional 1993
Tour Ranking 5th

BEST FINISH IN MAJORS
Tied 2nd BRITISH OPEN 2000

TOUR VICTORIES
EUROPEAN: 6
   1996 Loch Lomond World Invitational
   1998 Heineken Classic,
        Peugeot Open de Espana
   1999 The Sarazen World Open
   2000 BMW International Open
   2001 Dubai Desert Classic
OTHER: 1
   1999 Dunlop Phoenix

RYDER CUP 1997
WORLD CUP 1996, 1997

A tall, elegant golfer, Björn topped the Challenge Tour in 1995, claiming four wins on the circuit. He joined the European Tour the following year and became the first Danish player to win on Tour, claiming victory at the prestigious Loch Lomond World Invitational. That season he was awarded the Rookie of the Year title. Since then he has won three further European Tour events, including the Sarazen World Open, in 1999, where he beat Paolo Quirici and Katsuyoshi Tomori by two strokes. In the same year, he won the Dunlop Phoenix tournament in Japan in a play-off against Sergio Garcia. He is a frequent visitor to the USPGA Tour where his best finish is T17 in the 1999 WGC-Andersen Consulting Match Play.

He was the first Dane to play in the Ryder Cup, in 1997 at Valderrama, where with Ian Woosnam he won his four-ball match and also came back from four holes down to halve with Justin Leonard.

Matthew Blackey

European Tour

Born 11 June 1971
Place of Birth Lytham St Anne's, England
Year turned Professional 1997
Tour Ranking 126th

Blackey qualified for the 2000 European Tour through the 1999 Qualifying School. Although his highest finish was T8 at the Canon European Masters, he struggled for most of the year and ended the season in 126th place on the Order of Merit.

2000 SEASON. It was a very good year for the long-hitting Dane. He won the BMW International Open by a three-stroke margin over Bernhard Langer and also posted two second places in the Heineken Classic and the European Masters. Björn also performed very well in the Major Championships, where he tied for second place in the 2000 British Open, albeit eight strokes behind Tiger Woods, and finished third in the USPGA, behind Tiger again!

2001 STOP PRESS. At his home course – The Emirates GC – Björn went head-to-head with Tiger Woods in the Dubai Desert Classic and won the closely contested battle when Woods double bogied the last after driving into the trees and finding water with his third shot.

Henrik Bjornstad

European Tour

Born 7 May 1979
Place of Birth Oslo, Norway
Year turned Professional 1997
Tour Ranking 34 (Qualifying School)

The 1996 Norwegian Amateur Champion, Bjornstad played one European Tour event in 2000 and his best finish on the Challenge Tour was ninth at Le Toquet Challenge. He qualified 34th at Qualifying School for the 2001 European Tour.

Jay Don Blake

US Tour

Born 28 October 1958
Place of Birth St George, Utah, USA
Year turned Professional 1981
Tour Ranking 82nd

BEST FINISH IN MAJORS
Tied 6th **US OPEN 1992**

TOUR VICTORIES
US: 1
  1991 Shearson Lehman Brothers Open
OTHER: 1
  1991 Argentine Open

A regular on the US Tour since 1987, the tall Blake's best year came in 1991 when he beat Bill Sander by two shots to win the Shearson Lehman Brothers Open and finish 21st on the Money List. He has been runner-up on five subsequent occasions, including losing a play-off to Tiger Woods at the 1998 Bell South Classic. Blake has suffered from recurring back problems, perhaps exacerbated by his love of drag racing. He is renowned as a fine putter and led the Tour putting average in 1991.

2000 SEASON. Blake's three top-10 finishes helped him to move 20 places up the Money List to 82nd.

John Bland

US Seniors Tour

Born 22 September 1945
Place of Birth Johannesburg, South Africa
Year turned Professional 1969
Tour Ranking 21st

TOUR VICTORIES
SENIOR TOUR: 5
1995 Ralph's Senior Classic
1996 Bruno's Memorial Classic, Northville
Long Island Classic, Puerto Rican
Senior Tournament, The Transamerica

Bland left the European Tour in 1995 to play on the US Senior Tour. Two weeks after joining, the unknown South African had won his first title, Ralph's Senior Classic, having Monday qualified. An accurate shot-maker and putter, Bland won four more events in 1996, was voted Rookie of the Year and collected $1.4 million in winnings. His last win on Tour was that year in The Transamerica when he beat Jim Colbert by one stroke. Bland was runner-up in the Majors three times in the 1990s. He lost the British Senior Open in a play-off against Gary Player in 1997 and came second to Graham Marsh in the US Senior Open that year. In 1999 he again finished in second place, this time behind Christy O'Connor. Bland has one win – the 1995 London Masters – on the European Senior Tour.

2000 SEASON. Bland ended the season back in the top-31, picking up eight top-10s with his highest finish T4 in the SBC Senior Open. His bridesmaid streak continued in the Majors as he again finished runner-up to Christy O'Connor in the British Senior Open.

Kellee Booth

US Ladies Tour

Born 23 April 1976
Place of Birth West Covina, California, USA
Year turned Professional 1999
Tour Ranking 46th

After a glittering amateur career – the highlights of which were consecutive appearances in the 1996 and 1998 Curtis Cups – Californian Booth qualified for the LPGA Tour in 1999 through winning the Qualifying School.

2000 SEASON. In her first season on Tour, Booth finished comfortably in the top-20 six times, with her highest finish being T7 at the Safeway LPGA Golf Championship. She ended the year inside the top-50 on the Money List.

Diego Borrego

European Tour

Born 29 January 1972
Place of Birth Malaga, Spain
Year turned Professional 1991
Tour Ranking 106th

BEST FINISH IN MAJORS
Missed Cut **BRITISH OPEN 1996**

TOUR VICTORIES
EUROPEAN: 1
1996 Turespana Masters Open

DUNHILL CUP 1996
WORLD CUP 1996

Borrego joined the European Tour from the Challenge Tour in 1995 and won the Turespana Masters Open in his rookie year. He lost his card in 1998, but regained it for 1999 via Qualifying School.

2000 SEASON. His best finish was T4 at the Scandinavian Masters.

Desvonde Botes

European Tour

Born 2 November 1974
Place of Birth Pretoria, South Africa
Year turned Professional 1992
Tour Ranking 1st (Qualifying School)

TOUR VICTORIES

SOUTH AFRICA: 8

1993 Mercedes Benz Golf Challenge
1997 Zambia Open
1998 Bosveld Classic, Platinum Classic,
    Vodacom Series: Western Cape
1999 Pietersburg Classic, South African
    Masters
2000 Vodacom Series: Free State

A tall (6 foot 3 inch) and powerful South African, Botes won the European Qualifying School tournament in 2000 by the margin of four strokes, at 26 the youngest player ever to win the qualifying event. An ex-South African Amateur Champion, Botes won the South African Masters in 1999 and has also collected seven other South African titles.

Elliot Boult

European Tour

Born 8 March 1966
Place of Birth Blenheim, New Zealand
Year turned Professional 1992
Tour Ranking 4th (Qualifying School)

TOUR VICTORIES

OTHER: 3

1995 New Caledonian Open
1996 Fiji Open, Vanuatu Open

New Zealand-born Boult played on the Australasian Tour for a number of years. He played on the European Tour in 1999 and re-qualified for the 2000 European Tour at Qualifying School. After struggling again, he revisited the Qualifying School at the end of the 2000 season and finished in fourth place, to restore his playing privileges for 2001. His best performance in 1999 was T12 at the West of Ireland Golf Classic.

2001 STOP PRESS. Boult got off to a fast start, finishing in third place at the Qatar Masters behind Tony Johnstone and Robert Karlsson.

Heather Bowie

US Ladies Tour

Born 23 March 1975
Place of Birth Washington DC, USA
Year turned Professional 1997
Tour Ranking 54th

Bowie played on the Futures Tour from 1997 to 1999 and qualified for the LPGA Tour in 1999 after making it through the Qualifying School.

2000 SEASON. Her top finish in her rookie year was T5 at the Jamie Farr Kroeger Classic, and she also posted two other top-10 finishes.

Pat Bradley

US Ladies Tour

Born 24 March 1951
Place of Birth Westford, Maine, USA
Year turned Professional 1973
Tour Ranking 105th

MAJORS VICTORIES

US OPEN 1981
LPGA 1986
DINAH SHORE 1986
DU MAURIER CLASSIC 1980, 1985, 1986

TOUR VICTORIES

US: 25

1976 Girl Talk Classic
1977 Bankers Trust Classic
1978 Hoosier Classic, Lady Keystone
    Classic, Rail Charity Classic
1980 Greater Baltimore Open
1981 Kemper Open
1983 Chrysler-Plymouth Championship
    Classic, Columbia Savings Classic,
    Mazda Classic, Mazda Japan Classic
1985 LPGA National Pro-Am, Rochester
    International
1986 Nestle World Championship, S&H
    Golf Classic
1987 Standard Register Turquoise Classic
1989 Centinela Hospital Classic

1990 Corning Classic, Oldsmobile LPGA Classic, Standard Register Turquoise Classic

1991 Centel Classic, MBS LPGA Classic, Rail Charity Golf Classic, Safeco Classic

1995 Healthsouth Inaugural

SOLHEIM CUP 1990, 1992, 1996

A supremely confident and aggressive player, Bradley has won 31 tournaments on the US Ladies Tour in a career spanning over 25 years. She claimed her Maiden Tour victory – the Girl Talk Classic – in 1976, and by 1981 had won a further nine times, including the US Women's Open that same year. Her finest year was undoubtedly in 1986 when she won three of the four Majors, plus two other events, to become Player of the Year and finish on top of the Money List. In 1991, she was elected to the LPGA Hall of Fame and passed $4 million in career earnings the same year. She now plays infrequently on the Tour.

2000 SEASON. Bradley captained the US team to a narrow defeat in the Solheim Cup at Loch Lomond, in Scotland, and her highest individual finish was T17 at the British Women's Open.

Gordon Brand Jr

European Tour

Born 19 August 1958
Place of Birth Kircaldy, Scotland
Year turned Professional 1981
Tour Ranking 51st

BEST FINISH IN MAJORS
Tied 5th BRITISH OPEN 1992

TOUR VICTORIES
EUROPEAN: 8
1982 Bob Hope British Classic, Coral Classic
1984 Celtic International, Panasonic European Open

1987 KLM Dutch Open, Scandinavian Enterprise Open

1989 Benson & Hedges International Open

1993 European Open

OTHER: 1

1988 South Australian Open

RYDER CUP 1987, 1989, 1993
DUNHILL CUP 1985, 1986, 1987, 1988, 1989, 1991, 1992, 1993, 1994, 1997
WORLD CUP 1984, 1985, 1988, 1989, 1990, 1992, 1994

A fine amateur youth player, the veteran Brand turned pro in 1981 and joined the European Tour in 1982. That year he won two tournaments, became Rookie of the Year and finished seventh in the Money List. Two years later, he again finished seventh on the Order of Merit. He was a consistent performer for the next ten years, and his last victory was at the European Open at East Sussex National where he led throughout and won by an impressive seven strokes. He is a particularly effective player in the wind and rain and has a good record in the British Open.

2000 SEASON. Brand seemed back to his old form, evidenced by his second place in the Italian Open and T14 in the Volvo Masters the following weekend.

Bill Brask

US Seniors Tour

Born 18 December 1946
Place of Birth Annapolis, Maryland, USA
Year turned Professional 1969
Tour Ranking 38th

A former club professional, Maryland-born Brask made only two appearances in the 1999 US Senior Tour. That year he played on the European Senior Tour where he had three top-2 places, including the PGA Seniors Championship, and finished seventh on the Order of Merit. He qualified for the

US Senior Tour with a seventh place at Qualifying School, his fourth attempt to do so.

2000 SEASON. Brask's highest finish was T2 at the Bank One Championship, where he shot 64 in his first round. He had one other top-10 place and finished 38th on the Money List.

Jeff Brehaut

US Tour

Born 13 June 1963
Place of Birth Mountain View, California, USA
Year turned Professional 1988
Tour Ranking Tied 31st (Qualifying School)

Brehaut played on the Nike Tour from 1993 to 1998, winning two tournaments. He joined the US Tour in 1999, finishing 180th, and played again in 2000. After shoulder surgery he made no cuts that year and was granted a medical extension for 2001. He also qualified T31 at Qualifying School.

Markus Brier

European Tour

Born 5 July 1968
Place of Birth Vienna, Austria
Year turned Professional 1995
Tour Ranking 67th

Brier is the first Austrian golfer to play on the European Tour. He qualified via the Challenge Tour in 1999, having played consistently well to notch up two second-place and three third-place finishes.

2000 SEASON. Brier was a surprising first-round leader at the Turespana Masters, shooting a blistering eight under par 64, but then slipped away over the remaining three rounds to finish in a disappointing T25. However, he achieved his best ever finish later in the season with a second place at the Spanish Open, three strokes behind Englishman Brian Davis.

Mark Brooks

US Tour

Born 25 March 1961
Place of Birth Fort Worth, Texas, USA
Year turned Professional 1983
Tour Ranking 90th

MAJORS VICTORIES
USPGA 1996

TOUR VICTORIES
US: 6
- 1988 Canon Sammy Davies Jr Greater Hartford Open
- 1991 Greater Greensboro Open, Greater Milwaukee Open
- 1994 Kemper Open
- 1996 Bob Hope Chrysler Classic, Shell Houston Open

PRESIDENTS CUP 1996

Brooks joined the US Tour in 1984 and won his first title, the Greater Hartford Open in 1988. In 1996 he won two tournaments, as well as the USPGA Championship, and had his best ever season, finishing in third place on the Money List. He won his only Major in a play-off with Kenny Perry when he birdied the first extra hole at Valhalla. Since then he has been winless on Tour and dropped out of the top-100 in 1997 and 1998.

2000 SEASON. Brooks had three top-10 finishes, his highest a T5 at the Shell Houston Open, to capture 90th spot on the Money List.

Olin Browne

US Tour

Born 22 May 1959
Place of Birth Washington DC, USA
Year turned Professional 1984
Tour Ranking 98th

BEST FINISH IN MAJORS
Tied 5th US OPEN 1997

US: 2

1998 Greater Hartford Open
1999 MasterCard Colonial

Browne was one of the most successful players on the Nike Tour with four victories. He has been a regular on the US Tour since 1994 and in 1998 won his first tournament – the Greater Hartford Open – in a play-off against Stewart Cink and Larry Mize. His second victory came the following year by one shot in the Colonial.

2000 SEASON. Browne had seven top-25 finishes, his best being T9 at the Greater Milwaukee Open. He ended the year sixth on the Tour statistics for driving accuracy, although 160th for distance.

Jerry Bruner
European Senior Tour

Born 4 January 1947
Place of Birth Birmingham, Alabama,USA
Year turned Professional 1982
Tour Ranking 18th

A small (5 foot 6 inch), long-hitting American, Bruner first played on the European Tour in 1999, having qualified through Qualifying School, and he made four T2 finishes. He was third on the Order of Merit that year.

2000 SEASON. He had two second places early in the season, coming runner-up to Tommy Horton at the season-opening Royal Westmoreland Barbados Classic, and second to Neil Coles at the Microlease Jersey Seniors Open, to finish in 18th position on the OM.

Bart Bryant
US Tour

Born 18 November 1962
Place of Birth Gatesville, Texas, USA
Year turned Professional 1986
Tour Ranking Tied 11 (Qualifying School)

Bryant picked up his card for the 2001 US Tour at the 2000 Qualifying School, the fourth time he has had to qualify. His best placing is seventh at the 1991 Honda Classic.

Bob Burns
US Tour

Born 5 April 1968
Place of Birth Mission Hills, California, USA
Year turned Professional 1991
Tour Ranking 125th

Burns played on the US Tour between 1994 and 1995, and rejoined in 1999, when he ended 177th on the Money List. He secured his card through Qualifying School for the 2000 Tour.

2000 SEASON. Burns just scraped his 2001 card, finishing 125th on the Money List. He was helped by two top-10 finishes, at the Sony Open and the Compaq Classic.

Brandie Burton
US Ladies Tour

Born 8 January 1972
Place of Birth San Bernardino, California, USA
Year turned Professional 1990
Tour Ranking 23rd

MAJORS VICTORIES
DU MAURIER CLASSIC 1993, 1998

TOUR VICTORIES
US: 3

1992 Ping Welch's Championship
1993 Jamie Farr Toledo Classic, Safeco Classic

SOLHEIM CUP 1992, 1994, 1996, 1998, 2000

Burton burst onto the LPGA Tour in 1991 ending the season as Rookie of the Year with eight top-10 finishes and 22nd on the Money List. Within two years she had won three tournaments, passed the $1 million earnings mark and had collected her first Major, the du Maurier Classic. However, she was subsequently plagued by injuries and fell down the Money List. She did not win again until 1998 when she had her second victory at the du Maurier Classic. She was off the Tour in 1999 due to a shoulder injury. She has represented the US in five Solheim Cups.

2000 SEASON. Burton was twice runner-up – at the Cup Noodles Hawaiian Open and the Longs Drugs Challenge – and passed $3 million in career earnings. She won all three of her matches at the Solheim Cup at Loch Lomond.

Robin Byrd
European Tour

Born 2 August 1960
Place of Birth Austin, Texas, USA
Year turned Professional 1983
Tour Ranking 147th

Tall American Byrd played on the Nike, Asian and Australasian Tours before joining the 2000 European Tour through Qualifying School.
2000 SEASON. Byrd gained his highest placing on Tour – T6 at the Brazil Rio 500 Years Open – but finished in 147th place on the Order of Merit.

Tom Byrum
US Tour

Born 28 September 1960
Place of Birth Onida, South Dakota, USA
Year turned Professional 1984
Tour Ranking 93rd

BEST FINISH IN MAJORS
9th **USPGA 1997**

TOUR VICTORIES
US: 1
 1989 Kemper Open

Younger brother of Curt Byrum, Tom won his only tournament – the Kemper Open – by five strokes in 1989, seven weeks before Curt also won his only event on the US Tour. His best year on Tour was in 1997, when he had two second places and ended 42nd on the Money List. He lost a play-off to Notah Begay III at the 1999 Michelob. Byrum is an accurate driver but relatively short off the tee.
 2000 SEASON. He made three top-10 finishes, his highest being T6 in the Southern Farm Bureau Classic. He also led after the third round of the five-round Invensys Classic, only to be overtaken by Billy Andrade in the fourth round, and he ended the tournament T9.

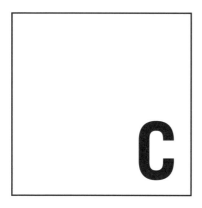

Angel Cabrera
European Tour

Born 12 September 1969
Place of Birth Cordoba, Argentina
Year turned Professional 1990
Tour Ranking 14th

BEST FINISH IN MAJORS
Tied 10th **MASTERS 2001**

TOUR VICTORIES
EUROPEAN: 1
   2001 Argentine Open

DUNHILL CUP 1997, 1998, 2000
WORLD CUP 1998, 1999, 2000

Cabrera – known on tour as 'the Duck' – was a caddy in his native Cordoba and turned pro at the age of 20 in 1990. He qualified for the European Tour in 1996 and claimed second place in the Oki Pro-Am that year. In 1999 he had two more second places – at the Murphy's Irish Open and the Benson & Hedges International Open – and finished tenth in the Order of Merit. He is a powerful, long-hitting player – second on the Tour for driving distance – although his putting is less than consistent.

2000 SEASON. He secured the fourth second place of his career when he was runner-up to Lee Westwood in the Smurfit European Open, and he followed this up with two more top-five finishes at the Dutch Open and the Volvo Masters. He played with his friend and mentor Eduardo Romero in the World Cup in Argentina at the end of the season and came very close to victory, only prevented from holding the trophy by a blistering last nine holes from Tiger Woods and David Duval.

2001 STOP PRESS. Cabrera finally won on the European Tour, beating Carl Pettersson by two shots at the Argentine Open. He also led the Masters to mid-way through the third round.

Mark Calcavecchia
US Tour

Born 12 June 1960
Place of Birth Laurel, New England, USA
Year turned Professional 1981
Tour Ranking 23rd

MAJORS VICTORIES
   BRITISH OPEN 1989

TOUR VICTORIES
US: 10
   1986 Southwest Golf Classic
   1987 Honda Classic
   1988 Bank of Boston Classic
   1989 Nissan Los Angeles Open, Phoenix Open
   1992 Phoenix Open
   1995 BellSouth Classic
   1997 Greater Vancouver Open
   1998 Honda Classic
   2001 Phoenix Open
AUSTRALASIAN: 1
   1988 Australian Open
OTHER: 3
   1993 Argentine Open
   1995 Argentine Open
   1997 Subaru Sarazen World Open

RYDER CUP 1987, 1989, 1991
DUNHILL CUP 1989, 1990
PRESIDENTS CUP 1998

In the late 1980s 'Calc' was one of the finest golfers in the world. An aggressive and competitive player, with a superb iron game, between 1986 and 1989 he won five USPGA titles, including the 1988 Honda Classic when he shot five birdies in the last seven holes to win by three strokes. He also played in two Ryder Cups and two Dunhill Cups. In 1988 he was on the final hole of the Masters and expecting a play-off with Sandy Lyle, when Lyle struck a superb shot from a fairway bunker over 150 yards to eight foot from the pin and sunk the winning birdie putt. He was more fortunate the following year at the British Open at Birkdale when, on the fourth hole of a play-off, Greg Norman overhit his drive into a bunker and Calcavecchia sent his 5-iron approach to within six feet of the flag and holed the putt for a birdie and victory.

He made his third appearance in the Ryder Cup in 1991 when, four up with four to play, he allowed Colin Montgomerie back into the game to halve the match. Since then he has won a further four tournaments and accumulated numerous top-10 finishes, and since 1986 has made at least one top-3 appearance per season. It is no surprise that he has amassed more than $9 million in prize money during his long career.

2000 SEASON. A second placing in the Greater Hartford Open brought him a further $300,000 and he also finished runner-up in the Pennsylvania Classic. He had five more top-10 appearances and finished T11 in the Tour Championship. He recorded a career-best earnings of over $1.5 million.

2001 STOP PRESS. Calc was in record-breaking form at the Phoenix Open, in Arizona, in January. He broke Mike Souchak's 46-year-old record for the lowest 72-hole score when he shot a 28 under par 256, including a second round 60. He also set a record for the number of birdies – 32 – in a 72-hole tournament. He eventually beat Rocco Mediate by eight strokes and later in the season secured third place at the Bob Hope Chrysler Classic.

Michael Campbell

European Tour

Born 23 February 1969
Place of Birth Hawere, New Zealand
Year turned Professional 1993
Tour Ranking 4th

BEST FINISH IN MAJORS
Tied 3rd **BRITISH OPEN 1995**

TOUR VICTORIES
EUROPEAN: 4
   2000 German Masters, Heineken Classic, Johnnie Walker Classic
   2001 Heineken Classic
AUSTRALASIAN: 3
   1993 Canon Challenge
   2000 Ericsson Masters, New Zealand Open

DUNHILL CUP 1995, 2000
PRESIDENTS CUP 2000

A descendant of Sir Logan Campbell, Mayor of Auckland in the 1840s, 'Cambo' was a golfing aristocrat in 1995, his rookie year on the European Tour. With his brisk but rhythmic swing and excellent putting ability, he burst on to the European golfing scene, having won the Canon Challenge on the Australasian Tour. He came second in both the British Masters and the Volvo PGA and took the third round lead in the British Open at St

Andrews, only to finish the tournament in fifth place. Fifth was also his position on the 1995 Order of Merit. He played on the US and European Tours the following year although his game suffered, partly because of tendinitis in his wrist and also because of some misguided swing changes, and he lost both Tour cards in 1997. However, he fought back in 1999 with three top-10 placings and secured 41st spot on the Order of Merit.

2000 SEASON. After working with new coach Jonathan Yarwood, Campbell was fully back to his golfing best. He won the first event of the European season – the Johnnie Walker Classic in Taiwan – as well as the New Zealand Open, the Ericsson Masters and the Heineken Classic, the latter by six shots with a 20 under par 268. He was number one on the ANZ Order of Merit. He beat Jose Coceres by one shot to pick up the Linde German Masters and finished second in the Volvo Scandinavian Masters, English Open and Lancome Trophy. Perhaps most impressive of all was his 12th place finish in the US Open at Pebble Beach.

2001 STOP PRESS. Campbell successfully defended his Heineken Classic title, winning by five strokes over Australians David Smail and Nick O'Hern.

Jose Canizares

Born 18 February 1947
Place of Birth Madrid, Spain
Year turned Professional 1967
Tour Ranking 12th

TOUR VICTORIES
SENIOR TOUR: 1
  2001 Toshiba Senior Classic

Canizares began his career as a caddie in his native Madrid. He played on the European Tour, winning seven tournaments, and co-holds the record for the lowest 9-hole score of 27. He made four Ryder Cup appearances for

Europe and he earned a critical one-hole victory over Ken Green in the 1989 competition at The Belfry.

He finished in seventh place on the 1997 European Order of Merit and joined the US Senior Tour in 1998, claiming the second place at Qualifying School. In his rookie year, Canizares made over $1 million and was placed T3 at the Senior PGA Championship. In 1999 he again passed the $1 million mark.

2000 SEASON. He still could not conjure up a victory on Tour, but for the third year in succession he earned $1 million, helped by ten top-10s and a T2 at the ACE Group Classic.

2001 STOP PRESS. Canizares finally won a tournament, the Toshiba Senior Classic, after a marathon 9-hole play-off against Gil Morgan. He also finished in second place behind Jim Colbert at the SBC Senior Classic.

Emanuele Canonica

Born 7 January 1971
Place of Birth Turin, Italy
Year turned Professional 1991
Tour Ranking 27th

DUNHILL CUP 1996, 1999
WORLD CUP 1999

A diminutive (5 foo 2 inch), stocky Italian, Canonica can nonetheless hit the golf ball a prodigious length off the tee and is regularly number one on the European Tour's Driving Distance statistics. He joined the European Tour in 1995 and has not yet won a tournament although he finished third in the Italian Open in 1995. He is coached by Butch Harmon.

2000 SEASON. Canonica achieved his career best placing at the Deutsche Bank Open, claiming the runner-up position, and he was also third at the European Grand Prix. He attended the USPGA Qualifying School and qualified for the 2001 US Tour, finishing tied 31st.

Raquel Carriedo
European Ladies Tour

Born 2 August 1971
Place of Birth Zaragoza, Spain
Year turned Professional 1995
Tour Ranking 5th

TOUR VICTORIES
EUROPEAN: 1
2001 Taiwan Ladies Open

SOLHEIM CUP 2000

Spaniard Carriedo (known as 'Poncho' on Tour) joined the European Tour in 1995. Her highest finish before 2001 was second at the French Open in 1996.
2000 SEASON. Carriedo finished second in the German Open and, with two other high finishes, she ended the year in sixth place on the Money List. In doing so, she also became the first Spanish player to be selected for the Solheim Cup.
2001 STOP PRESS. Carriedo won her first tournament by parring the final hole of the Taiwan Ladies Open to beat Sweden's Anna Berg and Elizabeth Esterl. She won again the next week when she finished T2 at the South African Ladies Masters.

David Carter
European Tour

Born 16 June 1972
Place of Birth Johannesburg, South Africa
Year turned Professional 1989
Tour Ranking 76th

BEST FINISH IN MAJORS
Tied 42nd **BRITISH OPEN 1998**

TOUR VICTORIES
EUROPEAN: 1
1996 Murphy's Irish Open
OTHER: 1
1996 Indian PGA

DUNHILL CUP 1998
WORLD CUP 1998

The son of a club professional, Carter joined the European Tour in 1995 and made his mark fairly shortly afterwards, in 1998, when he won the Murphy's Irish Open at Druid's Glen, holding his nerve to defeat the European number one at the time Colin Montgomerie in a sudden-death play-off in front of a large, vocal crowd. The following year, playing alongside Nick Faldo, he helped to secure the country's first win in the World Cup. His solid performances were even more impressive given the fact that the previous year, in 1997, he had to undergo brain surgery after collapsing in his hotel room in Dubai. He has been runner-up on four occasions in his career, including the European Grand Prix in 1999.
2000 SEASON. Carter's form was disappointing and his highest placing was T10 at the Irish Open. He declined from 27th on the 1999 OM to 76th.

Jim Carter
US Tour

Born 24 June 1961
Place of Birth Spring Lake, North Carolina, USA
Year turned Professional 1985
Tour Ranking 48th

BEST FINISH IN MAJORS
Tied 46th **USPGA 1999**

TOUR VICTORIES
US: 1
2000 Touchstone Energy Tucson Open

A consistent golfer with something of a talent for bunker play, Carter is a long-standing member of the US Tour, although he played on the Nike Tour from 1991 to 1994. His best year was in 1989 when he finished 33rd on the Money List. He is one of the shorter drivers on Tour. Prior to 2000 he made four top-3 finishes in his career.

2000 SEASON. Carter won the Tucson Open to record his first Tour victory, when he overtook Tom Scherrer over the last few holes, to win by two shots. He finished 48th on the Money List – his first top-50 placing since 1989.

Silvia Cavalleri
European Ladies Tour

Born 10 October 1972
Place of Birth Milan, Italy
Year turned Professional 1997
Tour Ranking 12th

TOUR VICTORIES
EUROPEAN: 1
1999 Royal Marie-Claire Open

The 1997 US Amateur Champion and leading amateur in the Weetabix Women's British Open the same year, Milan-born Cavalleri turned professional with something of a reputation to live up to and immediately joined the European Tour. She finished fifth at the Austrian Open in 1999 and also played on the LPGA Tour, where her highest finish was T9 at the Philips Invitational. She narrowly missed out on her exempt status for 2000 by one shot at the Qualifying School.

2000 SEASON. She played in seven European events, finishing T2 at the Italian Open and T7 at the *Daily Telegraph* Women's British Masters, to take 12th place on the Money List. Cavalleri also finished T10 at the First Union Betsy King Classic in America.

Francisco Cea
European Tour

Born 20 March 1974
Place of Birth Malaga, Spain
Year turned Professional 1995
Tour Ranking 105th

Spanish Amateur Champion at the age of 21, Cea turned pro in 1995. He joined the European Tour the following year and retained his card by a narrow margin at the end of the season, finishing 124th out of the 125 players who automatically regain their Tour membership for the following season. He was not so fortunate the next year but returned to the Tour in 1999 via the Qualifying School. That season he led the PGA European Tour's statistics for driving accuracy, although the accuracy is at the expense of length off the tee.

2000 SEASON. Cea was fifth in the Turespana Open and third in the Italian Open (his highest career finish), thereby retaining his card for the 2001 season.

Alexander Cejka
European Tour

Born 2 December 1970
Place of Birth Marienbad, Czechoslavakia
Year turned Professional 1989
Tour Ranking 70th

BEST FINISH IN MAJORS
Tied 11th **BRITISH OPEN 1996**

TOUR VICTORIES
EUROPEAN: 3
1995 Turespana Open, Hohe Brucke Open, Volvo Masters

DUNHILL CUP 1994, 1995, 1997, 1998
WORLD CUP 1995, 1996, 1997, 1999

The slightly-built Cejka, who as a young boy fled Czechoslovakia to settle in Munich, had his finest year in 1995. He won three tournaments – the Turespana Open, Hohe Brucke Open and the Volvo Masters – that year and was sixth on the Order of Merit. He was 17th on the Money List in 1999.

2000 SEASON. Cejka made the cut in only 12 European Tour tournaments in 2000, and his best finish was T4 at the Lancome Trophy.

Christian Cevaer
European Tour

Born 10 April 1970
Place of Birth Noumea, New Caledonia
Year turned Professional 1993
Tour Ranking 8th (Challenge Tour)

The tall, blonde Frenchman from the Pacific island of New Caledonia was World Junior Champion at the age of 16. He missed joining the 2000 European Tour by one place and, despite being touted as a star of the future, had to visit the Qualifying School five times in the 1990s. He qualified for the 2000 Tour by finishing in eighth place on the Challenge Tour Order of Merit with a win at the Finnish Masters and a runner-up place at the Luxembourg Open.

Greg Chalmers
US Tour

Born 11 October 1973
Place of Birth Sydney, Australia
Year turned Professional 1995
Tour Ranking 41st

BEST FINISH IN MAJORS
Tied 4th USPGA 2000

TOUR VICTORIES
AUSTRALASIAN: 2
1997 ANZ Players Championship
1998 Australian Open

A young, left-handed Australian, the long-hitting Chalmers joined the US Tour in 1999 and made an immediate impression, recording seven top-25 finishes.
2000 SEASON. Chalmers had two top-4 finishes – at the Kemper Open (T2, his highest career placing on the US Tour) and the Canadian Open – and claimed fourth spot at the USPGA Championship, only his third Major. He also tied for ninth place at the Players Championship.

Brandell Chamblee
US Tour

Born 2 July 1962
Place of Birth St Louis, Missouri, USA
Year turned Professional 1985
Tour Ranking 99th

BEST FINISH IN MAJORS
Tied 18th US MASTERS 1999

TOUR VICTORIES
US: 1
1998 Greater Vancouver Open

A member of the inaugural Ben Hogan Tour in 1990, Chamblee won the New England Classic that very same year. He received his US Tour card in 1991 and has been a regular, if unspectacular, member of the Tour ever since. He was runner-up to Paul Stankowski in the 1996 BellSouth Classic and achieved two more second places in 1997. He won his only PGA Tour title in 1998 when he beat Payne Stewart by three strokes to claim the Greater Vancouver Open.

With the exception of 1998, when he finished in 37th place, Chamblee has never ended the season in the top-70 on the Money List, although he has been in the top-100 since 1995.
2000 SEASON. Not a particularly impressive season for Chamblee, in spite of three top-10 finishes.
2001 STOP PRESS. Chamblee tied for second place with four other players at the Nissan Open, in California, after being defeated on the first play-off hole by Australia's play-off maestro Robert Allenby.

Roger Chapman
European Tour

Born 1 May 1959
Place of Birth Nakuru, Kenya
Year turned Professional 1981
Tour Ranking 33rd

TOUR VICTORIES

EUROPEAN: 1

    2000 Rio de Janeiro Open

OTHER: 1

    1988 Zimbabwe Open

Ex-English Amateur Champion, journeyman Chapman has been a member of the European Tour since 1981, although he had to attend Qualifying School to retain his card for the 2000 season. His most successful year was 1988 when he finished 17th on the Order of Merit and he has finished runner-up on six occasions in his long career. He is a consistent and accurate striker of the ball.

2000 SEASON. Chapman lifted his first European Tour trophy in 472 tournaments when he beat Padraig Harrington on a second-hole play-off at the Rio de Janeiro 500 Years Open.

Bob Charles
US Seniors Tour

Born 14 March 1936

Place of Birth Carterton, New Zealand

Year turned Professional 1960

Tour Ranking 60th

TOUR VICTORIES

SENIOR TOUR: 23

    1987 GTE Classic, Sunwest/Charley Pride Classic, Vintage Chrysler Invitational

    1988 NYNEX/*Golf Digest* Commemorative, Pepsi Senior Challenge, Rancho Murieta Senior Gold Rush, Sunwest/Charley Pride Classic, Vantage Bank One Senior Golf Classic

    1989 Digital Seniors Classic, Fairfield Barnett, GTE Suncoast Classic, NYNEX/*Golf Digest* Commemorative, Sunwest/Charley Pride Classic

    1990 Digital Seniors Classic, Kaanapali Classic

    1991 GTE Suncoast Classic

    1992 Raley's Senior Gold Rush, Transamerica Senior Golf Championship

    1993 Bell Atlantic Classic, Doug Sanders Celebrity Classic, Quicksilver Classic

    1995 Kaanapali Classic

    1996 Kaanapali Classic

New Zealander Charles had worldwide success before joining the Seniors Tour in 1986, which he dominated until the arrival of Lee Trevino. He amassed five USPGA Tour wins and eight European titles, and he won the British Open in 1963, beating Bill Rogers by eight strokes in a 36-hole play-off. Naturally right-handed, Charles plays golf left-handed and is the only left-handed player ever to have won a Major. He was awarded an OBE in 1972 and a CBE in 1992.

Between 1987 and 1990 Charles won 15 tournaments on the Senior Tour and he topped the Money List from 1988 till 1990. In 1988 he became the first player to earn over $500,000 in one season. He also won the Senior British Open in 1989 and again in 1993. One of the greatest-ever putters and an accurate shot-maker, Charles won his last title, his 24th, in 1996 when he defeated newcomer and heir apparent Hale Irwin at the Kaanapali Classic in Hawaii. In 1998 he eventually slipped out of the top 31 for the first time. He has earned more than $8 million in his Senior career.

2000 SEASON. His best finish was T9 at the Bank One Championship.

Barry Cheeseman
US Tour

Born 29 August 1959
Place of Birth Galesburg, Illinois, USA
Year turned Professional 1986
Tour Ranking 141st

Atall mid-Westerner, Cheeseman had his best year on the US Tour in 1998 when he achieved his highest-ever placing, T3 at the Michelob Championship. He finished the season in 95th spot on the Money List, the only year he has been inside the top 125.
2000 SEASON. Cheeseman had six top-25 finishes, his highest being T20 at the Bell Canadian Open.

Neil Cheetham
European Tour

Born 19 August 1967
Place of Birth Sheffield, England
Year turned Professional 1985
Tour Ranking 12th (Qualifying School)

Cheetham – an ex-schoolboy soccer player with Sheffield Wednesday – won twice on the Challenge Tour in 1998 and played again on the Tour in 2000, where his best finish was at the Formby Hall Challenge. He qualified for the 2001 European Tour with a 12th place at Qualifying School.

KJ Choi
US Tour

Born 5 September 1970
Place of Birth Seoul, South Korea
Year turned Professional 1994
Tour Ranking Tied 31 (Qualifying School)

Choi joined the US Tour in 2000 from Qualifying School, the first Korean to join the Tour, but had to requalify for the 2001 season, which he did with a T31 place. His highest finish was T8 at the Air Canada Championship.

Stewart Cink
US Tour

Born 21 May 1973
Place of Birth Huntsville, Alabama, USA
Year turned Professional 1995
Tour Ranking 10th

BEST FINISH IN MAJORS
3rd **US OPEN 2001**

TOUR VICTORIES
US: 2
    1997 Greater Hartford Open
    2000 MCI Heritage Classic
OTHER: 1
    1996 Mexican Open

PRESIDENTS CUP 2000

A6 foot 4 inch tall Southerner and noted short hole expert, Cink arrived on the US Tour in 1997, having won the Mexican Open and Nike Player of the Year title the previous year. In his first season he shot a final round 66 at the Greater Hartford Open to win the competition by one stroke from Jeff Maggert, Brandell Chamblee and Tom Byrum. He ended the season as Rookie of the Year, and his impressive run of form continued in 1998 with seven top-10 finishes. In 1999 Cink confirmed his status as one of the rising stars of North American golf when he finished third in the USPGA tournament and secured 32nd place on the Money List.

2000 SEASON. The consistent Cink won his only tournament of the season when he captured the MCI Heritage Classic trophy, surging through with a last round 65 to beat Tom Lehman by two strokes. On his birthday at the Colonial tournament in Texas, he threw away a three-shot lead at the beginning of the final round, to eventually lose by two strokes to Phil Mickelson. Cink had an excellent Presidents Cup, however, notching up three wins with partner Kirk Triplett and defeating Greg Norman in his singles match.

Tim Clark

US Tour

Born 17 December 1975
Place of Birth Durban, South Africa
Year turned Professional 1998
Tour Ranking 3rd (Buy.Com Tour)

South African Clark won the Public Links Amateur Championship in 1997 and qualified for the Masters, where he missed the cut. He played in South Africa early in 2000 and joined the Buy.Com Tour, where he notched up two wins and seven second places to end in third place on the Money List. 2001 is his rookie year on the US Tour.

Michael Clark II

US Tour

Born 4 May 1968
Place of Birth Kingsport, Tennessee, USA
Year turned Professional 1992
Tour Ranking 56th

BEST FINISH IN MAJORS
Tied 15th USPGA 2000

TOUR VICTORIES
US: 1
  2000 John Deere Classic

Graduating in 11th place from Qualifying School in 1999, Clark left the Nike Tour for the PGA Tour in 2000. In his first season he won the John Deere Classic when his 12-foot birdie putt on the fourth play-off hole defeated Kirk Triplett. His previous best finish had been T13 at the Compaq Classic. He also finished T4 in the Air Canada Championship, when he finished with a 63, and tied for 15th place in his first Major, the USPGA at Valhalla. His 56th place on the Money List guaranteed him the Rookie of the Year award.

Darren Clarke

European Tour

Born 14 August 1968
Place of Birth Dungannon, Northern `Ireland
Year turned Professional 1990
Tour Ranking 2nd

BEST FINISH IN MAJORS
Tied 2nd BRITISH OPEN 1997

TOUR VICTORIES
EUROPEAN: 6
  1993 Alfred Dunhill Open
  1996 German Masters
  1998 Benson & Hedges International Open, Volvo Masters
  1999 English Open
  2000 English Open
OTHER: 1
  2000 WGC-Andersen Consulting Match Play

RYDER CUP 1997
DUNHILL CUP 1994, 1995, 1996, 1997, 1998, 1999, 2000
WORLD CUP 1994, 1995, 1996

A large, genial Northern Irishman, Clarke has a taste for big cigars and fast sports cars. Long off the tee, he is also accurate with his iron play and a steady putter. He learnt to play his golf at the famous Royal Portrush links in Northern Ireland. He joined the European Tour in 1991 and has been ever-present since. In 1998 he won the Benson & Hedges International Open and followed it up with a last round 63 in the Volvo Masters to win that tournament and finish second in the Order of Merit behind Colin Montgomerie. He was in the top-10 in the Order of Merit every year between 1996 and 1999.

2000 SEASON. Clarke had the biggest, and most lucrative, victory of his career in California in February 2000 when he took on Tiger Woods in the WGC-Andersen Consulting Match Play Championship and trumped the prodigy by 4&3 to collect $1 million. He qualified for the final by beating David Duval and Hal Sutton. He also successfully defended his English Open title and recorded six other top-5 finishes including a second at the Volvo Masters. He battled throughout the season with his friend and stablemate Lee Westwood for the Order of Merit title, but Clarke's challenge faded away at the very end and he had to content himself with second place.

Russell Claydon
European Tour

Born 19 November 1965
Place of Birth Cambridge, England
Year turned Professional 1989
Tour Ranking 125th

BEST FINISH IN MAJORS
Tied 11th **BRITISH OPEN 1994**

TOUR VICTORIES
EUROPEAN: 1
1998 BMW International Open

DUNHILL CUP 1997

The large, amiable Claydon was English Amateur Champion in 1988 and joined the European Tour the following year. A very popular figure among his fellow pros, Claydon possesses an unorthodox grip and an even more idiosyncratic swing. He won his only tournament in 1998, at the BMW International Open in Germany, and he has finished as runner-up numerous times.

2000 SEASON. Claydon struggled with his game and fell outside the top-115 for the first time since 1989. He considered quitting the game, but has since decided to continue competing. His highest finish was eighth at the Dubai Desert Classic.

Keith Clearwater
US Tour

Born 1 September 1959
Place of Birth Long Beach, California, USA
Year turned Professional 1983
Tour Ranking Tied 27 (Qualifying School)

TOUR VICTORIES
US: 2
1987 Colonial, Centel Classic

Clearwater had an exceptional start to his US Tour career, winning two tournaments – the Colonial and the Centel Classic – in his rookie season of 1987. He was named Rookie of the Year and finished 31st on the Money List. Since then he has not won anything and he had to go back to Qualifying School in 2000. He ended the tournament T27 and regained his card for the 2001 US Tour season.

Jose Coceres
European Tour

Born 12 August 1963
Place of Birth Chaco, Argentina
Year turned Professional 1986
Tour Ranking 13th

BEST FINISH IN MAJORS
Tied 36th **BRITISH OPEN 2000**

TOUR VICTORIES
US: 1
    2001 Worldcom Classic
EUROPEAN: 2
    1994 Heineken Open Catalonia
    2000 Dubai Desert Classic

DUNHILL CUP 1993, 1995, 1997, 2000
WORLD CUP 1989, 1997

A former caddie from a poor background in Argentina, Coceres has won six tournaments on the sub-continent. His first European Tour victory came in 1994, at the Heineken Open Catalonia, and he has recorded 23 top-10 finishes in his career. He famously once carded 105 in a British Open qualifying match in gale force conditions. He is a powerful and accurate low-ball hitter from tee and fairway and is ranked second on the Tour's driving accuracy statistics.

2000 SEASON. It was an excellent year for Coceres, who led from the start to win the Dubai Desert Classic, in spite of a double bogey at the 18th, ahead of Paul McGinley and Patrik Sjoland. It was his first win for 210 tournaments. He also finished third at the Rio De Janeiro Open and T3 at the Benson & Hedges. He recorded his best-ever placing in a Major with T36 at the British Open.

2001 STOP PRESS. Coceres was T2 behind Darren Fitchardt at the Sao Paulo Brazilian Open. He also collected his first win on the US Tour when he defeated Billy Mayfair on the fifth play-off hole of the Worldcom Classic.

Russ Cochran
US Tour

Born 31 October 1958
Place of Birth Paducah, Kentucky, USA
Year turned Professional 1979
Tour Ranking 83rd

BEST FINISH IN MAJORS
Tied 10th **USPGA 1984**

TOUR VICTORIES
US: 1
    1991 Centel Western Open

Left-hander Cochran has been a member of the US Tour since 1983. His only victory was at the 1991 Western Open when Greg Norman threw away a five stroke lead with eight holes to play, and allowed Cochran to win the title by two strokes. Also in 1991, he reached the play-off in the lucrative and prestigious Tour Championship, but was defeated by Craig Stadler. He had to return to Qualifying School in 1995, but was back on Tour in 1996, where he went on to lead the USPGA Championship, scoring 65 in the third round. However, a final round 77 cost him his chances of the title.

2000 SEASON. Although Cochran had four top-10 finishes, the fact that he missed the cut in more than half the events he entered meant he finished the season in a lowly 83rd place on the Money List. His best place was T4 at the Nissan Open and the FedEx St Jude Classic.

Dawn Coe-Jones
US Ladies Tour

Born 19 October 1960
Place of Birth Campbell, British Columbia, Canada
Year turned Professional 1983
Tour Ranking 53rd

TOUR VICTORIES
US: 3
    1992 Women's Kemper Open

1994 Healthsouth Palm Beach Classic
1995 Chrysler-Plymouth Tour Championship

The 1983 Canadian Amateur Champion, Coe-Jones took up golf when she was 12 and, after qualifying for the Tour at her first attempt, has now won three events. Her last victory was the 1995 Chrysler-Plymouth Tour Championship. In 1997 she passed the $2 million career earnings mark.

2000 SEASON. An inconsistent year overall for Coe-Jones. Although she recorded two top-10 finishes, including a tie for sixth, at the Philips Invitational, she struggled for most of the season.

Jim Colbert
US Seniors Tour

Born 9 March 1941
Place of Birth Elizabeth, New Jersey, USA
Year turned Professional 1965
Tour Ranking 24th

MAJORS VICTORIES
SENIOR PLAYERS CHAMPIONSHIP 1993

TOUR VICTORIES
SENIOR TOUR: 19
1991 Kaanapali Classic, Southwestern Bell Classic, Vantage Championship
1992 GTE Suncoast Classic, Vantage Championship
1993 Royal Caribbean Classic
1994 Kroger Senior Classic, Southwestern Bell Classic
1995 Bell Atlantic Classic, Las Vegas Senior Classic, Senior Tour Championship, Senior Tournament of Champions
1996 Las Vegas Senior Classic, Nationwide Championship, Raley's Gold Rush Classic, Toshiba Senior Classic, Vantage Championship
1998 The Transamerica
2001 SBC Senior Classic

Colbert played on the USPGA Tour and picked up eight titles, the last being the Texas Open in 1983. After spells in business and broadcasting, he joined the Senior Tour in 1991 and immediately made his mark, winning three times and finishing third on the Money List. This confident and competitive player – known as 'Bulldog' on Tour – was also voted Rookie of the Year. His most fruitful years were in 1995 and 1996 when he was twice Player of the Year and topped the Money Lists. He also won nine events in the two years. In 1997 he was out for four months recuperating from prostate cancer, but still contrived to finish in the top-31. He was voted Comeback Player of the Year in 1998. He is identifiable by his bucket hat and his turned-up shirt collar.

2000 SEASON. The remarkably consistent Colbert achieved eight top-10 placings and remained in the top-31 for the tenth year in succession. Colbert has won more than $9 million in his Senior career.

2001 STOP PRESS. Colbert won his 20th Tour event, beating Jose Canizares by one stroke at the SBC Senior Classic. The win took his Senior Tour earnings to $9.9 million, second only to Hale Irwin.

Neil Coles
European Senior Tour

Born 26 September 1934
Place of Birth London, England
Year turned Professional 1950
Tour Ranking 9th

TOUR VICTORIES
SENIOR TOUR: 13
1985 Forte PGA Seniors
1986 Forte PGA Seniors
1987 Forte PGA Seniors, Senior British Open
1989 Forte PGA Seniors
1992 Collingtree Homes Seniors Classic
1993 Gary Player Seniors Classic

1995 Collingtree Seniors
1997 Ryder Collingtree Seniors Classic
1998 Philip's PFA Golf Classic
1999 Energis Senior Masters, Scottish
Seniors Open
2000 Microlease Jersey Seniors Open

Coles was one of the main figures behind the development of European golf. A supremely consistent golfer, he played on the European Tour since its formation and was ranked in first place in 1963 and 1970. He won 25 titles in his career and he became the oldest golfer ever to win a Tour event when he claimed the Sanyo Open in 1982 at the age of 48. Regarded as a supreme striker of the ball, Coles has also represented Britain and Ireland in eight Ryder Cups. He is now Chairman of the European Tour Board of Directors.

He joined the European Senior Tour in 1992, the year of its official formation, and he has won 13 tournaments, including the Senior British Open. He won twice in 1999 to finish fourth on the Order of Merit.

2000 SEASON. Coles won the Microlease Jersey Seniors Open, beating his own oldest player record set the previous year, at the pensionable age of 65, to win on the Senior Tour. His victory also meant that he is the only player to have won a professional golf tournament in six different decades. He went on to finish the season in ninth place on the Order of Merit.

Robert Coles
European Tour

Born 2 September 1972
Place of Birth Hornchurch, England
Year turned Professional 1994
Tour Ranking 3rd (Qualifying School)

Coles played on the European Tour from 1996 to 1998, his best position being T8 at the 1997 Peugeot Open de France in 1997. He played again on the 2000 European Tour, posting a seventh place at the Novotel Perrier Open de France and an eighth at the Celtic Manor Wales Open. He retained his Tour card for 2001 by finishing third at Qualifying School.

Nicholas Colsaerts
European Tour

Born 14 November 1982
Place of Birth Brussels, Belgium
Year turned Professional 2000
Tour Ranking 5th (Qualifying School)

At 19 years old, he became the youngest player to finish in the top-5 at the European Qualifying School, and was also the leader at the halfway stage of the tournament. Belgian-born Colsaerts played as an amateur in one Challenge Tour tournament – the Luxembourg Open – and lost in a play-off to eventual Tour winner, Henrik Stenson.

Andrew Coltart
European Tour

Born 12 May 1970
Place of Birth Dumfries, Scotland
Year turned Professional 1991
Tour Ranking 17th

BEST FINISH IN MAJORS
Tied 18th BRITISH OPEN 1999

TOUR VICTORIES
EUROPEAN: 1
 1998 Qatar Masters
AUSTRALASIAN: 2
 1994 Australian PGA
 1997 Australian PGA

RYDER CUP 1999
DUNHILL CUP 1994, 1995, 1996, 1998, 2000
WORLD CUP 1994, 1995, 1996, 1998

A tall, lean Scotsman, Coltart played on the European Tour in 1993 but had to return to Qualifying School at the end of the season. He re-joined in 1994 and he has been a regular fixture on Tour since. Along with Colin Montgomerie and Sam Torrance he helped Scotland to its first Dunhill Cup win in 1995, his hole-in-one at the eighth in the final against Zimbabwe contributing to the victory. He won two tournaments on the Australasian Tour – the PGA in 1994 and 1997 – and was awarded the Australasian Order of Merit in 1998. That same year he won his first European tournament, the Qatar Masters.

In the 1999 Ryder Cup, where he was one of captain Mark James' wild card picks, Coltart only played in the last day singles and was well beaten by Tiger Woods as the European lead evaporated. Coltart is Lee Westwood's brother-in-law, Westwood having married Coltart's sister Laurae.

2000 SEASON. He posted four top-5 finishes, with his best placing being T2 at the Volvo PGA Championship.

Frank Conner
US Seniors Tour

Born 11 January 1946
Place of Birth Vienna, Austria
Year turned Professional 1972
Tour Ranking 59th

A ustrian-born Conner played on the Ben Hogan/Nike Tour from 1990 until 1995, and joined the US Seniors Tour in 1996, finishing in eighth place at the Qualifying School. His best performance on the Tour is T2, at the 1997 Transamerica and the 1999 Kroger Senior Classic. An exceptional all-round athlete, Conner has played in the US Open in both golf and tennis.

2000 SEASON. He fell outside the top-50 for the first time, but he passed $3 million in career earnings.

John Cook
US Tour

Born 2 October 1957
Place of Birth Toledo, Ohio, USA
Year turned Professional 1979
Tour Ranking 89th

BEST FINISH IN MAJORS
2nd BRITISH OPEN 1992

TOUR VICTORIES
US: 10
 1981 Bing Crosby National Pro-Am
 1983 Canadian Open
 1987 The International
 1992 Bob Hope Chrysler Classic, Las Vegas Invitational, United Airlines Hawaiian Open
 1996 CVS Charity Classic, FedEx St Jude Classic
 1997 Bob Hope Chrysler Classic
 1998 GTE Byron Nelson Classic
OTHER: 2
 1982 Sao Paulo Open
 1995 Mexican Open

RYDER CUP 1983
WORLD CUP 1983

The 1978 US Amateur Champion, Cook has played on the US Tour since 1980, the year after he turned professional. He has won ten times on Tour, but is in that select, but unenvied, group of top players never to have won a Major. He had his opportunity at the British Open in 1992 but, two shots ahead with two holes to play, he missed a short putt on the 17th and bogeyed the 18th to hand the title to Nick Faldo. He also finished second in the 1992 PGA and fourth in the same tournament in 1994, and he took fifth place in the 1994 US Open. However, a Major continues to elude him.

He went through something of a slump from 1992 till 1995 – dropping from third to 97th on the Money List – but he won the 1997 Bob Hope Classic in 1997, shooting 62 and 63 in the final two rounds. The following year he won his last title - the Byron Nelson Classic - with a last round 65 to defeat Fred Couples, Harrison Frazar and Hal Sutton. One of the best iron players on Tour, his putting has not matched his iron accuracy over his career.

2000 SEASON. Although straight and accurate on the tee and fairway, Cook has had an indifferent season largely due to his bad putting (175th on the statistics), but he did manage two T5s – in the Buick Classic and the Invensys Classic.

Richie Coughlan
US Tour

Born 7 April 1974
Place of Birth Birr, Ireland
Year turned Professional 1997
Tour Ranking Tied 8th (Qualifying School)

Irishman Coughlan was a member of the 1997 Great Britain and Ireland Walker Cup team and qualified via Qualifying School for the US Tour in 1998. He ended the season in

151st place. He has also played on the European Tour. He gained his 2001 US Tour card by finishing T8 at Qualifying School. His highest finish on Tour is T9 at the 1998 BC Open.

Fred Couples
US Tour

Born 3 October 1959
Place of Birth Seattle, Washington, USA
Year turned Professional 1980
Tour Ranking 47th

MAJORS VICTORIES
US MASTERS 1992

TOUR VICTORIES
US: 13
  1983 Kemper Open
  1984 Tournament Players Championship
  1987 Byron Nelson Golf Classic
  1990 Nissan Los Angeles Open
  1991 BC Open, Federal Express St Jude Classic
  1992 Nestle Invitational , Nissan Los Angeles Open
  1993 Honda Classic
  1994 Buick Open
  1996 The Players Championship
  1998 Bob Hope Chrysler Classic, Memorial Tournament
EUROPEAN: 4
  1991 Johnnie Walker World Championship
  1995 Dubai Desert Classic, Johnnie Walker Classic, Johnnie Walker World Championship

RYDER CUP 1989, 1991, 1993, 1995, 1997
DUNHILL CUP 1991, 1992, 1993, 1994
PRESIDENTS CUP 1994, 1996, 1998
WORLD CUP 1992, 1993, 1994, 1995

The laid-back Fred 'Boom Boom' Couples possesses a smooth, deceptively languid swing which can nonetheless propel the golf-ball a long way. His first US Tour victory was in the 1983 Kemper Open and he has won a further 12 tournaments on Tour, as well as securing victory in the 1992 Masters by a two stroke margin over Ray Floyd. He won four titles in 1991 and 1992 and was voted PGA Player of the Year both years. In 1995 he won two tournaments in succession on the European Tour, but back problems forced him of both Tours for two months. He returned the following year to win the Players Championship for the second time with a final round 64 at Sawgrass, and won two more events in 1998 – the Byron Nelson Classic and The Memorial, the latter by four strokes over Andrew Magee – in spite of only making 17 starts.

He has competed in five Ryder Cups, the highlight being 1991, when he played all five matches and only lost one. With Davis Love III he won all four World Cups between 1992 and 1995, and has represented his country in three Presidents Cups. This hugely popular player is one of the finest golfers of his generation, and his Players Championship victory assures him of exempt status until 2006, by when he could well have added to his impressive collection of silverware – if his back holds out.

2000 SEASON. Not a particularly brilliant season for Fred, although he did secure two top-5 finishes. His habit of doing well in the Majors continued with a T11 in the Masters, a T16 in the US Open and a sixth in the British Open, but he missed the cut in the USPGA.

Jane Crafter
US Ladies Tour

Born 14 December 1955
Place of Birth Perth, Australia
Year turned Professional 1981
Tour Ranking 56th

TOUR VICTORIES
US: 1
1990 Phar-Mor at Inverary

Known as 'Crafty' on the LPGA Tour, Crafter had an outstanding amateur career in Australia. She won her only US event when she sunk a 40-foot putt at the last hole at the 1990 Phar-Mor at Inverary. She has also won the Australian Ladies Open, in 1992, 1996 and 1997. She is a qualified pharmacist and writes for *Golf Digest* as well as commentating for ESPN and CBS.

2000 SEASON. Crafter posted eight top-20s, her highest being T5 at the Jamie Farr Kroger Classic.

2001 STOP PRESS. Crafter was third in the Australian Women's Open.

David Creamer
European Senior Tour

Born 9 December 1942
Place of Birth Middlesex, England
Year turned Professional 1966
Tour Ranking 10th

TOUR VICTORIES
SENIOR TOUR: 1
2000 Energis Senior Masters

Creamer has played on the European Senior Tour since 1993 and has four runner-up finishes. He had to qualify through Qualifying School for season 2000 and ended the tournament in third place.

2000 SEASON. He recorded his first win on the European Senior Tour at the Energis Senior Masters at Wentworth when he sank a 30-foot birdie putt on the last hole to edge one stroke clear of Ian Stanley and finish in tenth place on the Order of Merit.

Ben Crenshaw
US Tour

Born 11 January 1952
Place of Birth Austin, Texas, USA
Year turned Professional 1973
Tour Ranking 240th

MAJORS VICTORIES

US MASTERS 1984, 1995

TOUR VICTORIES

US: 16

1973 San Antonio Texas Open
1976 Bing Crosby National Pro-Am, Hawaian Open, Ohio Kings Island Open
1977 Colonial National Invitational
1979 Phoenix Open
1980 Anheuser-Busch Classic
1983 Byron Nelson Classic
1986 Buick Open, Vantage Championship
1987 USF&G Classic
1988 Doral Ryder Open
1990 Southwestern Bell Colonial
1992 Centel Western Open
1993 Nestle Invitational
1994 Freeport-McMoran Classic

EUROPEAN: 1

1976 Irish Open

OTHER: 2

1981 Mexican Open
1988 World Cup (indiv)

RYDER CUP 1981, 1983, 1995
DUNHILL CUP 1995
WORLD CUP 1987, 1988

An enthusiastic golf historian and twice Majors winner, 'Gentle Ben' Crenshaw is one of the most respected and popular veteran players on the US Tour. He won his first tournament – the San Antonio Texas Open – in 1973 and he has won a total of 16 events, excluding his two Masters triumphs. The first of these came in 1984 when he defeated Tom Watson by two strokes to don the green jacket. The second was in 1995 when he beat Davis Love III by one shot, and an emotional Crenshaw dedicated his victory to his friend and coach Harvey Pennick, who had died earlier that week. A peerless putter, although tending to inaccuracy off the tee, Crenshaw has not won on Tour since the last Masters

triumph. He was captain of the 1999 US Ryder Cup team which won back the Ryder Cup for the first time since 1993, coming back on the last day from four points behind to score 8½ points in the singles.

2000 SEASON. He made only one cut, finishing T77 at the GTE Byron Nelson Classic. He is exempt on the US Tour until 2005 because of his 1995 Masters victory.

Stefania Croce
US Ladies Tour

Born 17 May 1970
Place of Birth Bergamo, Italy
Year turned Professional 1989
Tour Ranking 55th

TOUR VICTORIES

EUROPEAN: 1

1992 Ford Ladies Classic

Italian-born Croce joined the European Tour in 1990 and won her only tournament, the Ford Ladies Classic, in 1992, finishing 12th on the Order of Merit. She qualified for the LPGA Tour in 1993 and her highest finish in the 1990s was T3 at the 1998 Safeway LPGA Championship.

2000 SEASON. Croce achieved the best finish of her career when she was second at the McDonald's LPGA Championship, losing the play-off to Juli Inkster. She was in 55th place on the Money List.

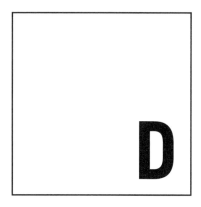

Diana D'Alessio
US Ladies Tour

Born 18 November 1974
Place of Birth Dover, New Jersey, USA
Year turned Professional 1997
Tour Ranking 76th

D'Alesio played on the Futures Tour in 1999 and ended the season with a 46th place at Qualifying School and non-exempt for 2000.

2000 SEASON. She played only 16 tournaments but came fourth at the du Maurier and the Cup Noodle Hawaian Open to clinch her card for 2001 at 76th on the Money List.

John Daly
US Tour

Born 28 April 1966
Place of Birth Carmichael, California, USA
Year turned Professional 1987
Tour Ranking 188th

MAJORS VICTORIES

BRITISH OPEN 1995
USPGA 1991

TOUR VICTORIES

US: 2
1992 BC Open
1994 BellSouth Classic

SOUTH AFRICA: 2
1990 AECI Charity Classic, Hollard Royal Swazi Sun Classic

DUNHILL CUP 1993, 1998, 2000
WORLD CUP 1998

When an unknown, stocky, long fair-haired John Daly appeared on the first tee of the Crooked Stick golf course for the start of the 1991 USPGA Championship, no-one could realize that he was going to grab golfing headlines for the rest of the decade. After all, he was ninth reserve for the competition, called out at the last moment. Although he had never played the course before and had driven through the night to get there, his second round 67 put him in the lead and he held on to win by three strokes over Bruce Lietzke. America had a new golfing hero and he was, unsurprisingly, Rookie of the Year in 1991.

His unpredictable temperament and his addiction to alcohol and junk food, however, were to dog him throughout the 1990s and his many conflicts with authority and other players and his stormy private life flawed his undoubted talent and gave him the nickname 'Wild Thing'. A regular at the top of the driving distance statistics, with an average of over 300 yards ('Grip it and Rip it' is his motto), he also possesses a deft touch around the greens. His game came together again in the 1995 British Open, at St Andrews, where he won his second Major tournament after a four-hole playoff with Costantino Rocca. His erratic nature, however, can be demonstrated by his taking 18 shots on the sixth hole of the 1998 Bay Hill Invitational, followed by a birdie two at the next.

Daly has not won a tournament anywhere in the world since St Andrews, but he represented the USA at the 1998 Dunhill Cup, alongside Mark O'Meara and Tiger Woods, and won all four of his matches. He was signed up by Callaway, who wrote off a large chunk of his gambling debts. His Open win gives him exempt status through to 2005.

2000 SEASON. Daly had a disappointing season, summed up by his final round 87 at the Bay Hill Invitational in March. His highest finish was T16 at the Honda Classic.

Robert Damron

US Tour

Born 27 October 1972
Place of Birth Pikeville, Kentucky, USA
Year turned Professional 1994
Tour Ranking 67th

BEST FINISH IN MAJORS
63rd **US OPEN 2000**

TOUR VICTORIES
US: 1
2001 Verizon Byron Nelson Classic

Long-hitting Damron joined the US Tour in 1997 from Qualifying School and, with two top-three finishes at the Buick Classic and the Fedex St Jude Classic, he ended the season in 53rd place. He was second to Stewart Cink as Rookie of the Year.

2000 SEASON. He made the cut for the first time in a Major and finished 63rd at the US Open, bringing up the rear of the field on the Sunday. His best finish was T3 in the prestigious Players Championship.

2001 STOP PRESS. Damron won his first US event, at the Byron Nelson Classic.

Beth Daniel

US Ladies Tour

Born 10 April 1955
Place of Birth Charleston, South Carolina, USA
Year turned Professional 1978
Tour Ranking 27th

MAJORS VICTORIES
LPGA 1990

TOUR VICTORIES
US: 31
1979 Patty Berg Classic
1980 Columbia Savings Classic, Golden Lights Championship, Patty Berg Classic, World Championship of Women's Golf
1981 Florida Lady Citrus, World Championship of Women's Golf
1982 American Express Sun City Classic, Bent Tree Ladies Classic, Birmingham Classic, Columbia Savings Classic, WUI Classic
1983 McDonald's Kids Classic
1985 Kyocera Inamori Classic
1989 Greater Washington Open, Konica San Jose Classic, Rail Charity Golf Classic, SAFECO Classic
1990 Centel Classic, Hawaiian Open, Kemper Open, Northgate Classic, Phar-Mor in Youngstown, Rail Charity Golf Classic
1991 McDonald's Championship, Phar-Mor at Inverary
1994 Corning Classic, JAL Big Apple Classic, Oldsmobile Classic, World Championship of Women's Golf
1995 Ping Welch's Championship

SOLHEIM CUP 1990, 1992, 1994, 1996, 2000

Before joining the LPGA Tour in 1979, the tall, fair-haired Beth Daniels was a successful amateur, winning the US Women's Amateur Championship in 1975 and 1977 and representing the USA in the Curtis Cup in 1976 and 1978. In her first year on the Tour she was voted Rookie of the Year. She won one tournament – the Patty Berg Classic – that year, ending the season tenth on the money list, and a further four in 1980. She was top of the Money List in 1980 and 1981.

Her finest year was in 1990 when she won six Tour tournaments and the LPGA Championship (her only Major victory) and she set a low scoring record with nine consecutive rounds in the 60s. Her last tournament win was the Ping Welch's Championship in Boston in 1995, and the following year she became only the third player to collect over $5 million in career earnings. She was elected to the LPGA Hall of Fame in 1999.

2000 SEASON. Daniel was inducted into the World Golf Hall of Fame. She had six top-10 finishes, her highest being fourth at the Jamie Farr Kroger Classic.

Eamon Darcy

European Tour

Born 7 August 1952
Place of Birth Delgany, Ireland
Year turned Professional 1968
Tour Ranking 137th

BEST FINISH IN MAJORS
Tied 5th **BRITISH OPEN 1991**

TOUR VICTORIES
EUROPEAN: 4
- **1977** Greater Manchester Open
- **1983** Spanish Open
- **1987** Belgian Open
- **1990** Emirates Airline Desert Classic

AUSTRALASIAN: 2
- **1980** New Zealand Open
- **1981** West Lakes Classic

RYDER CUP 1975, 1977, 1981, 1987
DUNHILL CUP 1987, 1988, 1991
WORLD CUP 1976, 1977, 1983, 1984, 1985, 1987, 1991

A 30-year veteran of the European Tour, Irishman Darcy has won four events, his most recent being the Emirates Airline Desert Classic in 1990. His best year was 1976 when he was twice runner-up and ended the season in second place on the Order of Merit. He has played in four Ryder Cups, his most memorable competition being in 1987 when his five-foot downhill putt on the 18th beat Ben Crenshaw by one hole and paved the way for Tony Jacklin's side's victory.

2000 SEASON. Darcy had his worst ever season on Tour, finishing in 137th place on the Order of Merit.

Laura Davies

US Ladies Tour

Born 5 October 1963
Place of Birth Coventry, England
Year turned Professional 1985
Tour Ranking 11th

MAJORS VICTORIES
US OPEN 1987
LPGA 1993, 1994, 1996
DU MAURIER CLASSIC 1996

TOUR VICTORIES
US: 14
- **1988** Circle K Tucson Open, Jamie Farr Toledo Classic
- **1989** Lady Keystone Open
- **1991** Inamori Classic
- **1994** Sara Lee Classic, Standard Register Ping Championship
- **1995** Chick-fil-A Charity Championship, Standard Register Ping Championship
- **1996** Standard Register Ping Championship, Star Bank Classic
- **1997** Standard Register Ping Championship

1998 PageNet Tour Championship
2000 Los Angeles Women's Championship, Philips Invitational

EUROPEAN: 31

1985 Belgian Open
1986 British Women's Open, Greater Manchester Tournament, McEwan's Wirral Classic, Spanish Open
1987 Italian Open
1988 Biarritz Open, Ford Classic, Italian Open
1989 Laing Charity Classic
1990 Biarritz Open
1991 Valextra Classic
1992 English Open, European Open, Italian Open
1993 English Open
1994 Irish Open, Scottish Open
1995 English Open, Evian Masters, Irish Open, Welsh Open
1996 English Open, Evian Masters, Italian Open
1997 Danish Open, Hennessy Cup
1998 Chrysler Open
1999 Chrysler Open, Compaq Open, WPGA Championship of Europe

AUSTRALASIAN: 2

1993 Australian Masters
1994 Australian Masters

OTHER: 6

1988 Itoki Classic
1993 Thailand Open
1994 Itoki Classic
1995 Itoen Tournament
1996 Itoen Tournament, Satake Japan Classic

SOLHEIM CUP 1990, 1992, 1994, 1996, 1998, 2000

The huge-hitting Davies, with her passion for soccer and fast cars, is the finest woman golfer Britain has produced. Self-taught, with little time or inclination for practice or the technicalities of the golf swing, she is occasionally inconsistent but is a brilliant striker of the ball, with a smooth and delicate touch around the green. But her power and length are her biggest assets. Since she emerged onto the European Tour in 1985, when she won Rookie of the Year and the Order of Merit, she has won 31 titles on Tour and has headed the Order of Merit on five occasions, most recently in 1999. She arrived on the LPGA Tour in 1987 and won the US Women's Open that year, and has collected 19 victories to date, including five majors, on the US Tour. She was also, in 1994 and 1996, number one on the US Money List and won the Golf Writers' Association of America LPGA Player of the Year Award in both years. She has played in every Solheim Cup and was the inspiration behind Europe's 1992 victory, winning all three of her matches.

In recent years her domination has been challenged by the emergence of a new generation of golfers, such as Annika Sorenstam and Karrie Webb, but Davies remains a major force in women's golf, not only in the US and Europe but also at her frequent attendances at competitions around the world. She was awarded the MBE in 1988 and the CBE in 2000.

2000 SEASON. Davies won twice in the US, but did not manage a victory on the European Tour, the first time in 16 years she has been winless in a European season. Her highest finish on the European Tour was third at the Australian Open.

Brian Davis
European Tour

Born 2 August 1974
Place of Birth London, England
Year turned Professional 1994
Tour Ranking 29th

BEST FINISH IN MAJORS
Tied 68th BRITISH OPEN 1999

TOUR VICTORIES
EUROPEAN: 1
2000 Spanish Open

DUNHILL CUP 2000

Afine driver of the ball, Davis spends his time alternating between England and Florida. His best performance before 2000 was tied for fourth place at the German Open in 1997, his rookie year. In 1998 he was in intensive care in Dubai after contracting a virus, but he survived and just missed out on his US Tour card in 1999. Davis is a long hitter and a very capable putter.

2000 SEASON. Davis began 2000 in fine form, making the cut on his first five tournaments, and won his first European Tour title – the Spanish Open – three shots ahead of Austria's Markus Brier. He was also third at the Portugese Open.

Mark Davis
European Tour

Born 4 July 1964
Place of Birth Brentwood, England
Year turned Professional 1986
Tour Ranking 116th

BEST FINISH IN MAJORS
Tied 30th BRITISH OPEN 1989

TOUR VICTORIES
EUROPEAN: 2
1991 Mitsubishi Austrian Open
1994 Hohe Brucke Open

Davis won the English Amateur Strokeplay Championship at the age of 19 and he joined the European Tour in 1987. He has won two Tour events, the 1991 Mitsubishi Austrian Open and the 1994 Hohe Brucke Open.

2000 SEASON. Despite finishing tied for second place in the Madeira Island Open, Davis just managed to retain his Tour card finishing 116th on the Order of Merit.

Rodger Davis
Australasian Tour

Born 18 May 1951
Place of Birth Sydney, Australia
Year turned Professional 1974
Tour Ranking 117th

BEST FINISH IN MAJORS
Tied 2nd BRITISH OPEN 1987

TOUR VICTORIES
EUROPEAN: 7
1981 State Express Classic
1986 Whyte & Mackay PGA Championship
1988 Wang Pro-Celebrity
1990 Peugeot Spanish Open, Wang
       Pro-Celebrity
1991 Volvo Masters
1993 Air France Cannes Open

DUNHILL CUP 1986, 1987, 1988, 1990, 1992, 1993
WORLD CUP 1985, 1987, 1991, 1993

With his moustache, long socks and his plus-twos, Davis is a hard figure to miss on the European Tour. His 19 tournament wins in Australia and New Zealand and his seven European Tour victories (the last in 1993 when he beat Mark McNulty in a play-off at the Cannes Open) have brought him over £2 million and 2001 season will find him adding to this on the US Seniors Tour. He has twice come close to winning the British Open. In 1979 at Royal Lytham he led with five holes to play but ended in fifth position, and in 1987, at Muirfield, he finished tied for second with Paul Azinger, one stroke behind winner Nick Faldo.

2000 SEASON. He occupied 117th position on the 2000 Money List.

Marco Dawson

US Tour

Born 17 November 1963
Place of Birth Freising, Germany
Year turned Professional 1986
Tour Ranking Tied 31st (Qualifying School)

Dawson was a regular on the US Tour from 1991 until 1997. His best year was in 1995 when he came second to Scott Hoch in the Greater Milwaukee Open and finished 71st on the Money List. He had back surgery in 2000 and only competed in 11 events, and was granted a medical extension for 2001. He also qualified from Qualifying School at T31.

Peter Dawson

European Senior Tour

Born 9 May 1950
Place of Birth Doncaster, England
Year turned Professional 1970
Tour Ranking 20th

Left-hander Dawson played on the European Tour, finishing seventh on the Order of Merit in 1977, but has spent the last 16 years as a golf coach in France and Switzerland. One of his more illustrious students was Thomas Björn. He played for Britain and Ireland in the 1977 Ryder Cup.

2000 SEASON. Dawson took John Grace to a play-off at the Belfry PGA Seniors Championship but was beaten at the first extra hole. He finished in 20th spot on the Order of Merit.

Glen Day

US Tour

Born 16 November 1965
Place of Birth Mobile, Alabama, USA
Year turned Professional 1988
Tour Ranking 75th

BEST FINISH IN MAJORS
Tied 15th **USPGA 1994**

TOUR VICTORIES
US: 1
  1999 MCI Heritage Classic
OTHER: 1
  1990 Malaysian Open

Day qualified through Qualifying School in 1993 having previously played on both the European and Asian Tours, where he won the Malaysian Open in 1990. He is known for the excellence of his short game and his putting, although his slow pace of play has earned him the nickname Glen 'All' Day. In 1994 he was third in the Rookie of the Year awards and, even more impressively, posted two holes-in-one at the Greater Hartford Classic. He finished second in the 1998 Players Championship at the TPC of Sawgrass Stadium Course, in Florida, and won his first trophy at the MCI Heritage Classic in 1999. His 35-foot birdie putt at the first play-off hole saw off the challenges of Payne Stewart and Jeff Sluman.

2000 SEASON. Day began the season well with a T8 at the opening Mercedes Championship, and he finished tied for 19th position at the Masters. He ended the season with a sixth place at the NCR Disney Classic. Otherwise, 2000 was not a particularly impressive year for Day, although he finished in the top-100 for the seventh year in succession.

Sally Dee

US Ladies Tour

Born 17 December 1970
Place of Birth Syracuse, New York, USA
Year turned Professional 1994
Tour Ranking 77th

The tall, blond-haired Dee played on the Futures Tour in 1994 and, after five failed attempts, qualified for the LPGA Tour in 1999, finishing T13 at Qualifying School.

2000 SEASON. She retained her card for 2001 by carding a career-best T3 at the Michelob Light Classic, taking fourth place at the Takefuji Classic and tieing for ninth at the Cup Noodles Hawaian Open.

Dorothy Delasin

US Ladies Tour

Born 28 August 1980
Place of Birth Lubbock, Texas, USA
Year turned Professional 1999
Tour Ranking 25th

TOUR VICTORIES
US: 1
2000 Giant Eagle LPGA Classic

Junior World Champion in 1998 and US Ladies Amateur Champion in 1999, the hugely talented Delasin qualified T4 at 1999 Qualifying School for the 2000 LPGA Tour.

2000 SEASON. She became the youngest winner on the LPGA Tour for 25 years when she lifted the Giant Eagle LPGA Classic title and, with seven top-20s and a T12 at the US Women's Open, was voted Rookie of the Year.

Jim Dent

US Seniors Tour

Born 9 May 1939
Place of Birth Augusta, Georgia, USA
Year turned Professional 1966
Tour Ranking 25th

TOUR VICTORIES
SENIOR TOUR: 12
1989 MONY Syracuse Senior Classic, Newport Cup
1990 Crestar Classic, Kroger Senior Classic, MONY Syracuse Senior Classic, Vantage at the Dominion
1992 Newport Cup
1994 Bruno's Memorial Classic
1995 BellSouth Senior Classic
1996 Bank of Boston Senior Classic
1997 The Home Depot Invitational
1998 The Home Depot Invitational

The 6 foot 3 inch, Afro-American Georgian – known on Tour as 'Big Boy' – began as a caddie at Augusta and joined the USPGA Tour in 1971. He was winless in his PGA career and, after a spell in the mini-tours, he joined the US Seniors in 1989. He won twice and was voted Rookie of the Year in 1989, and won a further four events in 1990, finishing in the top-10 of the Money List. A long hitter, he topped the driving distance statistics in 1994 for the sixth year in succession. He has won a total of 12 tournaments and has earned over $7 million in his career.

2000 SEASON. Dent enjoyed his most profitable season since 1994, finishing seven times in the top-10 with his highest placing T2 at the Coldwell Banker Burnett Classic behind Hale Irwin. He was also on second place in the over-60, Super Senior Money List behind George Archer. It was his 12th successive season in the top-30.

Laura Diaz
US Ladies Tour

Born 27 April 1975
Place of Birth Scotia, New York, USA
Year turned Professional 1997
Tour Ranking 33rd

Known as Laura Philo until the 2000 season, Diaz played regularly on the Future Tour between 1997 and 1998 and was very successful, notching up three wins on the circuit. In 1998, she was Rookie of the Year on the European Ladies Tour, and joined the US Ladies Tour in 1999, when her best finish was T6 at the Michelob Light Classic.

2000 SEASON. Diaz had her best LPGA finish at the Giant Eagle Classic, finishing T3, and collected three other top-10s, including sixth at the British Women's Open.

2001 STOP PRESS. Diaz finished T2 at Welch's Circle K Championship and was also runner-up to Korea's Se Ri Pak at the Longs Drugs Challenge.

Alicia Dibos
US Ladies Tour

Born 1 March 1960
Place of Birth Lima, Peru
Year turned Professional 1988
Tour Ranking 87th

Peruvian Dibos was a three-time South American Junior Champion before she joined the European Tour in 1988. In 1992 she finished 11th on the Order of Merit and qualified for the LPGA Tour in 1992. Her best ever finish on Tour was T2 at the Children's Medical Center Classic in 1994.

2000 SEASON. Her best performance of the season was T17 at the Giant Eagle LPGA Classic, and she ended the season in 87th position on the Money List. During the year, Dibos made 16 successive cuts, but failed to break into the top-10 in any tournament she entered.

Bob Dickson
US Seniors Tour

Born 25 January 1944
Place of Birth McAlaster, Oklahoma, USA
Year turned Professional 1968
Tour Ranking 67th

TOUR VICTORIES
SENIOR TOUR: 1
1998 Cadillac NFL Golf Classic

Holder of both the 1967 US and British Amateur Championships before he turned professional, the tall (6 foot 3 inch) Oklahoman joined the USPGA Tour in 1968 and went on to win twice during his career. After deciding to put the clubs away for a while, he went on to become a PGA Tour employee, where he took on the role of Tournament Director for the fledgling Ben Hogan Tour in 1989 before dusting down his clubs and joining the US Senior Tour, this time as a player, in 1994. He has one victory on the Senior Tour to date, beating Larry Nelson and Jim Colbert on the first play-off hole at the 1998 Cadillac NFL Golf Classic.

2000 SEASON. Dickson had another solid season with two top-20 finishes, his highest being T14 at the GTE Classic.

Tobias Dier
European Tour

Born 22nd September 1976
Place of Birth Nurnberg, Germany
Year turned Professional 1998
Tour Ranking 6th (Challenge Tour)

An engineering graduate from Frankfurt University, Dier qualified for the 2001 European Tour by finishing in a creditable sixth place on the 2000 Challenge Tour, his best placing being third at the Le Touquet Challenge and the Finnish Masters. He has a solid all-round game and is known as a very good putter

Terry Dill
US Seniors Tour

Born 13 May 1939
Place of Birth Fort Worth, Texas, USA
Year turned Professional 1962
Tour Ranking 61st

TOUR VICTORIES
SENIOR TOUR: 1
1992 Bank One Classic

A tall, long-hitting Texan, ex-law teacher Dill joined the US Senior Tour in 1989. He recorded his only win in 1992 when he won the Bank One Classic by four strokes, and his best season was 1998 when he had eight top-10 finishes and secured 20th place on the Money List.

2000 SEASON. Dill topped the driving distance statistics, at 61 years of age the oldest player to do so. His best finish was T6 at the Audi Senior Classic.

Chris DiMarco
US Tour

Born 23 August 1968
Place of Birth Huntington, New York, USA
Year turned Professional 1990
Tour Ranking 19th

BEST FINISH IN MAJORS
T10 **MASTERS 2001**

TOUR VICTORIES
US: 1
2000 SEI Pennsylvania Classic

D iMarco arrived on the US Tour in 1994 from the Canadian and Nike Tours. His best year before 2000 was in 1999 when he came second to Brian Henninger in the Southern Farm Bureau Classic and tied for third place in the Byron Nelson Classic, shooting four sub-70 rounds. He is an advocate of the 'split grip' putting technique, where the thumbs point upward on the grip rather than downward, a method he learned from fellow Tour Pro Skip Kendall.

2000 SEASON. He enjoyed another good season, winning the Pennsylvania Classic by six shots and T15 in the USPGA Championship, but missed the cut in the British Open.

2001 STOP PRESS. DiMarco led the Masters for the first two rounds in his first appearance at the tournament. He faded away in the final round, shooting a 73, and ended tied for tenth place.

Priscillo Diniz
European Senior Tour

Born 12 December 1948
Place of Birth Sao Paulo, Brazil
Year turned Professional 1977
Tour Ranking 6th

TOUR VICTORIES
SENIOR TOUR: 2
2000 European Seniors Matchplay Championship
2001 Royal Westmoreland Barbados Open

A sometime lawyer from Sao Paulo, Brazil, Diniz played briefly on the European Tour in the late 1970s, but mainly concentrated on the South American golfing circuit. He joined the European Senior Tour in 2000 having qualified T3 at Qualifying School. Eight other members of his immediate family are golf professionals.

2000 SEASON. He won his first Tour event at the *Daily Telegraph* European Seniors Match Play Championship when he beat Australia's Ian Stanley 3&2, and he finished in second place to Denis O'Sullivan at the Abu Dhabi Championship. He ended the season in sixth place on the Order of Merit.

2001 STOP PRESS. Diniz claimed his second Senior title when he led wire-to-wire at the Royal Westmoreland Barbados Open to win the tournament with a 16 under par total.

Stephen Dodd
European Tour

Born 15 July 1960
Place of Birth Cardiff, Wales
Year turned Professional 1990
Tour Ranking 18th (Qualifying School)

British Amateur Champion at Birkdale in 1989, Dodd played in the 1990 Masters, but not surprisingly comfortably missed the cut. His best finish on the Challenge Tour in 2000 was third in the Credit Suisse Open and he was placed 18th at the 2000 Qualifying School to gain his 2001 European Tour card.

Wendy Doolan
US Ladies Tour

Born 16 December 1968
Place of Birth Sydney, Australia
Year turned Professional 1991
Tour Ranking 30th

Doolan represented Australia seven times as an amateur international, and she played mainly on the European and Asian Tour circuits between 1992 and 1995. She qualified for the LPGA Tour in 1996, but has to date been without a win.

2000 SEASON. Doolan came very close to claiming her maiden Tour win when she had her highest-ever finish, second at the Wegmans Rochester International, and also a T3 at the Electrolux USA Championship.

Ed Dougherty
US Seniors Tour

Born 4 November 1947
Place of Birth Chester, Pennsylvania, USA
Year turned Professional 1969
Tour Ranking 17th

TOUR VICTORIES
SENIOR TOUR: 1
 2000 Coldwell Banker Burnett Classic

Apopular figure on the US Senior Tour, 'Doc' Dougherty played his first full year in the Seniors in 1999, when he led the Senior Open for three rounds, eventually losing to Dave Eichelberger, and picked up four second places. Dougherty's unusual hobby is collecting model trains and old pinball machines.

2000 SEASON. Dougherty won his first tournament on Tour at the Coldwell Banker Burnett Classic when he shot 19 under par to defeat Hale Irwin and Gil Morgan. He also had seven other top-10s. In two seasons he has earned nearly $2 million.

2001 STOP PRESS. Dougherty had two T3 finishes, at the MasterCard Championship and the SBC Senior Classic.

Dale Douglass
US Seniors Tour

Born 5 March 1936
Place of Birth Wewoka, Oklahoma, USA
Year turned Professional 1960
Tour Ranking 62nd

MAJORS VICTORIES
US SENIOR OPEN 1986

TOUR VICTORIES
SENIOR TOUR: 10
 1986 Fairfield Barnett Classic, Johnny Mathis Senior Classic, Vantage Invitational
 1988 GTE Suncoast Classic
 1990 Bell Atlantic Classic
 1991 Showdown Classic
 1992 Ameritech Senior Open, NYNEX Commemorative
 1993 Ralphs Senior Classic
 1996 Bell Atlantic Classic

The tall Douglass had three US Tour wins in the 1960s and became VP of the PGA in 1972. He joined the US Senior Tour in 1986 and in his rookie year he claimed third spot on the Money List, helped by four tournament victories, including the US Senior Open by one stroke over Gary Player. The last of his 12 wins was in a play-off at the Bell Atlantic Classic in 1996, and by 1999 he had exceeded $6 million earnings on Tour.

2000 SEASON. Douglass's highest finish was T9 at the Kroger Senior Classic.

Allen Doyle
US Seniors Tour

Born 26 July 1948
Place of Birth Woonsocket, Rhode Island, USA
Year turned Professional 1995
Tour Ranking 7th

MAJORS VICTORIES
  PGA SENIORS CHAMPIONSHIP 1999

TOUR VICTORIES
SENIOR TOUR: 4
  1999 ACE Group Classic, Cadillac NFL Golf Classic, TD Waterhouse Championship
  2000 Toshiba Senior Classic

Doyle's route to the US Senior Tour was an unconventional one. He played as an amateur until 1994 and then joined the Nike Tour, moving up to the PGA Tour in 1996, where he became the oldest rookie the in history of the Tour. He joined the US Seniors in 1998 when he won the Qualifying School tournament, setting another record as the only player to have finished first on both the PGA and Senior Qualifying Schools.

His accurate, if unorthodox, ice hockey-like swing brought him four victories in his rookie year of 1999, including a final round 64 and a two-shot win over Vicente Fernandez in the PGA Senior Championship. He finished his first year in THIrd spot on the Money List, enough to allow him to refurbish his driving range in Georgia.

2000 SEASON. Doyle achieved 17 top-10 finishes and he won the rain-shortened Toshiba

Senior Classic by one shot ahead of Howard Twitty and Jim Thorpe. He earned over $1 million.

2001 STOP PRESS. Doyle finished T2 behind Hale Irwin at the Siebel Classic and was third at the Toshiba Senior Classic. He was also T3 at the Las Vegas Senior Classic.

Bradley Dredge
European Tour

Born 6 July 1973
Place of Birth Newport, Gwent, Wales
Year turned Professional 1996
Tour Ranking 107th

An inconsistent player, Welshman Dredge joined the European Tour in 1998 from the Challenge Tour, but lost his card at the end of the season. An eighth place on the 1999 Challenge Tour regained him his card for 2000.

2000 SEASON. He scored his first top-10 places with a T8 at the Moroccan Open, a T7 at the Madeira Island Open and a T6, his highest finish on Tour, at the Irish Open.

Doug Dunakey
US Tour

Born 7 July 1963
Place of Birth Waterloo, Iowa, USA
Year turned Professional 1987
Tour Ranking 124th

Dunakey joined the US Tour in 1999 from the Buy.Com Tour, where he shot a 59 in 1998 at the Miami Valley Open. He lost his card at the end of the season in spite of tieing for third place, his highest career finish, at the Honda Classic, but regained it at Qualifying School.

2000 SEASON. Although he failed to make several cuts, he was T5 in the Greater Greensboro Classic and T4 in the Reno-Tahoe Open. He just made his card for 2001, ending 124th on the Money List.

Scott Dunlap

US Tour

Born 16 August 1963
Place of Birth Pittsburgh, Pennsylvania, USA
Year turned Professional 1985
Tour Ranking 44th

BEST FINISH IN MAJORS

Tied 9th USPGA 2000

TOUR VICTORIES

SOUTH AFRICA: 2
    1995 South African Masters
    1999 Dimension Data Pro-Am
OTHER: 7
    1994 Manitoba Open
    1995 Canadian Open
    1996 Litoral Open
    1998 Peru Open
    1999 Argentine Open, Peru Open
    2000 Peru Open

Golf runs in Dunlap's family, with his sister Page a sometime member of the USPGA Ladies Tour. Dunlap has been on the US Tour since 1996 and has not yet won a tournament, although he has won internationally, particularly in South Africa and South America. He won the Canadian Open in 1995 by ten strokes and was second on the Canadian Order of Merit in 1995. He had a particularly good year in 1999, finishing tied for third in the Doral-Ryder Open and tied for tenth in the British Open at Carnoustie. He played in the South African Open early in the season, finishing second and posting a course record 65. The predictable headline in the next day's newspaper – 'Dunlap 65'.

2000 SEASON. Dunlap had his best finish in a Major with a tied ninth at the USPGA Championship. He also recorded five top-5 finishes, the most lucrative by some margin being his T3 at the Players Championship. He entered the top-50 on the Money List for the first time, earning just over $1 million.

Moira Dunn

US Seniors Tour

Born 3 August 1971
Place of Birth Utica, New York, USA
Year turned Professional 1994
Tour Ranking 47th

Dunn joined the LPGA Tour in 1995 but has yet to win a tournament. Her highest finish is T2 at the 1999 Sunrise Hawaian Ladies Open.

2000 SEASON. Dunn claimed T3 at the Philips Invitational and three other top-10s to make 47th place on the Money List.

Joe Durant

US Tour

Born 7 April 1964
Place of Birth Pensacola, Florida, USA
Year turned Professional 1987
Tour Ranking 76th

BEST FINISH IN MAJORS

Tied 24th US OPEN 2001

TOUR VICTORIES

US: 3
    1998 Motorola Western Open
    2001 Bob Hope Chrysler Classic, Genuity Championship

Durant played on the US Tour in 1993 but spent the next three seasons on the Nike Tour, winning one tournament, before rejoining the main Tour in 1997. In 1998 he won his first Tour event when he shot 66 in the final round, birdieing three of the last five holes, at the Motorola Western Open to beat Vijay Singh by two shots. An extremely accurate golfer, in 1999 and 2000 he was second in the green in regulation statistics, but he was let down by poor putting. Considered something of a journeyman golfer, he quit the sport briefly in 1991 to sell insurance, a career change which was markedly unsuccessful by his own admission.

2000 SEASON. His best result was fifth in the Tampa Bay Classic and he also gained three other top-10 finishes. He was second in driving accuracy stats.

2001 STOP PRESS. Durant, who had been considering quitting golf to sell insurance, was encouraged by his wife to adopt a more positive attitude. He buried the 'journeyman' tag and struck gold at the 90-hole Bob Hope Chrysler Classic, winning the second tournament of his career, four shots ahead of Paul Stankowski. He then won the next tournament he entered – the Genuity Championship – when he shot a 7 under par last round 65 in wet and windy conditions. The win moved him to the top of the Money List and guaranteed him a place in the Masters. He then came T2 at the Shell Houston Open behind Hal Sutton.

Bob Duval
US Seniors Tour

Born 9 October 1946
Place of Birth Schenectady, New York, USA
Year turned Professional 1968
Tour Ranking 85th

TOUR VICTORIES
SENIOR TOUR: 1
1999 Emerald Coast Classic

Duval, who was a teaching professional and had never played on the US Tour, joined the US Senior Tour in 1997, earning over $500,000 in his rookie year. The following season he finished 17th on the Money List, his highest ever placing. He won his only tournament – the Emerald Coast Classic – in 1999, on the same weekend that his son, David, won the Players Championship.

2000 SEASON. He injured his elbow, underwent surgery, and spent most of the season recuperating.

David Duval
US Tour

Born 9 November 1971
Place of Birth Jacksonville, Florida, USA
Year turned Professional 1993
Tour Ranking 7th

MAJORS VICTORIES
BRITISH OPEN 2001

TOUR VICTORIES
US: 12
1997 Michelob Championship, The Tour Championship, Walt Disney World/Oldsmobile Classic
1998 Michelob Championship, NEC World Series of Golf, Shell Houston Open, Tucson Chrysler Classic
1999 BellSouth Classic, Bob Hope Chrysler Classic, Mercedes Championship, The Players Championship
2000 Buick Challenge

RYDER CUP 1999
PRESIDENTS CUP 1996, 1998, 2000
WORLD CUP 2000

Duval, sporting his collarless shirt, distinctive wrap-around sunglasses and baggy chinos, became one of the world's top players within two years of joining the US Tour. A graduate of the Nike Tour, he made a sensational start in his Rookie Year in 1995 when he achieved eight top-10 finishes to amass nearly $900,000 and end the season in 11th place on the Money List. In 1997 he won three trophies back-to-back and was tenth on the Money List. The following year he consolidated his position as the best golfer in the world with four tournament victories, topping the money list ahead of Tiger Woods and recording the lowest scoring average (69.13). That year he won the Tucson Open, helped by his second round front nine score of 28. In 1999, he claimed another four tournaments, including the Bob Hope Classic when he scored a 59 in the final round to win by one shot and equal the Tour record for lowest-ever score. Also in that year he won the prestigious Players Championship, beating Scott Gump by two strokes to earn himself a five-year exemption on Tour. He was PGA Player of the Year in both 1998 and 1999.

He played in the 1999 Ryder Cup, and beat Jesper Parnevik in the Sunday singles matchplay by the 14th hole to atone for his previously disappointing fourball failure against the Europeans. The emotion he displayed after the win surprised many who viewed him previously as a rather distant and cold figure. He has not won a Major, although he came close in 1998 when he sat in the clubhouse in Augusta to watch Mark O'Meara birdie the 18th to beat him to the Masters green jacket by one stroke.

2000 SEASON. Duval embarked on a fitness training programme before the season began, but injured his back in the late summer and did not win a tournament until the Buick Challenge in October when he finished two strokes ahead of Jeff Maggert and Nick Price. He was T3 in the Masters, T8 in the US Open and T11 in the British Open, where he was head-to-head with Tiger Woods on the final day, but took four shots to get out of the infamous 17th hole bunker. However, he still could not land that elusive Major. With his superb long game, putting ability and his obvious determination,

a Major victory for Duval cannot be far away.

2001 STOP PRESS. Duval had a disappointing start to the season but came second in the Masters to Tiger Woods. The Open at Royal Lytham & St Anne's saw Duval go one better. He emerged from the pack on the final day to claim his first Major victory.

Simon Dyson
European Tour

Born 22 December 1977
Place of Birth York, England
Year turned Professional 1999
Tour Ranking 33rd (Qualifying School)

TOUR VICTORIES
OTHER: 3
2000 Macau Open, Omega Hong Kong Open, Volvo China Open

Nephew of Terry Dyson, right-winger in Tottenham Hotspur's 1969 Double-winning team, Dyson's amateur career included playing in the winning 1999 Walker Cup team. Finnish Amateur Champion in 1999, he turned professional that year and joined the Asian Tour. He won three tournaments – the Macau Open, Volvo China Open and Hong Kong Open – and won the Asian Order of Merit and the Rookie of the Year award. He played in eight European Tour events that year and qualified for the 2001 season by finishing 33rd at Qualifying School.

other top-10 finishes. He remained in the top-100 in the Order of Merit from joining the Tour in 1993 until the 1999 season. He finished third behind Colin Montgomerie and Mark James in the 1999 Volvo PGA Championship. A former assistant professional at the famous Royal Lytham & St Annes links course, in Lancashire, Eales is not known for his length off the tee, but he is an accurate driver. However, his game is often let down by his poor putting. For obvious reasons, the popular Eales is known as 'Slippery' on Tour. He is also a regular radio commentator on golf.

2000 SEASON. Eales started the season brightly with two T13s, but then virtually disappeared from sight. However, his T12 in the Italian Open in October helped to secure his card for 2001. He finished 112 in the Order of Merit.

Paul Eales

European Tour

Born 2 August 1963
Place of Birth Epping, England
Year turned Professional 1985
Tour Ranking 112th

BEST FINISH IN MAJORS
Made Cut BRITISH OPEN 2000, 1999, 1996,1994, 1993

TOUR VICTORIES
EUROPEAN: 1
1994 Open de Extremadura

Bob Eastwood

US Seniors Tour

Born 9 February 1946
Place of Birth Providence, Rhode Island, USA
Year turned Professional 1969
Tour Ranking 49th

TOUR VICTORIES
SENIOR TOUR: 2
1997 Bell Atlantic Classic, Raley's Gold Rush Classic

Eales' best year was in 1994, his second full season on the European Tour, when he won the Open de Extremadura and had four

Eastwood had three wins in his USPGA Tour career, and joined the US Senior Tour in 1997. In his rookie year he won twice, the first at the rain-shortened Bell Atlantic Classic by one stroke and then wire-to-wire at Raley's Gold Rush Classic. Eastwood is a short game specialist and a fine bunker player.

2000 SEASON. His highest place was T4 at the Emerald Coast Classic and he passed the $2 million career earnings mark.

2001 STOP PRESS. McGinnis had his highest finish since his 1997 Raley's win when he was T3 at the Royal Caribbean Classic.

Anna Jane J Eathorne
US Ladies Tour

Born 12 July 1976
Place of Birth Calgary, Alberta
Year turned Professional 1998
Tour Ranking 35th

Anna Jane was Canadian Ladies Champion in 1997 and played on the 1998 Futures Tour. She joined the 1999 LPGA Tour full of confidence after winning the Qualifying School, and she turned that confidence into a string of good results, the most notable of which was a T3 at the Longs Drugs Challenge.

2000 SEASON. Eathorne continued where she left off in 1999 by posting seven top-10 finishes, her highest being fourth at the Firstar LPGA Classic. She ended the season in a respectable 35th position on the Money List.

Seiji Eblhara
European Senior Tour

Born 4 February 1949
Place of Birth Chiba, Japan
Year turned Professional 1969
Tour Ranking 15th

TOUR VICTORIES
SENIOR TOUR: 1
2001 AIB Irish Seniors Open

Japanese Ebihara has won several tournaments in Japan and competed in the Senior British Open in 1999, finishing 26th. He qualified for the 2000 European Senior Tour by finishing in second place at Qualifying School.

2000 SEASON. Ebihara carded two runner-up spots early in the season. He tied with Denis Durnian for second at the Coca Cola Kaiser Karl European Trophy, and the following weekend he was second again at the Total Fina Elf Seniors Open in France.

2001 STOP PRESS. Ebihara won his first tournament at the AIB Irish Seniors Open.

Olivier Edmond
European Tour

Born 29 January 1970
Place of Birth Paris, France
Year turned Professional 1990
Tour Ranking 109th

DUNHILL CUP 1998

The French Amateur Champion in 1990, Edmond demonstrated his grit and determination by eventually qualifying for the European Tour in 1997 after four previous failed attempts. In his first season, Edmond tied for second in the French Open on home soil and went on to receive the Rookie of the Year award. As he was beginning to settle comfortably into life as a Tour regular, however, he had to take nine months off from golf in 1999 to undergo chemotherapy for testicular cancer.

2000 SEASON. Back to full health, Edmond had three top-20 finishes and ended the season 109th on the Order of Merit.

Joel Edwards
US Tour

Born 2 November 1961
Place of Birth Dallas, Texas, USA
Year turned Professional 1978
Tour Ranking 73rd

BEST FINISH IN MAJORS
Tied 62nd US OPEN 1993

A veteran US Tour member between 1989 and 1997, Edwards rejoined the Tour in 2000 after finishing second in the Buy.Com Tour after claiming one victory and eight top-10 finishes.

2000 SEASON. He earned his 2001 card convincingly with a T2 at the Shell Houston Open and a T5 in the Buick Challenge. He also claimed six other top-20 places to finish in the top-100 for only the second time in his long tournament career.

Dale Eggeling
US Ladies Tour

Born 21 April 1954
Place of Birth Statesboro, Georgia, USA
Year turned Professional 1974
Tour Ranking 52nd

TOUR VICTORIES
US: 3

1980 Boston Five Classic
1995 Oldsmobile Classic
1998 Los Angeles Women's Championship

A veteran of the LPGA Tour, Eggeling holds the record for the length of time between victories. She won her first tournament – the Boston Five Classic – in 1980 and claimed her second event 15 years later at the Oldsmobile Classic, where she shot a second round 63. She won her third title at the 1998 Los Angeles Women's Championship, beating Hiromi Kobayashi in a play-off. She has had six holes-in-one in her career.

2000 SEASON. Another solid season saw her finish third at the Wegmans Rochester International and tied for third place at the Subaru Memorial of Naples, in Florida.

Dave Eichelberger
US Seniors Tour

Born 3 September 1943
Place of Birth Waco, Texas, USA
Year turned Professional 1966
Tour Ranking 40th

MAJOR VICTORIES
US SENIOR OPEN 1999

TOUR VICTORIES
SENIOR TOUR: 5

1994 Quicksilver Classic
1996 VFW Senior Championship
1997 The Transamerica
1999 Novell Utah Showdown, US Senior Open

The long-driving, if inconsistent, 'Ike' Eichelberger won four times on the USPGA Tour between 1971 and 1981 and joined the US Seniors in 1994. In his rookie year he won the Quicksilver Classic and, with six other top-10 placings, he finished 20th on the Money List. His best year was 1999 when he beat Ed Dougherty by three shots to win the US Senior Open and collect $315,000, and three weeks later he defeated Dana Quigley in a play-off at the Novell Utah Showdown.

2000 SEASON. He collected three top-10s, his highest being T5 at the Toshiba Senior Classic.

Brad Elder
US Tour

Born 17 March 1975
Place of Birth Tulsa, Oklahoma, USA
Year turned Professional 1998
Tour Ranking 68th

Six foot three inch Brad Elder is a relative newcomer to the US Tour, having joined from the Buy.Com Tour in 2000, where he won two tournaments in 1999. A golfer of no mean ability, he was Jack Nicklaus College Player of the Year in 1997.

2000 SEASON. Elder had an impressive rookie year on Tour with six top-20 finishes, including a T2, six strokes behind Chris DiMarco in the Pennsylvania Classic and a T6 in the Southern Farm Bureau Classic. This tall, powerful young golfer is definitely a player to look out for in the future.

Steve Elkington
US Tour

Born 8 December 1962
Place of Birth Inverell, Australia
Year turned Professional 1985
Tour Ranking 154th

MAJORS VICTORIES
USPGA 1995

TOUR VICTORIES

US: 9

1990 Kmart Greater Greensboro Open
1991 The Players Championship
1992 Infiniti Tournament of Champions
1994 Buick Southern Open
1995 Mercedes Championships
1997 Doral-Ryder Open, The Players Championship
1998 Buick Challenge
1999 Doral-Ryder Open

AUSTRALASIAN: 1

1992 Australian Open

OTHER: 1

1996 Honda Invitational

DUNHILL CUP 1994, 1995, 1996, 1997
PRESIDENTS CUP 1994, 1996, 1998, 2000
WORLD CUP 1994

Tall, powerfully-built Australian Steve Elkington has one of the most elegantly effective swings on the US Tour. He won the Australian Amateur Championship in 1981 and joined the Tour in 1987, picking up his first tournament win – the Greater Greensboro Open – in 1990. He secured a ten-year exemption by winning the Players Championship in 1991, holding off Fuzzy Zoeller by one stroke, and he won the tournament again in 1997, this time by a comprehensive seven strokes. In the 1995 USPGA Championship he shot a final round 64 to force a play-off with Colin Montgomerie, and he won the title by sinking a 25-foot birdie putt on the first hole in the play-off.

'The Elk' has played in four Presidents Cups, winning five points out of a possible six in 1998 to help the International team to a deserved victory. His last tournament win was in 1999 at the Doral-Ryder Open, when he shot ten birdies in his final round 64 to defeat Greg Kraft. His career, successful though it is, has been hampered by recurring sinus problems and allergies.

2000 SEASON. Illness dogged Elkington again in 2000 and he had to pull out of the US Open, USPGA and the Players Championship, and the highest finish he could achieve was T10 in the Buick Challenge in only 17 appearances. However, he had hip surgery in the autumn and is reportedly feeling better than ever. Watch out for him in 2001.

Danny Ellis

US Tour

Born 15 September 1970
Place of Birth Orlando, Florida, USA
Year turned Professional 1994
Tour Ranking Tied 27th (Qualifying School)

Ellis was runner-up in the 1993 US Amateur Championship and competed in the 1994 Masters, missing the cut. He turned professional, played on the Canadian and Asian Tours and was a member of the 1996 and 1997 Nike Tour. He gained his 2001 US Tour card by finishing T27 at Qualifying School.

Ernie Els

US Tour

Born 17 October 1969
Place of Birth Johannesburg, South Africa
Year turned Professional 1989
Tour Ranking 3rd

MAJORS VICTORIES
US OPEN 1994, 1997

TOUR VICTORIES
US: 6
- **1995** GTE Byron Nelson Classic
- **1996** Buick Classic
- **1997** Buick Classic
- **1998** Bay Hill International
- **1999** Nissan Open
- **2000** The International

EUROPEAN: 6
- **1994** Dubai Desert Classic
- **1995** South African PGA
- **1997** Johnny Walker Classic
- **1998** South African Open
- **1999** South African PGA
- **2000** Loch Lomond International

AUSTRALASIAN: 1
- **1997** Johnnie Walker Classic

SOUTH AFRICA: 11
- **1992** Goodyear Classic, Royal Swazi Sun Classic, South African Masters, South African Open, South African PGA, South African Players Championship
- **1995** Bells Cup, South African PGA
- **1996** South African Open
- **1998** South African Open
- **1999** Alfred Dunhill PGA Championship

OTHER: 3
- **1993** Dunlop Phoenix Tournament
- **1994** Sarazen World Open
- **2000** Nedbank Challenge

DUNHILL CUP 1992, 1993, 1994, 1995, 1996, 1997, 1998, 1999, 2000
PRESIDENT'S CUP 1996, 1998
WORLD CUP 1992, 1993, 1996, 1997

South African Els is one of the finest golfers in the world, possessing the ability to hit the golf ball a prodigious distance, yet retaining a delicate and accurate touch around the green and from the sand. Known as 'the Big Easy' for his calm, unruffled manner and his fluid, powerful swing, he has already won two Majors, six US Tour and six European Tour events, as well 18 other tournaments around the world, and he is still only in his early thirties.

A naturally gifted, all-round young sportsman, he opted for golf at the age of 14 and played in the British Open in 1989, missing the cut. In 1992 he won the South African Open, PGA and Masters, the first player to achieve the feat since Gary Player more than a decade before. His first European win came in the 1994 Dubai Desert Classic and he followed that up with his first Major, the US Open, when he won a play-off against Colin Montgomerie and Loren Roberts. He finished off that season with victory in the World Match Play Championship at Wentworth, a title he was to win again in the following two seasons. He won the US Open again in 1997, when he beat Colin Montgomerie by one stroke at Congressional. He was given honorary life membership of the European Tour in 1999.

2000 SEASON. Els finished second in three Majors in 2000. He was runner-up to Vijay Singh in the Masters and to Tiger Woods in the US and British Open. He had five top-5 finishes on the USPGA Tour, including losing to Tiger Woods in a play-off at the season-opening Mercedes Championship, and was victorious in The International when he led from the beginning and shot three birdies over the last five holes. On the European Tour, at the Loch Lomond International, he beat defending champion Tom Lehman by one shot. In the Dunhill Cup at St Andrews he won all five games he played, helping South Africa to second place, although in the Presidents Cup he lost all five. Perhaps he is too easy-going for his own good, particularly in the Tiger Woods era, but there are still plenty of tournament victories and maybe a Major or two ahead for Els.

2001 STOP PRESS. Els recorded two third places before the Masters, T3 at the Mercedes Championship and third at the Sony Open.

Gary Emerson

European Tour

Born 26 September 1963
Place of Birth Bournemouth, England
Year turned Professional 1982
Tour Ranking 97th

Emerson joined the European Tour in 1995 straight from working as a club professional. In his first two seasons, he secured his card by finishing within the top-125 on the Order of Merit, but had to revisit the Qualifying School in 1997 and 1998. He broke into the top-100 in 1999 and stayed there in 2000 thanks to his four top-20 finishes, the highest being T7 at the North West of Ireland Open.

Elisabeth Esterl

European Ladies Tour

Born 29 August 1976
Place of Birth Dingolfing, Germany
Year turned Professional 1997
Tour Ranking 20th

German Esterl joined the European Ladies Tour in 1998. In 1999 she posted two T2 finishes and four other top-20s.

2000 SEASON. Esterl missed just one cut out of the 15 events she played in. Her best place was T3 at the Waterford Crystal Irish Ladies Open and she had three top-10s. She finished the season 20th on the Money List.

2001 STOP PRESS. She finished tied for second place at the South African Ladies Masters.

Bob Estes

US Tour

Born 2 February 1966
Place of Birth Graham, Texas, USA
Year turned Professional 1988
Tour Ranking 88th

BEST FINISH IN MAJORS
Tied 4th US MASTERS 1999

TOUR VICTORIES
US: 2
   1994 Texas Open
   2001 Fedex St Jude Classic

A popular player on the US Tour, Estes graduated from Qualifying School in 1988 and notched up his only tournament victory in 1994, when he led from the beginning and shot a course record 62 in the first round to win the Texas Open. His most successful year was 1999, when he achieved nine top-10 finishes, including tied fourth at the Masters and tied sixth at the USPGA Championship. He was 26th on the Money List and made 27 out of 28 cuts. He is known for his consistency and, unusually, he does not wear a golf glove.

2000 SEASON. Estes performed well at the Masters (T19) and British Open (T20), but otherwise he slipped dramatically down the Money List from 1999's 26th to 88th. His best performances were six at the Byron Nelson Classic and T6 at the Colonial.

2001 STOP PRESS. Estes won his second title, leading from the start again to beat Germany's Bernhard Langer by one stroke at the Fedex St Jude Classic.

Michelle Estill

US Ladies Tour

Born 1 November 1962
Place of Birth Scottsdale, Arizona, USA
Year turned Professional 1989
Tour Ranking 63rd

TOUR VICTORIES
US: 1
   1991 Ping-Cellular One Championship

A former member of the US Junior Olympic basketball team, Estill won her only tournament – the Ping-Cellular One LPGA Golf Championship – in 1991, but was pipped to the Rookie of the Year award by

Brandie Burton. She has played on the European Tour and in 1998 passed US career earnings of $1 million.

2000 SEASON. Estill had two top-10 finishes, her highest being T4 at the ShopRite LPGA Classic.

Gary Evans
European Tour

Born 22 February 1969
Place of Birth Rustington, England
Year turned Professional 1991
Tour Ranking 86th

BEST FINISH IN MAJORS
Tied 35th **BRITISH OPEN 1994**

In his rookie year of 1992, Evans finished second in the Turespana Masters, 35th on the Order of Merit and was just pipped by Jim Payne for the Rookie of the Year award. He remained in the top-100 and ended 1999 in 42nd place after four top-10 finishes. He is a talented but inconsistent golfer.

2000 SEASON. Evans landed two top-10 finishes – in the Spanish and European Opens – to leave him on 86th position on the Order of Merit.

Nick Faldo

US Tour

Born 18 July 1957
Place of Birth Welwyn Garden City, England
Year turned Professional 1976
Tour Ranking 142nd

MAJORS VICTORIES

US MASTERS 1989, 1990, 1996
BRITISH OPEN 1987, 1990, 1992

TOUR VICTORIES

US: 3
1984 Sea Pines Heritage
1995 Doral-Ryder Open
1997 Nissan Open
EUROPEAN: 29
1977 Skol Lager
1978 Colgate PGA Championship
1980 Sun Alliance PGA Championship
1981 Sun Alliance PGA Championship
1982 Haig Whisky TPC
1983 Car Care Plan International, Ebel
  Swiss Open-European Masters,
  Lawrence Batley International,
  Martini International, Paco Rabanne
  French Open
1984 Car Care Plan International
1987 Peugeot Spanish Open
1988 Peugeot French Open, Volvo Masters
1989 Dunhill British Masters,
  Peugeot French Open, Suntory World
  Match Play Championship, Volvo
  PGA Championship
1990 Johnnie Walker Classic (Hong Kong)
1991 Carroll's Irish Open
1992 Carroll's Irish Open, GA European
  Open, Johnnie Walker World
  Championship of Golf, Scandinavian
  Masters, Toyota World Match Play
  Championship
1993 Carroll's Irish Open, Johnnie Walker
  Classic
1994 Alfred Dunhill Open
1996 World Cup of Golf
SOUTH AFRICA: 2
1979 ICL International
1994 Nedbank Million Dollar Challenge

RYDER CUP 1977, 1979, 1981, 1983, 1985, 1987,
  1989, 1991, 1993, 1995, 1997
DUNHILL CUP 1985, 1986, 1988, 1991, 1993
WORLD CUP 1977, 1991, 1996

Over the last two decades Faldo was the finest British golfer of his generation. Six times a Majors winner, and holder of 34 international titles, the tall, single-minded Englishman was one of the most consistent and determined golfers in the world.

He took up golf when, at the age of 14, he watched the Masters on TV and was rivetted by the sport. He was English Amateur Champion in 1975 and turned pro in 1976, but his greatest victories came after he employed David Leadbetter in 1983 to remodel his swing. His first Majors triumph was at the 1987 British Open when he parred every hole on the last day to overcome Paul Azinger. In 1989 he won the Masters, coming from five strokes behind on the last day to force a play-off with Scott Hoch, who missed a two-foot putt on the second extra hole to hand the title to Faldo. The following year he became only the second player after Jack Nicklaus to win consecutive Masters, beating Ray Floyd in the play-off, and he won the British Open again three months later at St Andrews when he shot an 18 under par 270 to beat Mark McNulty and Payne Stewart by five strokes. He collected the claret jug for the third time in 1992 when his two birdies on the last four holes helped him to beat John Cook by one shot. His last Majors title – and probably his most memorable – came at the Masters in 1996 when, in an epic, gladiatorial battle, he overcame a five stroke deficit on the last round to crush a disbelieving Greg Norman by six shots.

Faldo also has a proud record in the Ryder Cup, having played in 11 tournaments in the competition. His finest moment came in 1975 when he recovered from being one down with two to play against Curtis Strange to beat the American and lead Europe to the brink of victory. In the World Cup Faldo and his partner David Carter won the trophy in 1996 for England's first victory in the competition.

Faldo joined the European Tour in 1977 and has accumulated 28 European Tour victories. He also played on the US Tour collecting three wins, his last – the Nissan Open – coming in 1997. In recent years Faldo's form has fallen off, partly because of lack of confidence in his swing and personal family disruptions, and he finished outside the US Money List in 1998 and 1999. Perhaps, at 44, age is beginning to have an impact on his golf, but it would be a brave man who would bet against this most intensely competitive of players from ever winning another tournament.

2000 SEASON. Faldo's highest finish on the US Tour was seventh at the US Open, while he also played in seven European Tour events, claiming two top-10 places.

Marc Farry
European Tour

Born 3 July 1959
Place of Birth Paris, France
Year turned Professional 1979
Tour Ranking 93rd

BEST FINISH IN MAJORS
Made Cut **BRITISH OPEN 1991, 1996, 1999, 2000**

TOUR VICTORIES
EUROPEAN : 1
  1996 BMW International Open

DUNHILL CUP 1990, 1992, 1997, 1999
WORLD CUP 1987, 1991, 1993, 1996, 1997, 1999

A tall Frenchman, Farry has been a regular on the European Tour since 1988. He has won one tournament on Tour, the rain-shortened BMW International Open in 1996, and in 1999 he had four top-10 finishes, his best-ever season.

2000 SEASON. He had some weeks off with bronchitis at the beginning of the season, but came back to record a T12 at the English Open. His T7 at the Belgacom Open allowed him to retain his card for 2001.

Niclas Fasth
European Tour

Born 29 April 1972
Place of Birth Gothenburg, Sweden
Year turned Professional 1993
Tour Ranking 45th

TOUR VICTORIES
EUROPEAN: 1
  2000 Madeira Island Open

For such a slow, unhurried player, Swedish golfer Fasth has had a hectic career. He started playing on the Asian Tour and joined the European Tour from the Challenge Tour in 1993. He lost his card in 1996, but won the qualifying tournament to return to the Tour. He then spent some time in the USA, but came back to qualify for the European Tour in 1999, finishing second to Alastair Forsyth in Qualifying School.

2000 SEASON. Fasth finished in the top-5 at the European Masters. At the Madeira Island

Open, he led from the start, with a first round 66, to beat fellow Swede Richard Johnson, Mark Davis and Ross Drummond by two shots for his first Tour victory.

Brad Faxon
_____ US Tour

Born 1 August 1961
Place of Birth Oceanport, New Jersey, USA
Year turned Professional 1983
Tour Ranking 46th

BEST FINISH IN MAJORS
5th **USPGA 1995**

TOUR VICTORIES
US: 8
  1986 Provident Classic
  1991 Buick Open
  1992 New England Classic,
        The International
  1997 Freeport McDermott Classic
  1999 BC Open
  2000 BC Open
  2001 Sony Open, Hawaii
AUSTRALASIAN: 1
  1993 Heineken Australian Open

RYDER CUP 1995, 1997
DUNHILL CUP 1997

An elegant player, Faxon is a long-term pro on the US Tour. He gained his card through Qualifying School in 1983 and he has been a regular on Tour ever since. He has won seven Tour tournaments, the last before 2000 being the BC Open in 1999 when he beat Fred Funk in a 2-hole play-off. He missed three months of that season with a broken wrist. His most successful seasons were 1992 and 1996 when he finished eighth on the money list. With his friend Billy Andrade he runs the Billy Andrade/Brad Faxon Charity for Children. An exceptional putter, he topped the PGA Tour putting statistics in 1999.

2000 SEASON. After three top-10 finishes in the Mercedes, Buick Open and Tampa Bay Classic, Faxon flew to Scotland for the British Open but failed to pre-qualify. He returned to the USA and successfully defended his BC Open title, beating Esteban Toledo by one shot. He topped the putting statistics again in 2000.

2001 STOP PRESS. Faxon won the Sony Open, shooting a final round 65 to beat Tom Lehman by four shots. He was also T4 at the Bob Hope Chrysler Classic.

Rick Fehr
_____ US Tour

Born 28 August 1962
Place of Birth Seattle, Washington, USA
Year turned Professional 1984
Tour Ranking 132nd

TOUR VICTORIES
US: 2
  1986 BC Open
  1994 Walt Disney/Oldsmobile Classic

Fehr won his first tournament at the BC Open in 1986 when he defeated Larry Mize by two shots and he won again by the same margin in 1994 at the Walt Disney. He had to qualify through Qualifying School in 1998 and 1999.

2000 SEASON. Revisiting Qualifying School again in 2000, although he had two top-10 finishes, his highest being T5 at the Tucson Open.

Jennifer Feldott
_____ US Ladies Tour

Born 30 May 1971
Place of Birth LaGrange, Illinois, USA
Year turned Professional 1995
Tour Ranking 75th

Feldott joined the LPGA Tour in 1998 and posted her highest finish that year with a T5 at the Sara Lee Classic.

2000 SEASON. Feldott had two T7s and one T8 to finish the 2000 season 75th on the Money List.

Ben Ferguson
US Tour

Born 30 March 1973
Place of Birth Sydney, Australia
Year turned Professional 1997
Tour Ranking Tied 17th (Qualifying School)

After playing as an amateur in Australia, Ferguson joined the Canadian Tour, winning one tournament and ending the 2000 season in sixth place on the Order of Merit. He earned his 2001 US Tour Card by finishing T17 at Qualifying School.

Vicente Fernandez
US Seniors Tour

Born 5 April 1946
Place of Birth Carmento, Argentina
Year turned Professional 1964
Tour Ranking 23rd

TOUR VICTORIES
SENIOR TOUR: 3
  1996 Burnett Senior Classic
  1997 Bank One Classic
  1999 Las Vegas Senior Classic

Argentinian 'Chino' Fernandez played on the European Tour, where he is most famous for sinking a 90-foot birdie putt to win the Murphy's English Open, and joined the US Senior Tour in 1996. As a Monday qualifier he won the Burnet Senior Classic by one shot, and he ended 1996 at the top of the putting statistics. He beat Isao Aoki to win the 1997 Bank One Classic and in 1999 finished in the top-10, helped by a two shot victory over Dave Eichelberger in the Las Vegas Senior Classic.

2000 SEASON. Fernandez produced six top-10 finishes and also won the unofficial Chrysler

Senior Match Play Challenge, beating Leonard Thompson to collect $240,000. He has already won over $4 million in his Senior career in just under five years.

Kenneth Ferrie
European Tour

Born 28 September 1978
Place of Birth Ashington, England
Year turned Professional 1999
Tour Ranking 24th (Qualifying School)

A massive 6 foot 4 inch, 17-stone Englishman, Ferrie turned professional in 1999 and won twice in succession on the 2000 Challenge Tour, at the Tessali Open del Sud and the Gula Sidorna Grand Prix. He qualified for the 2001 European Tour by virtue of his 24th-place finish at the Qualifying School.

Cindy Figg-Currier
US Ladies Tour

Born 23th February 1960
Place of Birth Mt Pleasant, Michigan, USA
Year turned Professional 1983
Tour Ranking 41st

TOUR VICTORIES
US: 1
  1997 State Farm Rail Classic

Now considered a veteran of the Ladies Tour, Figg-Currier joined the circuit in 1984, but had to wait an agonizing 13 seasons for her first victory, when a birdie putt on the first sudden death play-off hole gave her the 1997 State Farm Rail Classic title. A solid rather than spectacular performer, she has finished in third place four times in her career.

2000 SEASON. Figg-Currier had a consistent year, finishing six times in the top-10, her best performance being T5 at the Rochester International.

Tina Fischer

European Ladies Tour

Born 29 September 1970
Place of Birth Bad Nauheim, Germany
Year turned Professional 1994
Tour Ranking 34th

TOUR VICTORIES
EUROPEAN: 2
   1996 McDonalds WPGA Championship
   2000 Mexx Open

European Ladies Amateur Champion in 1994, Fischer secured her first win on the European Tour in 1996 with the McDonald's WPGA Championship. That year she also finished T2 at the Italian Open.

2000 SEASON. She collected her second Tour victory in September when she won the Mexx Open by three strokes over Trish Johnson, one of only seven events she played.

Darren Fitchardt

South African Tour

Born 13 May 1975
Place of Birth Pretoria, South Africa
Year turned Professional 1994
Tour Ranking 8th

TOUR VICTORIES
EUROPEAN: 1
   2001 Sao Paulo Brazil Open
SOUTH AFRICA: 3
   1997 Highveld Classic
   1999 South African PGA Cup
   2001 South African Tournament Players
        Championship

Leader of the 1999–2000 South African Order of Merit, Fitchardt failed to qualify for the 2001 European Tour through Qualifying School. He did, however, play in the Sao Paulo Brazil Open, which was shortened to three rounds because of lightning, and took advantage by winning the tournament by a comfortable five strokes. Earlier in the year he won the South African Tournament Players Championship by four shots.

Bruce Fleisher

US Seniors Tour

Born 16 October 1948
Place of Birth Union City, Tennessee, USA
Year turned Professional 1970
Tour Ranking 2nd

TOUR VICTORIES
SENIOR TOUR: 12
   1999 American Express Invitational,
        BellSouth Senior Classic, Kaanapali
        Classic, Lightpath Long Island Classic,
        Royal Caribbean Classic, The Home
        Depot Invitational, The Transamerica
   2000 GTE Classic, Lightpath Long Island
        Classic, Royal Caribbean Classic, The
        Home Depot Invitational
   2001 Las Vegas Senior Classic

Fleisher is a classic example of how a journeyman USPGA Tour player can blossom into a multiple winner on the US Senior Tour. With only one PGA Tour victory under his belt from over 400 starts, Fleisher quit the regular PGA Tour in 1984 to become a club pro in North Miami Beach. He joined the US Senior Tour in 1999, finishing second at Qualifying School. In his debut season he won an unbelievable seven tournaments and became the first Senior player to win his first two tournaments – the Royal Caribbean Classic and the American Express Invitational. Indeed, he nearly won his third, only losing to Larry Nelson by two shots in the Verizon Classic. Fleisher carded seven other second places and he became the first rookie to top the Money List since Lee Trevino in 1990. He was also named both Player of the Year and Rookie of the Year.

2000 SEASON. 'Flash' Fleisher won a further four tournaments and was runner-up on four occasions. He led the US Senior Open for three rounds but was overhauled by Hale Irwin, and he earned over $2.3 million in the season.

2001 STOP PRESS. Fleisher picked up his first win of the year at the Las Vegas Senior Classic.

Steve Flesch
US Tour

Born 23 May 1967
Place of Birth Cincinnati, Ohio, USA
Year turned Professional 1990
Tour Ranking 13th

BEST FINISH IN MAJORS
Tied 13th **USPGA 1998**

TOUR VICTORIES
OTHER: 1
1996 Malaysian Open

Left-hander Flesch played on the Asian Tour between 1993 and 1996, featuring in the top-10 in the Order of Merit in 1996. In 1998, he secured his US Tour card through the Nike Tour. He finished second behind England's Lee Westwood at the 1998 Freeport-McDermott Classic in Louisiana and his position of 35th in the end of season Money List earned him the Rookie of the Year award that year. He demonstrated good consistency by making 23 out of 29 cuts that season.

2000 SEASON. Flesch finished T5 in three tournaments – Nissan Open, Memorial and Greater Hartford Open – and finished in second place, one stroke behind winner Duffy Waldorf, in the NCR Walt Disney Classic. He had a remarkably consistent season and his game continues to improve. It would be surprising if he did not collect his first tournament victory in the near future.

Massimo Florioli
European Tour

Born 14 February 1972
Place of Birth Mantova, Italy
Year turned Professional 1992
Tour Ranking 132nd

BEST FINISH IN MAJORS
Missed Cut **BRITISH OPEN 1996**

WORLD CUP 1997, 1998

Florioli, who played regularly on the European Tour between 1997 and 2000, had his best season in 1998, when he had four top-10 finishes. His highest placing was T2 at the French Open and he was 49th on the Order of Merit.

2000 SEASON. It was a disappointing year for the Italian who finished in 132nd place on the Order of Merit.

Ray Floyd
US Seniors Tour

Born 4 September 1942
Place of Birth Fort Bragg, North Carolina, USA
Year turned Professional 1961
Tour Ranking 26th

MAJORS VICTORIES
PGA SENIORS CHAMPIONSHIP 1995
SENIOR PLAYERS CHAMPIONSHIP 2000
SENIOR PLAYERS CHAMPIONSHIP 1996
THE TRADITION 1994

TOUR VICTORIES

SENIOR TOUR: 10

- **1992** GTE North Classic, Ralph's Senior Classic, Senior Tour Championship
- **1993** Gulfstream Aerospace Invitational, Northville Long Island Classic
- **1994** Cadillac NFL Golf Classic, Las Vegas Senior Classic, Senior Tour Championship
- **1995** Burnett Senior Classic, Emerald Coast Classic

A formidable competitor with nerves of steel, Floyd has been a dominant figure in American and world golf since the late 1960s. He has 22 USPGA titles to his name, and his best years were 1981 and 1982 when he was second on the Money List and ran up three victories each year. He has also won four Majors, his first in 1969 when he held off Gary Player by one stroke to win the USPGA Championship. He then claimed the Masters in 1976, shooting 65 in his first round and led wire-to-wire to defeat Ben Crenshaw by a massive eight strokes. In 1982 he won the PGA again, three shots ahead of Lanny Wadkins. His last Major triumph, though, came in 1986 at the US Open, at Shinnecock Hills when he beat Wadkins and Chip Beck by two strokes and became, at the age of 44, the oldest player ever to win the title. Floyd also played in seven Ryder Cups. In his last appearance in the competition in 1993, at the age of 51, he won three out of his four matches.

Floyd, whose son Robert is now a professional golfer, started playing on the US Senior Tour in 1992 and won two tournaments, the first – the GTE Classic – 16 days after his 50th birthday. In 1993, he only played 14 events but was ninth on the Money List, and the following year he had another four wins, earning himself over $1 million. He rose to second place behind Jim Colbert in 1995 and picked up the Senior PGA title. In 1996 he again exceeded $1 million in earnings and the following year he carded ten top-10s, but was winless for the first season in his Senior career.

2000 SEASON. Comeback Player of the Year Floyd consolidated his top-31 place for the ninth year in succession and brought his all-time career earnings to over $13 million. He won his first tournament for four years, the Senior Players Championship, beating Larry Nelson and Dana Quigley by one stroke, and was T4 in the Senior Open. He also made occasional appearances on the PGA Tour.

Dan Forsman

US Tour

Born 15 July 1958
Place of Birth Rhinelander, Wisconsin, USA
Year turned Professional 1982
Tour Ranking 128th

BEST FINISH IN MAJORS
Tied 7th US MASTERS 1993

TOUR VICTORIES

US: 4

- **1985** Lite Quad Cities Open
- **1986** Hertz Bay Hill Classic
- **1990** Lehman Hutton Open
- **1992** Buick Open

B ig Dan Forsman – all 6 feet 4 inches of him – has played on the US Tour since 1983 and retained his card every year between then and 1999. He last won a tournament – the Buick Open – in 1992. Along with three second places, he ended that season in his highest ever position of tenth on the Money List.

He is probably best known, however, for leading The Masters in 1993 before running up a quadruple bogey seven on the par-3 12th hole after hitting two tee shots into the creek in front of the green

2000 SEASON. He was on 125th spot before the Southern Farm Bureau Classic, the last tournament of the season, but missed the cut and ended 127th.

Alastair Forsyth
European Tour

Born 5 February 1976
Place of Birth Glasgow, Scotland
Year turned Professional 1998
Tour Ranking 46th

Touted by many observers as a superstar of the future, the heavily-built Forsyth won the 1999 Qualifying School and gained his European Tour card. The Glaswegian is an accurate, medium length player with a delicate and effective short game.

2000 SEASON. In only his second Tour event, Forsyth finished in third place in the Heineken Classic (one stroke ahead of Ernie Els) and then achieved a T7 at the Dubai Desert Clas-

sic and a T6 at the Brazil Rio De Janeiro 500 Years Open, leading the last tournament at the halfway stage. Towards the season's end he shot four rounds in the 60s to finish T5 at the Belgacom Open.

Peter Fowler
European Tour

Born 9 June 1959
Place of Birth Sydney, Australia
Year turned Professional 1977
Tour Ranking 142nd

BEST FINISH IN MAJORS
48th **BRITISH OPEN 1990**

TOUR VICTORIES
EUROPEAN: 1
  1993 BMW International Open
AUSTRALASIAN: 4
  1983 Australian Open
  1985 Queensland PGA Championship
  1986 Australian Matchplay Championship
  1993 New Zealand Open
OTHER: 1
  1987 Singapore Open

WORLD CUP 1989

Australian Fowler joined the European Tour in 1983, but had to wait some ten years for his first win, the BMW International Open in Germany, shooting a 63 in his last round. However, he lost his card the following season. He won the individual World Cup award in 1989.

2000 SEASON. He finished in 142nd place on the Order of Merit.

Carlos Franco
US Tour

Born 24 May 1965
Place of Birth Asuncion, Paraguay
Year turned Professional 1986
Tour Ranking 30th

BEST FINISH IN MAJORS
Tied 6th US MASTERS 1999

TOUR VICTORIES
US: 3
1999 Compaq Classic, Greater Milwaukee Open
2000 Compaq Classic
OTHER: 6
1994 Jun Classic
1995 Tokyo Open
1996 ANA Open
1998 Fuji Sankei Classic, Just System KSB Open
1999 Philippines Open

DUNHILL CUP 1991, 1993, 1994, 1999
PRESIDENTS CUP 1998, 2000
WORLD CUP 1992, 2000

One of six Paraguayan professional golfer brothers from a poverty-stricken background, Franco broke through to the US Tour in 1999 after earning his card at the Qualifying School. He made a bright start, ending the season as Rookie of the Year and finishing an impressive 11th on the Money List. He won two tournaments in 1999 – the Compaq Classic, beating Harrison Frazar and Steve Flesch by two strokes, and the Greater Milwaukee Classic, two shots ahead of Tom Lehman – and picked up three third places.

In 1993 Paraguay pulled off a surprise result in the Dunhill Cup by eliminating Scotland, and Franco played his part by defeating Sam Torrance. Not particularly long or accurate off the tee, Franco does have an excellent short game and putting ability.

2000 SEASON. Franco successfully defended his title when he beat Blaine McAllister in a two-hole play-off at the Compaq Classic. He also finished tied for seventh place at the Masters and opened the season with a T6 at the Mercedes and a T9 at the Sony Open. In the Presidents Cup he beat Hal Sutton 6&5 in the singles.

Harrison Frazar
US Tour

Born 29 July 1971
Place of Birth Dallas, Texas, USA
Year turned Professional 1996
Tour Ranking 79th

BEST FINISH IN MAJORS
Missed Cut USPGA 1998, 1999, 2000

An ex-college room-mate of Justin Leonard, Frazar worked in the real estate business for a year before deciding to attend the Qualifying School at the end of 1996. He made it onto the Tour in 1998 and, with three top-10 finishes, was nominated for Rookie of the Year. His strength is his length (seventh on the Tour statistics for distance) and accuracy off the tee. His highest finish on Tour is T2, at the 1998 Byron Nelson Classic and the 1999 Compaq Classic.

2000 SEASON. Frazar had a T3 finish at the Bell South Classic and a third place at the Compaq Classic.

Robin Freeman
US Tour

Born 7 May 1959
Place of Birth St Charles, Minnesota
Year turned Professional 1992
Tour Ranking 115th

BEST FINISH IN MAJORS
Tied 49th USPGA 1995

Freeman has dipped in and out of the US Tour since 1988, with his best season coming in 1995 when he tied for second place, three strokes behind Ernie Els, at the Byron Nelson Classic. He qualified for the 2000 season through his T7th place at Qualifying School.

2000 SEASON. He finished third in the Nissan Open, one stroke behind Jesper Parnevik and two behind winner Kirk Triplett and had five other top-25 placings.

David Frost

US Tour

Born 11 September 1959
Place of Birth Cape Town, South Africa
Year turned Professional 1981
Tour Ranking 177th

BEST FINISH IN MAJORS
6th BRITISH OPEN 1987

TOUR VICTORIES
US: 10
  1988 Southern Open, Tucson Open
  1989 NEC World Series of Golf
  1990 USF&G Classic
  1992 Buick Classic, Hardee's Golf Classic
  1993 Canadian Open, Hardee's Golf Classic
  1994 Canon Greater Hartford Open
  1997 MasterCard Colonial
EUROPEAN: 1
  1984 Air France Cannes Open
SOUTH AFRICA: 8
  1982 Gordon's Gin Classic
  1986 South African Open
  1987 South African Masters
  1989 Sun City Million Dollar Challenge
  1990 Sun City Million Dollar Challenge
  1992 Sun City Million Dollar Challenge
  1994 Lexington PGA Championship
  1999 South African Open Championship
OTHER: 2
  1992 Dunlop Phoenix
  1993 Hong Kong Open

DUNHILL CUP 1991, 1992, 1993, 1994, 1995, 1997, 1998
PRESIDENTS CUP 1994, 1996

Three-time winner of the Sun City Million Dollar Challenge and winner of 21 tournaments worldwide, South African Frost is, not surprisingly, also in the top-50 of the PGA Tour Career Money List. After playing for two years and winning one trophy on the European Tour, he qualified for the US Tour in 1984 and won twice in 1988, finishing ninth on the Money List. One of David Leadbetter's original pupils, 'Frosty' has won a total of ten US tournaments, his last victory coming in 1997, at the MasterCard Colonial, when he shot a front-nine 32 in his last round to win by two shots. Major Championships, however, have somehow eluded him over the years. His last international win came at the South African Open in 1999 when he overtook Germany's Sven Struver on the last two holes to win by one stroke. He captained South Africa to victory in 1997 and 1998 at the Dunhill Cup. Frost owns a 300-acre vineyard in South Africa.

2000 SEASON. He had his best finish – T8 – at the John Deere Classic and he also picked up three top-5 places on the South African Tour.

Amy Fruhwirth

US Ladies Tour

Born 23 July 1968
Place of Birth Cypress, California, USA
Year turned Professional 1992
Tour Ranking 42nd

TOUR VICTORIES
US: 1
  1998 Friendly's Classic

The petite Fruhwirth, known as 'Giggles' on the LPGA Tour, was US Women's Amateur Champion in 1991 and Public Links Champion in 1992. That year she played in the Curtis Cup and was low amateur at the Nabisco Dinah Shore. Her best season was in 1997, when her accurate driving helped her to pick up seven top-10 placings, including a T3 at the Nabisco, and the following year she won her only tournament, the Friendly's Classic by two strokes.

2000 SEASON. Fruhwirth had six top-20 finishes, her best being T2 at the Chick-fil-A Charity Championship. She also won the unofficial JC Penney Classic along with PGA Tour member Clarence Rose.

Edward Fryatt

US Tour

Born 8 April 1971
Place of Birth Rochdale, England
Year turned Professional 1994
Tour Ranking 77th

BEST FINISH IN MAJORS
Tied 24th US OPEN 1997

TOUR VICTORIES
OTHER: 4
1996 Indonesian Open
1997 India Open
1998 China Open, Malaysian Open

Son of a former English professional soccer player, the tall, powerful Fryatt joined the US Tour in 2000. He had played in Asia – winning four competitions – and graduated through the Nike Tour. He secured his best-ever finish at T3 in the MCI Classic, five strokes behind leader Stewart Cink, and a T5 at the Greater Hartford Open. His consistent golf in his rookie year has meant he retains playing privileges for 2001.

Akiko Fukushima

US Ladies Tour

Born 29 June 1973
Place of Birth Kanagawa, Japan
Year turned Professional 1992
Tour Ranking 67th

TOUR VICTORIES
US: 2
1999 AFLAC Champions, Philips Invitational

Fukushima played on the Japan Tour between 1992 and 1998, finishing as the top player in 1997 with 14 wins. She joined the LPGA Tour in 1999 and claimed two tournaments, beating Charlotta Sorenstam by one stroke at the Philips Invitational and finishing one shot ahead of Maria Hjorth and Karrie Webb at the AFLAC Champions. She was second to Mi Hyun Kim as Rookie of the Year.

2000 SEASON. Her highest finish was T4 at the Mizuno Classic.

Pierre Fulke

European Tour

Born 21 February 1971
Place of Birth Nykoping, Sweden
Year turned Professional 1989
Tour Ranking 12th

BEST FINISH IN MAJORS
Tied 7th BRITISH OPEN 2000

TOUR VICTORIES
EUROPEAN: 3
1999 Trophee Lancome
2000 Scottish PGA Championship, Volvo Masters

The small, stocky Swede with the French name joined the European Tour from the Challenge Tour in 1993, but had to wait until 1999 for his first tournament victory, the Trophee Lancome. Shortly after this win he developed a pain in his right wrist which saw him out of action until June 2000, his injury by then having been successfully attended to by a yogic chiropractor.

2000 SEASON. By mid-July Fulke had run up his highest-ever placing in a Major – T7 at the British Open – and he followed this up a month later with a two-stroke win at Gleneagles in the Scottish PGA, setting a new course record of 63. He finished in the top-20 in four more tournaments, but his most prestigious victory was to come in November at the Volvo Masters in Montecastillo. Level with Darren Clarke at the beginning of the last round, Fulke kept his head to fire a 67 and edge in front of Clarke by one stroke bringing the Swede a £333,000 cheque and 12th place in the Order of Merit. That round contained the Canon Shot of the Year when, on the 16th, Fulke hit a magnificent 5-wood 215 yards to within 25 feet of the pin. He putted for his eagle and effectively won the tournament. An excellent all-round golfer, Fulke is fifth for driving accuracy and second for putting on the Tour statistics.

2001 STOP PRESS. Fulke secured his 2001 Ryder Cup place when he came 2nd to Steve Stricker in the WGC Accenture Match Play Championship and collected a cheque for $500,000.

Fred Funk
US Tour

Born 14 June 1956
Place of Birth Takoma Park, Maryland, USA
Year turned Professional 1981
Tour Ranking 58th

BEST FINISH IN MAJORS
Tied 7th US OPEN 1993

TOUR VICTORIES
US: 5
   1992 Shell Houston Open
   1995 Buick Challenge, Ideon Classic at
         Pleasant Valley
   1996 BC Open
   1998 Deposit Guaranty Golf Classic
OTHER: 1
   1993 Mexican Open

Consistently in the top-100 of the US Tour Money List since 1990, Funk has won five tournaments on Tour in that period. He is one of the busiest players on Tour and his short but deadly accurate driving has kept him on the Money List and landed him with the nickname 'Fairway Fred'. He was top of the driving accuracy statistics in 1999. His most successful season came in the same year when he claimed the runner-up spot in three tournaments making over $1.6 million and 16th in the Money List.

2000 SEASON. He was again top of the driving accuracy ratings, but could not parlay this into winning a sixth tournament, partly because of his poor putting. The closest he got was a T4 at the NCR Walt Disney Classic and he had two other top-10 finishes. He finished a respectable T9 in the USPGA and T37 in the Masters, but missed the cut in both the British and US Opens. Now aged 44, his chances of another victory seem increasingly remote.

Jim Furyk
US Tour

Born 12 May 1970
Place of Birth West Chester, Pennsylvania, USA
Year turned Professional 1992
Tour Ranking 17th

BEST FINISH IN MAJORS
4th US MASTERS 1998

TOUR VICTORIES
US: 6
   1995 Las Vegas Invitational
   1996 United Airlines Hawaiian Open
   1998 Las Vegas Invitational
   1999 Las Vegas Invitational
   2000 Doral Ryder Open
   2001 Mercedes Championship
OTHER: 1
   1997 Argentine Open

RYDER CUP 1997, 1999
PRESIDENTS CUP 1998, 2000

Furyk is a supremely consistent and accurate golfer, in spite of having a swing resembling, according to David Feherty, an octopus falling out of a tree, and an unusual cross-handed putting style. He seems to have an affinity with Las Vegas, having won that city's Invitational tournament three times between 1995 and 1999, the last by one stroke over Jonathan Kaye. This tall, balding, unorthodox golfer did not win a tournament in 1997, yet still finished fourth on the Money List with eight top-10 finishes in successsion out of a total of 13 that year. Although he has never won a Major, he finished in fourth place at the British Open in 1997 and finished T4 the following year, the same year he finished fourth in the Masters. He played for the USA in their victorious Ryder Cup in 1999 and he helped the American cause by beating Sergio Garcia 4&3 in the Sunday singles. He keeps the ball low and is particularly effective in the wind.

2001 STOP PRESS. Furyk won the season-opening Mercedes Championship beating Rory Sabbatini, who missed a 3-foot putt to get into a play-off, on the final green.

2000 SEASON. Furyk picked up his fifth tournament trophy at the Doral-Ryder Open. Six strokes behind Franklin Langham with seven holes to play in the last round, Furyk shot six birdies to card 30 on the back nine and beat Langham by two strokes. He equalled the tournament record with a 23 under par 265. He also had seven top-10 finishes and was T15 at the Masters. He is caddied by Mike 'Fluff' Cowan, formerly employed by Tiger Woods.

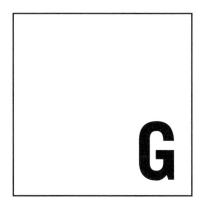

A member of the US Tour in 1996 and 1998–99, Gallagher played the Buy.Com Tour in 2000 where he won a tournament and had five other top-10 finishes to end 12th on the Money List. His brother is US Tour member Jim Gallagher Jr and his sister, Jackie Gallagher-Smith plays on the LPGA Tour. His highest finish on the US Tour is T6 at the 1998 Nissan Open.

Jackie Gallagher-Smith
US Ladies Tour

Born 11 December 1967
Place of Birth Marion, Indiana, USA
Year turned Professional 1992
Tour Ranking 57th

TOUR VICTORIES
US: 1
    1999 Giant Eagle LPGA Classic

W ith brothers Jim and Jeff on the PGA Tour, golf is in the blood in Jackie's family. Even her husband and manager, Eddie Smith, was an assistant professional at the TPC of Sawgrass, in Jacksonville, Florida. Gallagher-Smith began her professional career on the Asian Tour and joined the US Ladies Tour in 1994. She competed on the Asian Tour again in 1996, finishing 12th on the Order of Merit. She won her only tournament, the Giant Eagle LPGA Classic, in 1999 when she beat Marnie McGuire by three strokes, shot 65 on her final round and set a Tour record of 17 under par 199.

2000 SEASON. Her best finish was T4 at the JAL Big Apple Classic.

Stephen Gallacher
European Tour

Born 1 November 1974
Place of Birth Dechmont, Scotland
Year turned Professional 1995
Tour Ranking 56th

BEST FINISH IN MAJORS
Missed Cut **BRITISH OPEN 1999**

N ephew of ex-Ryder Cup captain Bernard Gallacher, Gallacher was an outstanding amateur golfer in Scotland and, under an intense media spotlight, turned pro in 1995. He moved straight on to the European Tour the following year. He is a long and accurate hitter. He lost his Tour card in 1997, but regained his playing rights via the Challenge Tour in 1998.

2000 SEASON. Gallacher posted his best-ever finish at the Dubai Desert Classic with a T4 and followed this up with a T5 at the Benson & Hedges International Open.

Jeff Gallagher
US Tour

Born 29 December 1964
Place of Birth Marion, Indiana, USA
Year turned Professional 1988
Tour Ranking 12th (Buy.Com Tour)

Robert Gamez
US Tour

Born 21 July 1968
Place of Birth Las Vegas, Nevada, USA
Year turned Professional 1989
Tour Ranking 145th

TOUR VICTORIES

US: 2

1990 Nestlé Invitational, Northern
    Telecom Tucson Open

OTHER: 1

1994 Casio World Open

Gamez made a sensational start on the US Tour in his rookie year of 1990. He won his first start on Tour at the Tucson Open, beating Mark Calcavecchia by four strokes. Later in the season he holed a 7-iron shot from 175 yards on the final hole of the Nestlé Invitational for an eagle, giving him a one-shot win over Greg Norman. He was Rookie of the Year. Gamez has not since won on Tour, although he was victorious at the 1994 Casio World Open in Japan.

2000 SEASON. His best finish was T12 at the Honda Classic.

Ian Garbutt

European Tour

Born 3 April 1972

Place of Birth Doncaster, England

Year turned Professional 1992

Tour Ranking 55th

BEST FINISH IN MAJORS

Tied 52nd **BRITISH OPEN 2000**

Former English Amateur Champion Garbutt joined the European Tour in 1993. He lost his card in 1995, but won the European Challenge Tour in 1996 to return to the main Tour. His best performance on Tour was tied for seventh place at the 1998 Dutch Open.

2000 SEASON. Garbutt had his best placing in a Major with a T52 at the British Open. He began the tournament with a 4-under-par 68. He had three other top-10 finishes – at the Greg Norman Holden International, English Open and Wales Open. Although he was top-5 for greens in regulation, he could only finish 55th in the Order of Merit.

Sergio Garcia

US Tour

Born 9 January 1980

Place of Birth Castellon, Spain

Year turned Professional 1999

Tour Ranking 42nd

BEST FINISH IN MAJORS

2nd **USPGA 1999**

TOUR VICTORIES

EUROPEAN: 2

1999 Linde German Masters, Murphy's
    Irish Open

US: 1

2001 MasterCard Colonial

RYDER CUP 1999

DUNHILL CUP 1999

Known as 'El Nino' on the US and European Tours, the young Spaniard Garcia burst on to the international golf scene in 1999. That year, after winning the British Amateur Championship and also finishing low amateur at the Masters, Garcia turned pro and won his first tournament – the Murphy's Irish Open – on only his sixth start on the European Tour. He then tied for second place at the Standard Life Loch Lomond, in Scotland, although he did prop up the leaderboard at the British Open, at Carnoustie a week later.

He also played on the US Tour, with a T3 at the Byron Nelson Classic on his first start. At the USPGA Championship at Medinah, he led after the first round and, on the last day, he was two shots behind Tiger Woods with three to play. With his ball nestling against a tree root, Garcia shut his eyes, audaciously smacked a 6-iron and the ball flew to the green. Garcia raced up the fairway to assess his effort which was deservedly voted the 'shot of the year', although Woods won the tournament by a stroke. He ended the season by winning the Linde German Masters and was named the European Tour Rookie of the Year. He also played in the Ryder Cup, winning three and a half out of five possible points and became the youngest–ever participant in the history of the competition. Garcia is a huge hitter although he can be inaccurate off the tee.

2000 SEASON. On the US Tour, Garcia had five top-10 finishes, with his third highest placing at the Buick Classic. He also ended T5 at the season-ending WGC-American Express Championship. His best European Tour finish was fifth at the Volvo PGA. His relative under-performance in 2000 was perhaps a reaction to the instant success of his rookie year.

2001 STOP PRESS. Garcia won his first USPGA Tour title – The MasterCard Colonial, in Texas, and also finished second in Jack Nicklaus' Memorial Tournament at Muirfield Village as well as T5 at Arnold Palmer's own tournament – The Bay Hill Invitational, in Orlando, Florida.

Ignacio Garrido
European Tour

Born 27 March 1972
Place of Birth Madrid, Spain
Year turned Professional 1993
Tour Ranking 43rd

BEST FINISH IN MAJORS
Tied 41st USPGA 1997

TOUR VICTORIES
EUROPEAN: 1
  1997 Volvo German Open
SOUTH AFRICA: 1
  1996 Hassan II Trophy

RYDER CUP 1997
DUNHILL CUP 1995, 1996, 1997
WORLD CUP 1995, 1996, 1997

Son of Antonio, who played for Europe in the 1979 Ryder Cup, Garrido followed in his father's footsteps with a fine performance in the 1997 Ryder Cup after having won the German Open, his only win to date on the European Tour. That year he finished sixth on the Order of Merit. A keen student of the martial art Taekwando, he was successful on the Challenge Tour four times. He is a long hitter off the tee but can be inaccurate.

2000 SEASON. His best finishes were fourth at the BMW International and T5 at the European Open.

Brian Gay
US Tour

Born 14 December 1971
Place of Birth Fort Worth, Texas, USA
Year turned Professional 1994
Tour Ranking 102nd

BEST FINISH IN MAJORS
Missed Cut US OPEN 1996 AND 2000

Gay re-qualified for the 2000 US Tour with a T10 at Qualifying School.

2000 SEASON. He guaranteed his 2001 Tour card in 2000 with seven top-20 placings and his best-ever finish, T4 in the Honda Classic. In that tournament, one shot off the lead, his ball sat on the lip of the 71st hole and dropped in after 13 seconds. As the rules stipulate a maximum of ten seconds before tapping in, he forfeited a shot, lost $88,000 and the chance of his first victory.

Jane Geddes

US Ladies Tour

Born 5 February 1960
Place of Birth Huntington, New York, USA
Year turned Professional 1983
Tour Ranking 70th

MAJORS VICTORIES
US OPEN 1986
LPGA CHAMPIONSHIP 1987

TOUR VICTORIES
US: 9
- **1986** Boston Five Classic
- **1987** Boston Five Classic, Glendale Federal Classic, Jamie Farr Toledo Classic, Kemper Open
- **1991** Atlantic City Classic, Jamaica Classic
- **1993** Oldsmobile Classic
- **1994** Chicago Challenge

SOLHEIM CUP 1996

Geddes joined the LPGA Tour in 1983 and her first win was a Major, the US Women's Open in 1986. The following week she won again, picking up the Boston Five Classic. She landed another Major, the Mazda LPGA Championship in 1987 and between then and 1994, when she won the Chicago Challenge, she added another nine titles to her belt. She has not won since. She represented the US in the 1996 Solheim Cup. A long hitter, she is known on Tour as 'Spanky' for the distance she achieves.

2000 SEASON. Her top finish was T6 at the Standard Register Ping and she recorded two other top-10s.

Al Geiberger

US Seniors Tour

Born 1 September 1937
Place of Birth Red Bluff, California, USA
Year turned Professional 1959
Tour Ranking 75th

TOUR VICTORIES
SENIOR TOUR: 10
- **1987** Hilton Head Senior International, Las Vegas Senior Classic, Vantage Championship
- **1988** Arizona Classic
- **1989** GTE North West Classic
- **1991** Kroger Senior Classic
- **1992** Infiniti Senior Tournament of Champions
- **1993** GTE Western Classic, Infiniti Senior Tournament of Champions
- **1996** Greater Naples IntelliNet Challenge

Winner of 11 USPGA Tour tournaments, including the 1966 PGA Championship, and veteran of two Ryder Cups, Geiberger's name will always be associated with his remarkable round of 59 – the first ever on the Tour – at the 1977 Memphis Classic. The round comprised 11 birdies and one eagle, and the tall, likeable Geiberger is still referred to as 'Mr 59'.

He joined the US Senior Tour in 1987 and ran up three victories in his rookie year, including the Las Vegas Senior Classic, when he shot a final round 62 to win by four strokes. By 1993 Geiberger had won another six events, but injury affected his golf for the following two years. In 1996 he was voted Comeback Player of the Year and beat Isao Aoki to win the Greater Naples IntelliNet Challenge, his last victory on Tour. He is the father of USPGA Tour player Brent Geiberger.

2000 SEASON. He broke through the $5 million Senior Tour earnings mark, helped by a T3 at the Foremost Insurance Championship.

Brent Geiberger

US Tour

Born 22 May 1968
Place of Birth Santa Barbara, California, USA
Year turned Professional 1993
Tour Ranking 85th

BEST FINISH IN MAJORS
Tied 71st USPGA 1998

TOUR VICTORIES
US: 1
1999 Canon Greater Hartford Open

A six foot four inch Californian, Geiberger is the son of Al Geigerber who, in 1977 at the Memphis Classic, became the first golfer to shoot a 59 in tournament play. Brent spent two years on the Nike Tour before joining the main Tour in 1996. His only Tour win to date came in 1999 when he beat Skip Kendall by three strokes in the Greater Hartford Open. He ended the season in 19th place on the Money List.

2000 SEASON. In 2000 Geiberger slipped to 85th on the Money List, with only four top-10 finishes to his name – T8 at the Mercedes and Air Canada Open, T5 in the Buick Challenge and T10 at the Buick Invitational. He missed the cuts in the three Major Championships he entered – Masters, US Open and USPGA.

Fred Gibson

US Seniors Tour

Born 12 September 1947
Place of Birth Washington DC, USA
Year turned Professional 1977
Tour Ranking 39th

TOUR VICTORIES
SENIOR TOUR: 1
1999 Vantage Championship

Former club professional Gibson qualified for the US Senior Tour in 1997 after finishing in seventh place at the Qualifying School and had to repeat the arduous process again in 1998, finishing in eighth place. He won his only Senior tournament in 1999 when he finished three shots clear of Bruce Fleisher to win the Vantage Championship, having Monday qualified, and banked $225,000.

2000 SEASON. Gibson had five top-10 finishes and ended the season in 39th spot on the Money List.

Gibby Gilbert

US Seniors Tour

Born 14 January 1941
Place of Birth Chattanooga, Tennessee, USA
Year turned Professional 1963
Tour Ranking 80th

TOUR VICTORIES
SENIOR TOUR: 6
1992 First of America Classic, Kroeger Senior Classic, Southwestern Bell Classic
1993 Las Vegas Senior Classic
1996 Boone Valley Classic
1997 Royal Caribbean Classic

A three-win journeyman on the USPGA Tour (although runner-up to Seve Ballesteros in the 1980 Masters), Gilbert ran a golf club before joining the US Senior Tour in 1991. In 1992 he recorded back-to-back wins, in the SouthwesternBell Classic and the Kroeger Senior Classic, and won again the following year. In 1996 he shot six birdies in the last 14 holes to force Hale Irwin into a play-off at the Boone Valley Classic, and Gilbert snatched victory. His last title came in 1997 when he led David Graham by four strokes to pick up the first full-field event of the season, the Royal Caribbean Classic, in Key Biscayne, Florida.

2000 SEASON. His best result ·was T18 in the Las Vegas Senior Classic.

Bob Gilder
US Seniors Tour

Born 31 December 1950
Place of Birth Corvallis, Oregon, USA
Year turned Professional 1973
Tour Ranking 206th

TOUR VICTORIES
US: 1
   2001 Verizon Classic

Gilder's last US Tour win was the Phoenix Open in 1983. He graduated from the Senior Qualifying School in 2000, shooting a record-breaking 19 under par 269.

2001 STOP PRESS. Gilder won the Verizon Classic in his rookie year.

David Gilford
European Tour

Born 14 September 1965
Place of Birth Crewe, England
Year turned Professional 1986
Tour Ranking 119th

BEST FINISH IN MAJORS
Tied 24th **US MASTERS 1995**

TOUR VICTORIES
EUROPEAN: 6
   1991 English Open
   1992 Moroccan Open
   1993 Moroccan Open, Portugese Open
   1994 European Open, Turespana Open de Tenerife

RYDER CUP 1991, 1995
DUNHILL CUP 1992
WORLD CUP 1992, 1993

The English Amateur Champion in 1984, Gilford's proudest moment to date came in the 1995 Ryder Cup in America, when he scored three points out of five, including a singles win over the highly-rated Brad Faxon. In his first Ryder Cup appearance – the famous 1991 encounter at Kiawah Island – Gilford missed his final day singles match after the American player, Steve Pate, was injured in an accident on the way to the course. A cattle farmer back home in Staffordshire, Gilford has played on the European Tour since 1987. Between 1988 and 1999 he remained in the top-100. His best year was 1994 when he notched up two victories and finished seventh in the Order of Merit.

2000 SEASON. Gilford had his worst year since 1987. He was T7 in the French Open and had two other top-5s, but he slumped to 119th place in the rankings.

Tom Gillis
European Tour

Born 16 July 1968
Place of Birth Lake Orion, Michigan, USA
Year turned Professional 1990
Tour Ranking 83rd

BEST FINISH IN MAJORS
Missed Cut **BRITISH OPEN 1999**

TOUR VICTORIES
OTHER: 1
   1994 Jamaican Open

One of the few Americans on the European Tour, Michigan-born Gillis joined the Tour in 1998 but lost his card in 1999. He graduated from Qualifying School in 2000 to rejoin the Tour. He has failed six times to qualify for the US Tour.

2000 SEASON. His best result was tied for third place with Padraig Harrington in the Belgacom Open. He was second round leader in the tournament thanks to opening rounds of 67-64.

Stewart Ginn

US Seniors Tour

Born 2 June 1949
Place of Birth Melbourne, Australia
Year turned Professional 1971
Tour Ranking 27th

Awidely-travelled Australian, Ginn has an impressive 16 international wins to his credit. An ex-Royal Melbourne caddie, he played in Australasia, Japan and on the European Tour in 1999, where he finished 40th on the Order of Merit. His only European Tour win so far was at the 1974 Martini International. In 1999 Ginn succeeded in securing a T2 place at the US Senior Tour Qualifying School.

2000 SEASON. His seven top-10 placings in his rookie year, his highest being T3 at the SBC Senior Classic, helped him to qualify for the Senior Tour Championship. He ended the season in 27th spot on the Money List.

2001 STOP PRESS. Ginn finished in third place at the ACE Group Classic and he was also second to Bruce Fleisher at the Las Vegas Senior Classic.

Bill Glasson

US Tour

Born 29 April 1960
Place of Birth Fresno, California, USA
Year turned Professional 1983
Tour Ranking 86th

BEST FINISH IN MAJORS
Tied 4th US OPEN 1995

TOUR VICTORIES
US: 7
1985 Kemper Open
1988 BC Open, Centel Classic
1989 Doral-Ryder Open
1992 Kemper Open
1994 Phoenix Open
1997 Las Vegas Invitational

Despite having suffered a series of medical problems and operations on his elbows, knees and forearm, Glasson has collected seven US Tour tournament wins in his career. He won his first event – the Kemper Open - in 1985, beating Larry Mize by one shot with a birdie putt, and his last win was at the Las Vegas Invitational in 1997. In 1997 he was voted Comeback Player of the Year. Glasson regularly flies his own plane to events.

2000 SEASON. Glasson had five top-20 finishes and was T3 at the BC Open. He slipped from 50th to 86th on the Money List.

Vicki Goetzee-Ackerman

US Ladies Tour

Born 17 October 1972
Place of Birth Michicot, Wisconsin, USA
Year turned Professional 1993
Tour Ranking 51st

Before joining the US Ladies Tour in 1994, the popular Goetzee-Ackerman was a star amateur, winning the US Women's Amateur Championship in 1989 and 1992 and playing in the 1990 and 1992 Curtis Cup. She was also low amateur at the US Women's Open in 1989, 1990 and 1992. However, she did not make the predicted impact on Tour and her best season in the 1990s was 1996, when she achieved seven top-20 places.

2000 SEASON. She finished in her career-best position of T2 in the LPGA Corning Classic, beaten by Betsy King after a play-off.

Matt Gogel

US Tour

Born 9th February 1971
Place of Birth Denver, Colorado, USA
Year turned Professional 1994
Tour Ranking 80th

BEST FINISH IN MAJORS
Tied 12th US OPEN 2001

The 2000 season was Gogel's first year on the US Tour, having failed to qualify via the Qualifying School for five years in succession between 1994 and 1998. However, in his four years on the Nike Tour between 1996 and 1999 he won six events and qualified for the main Tour by finishing seventh on the Money List in 1999.

2000 SEASON. Gogel started his rookie year well on the West Coast Swing, finishing T7 in only his second tournament, the Bob Hope Classic. He was then co-leader with Mark Brooks for the first three rounds in the AT&T Pro-Am at Pebble Beach. On the last round he birdied five of the first seven holes, but took a 40 on the back nine, while Tiger Woods came from ten shots behind to win by one stroke. Gogel picked up $350,000 for his second place finish. His only other top-20 placement came at the Shell Houston Open, but his first two top-10s had already secured his Tour card for 2001.

Thomas Gögele
European Tour

Born 17 November 1970
Place of Birth Hamburg, Germany
Year turned Professional 1986
Tour Ranking 81st

BEST FINISH IN MAJORS
Missed Cut **BRITISH OPEN 1997**

DUNHILL CUP 1996, 1997, 1998, 2000
WORLD CUP 1998

A powerful, long-hitting German, Gögele has been a regular on the European Tour since 1996, having earlier failed to retain his card. His highest finish on Tour is T2 at the 1996 German Open. A keen soccer and tennis fan, he is coached by leading Tour swing guru, Denis Pugh.

2000 SEASON. His only top-10 finish of the year came in the Madeira Island Open and he had two T13s at the BMW International and the Canon European Masters.

Matthew Goggin
US Tour

Born 13 June 1974
Place of Birth Hobart, Australia
Year turned Professional 1994
Tour Ranking 117th

TOUR VICTORIES
AUSTRALASIAN: 1
 1998 Australasian Tour Championship
OTHER: 1
 1997 Sao Paulo Open

The 1995 Australian Amateur of the Year, Goggin joined the USPGA Tour in 2000 having finished 1999 in fourth place on the Buy.Com Tour. He had a dispiriting and frustrating start to his first year on Tour however, making only two out of his first 17 cuts, but rallied in the summer to post a T3 at the Greater Milwaukee Open and a ninth place at the BC Open, in September. He hits the ball a very long way (ninth in driving distance), but also tends to be wayward off the tee.

Kate Golden
US Ladies Tour

Born 9 February 1967
Place of Birth Beaumont, Texas, USA
Year turned Professional 1989
Tour Ranking 66th

Texan Golden joined the LPGA Tour in 1990 from the Futures Tour, and her best finish was fourth at the 1997 Diet Dr Pepper National Pro-Am.

2000 SEASON. Golden enjoyed her best ever season on Tour, with five top-20 spots. She finished in the top-100 for the first time in her career.

Ricardo Gonzalez
European Tour

Born 24 October 1969
Place of Birth Corrientes, Argentina
Year turned Professional 1986
Tour Ranking 34th

BEST FINISH IN MAJORS
Missed Cut **BRITISH OPEN 1990**

DUNHILL CUP 1990, 1998
WORLD CUP 1996, 1998

An ex-caddie in Argentina, Gonzalez arrived on the European Tour in 1992, lost his card at the end of the season and did not re-qualify until 1999. His three top-10 finishes ensured his place on Tour in 2000. He partnered Angel Cabrera to third place in the 1998 World Cup. Gonzalez is one of the longest drivers on Tour, ranked fourth in the driving distance statistics.

2000 SEASON. He had his best-ever finish in the South African Open when he missed an eagle putt on the 18th which would have forced a play-off with Matthias Gronberg, and he had to settle for T2. He also finished T4 with Lee Westwood in the English Open. His only other top-10 finish was T7 in the Volvo Masters, five strokes behind the winner, Pierre Fulke.

David Good
European Senior Tour

Born 18 December 1947
Place of Birth Tasmania, Australia
Year turned Professional 1971
Tour Ranking 25th

Tasmanian-born Good qualified for the 2000 European Senior Tour in sixth place at 1999 Qualifying School.

2000 SEASON. Good finished the season in 25th place on the Order of Merit to retain full playing privileges for 2001.

Retief Goosen
European Tour

Born 3 February 1969
Place of Birth Pietersburg, South Africa
Year turned Professional 1990
Tour Ranking 15th

MAJOR VICTORIES
US OPEN 2001

TOUR VICTORIES
EUROPEAN: 4
1996 Slaley Hall Challenge
1997 French Open
1999 French Open
2000 Trophee Lancome
SOUTH AFRICA: 6
1991 Iscor Newcastle Classic
1992 Bushveld Classic, Spoornet Classic, Witbank Classic
1993 Mount Edgecombe Trophy
1995 South African Open

DUNHILL CUP 1995, 1996, 1997, 1998, 1999, 2000
PRESIDENTS CUP 2000
WORLD CUP 1993, 1995, 1998

Holder of six South African titles, Goosen joined the European Tour in 1993 and won his first title in 1996. The following year he led all the way to capture the French Open, in spite of double bogeying the last hole, and won it again in 1999 on the second play-off hole against Greg Turner. He finished 1999 fifth on the Order of Merit. He was one of the South African team (the others being Ernie Els and David Frost) who won the Dunhill Cup twice in succession in 1997 and 1998. 'The Goose' hits the ball a long way and is fairly accurate.

2000 SEASON. Goosen won the Lancome Trophy and also had four other top-5 finishes, two in South Africa. He also tied for a creditable 12th place in the US Open.

2001 STOP PRESS. Goosen claimed his first Major when, as a 125-1 outsider, he won the US Open at Southern Hills in an 18-hole play-off with Mark Brooks. The shy South African led from the start and would have won on the final day if he had not three-putted the last hole.

Jason Gore
US Tour

Born 17 May 1974
Place of Birth Van Nuys, California, USA
Year turned Professional 1997
Tour Ranking Tied 14th (Qualifying School)

A member of the US 1997 Walker Cup team, Gore played on the Buy.Com Tour between 1998 and 2000, winning once. He qualified for the 2001 US Tour by finishing T14 at Qualifying School. His highest finish on Tour is T26 at the 1999 Buick Invitational.

Asa Gottmo
European Ladies Tour

Born 22 June 1971
Place of Birth Kalmar, Sweden
Year turned Professional 1992
Tour Ranking 27th

Gottmo joined the European Ladies Tour in 1993, her best finish since then being second at the 1995 Irish Open.

2000 SEASON. Gottmo finished the season in 22nd place on the Money List, with her best placing being T2 at the French Open.

Paul Gow
US Tour

Born 11 October 1970
Place of Birth Sydney, Australia
Year turned Professional 1994
Tour Ranking 9th (Buy.Com Tour)

BEST FINISH IN MAJORS
Missed Cut **US OPEN 2000**

TOUR VICTORIES
AUSTRALASIAN: 1
2000 Canon Challenge

Winner of the 2000 Canon Challenge on the Australasian Tour, Gow finished the 1999–2000 season in sixth place on the ANZ Order of Merit. He played on the Buy.Com Tour in the USA from 1997 to 2000, achieving nine top-10 placings in 2000, which included one victory. Gow also established a new Australasian Tour record when he shot a 12 under par 60 in the first round of the 2000–01 season Canon Challenge. He was a rookie on the USPGA Tour in 2001.

Paul Goydos
US Tour

Born 20 June 1964
Place of Birth Long Beach, California, USA
Year turned Professional 1989
Tour Ranking 121st

BEST FINISH IN MAJORS
Tied 12th **US OPEN 1999**

TOUR VICTORIES
US: 1
1996 Bay Hill Invitational

Goydos joined the US Tour in 1993 from the Ben Hogan Tour and made only three top-10 finishes in three years until, out of nowhere, he won the prestigious Bay Hill Invitational in Orlando, Florida, in 1996 by one stroke from Jeff Maggert. Since then, he has managed two second places on Tour. In 1999 he shot a five under par 67 at Pinehurst to become joint first round leader in the US Open and he went on to finish the tournament tied for 12th place. He is known, rather sarcastically, on the US Tour as 'Mr Sunshine'.

2000 SEASON. Goydos slumped to 121st on the Money List although he collected three T10 placings – at the Bay Hill Invitational, BC Open and Buick Challenge.

John Grace
European Senior Tour

Born 16 April 1948
Place of Birth Fort Worth, Texas, USA
Year turned Professional 1998
Tour Ranking 2nd

TOUR VICTORIES
SENIOR TOUR: 3
2000 Belfry PGA Seniors Championship, Monte Carlo Invitational, Ordina Legends of Golf

American Grace, who in 1975 played in the victorious US Walker Cup team alongside Craig Stadler, Jay Haas and Curtis Strange, turned pro in 1998 at the age of 50, having had an illustrious amateur career. He played only three events on the 1999 European Tour, but was successful enough in these to gain exemption for the 2000 season.

2000 SEASON. Grace won his first European Senior Tour event when he birdied the first hole of a play-off to beat Peter Dawson in the Belfry PGA Seniors Championship. He won again a fortnight later, finishing one ahead of David Jones at the Ordina Legends of Golf, to go top of the Order of Merit. He won his third event at the Big 3 Records Monte Carlo Invitational, when he shot an 8 under par 199 to beat Maurice Bembridge by five shots. At the final event of the season – the Abu Dhabi Championship – he could not finish high enough on the leaderboard to claim the Order of Merit title, which went to Noel Ratcliffe.

David Graham
US Seniors Tour

Born 23rd May 1946
Place of Birth Windsor, Australia
Year turned Professional 1962
Tour Ranking 42nd

TOUR VICTORIES
SENIOR TOUR: 5
1997 Comfort Classic, GTE Classic, South West Bell Dominion
1998 Royal Caribbean Classic
1999 Raley's Gold Rush Classic

The long-hitting Australian Graham won 20 tournaments worldwide, eight on the USPGA Tour, before joining the US Senior Tour in 1996. This tally included the 1979 USPGA Championship, when he beat Ben Crenshaw on the third play-off hole, and the 1981 US Open, shooting a three under par last round 67 to defeat George Burns and Bill

Rogers by 3 strokes. In the latter tournament he became the first Australian to lift the trophy.

In his first full Senior season in 1997 he won three times and ended fifth on the Money List, earning $1 million. He has won two more tournaments, his last being the Rayley's Gold Rush Classic in 1999 when he beat Larry Nelson by four shots and shot a 17 under par tournament record 199. Marsh is involved in course design and architecture and he received the Order of Australia in 1992 for his contribution to the game.

2000 SEASON. Graham produced three top-10s, his best being third at the Boone Valley Classic behind Tom Watson and Larry Nelson. He is in the top-31 on the All Time List.

Gail Graham

US Ladies Tour

Born 16 January 1964
Place of Birth Vanderhoof, British Columbia
Year turned Professional 1988
Tour Ranking 81st

TOUR VICTORIES

US: 2

1995 Fieldcrest Cannon Classic
1997 Australian Ladies Masters

Married to a Canadian golf professional, Graham was low amateur at the 1987 du Maurier Classic and joined the LPGA Tour in 1990. She has won twice on Tour – the 1995 Fieldcrest Cannon Classic and the 1997 Australian Ladies Masters, when she beat Karrie Webb in Queensland.

2000 SEASON. Illness curtailed her season.

Hubert Green

US Seniors Tour

Born 28 December 1946
Place of Birth Birmingham, Alabama, USA
Year turned Professional 1969
Tour Ranking 9th

TOUR VICTORIES

SENIOR TOUR: 3

1998 Bruno's Memorial Classic
2000 Audi Senior Classic, Kroger Senior Classic

A plain-speaking, often abrasive individual with an unorthodox swing, Green had a highly successful USPGA Tour career, winning 19 tournaments between 1971 and 1985 as well as two Major titles. He won the 1977 US Open by two strokes over Lou Graham, also finishing third that year at the British Open, and he beat Lee Trevino by two shots to collect the 1985 USPGA Championship. Known as 'the Doberman' for his appearance and on-course aggression, he joined the US Senior Tour in 1997, finishing in the top 31, and won his first title the following year when he shot a final round 64 at Bruno's Memorial Classic, at his home town of Birmingham, Alabama, to edge Hale Irwin by one shot and overturn a four stroke deficit. Green has represented the USA at three Ryder Cups.

2000 SEASON. His lightning quick, although accurate, swing earned Green another two victories. He shot a final round 62 to win the Audi Classic by a margin of five strokes, and he collected the Kroger Senior Classic, beating Larry Nelson by one shot. He was also third at the British Senior Open. These victories, and his 14 other top-10 placings propelled him into ninth spot on the end of season Money List.

Jimmy Green

US Tour

Born 6 August 1969
Place of Birth Meridian, Mississippi, USA
Year turned Professional 1992
Tour Ranking 116th

BEST FINISH IN MAJORS

Tied 57th US OPEN 2000

Green played on the US Tour in 1997 and 1999, when his best finish was T7 at the Sony Open in Hawaii, and he qualified for 2000 through the Qualifying School. He won the Buy.Com Buffalo Open with his wife by his side as caddie.

2000 SEASON. Playing in his second tournament of the season, Green shot two successive 68s to finish T4 at Pebble Beach, in California. However, his only other top-20 placings of the season were at the Greater Greensboro Classic (T16) and later at the Buick Classic (T13).

Nathan Green
Australasian Tour

Born 30 May 1975
Place of Birth Waratah, Australia
Year turned Professional 1998
Tour Ranking 6th

Green produced two second-place finishes on the 2000–01 Australasian Tour to end the season in sixth place on the Order of Merit. He was runner-up at the lucrative Ericsson Masters, where he scored a hole in one at the 12th hole on his final round to win Aus$500,000.

Richard Green
European Tour

Born 19 February 1971
Place of Birth Melbourne, Australia
Year turned Professional 1992
Tour Ranking 54th

BEST FINISH IN MAJORS
Missed Cut **BRITISH OPEN 1997, 1999**

TOUR VICTORIES
EUROPEAN: 1
1997 Dubai Desert Classic

WORLD CUP 1998

The tall, left-handed Australian won his first tournament – the Dubai Desert Classic – in 1997, his second year on the European Tour, beating Ian Woosnam and Greg Norman in a play-off. However, his golf went somewhat downhill in the following two years and he finished 165th and 102nd on the European Order of Merit. He is an accurate player with a suspect short game.

2000 SEASON. His form picked up in 2000 with four top-20 finishes, a T5 at the Volvo PGA and a T3 at the Italian Open. At the Standard Life Loch Lomond, he was half-way leader with Ernie Els, but a final round of 76 saw him finish in 22nd place. On the Australasian Tour he was second at the Victorian Open and third at the Australian Open, leaving him on 13th place on the Order of Merit.

Tammie Green
US Ladies Tour

Born 17 December 1959
Place of Birth Somerset, Ohio, USA
Year turned Professional 1986
Tour Ranking 118th

MAJORS VICTORIES
DU MAURIER CLASSIC 1989

TOUR VICTORIES
US: 6
1993 Healthsouth Palm Beach Classic, Rochester Invitational
1994 Youngstown-Warren Classic
1997 Giant Eagle Classic, Sprint Title holders Championship
1998 Corning Classic

SOLHEIM CUP 1994, 1998

Green won ten times on the Futures Tour before joining the LPGA in 1987, becoming Rookie of the Year. She won her first Major in 1989 and to date has won six other tournaments. Her last victory was at the 1998 LPGA Corning Classic, where she won by seven strokes from Brandie Burton and Emilee Klein, and received an exemption for the 2001 season.

2000 SEASON. Her highest finish was T16 at the Philips Invitational.

Malcolm Gregson
European Senior Tour

Born 15 August 1943
Place of Birth Leicester, England
Year turned Professional 1961
Tour Ranking 23rd

TOUR VICTORIES

SENIOR TOUR: 3
1994 Tandem Open
1996 Lawrence Batley Seniors
1998 Is Molas Open

In 1967 Gregson was placed first on the European Tour Order of Merit, claiming three Tour victories and playing in his only Ryder Cup competition, and he won two other tournaments in the 1960s. He first played on the European Senior Tour in 1994 and won the Tandem Open that year. He has subsequently won two more Senior events.

2000 SEASON. His best performance was fourth at the Scottish Seniors Open and he had seven other top-10 placings to finish in 23rd on the Order of Merit at the end of the season.

Mathias Gronberg
European Tour

Born 12 March 1970
Place of Birth Stockholm, Sweden
Year turned Professional 1990
Tour Ranking 20th

BEST FINISH IN MAJORS

Missed Cut **US OPEN 1999, 2001**

TOUR VICTORIES

EUROPEAN: 2
1995 Canon European Masters
1998 Smurfit European Open
SOUTH AFRICA: 1
2000 South African Open

DUNHILL CUP 1998, 2000
WORLD CUP 1998

The long-hitting Gronberg joined the European Tour in 1994 and won his first title, the European Masters, the following year. His best season came in 1998 when he won the European Open at the K Club by an amazing ten strokes and finished tenth on the Order of Merit. At the end of the 1999 season, Gronberg failed to qualify for the US Tour by just one shot. Married to an American, the US Tour would seem to be his ultimate ambition.

2000 SEASON. Five shots behind leader Darren Fischardt at the beginning of the last round of the South African Open, Gronberg rallied to win the tournament by one stroke. He also had a hot streak in July, with a T4 at the European Open and then a T3 at the Dutch Open, his only other top-10 finish coming at the Rio De Janeiro Open. In the Dunhill Cup he won two out of his three games for Sweden.

2001 STOP PRESS. Gronberg lost a four-way sudden-death play-off in the Victor Chandler British Masters at Woburn.

Sofia Gronberg Whitmore
European Ladies Tour

Born 25 May 1965
Place of Birth Falkoping, Sweden
Year turned Professional 1987
Tour Ranking 21st

TOUR VICTORIES

EUROPEAN: 3
1989 Rome Classic
1999 Biarritz Open, Laura Davies Invitational

A veteran of the European Ladies Tour, Whitmore won her first title, the Rome Classic, in 1989 and won twice again in 1999, claiming the Air France Open and beating Trish Johnson in an exciting sudden-death play-off at the Laura Davies Invitational at Brocket Hall Golf Club.

2000 SEASON. Her highest placing was T3 at the *Daily Telegraph* British Women's Masters and she ended the year in 26th position on the Money List.

Kelly Grunewald
US Tour

Born 24 September 1968
Place of Birth Arlington, Texas, USA
Year turned Professional 1992
Tour Ranking 14th (Buy.Com Tour)

A rookie on the 2001 US Tour, the burly Grunewald joined the 2000 Buy.Com Tour and had six top-5s and three top-10s to claim 14th place on the Money List

Sophie Gustafson
US Ladies Tour

Born 27th December 1973
Place of Birth Saro, Sweden
Year turned Professional 1992
Tour Ranking 13th

TOUR VICTORIES

US: 2
  2000 Chick-fil-A Charity Classic
  2001 Subaru Memorial of Naples
EUROPEAN: 7
  1996 Swiss Open
  1998 Irish Ladies Open, Marrakech
        Palmeraie Open
  2000 British Women's Open, Irish Ladies
        Open, Italian Ladies Open
  2001 Australian Women's Open

SOLHEIM CUP 1998, 2000

Sweden's Gustafson joined the European Tour in 1994 and won the Swiss Open in 1996 to end 12th on the Order of Merit. In 1998 she collected the Irish Ladies Open and the Marrakech Open and moved to second on the Order of Merit.

2000 SEASON. Gustafson won her first tournament on the LPGA Tour when a birdie putt on the final hole gave her victory in the Chick-fil-A Charity Classic. She also won the co-sanctioned Weetabix British Women's Open ahead of Kirsty Taylor and Becky Iverson. She won the Italian Open by three strokes and the Irish Open, when she sunk a birdie putt at the last hole for a 69. She ended 13th on the LPGA Money List and first on the European Order of Merit.

2001 STOP PRESS. Gustafson won her second US event, the Subaru Memorial of Naples. She also won the Australian Women's Open on the European Tour, beating Karrie Webb by one stroke.

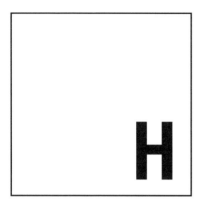

Hunter Haas

US Tour

Born 1 December 1976
Place of Birth Fort Worth, Texas, USA
Year turned Professional 2000
Tour Ranking Tied 8th (Qualifying School)

Winner of the 1999 Amateur Public Links Championship, but with no Buy.Com or US Tour experience, Haas qualified in T8th position at Qualifying School for the 2001 US Tour. He is no relation to Jay Haas.

Jay Haas

US Tour

Born 2 December 1953
Place of Birth St Louis, Missouri, USA
Year turned Professional 1976
Tour Ranking 144th

BEST FINISH IN MAJORS
Tied 3rd USPGA 1999

TOUR VICTORIES
US: 9
1978 Andy Williams-San Diego Open Invitational
1981 BC Open, Greater Milwaukee Open
1982 Hall of Fame, Texas Open
1987 Houston Open

1988 Bob Hope Chrysler Classic
1992 Federal Express St Jude Classic
1993 HEB Texas Open

RYDER CUP 1983, 1995
PRESIDENTS CUP 1994

Nine-time US Tour winner Haas was in the top-100 on the Money List every year between 1977 and 1999. His best years were 1981 and 1982, when he was respectively 15th and 13th on the List and he won four tournaments. His last win was at the 1993 Texas Open. Good performances seem few and far between, but he consistently plays well in The Masters at Augusta National.

2000 SEASON. This was Haas' worst-ever season. He made only half his cuts, his highest finish was T12 at the Nissan Open, and he fell from 60th to 144th on the Money List.

Joakim Haeggman

European Tour

Born 28 August 1969
Place of Birth Kalmar, Sweden
Year turned Professional 1989
Tour Ranking 104th

TOUR VICTORIES
EUROPEAN: 2
1993 Peugeot Open de Espana
1997 Scandinavian Masters

RYDER CUP 1993
DUNHILL CUP 1993, 1997
WORLD CUP 1993, 1994, 1997

A keen ice-hockey fan, Haeggman was the first Swedish golfer to play in the Ryder Cup in 1993. He also won his first European Tour event – the Spanish Open – that year and ended the season 15th in the Order of Merirt. He won the Scandinavian Masters in 1997 and also equalled the world record of 27 strokes for nine holes in the Dunhill Cup.

2000 SEASON. Haeggman seemed to be returning to his form of the mid-1990s when he clinched four top-20 finishes, his highest being T4 in the Rio De Janeiro Open.

Craig Hainline
European Tour

Born 29 January 1970
Place of Birth Wichita, Kansas, USA
Year turned Professional 1993
Tour Ranking 124th

BEST FINISH IN MAJORS
70th **US OPEN 1999**

Texan Hainline joined the European Tour through the Challenge Tour in 1998. He retained his card with three top-10 finishes and played again in 1999, finishing 87th on the Order of Merit.
2000 SEASON. Hainline had his best-ever finish with a T2 at the Malaysian Open, but finished outside the top-115 on the Order of Merit.

Caroline Hall
European Ladies Tour

Born 14 November 1973
Place of Birth Bristol, England
Year turned Professional 1992
Tour Ranking 29th

TOUR VICTORIES
EUROPEAN: 1
1995 Danish Open

Hall turned pro in 1992 and won the Danish Open in 1995, and was second the same year in the Maredo Ladies Open.
2000 SEASON. She played in all 15 events on the European Ladies Tour and her highest placing was T4 at the Italian Open, her best finish since 1995. She also played on the Asian Tour, ending the year eighth on the Order of Merit.

Walter Hall
US Seniors Tour

Born 12 June 1947
Place of Birth Winston-Salem, North Carolina, USA
Year turned Professional 1994
Tour Ranking 20th

TOUR VICTORIES
SENIOR TOUR: 1
1997 Belfry Senior PGA Championship

Hall played on the European Senior Tour in 1997, winning the Belfry PGA Senior Championship and finishing eighth at the British Senior Open. He then crossed the Atlantic to join the US Senior Tour in 1998, and showed that he had the game to challenge for tournaments by immediately posting three second-place spots. He twice finished in third place in 1999.
2000 SEASON. Hall was runner-up at the Cadillac NFL, the ACE Group Classic and the SBC Senior Classic and secured five other top-10s. He ended 2000 in the top-31.

Kyi Hli Han
European Tour

Born 13 February, 1961
Place of Birth Myanmar, Burma
Year turned Professional 1982
Tour Ranking 149th

BEST FINISH IN MAJORS
Missed Cut **BRITISH OPEN 2000**

A member of both the Asian and European Tours, Han played in ten European Tour events in 2000, his highest finish being T17 at the Johnnie Walker Classic.
2000 SEASON. Of the ten events he entered in Europe in 2000, Han made the cut six times. On the Asian Tour, where he played more regularly, he competed in 14 events, finishing 35th on the Davidoff Order of Merit

Christopher Hanell

European Tour

Born 30 May 1973
Place of Birth Vastervik, Sweden
Year turned Professional 1997
Tour Ranking 65th

BEST FINISH IN MAJORS
Missed Cut **BRITISH OPEN 1999**

Swedish golfer Hanell, attended the same University – Arizona State – as fellow compatriot Per-Ulrik Johansson, and is coached by leading American teacher and commentator Peter Kostis. He competed against Tiger Woods in his college days and joined the European Tour from the Challenge Tour in 1999, ending the season 62nd in the Order of Merit. He had two top-10 finishes in his rookie season, finishing T5 in the Qatar Masters and third in the British Masters at Woburn.

2000 SEASON. Hanell demonstrated his consistency with six top-20 finishes to leave him 65 in the Order of Merit.

Anders Hansen

European Tour

Born 16 September 1970
Place of Birth Sonderborg, Denmark
Year turned Professional 1995
Tour Ranking 53rd

Former Danish Amateur Champion Hansen (no relation to Soren) is one of the straightest and most accurate drivers on the European Tour. An alumni of the University of Houston, he graduated in third place from Qualifying School in 1998 and ended the 1999 season 107th on the Order of Merit.

2000 SEASON. Hansen rose rapidly up the Order of Merit, with three top-10 finishes, his best being T6 at the Greg Norman Holden International, and he made the cut in 16 of his first 21 tournaments.

Soren Hansen

European Tour

Born 21 March 1974
Place of Birth Copenhagen, Denmark
Year turned Professional 1997
Tour Ranking 73rd

WORLD CUP 1998

Hansen (no relation to Anders) graduated from the Challenge Tour in 1998 and kept his card for 2000 by finishing 112th on the Order of Merit.

2000 SEASON. He made two top-10 finishes – T7 in both the French and Belgacom Opens, shooting a third round 63 in the latter to share second place.

2001 STOP PRESS. Hansen finished T3 at the Spanish Open.

Peter Hanson

European Tour

Born 4 October 1977
Place of Birth Boksogen, Sweden
Year turned Professional 1998
Tour Ranking 14th (Qualifying School)

A towering (6 foot 3 inch) Swede, Hanson won the amateur Brabazon Trophy in 1998 and turned professional. His best placing on the 2000 Challenge Tour was sixth at the Luxembourg Open and he later gained his card for the 2001 European Tour through Qualifying School.

Padraig Harrington

European Tour

Born 31 August 1971
Place of Birth Dublin, Ireland
Year turned Professional 1995
Tour Ranking 7th

BEST FINISH IN MAJORS
Tied 5th **BRITISH OPEN 1997, US OPEN 2000**

TOUR VICTORIES
EUROPEAN: 3
  1996 Peugeot Open de Espana
  2000 Brazil Sao Paulo 500 Years Open,
    Turespana Masters

RYDER CUP 1999
DUNHILL CUP 1996, 1997, 1998, 1999, 2000
WORLD CUP 1996, 1997, 1998, 1999

A qualified accountant, Harrington played in three Walker Cups before joining the European Tour in 1996. He made an immediate impression, winning the Peugeot Open de Espana in only his tenth start and finishing in 11th place in the Order of Merit. Since then the amiable Irishman has never been out of the top-30. In 1997 at Kiawah, Harrington along with Paul McGinley won the World Cup for Ireland for only the second time in the country's history. He also qualified for the European Ryder Cup team in the controversial 1999 clash at Brookline and beat Mark O'Meara in the singles.

2000 SEASON. It was a very successful year for Harrington. He finally broke his run of seven second places in 11 months with victory in the Sao Paulo 500 Years Open, beating Gerry Norquist by two strokes. In May, Harrington was five shots clear of the pack at the beginning of the final round of the Benson & Hedges International Open when it was dis-

covered that he had omitted to sign his first round card. Under Rule 6.6b, he was disqualified and Jose Maria Olázàbal went on to win the tournament. However, he made up for this blow by winning the Turespana Masters in October, two shots ahead of Gary Orr. He also had a successful season in the Majors, carding a T5 in his debut appearance at the US Open, T19 in the Masters, T20 in the British Open and T59 in the USPGA. In the WGC American Express at the end of the season he finished T5. He finished in seventh place in the Order of Merit for the second year in succession. He is coached by Sam Torrance's father, Bob.

2001 STOP PRESS. Harrington was defeated by Vijay Singh at the third play-off hole at the Carlsberg Malaysian Open. He was also second, tied with Tiger Woods, behind Thomas Björn at the Dubai Desert Classic. He came second again at the Portugese Open, two strokes behind Philip Price, and also finished T5 at the Deutsche Bank-SAP Open, in Germany.

Dudley Hart
US Tour

Born 4 August 1968
Place of Birth Rochester, New York, USA
Year turned Professional 1990
Tour Ranking 43rd

BEST FINISH IN MAJORS
Tied 6th USPGA 1993

TOUR VICTORIES
US: 2
  1996 Bell Canadian Open
  2000 Honda Classic
OTHER: 1
  1998 Subaru Sarazen World Open

Known earlier in his career as 'mini volcano' because of his temper, Hart joined the US Tour in 1991. The son of a golf coach (his sister Cathy is also a golf professional), he won his first tournament in 1996 when he defeated David Duval by one shot at the rain-shortened Bell Canadian Open. He won the Subaru Sarazen World Open in 1998. His eight top-10 and three top-3 finishes in 1999 brought him the number 29 slot on the Money List and he earned over $1.2 million.

2000 SEASON. Hart won his second tournament when, at the Honda Classic in March, he birdied the last four holes to catch up a three-stroke deficit. He also had a T3 at the Greater Greensboro Classic and a T6 in the Buick Open to end the season in 43rd place on the Money List, earning over $1 million in the process. It was his fifth year in succession in the top-60.

Jeff Hart

US Tour

Born 5 May 1960
Place of Birth Pomona, California, USA
Year turned Professional 1983
Tour Ranking 15th (Buy.Com Tour)

Hart has played on both the US Tour and the Nike Tour in his career. He played on the Buy.Com Tour in 2000 and won his first tournament, allowing him to finish the season in 15th place and, in turn, claim his US Tour card for 2001. His highest placing on the US Tour is T4 at the 1988 Deposit Guaranty Golf Classic.

Gregory Havret

European Tour

Born 25 November 1976
Place of Birth Bussy St Georges, France
Year turned Professional 1999
Tour Ranking 21st (Qualifying School)

Three-time French Amateur Champion, Havret also became European Amateur Champion in 1999. He qualified for the 2001 European tour by finishing 21st at Qualifying School.

J.P. Hayes

US Tour

Born 2 August 1965
Place of Birth Appleton, Wisconsin, USA
Year turned Professional 1989
Tour Ranking 57th

BEST FINISH IN MAJORS
Tied 19th **USPGA 2000**

TOUR VICTORIES
US: 1
1998 Buick Classic

An adopted Texan, John Patrick Hayes played on both the Nike Tour and the US Tour in the 1990s, and had to visit the Qualifying School four times during that decade. His one victory on Tour came as something of a shock result when he beat Jim Furyk in a play-off at the 1998 Buick Classic. He ended that season in 51st place on the Money List, his best-ever finish.

2000 SEASON. Hayes had a good year, achieving five top-10 finishes, including a T3 in the Greater Milwaukee Open and a T2 in the Honda Classic. Although he missed the cut in the US Open, he finished a respectable T19 in the USPGA.

Mark Hayes

US Seniors Tour

Born 12 July 1949
Place of Birth Stillwater, Oklahoma, USA
Year turned Professional 1972
Tour Ranking 68th

Hayes qualified for the 2000 US Senior season with a place in the Qualifying School top-eight, having already won three times on the USPGA Tour during his career. He had six top-25 finishes and re-qualified with a T7 at 2000 Qualifying School. In addition to his playing commitments, he also runs a golf course design business.

Johanna Head
European Ladies Tour

Born 28 February 1973
Place of Birth Ascot, England
Year turned Professional 1995
Tour Ranking 16th

TOUR VICTORIES
OTHER: 1
1999 Malaysian Open

Twin sister of fellow ELPGA Tour Professional, Samantha, Head's highest finish on the European Tour was T2 at the 1998 Compaq Open, and her best season was in 1999 when she was fourth at the Austrian Open and sixth at the German Open. In 1999 she also played on the Asian Tour, winning the Malaysian Open.

2000 SEASON. She made all 14 of her cuts and managed seven top-15 places, her highest being T4 at the Mexx Open.

Samantha Head
European Ladies Tour

Born 28 February 1973
Place of Birth Ascot, England
Year turned Professional 1995
Tour Ranking 14th

TOUR VICTORIES
EUROPEAN: 2
1999 Italian Open
2001 South African Ladies Masters

Head joined the Tour in 1995, and first won in 1999 when she captured the Italian Open beating Trish Johnson by one shot. Her twin sister Johanna also plays on Tour.

2000 SEASON. She was second to Carin Koch in the Chrysler Open and had two other top-10s to finish 17th on the Money List.

2001 STOP PRESS. Head won the South African Ladies Masters to claim her second European Tour victory.

Lisa Hed
European Ladies Tour

Born 5 July 1973
Place of Birth Gothenburg, Sweden
Year turned Professional 1995
Tour Ranking 27th

Swede Hed gained her European Ladies Tour card in 1999, after finishing T5 at the Qualifying School.

2000 SEASON. She had an impressive Rookie season, posting three top-10 finishes, including a T2 at the Austrian Open, one stroke behind winner Patricia Meunier Lebouc. She finished the year 27th on the Money List.

Fredrik Henge
European Tour

Born 30 December 1974
Place of Birth Lund, Sweden
Year turned Professional 1997
Tour Ranking 7th (Challenge Tour)

Henge played on the main Tour in 1998 and regained his card after finishing 7th on the 2000 Challenge Tour, winning the Danish Open and the Formby Hall Challenge.

Nic Henning
European Tour

Born 26 April 1969
Place of Birth Pretoria, South Africa
Year turned Professional 1992
Tour Ranking 15th (Qualifying School)

TOUR VICTORIES
SOUTH AFRICA: 1
1999 Vodacom Players Championship

Henning's finest win was in 1999 when he beat Darren Clarke in a play-off at the South African Tour's Vodacom Players Championship. In 2000, his highest finish on the European Tour was tenth at the Alfred Dunhill and he qualified for the 2001 Tour with a 15th placing at Qualifying School

Brian Henninger
US Tour

Born 19 October 1962
Place of Birth Sacramento, California, USA
Year turned Professional 1987
Tour Ranking 91st

BEST FINISH IN MAJORS
Tied 10th **US MASTERS 1995**

TOUR VICTORIES
US: 2
　1994 Deposit Guaranty Golf Classic
　1999 Southern Farm Bureau Classic

Henninger, who graduated from college with a degree in psychology, joined the US Tour from the Nike Tour in 1993, having secured three victories in 1992, and has played every year since. He has become a master at winning rain-shortened tournaments. He won his first tournament – the Deposit Guaranty Classic, shortened to 54 holes due to thunderstorms – in 1994 and won the same tournament – now renamed the Southern Farm Bureau Classic – in 1999. This latter tournament was also shortened to

54 holes. He finished 55th in the Money List in 1999, his best career finish. In his third year on Tour – 1995 – he achieved a T10 in the Masters. Henninger is known as an average driver but an excellent putter.

2000 SEASON. Henninger retained his card for 2001 by posting a T6 at the Advil Western Open and a T4 at the Reno-Tahoe Open, where he also shot a course record 63 to take the halfway lead.

JJ Henry
US Tour

Born 2 April 1975
Place of Birth Fairfield, Connecticut, USA
Year turned Professional 1998
Tour Ranking 13th (Buy.Com Tour)

Six foot three Henry joined the Buy.Com Tour in 2000 and had one win and four top-10 finishes. He earned his 2001 rookie US Tour card by virtue of his 13th place in the tour's Money List. His best finish on the main PGA Tour is T56 at the 1998 Greater Hartford Open.

Mark Hensby
US Tour

Born 29 June 1971
Place of Birth Melbourne, Australia
Year turned Professional 1994
Tour Ranking 2nd (Buy.Com Tour)

Australian Hensby played on the Nike Tour from 1997 until 2000. He won two tournaments during that period and led the 2000 Money List until the end of the season, when Spike McRoy overhauled him at the Tour Championship. He finished in second place, however. A long hitter, he also topped the greens in regulation statistics. Although 2001 is his rookie year on the US Tour, his highest finish is T41 at the 1996 Quad City Classic.

Tim Herron
_____
US Tour

Born 16- February 1970
Place of Birth Minneapolis, Minnesota, USA
Year turned Professional 1993
Tour Ranking 65th

BEST FINISH IN MAJORS
6th US OPEN 1999

TOUR VICTORIES
US: 3
  1996 Honda Classic
  1997 LaCantera Texas Open
  1999 Bay Hill Invitational

Known as 'Lumpy' because of his comfortable girth, Herron joined the US Tour in 1996 from the Nike Tour and won a tournament in his rookie year. At the Honda Classic, he shot a course record 62 in the first round and went wire-to-wire to win. The following year he captured the LaCantera Texas Open by two strokes, and he claimed his third victory in 1999 when he birdied the second playoff hole to defeat Tom Lehman at the Bay Hill Invitational. He was also twice runner-up and he finished the season in a best-ever 22nd place on the Money List. He is a long hitter, but not particularly accurate. Herron's father and grandfather were also professional golfers.

2000 SEASON. Herron had seven top-20 finishes – his best being seventh at the John Deere Classic – but slumped to 65th on the Money List. He entered all four Majors, but missed the cut in each.

David Higgins
_____
European Tour

Born 1 December 1972
Place of Birth Cork, Ireland
Year turned Professional 1994
Tour Ranking 2nd (Challenge Tour)

Son of Liam who plays on the European Senior Tour, Higgins won the Irish Amateur Championship in 1994. He had three victories on the 2000 European Challenge Tour – the NCC Open, Rolex Trophy and Gunther Hamburg Classic – and one top-3 place to finish second behind Henrik Stenson.

Mike Hill
_____
US Seniors Tour

Born 27 January 1939
Place of Birth Jackson, Mississippi, USA
Year turned Professional 1968
Tour Ranking 66th

MAJORS VICTORIES
US SENIOR OPEN 1991

TOUR VICTORIES
SENIOR TOUR: 17
  1990 Fairfield Barnett Space Coast Classic, GTE North Classic, GTE Suncoast Classic, New York Life Champions, Security Pacific Senior Classic
  1991 Doug Sanders Celebrity Classic, GTE Northwest Classic, Nationwide Championship, New York Life Champions
  1992 Digital Seniors Classic, Doug Sanders Celebrity Classic, Vintage Arco Invitational

1993 Better Homes and Gardens Real Estate
     Challenge, Paine Webber Invitational
1994 The IntelliNet Challenge
1995 Kroger Senior Classic
1996 Bank One Classic

Hill left the USPGA Tour with three titles and joined the US Senior Tour in 1989. In his rookie year he finished ninth on the Money List and the following season he won five tournaments and ended in second place behind Lee Trevino on the Money List. In 1991 he earned $1 million, was co-Player of the Year with George Archer and topped the List. By 1997 his efforts had earned him over $5 million, but the following year he fell outside the top-31 for the first time in his career. He has won 18 times on Tour and is on the top-31 All-Time Money List.

2000 SEASON. Hill was third on the Super Seniors for the second successive year, and his best Tour finish was T5 at the Foremost Insurance. He has passed the $7 million mark in Tour winnings.

Gabriel Hjertstedt
                                                    US Tour

Born 5 December 1971
Place of Birth Umea, Sweden
Year turned Professional 1990
Tour Ranking 138th

BEST FINISH IN MAJORS
Tied 16th USPGA 1999

TOUR VICTORIES
US: 2
    1997 BC Open
    1999 Touchstone Energy Tucson Open

DUNHILL CUP 1994, 1999

Australasian Tour Rookie of the Year in 1990, Hjertstedt joined the European Tour in 1993. After enjoying little success there, he surprised a lot of people when he qualified for the USPGA Tour in 1997. The American lifestyle appears to suit him as he went on to win his first tournament – the BC Open – in 1997 by one stroke, then, in 1999, he became the first Swede to win twice on Tour when he picked up the Tucson Open, beating Tommy Armour III in a play-off.

2000 SEASON. His best finish was T14 at the Greater Hartford Open and he slumped from 41st to 138th on the Money List.

Maria Hjorth
                                                 US Ladies Tour

Born 15 October 1973
Place of Birth Falun, Sweden
Year turned Professional 1996
Tour Ranking 50th

TOUR VICTORIES
US: 2
    1999 Mizuno Classic, Safeco Classic

Swedish powerhouse Hjorth had a very successful amateur career, winning the 1995 European Ladies Amateur Championship and has since developed into one of the world's finest golfers. She played on the European and Asian Tours in 1996 and 1997 before joining the LPGA Tour in 1998. She won twice on the US Tour in 1999, at the Safeco Classic and the Mizuno Classic, and finished the season 11th on the Money List.

2000 SEASON. She was runner-up at the Subaru Memorial of Naples, losing to Nancy Scranton on a playoff, and tied for 6th place at the Australian Ladies Masters.

Glen Hnatiuk
                                                    US Tour

Born 15 May 1965
Place of Birth Selkirk, Manitoba, USA
Year turned Professional 1990
Tour Ranking 101st

Tall Canadian Hnatiuk spent most of the 1990s on the Nike Tour, where he won four tournaments. He qualified in 1997 for the US Tour but could not retain his card, but he qualified again for season 2000. He is accurate - 7th for greens in regulation - but short off the tee. His best finish was T3 with Bill Glasson at the B.C. Open and he also achieved a T6 at the International.

Justin Hobday
European Tour

Born 12 August 1963
Place of Birth England
Year turned Professional 1985
Tour Ranking 7th (Qualifying School)

TOUR VICTORIES
SOUTH AFRICA: 7

1991 Goodyear Classic
1993 Spoornet Classic, Sun City Classic
1995 FNB Series: Free State
1996 IDC Development Tourism Classic
1998 FNB: Botswana Open, Royal Swazi Sun Classic

Nephew of Simon Hobday, the ex-European, PGA and currently US Senior Tour player, the bespectacled Hobday won seven times on the South African Tour. He played three tournaments on the 2000 European Tour and gained his card through Qualifying School for the 2001 European Tour.

Simon Hobday
US Seniors Tour

Born 23 June 1940
Place of Birth Mafeking, South Africa
Year turned Professional 1969
Tour Ranking 65th

MAJORS VICTORIES
SENIOR PLAYERS CHAMPIONSHIP 1993
US SENIOR OPEN 1994

TOUR VICTORIES
SENIOR TOUR: 3

1993 Kroger Senior Classic
1994 GTE Northwest Classic
1995 Brickyard Crossing Championship

An ex-rancher from South Africa, Hobday joined the US Senior Tour in 1990 by winning the Qualifying School. He won his first two tournaments, including the Senior Tour Championship, in 1993, and, in 1994, he was victorious in the US Senior Open when he finished one shot ahead of Jim Albus and Graham Marsh. He won his fifth and last tournament in 1995, collecting the Brickyard Crossing Championship. An eccentric, forthright character, he is known on Tour as 'Scruffy', for obvious reasons. Like many South African golfers Hobday has a tremendous short game and is a consumate bunker player.

2000 SEASON. He passed the Tour $4 million mark and his best finish was T15. He joined the over-60 Georgia-Pacific Super Senior tour.

Scott Hoch
US Tour

Born 24 November 1955
Place of Birth Raleigh, North Carolina, USA
Year turned Professional 1979
Tour Ranking 33rd

BEST FINISH IN MAJORS
2nd **US MASTERS 1989**

TOUR VICTORIES
US: 9

1980 Quad Cities Open
1982 USF&G Classic
1984 Lite Quad Cities Open
1989 Las Vegas Invitational
1994 Bob Hope Chrysler Classic
1995 Greater Milwaukee Open
1996 Michelob Championship
1997 Greater Milwaukee Open
2001 Greater Greensboro Chrysler Classic

EUROPEAN: 1

1995 Heineken Dutch Open

OTHER: 5

1982 Casio World Open, Pacific Masters

1986 Casio World Open

1990 Korean Open

1991 Korean Open

RYDER CUP 1997

PRESIDENTS CUP 1994, 1996, 1998

One of the most consistent and longest-serving players on the US Tour, Hoch is probably best known for missing a 2-foot birdie putt on the first play-off hole of the 1989 Masters that would have given him the green jacket. Nick Faldo won the next hole and claimed the title. Hoch became known as 'Hoch the Choke' as a result. He has accumulated over $10 million in prize money in his 20-year career as well as eight Tour and six international victories. His last Tour win was the 1997 Greater Milwaukee Open when he chipped in to eagle the final hole and pip Loren Roberts to the trophy, and he ended the season in sixth place on the Money List. Hoch has won the Casio World Open twice, in 1982 and 1986. Never slow to voice his opinions, he once famously described St Andrews Old Course as 'a goat field' and has often chosen not to travel to the British Isles to qualify for the British Open.

2000 SEASON. Hoch maintained his solid, all-round game to post 12 top-20 finishes, but could not win a tournament, although he earned over $1 million. He was T2 in the inaugural Pennsylvania Classic and finished T16 in the US Open. He had a good World Match Play competition, beating Stuart Appleby and Lee Westwood before eventually being eliminated by Jesper Parnevik.

2001 STOP PRESS. Hoch collected his ninth Tour victory and his first in 94 tournament starts when he won the Greater Greensboro Chrysler Classic.

Jim Holtgrieve

US Seniors Tour

Born 26 December 1947

Place of Birth St Louis, Missouri, USA

Year turned Professional 1998

Tour Ranking 64th

In 1999 Holtgrieve earned over $250,000 in prize money, largely through sponsor invites into tournaments and he also received a partial exemption for the 2000 season.

2000 SEASON. His best finish was T10 at the Novell Utah and he went back again to Qualifying School where he was 13th and qualified for 2001.

Tommy Horton

European Senior Tour

Born 16 June 1941

Place of Birth St Helens, England

Year turned Professional 1957

Tour Ranking 4th

TOUR VICTORIES

SENIOR TOUR: 24

1992 Forte PGA Seniors

1993 Collingtree Seniors, Lexus Trophy, Scottish Seniors Open, Senior Zurich Pro-Am

1994 Irish Seniors Open, St Pierre Senior Classic

1995 De Vere Hotels Senior Classic

1996 European Seniors Classic, Northern Electric Seniors, Stella Seniors Open, The Player Championship

1997 Clubhaus Seniors Classic, Irish Seniors Open, Jersey Seniors Open, Scottish Seniors Open, The Player Championship, Turkish Seniors Open

1998 De Vere Hotels Seniors Classic, El Bosque Seniors Open, The Belfry PGA Seniors Championship

1999 Beko Classic, Monte Carlo Invitational

2000 Barbados Open

The seemingly impregnable Horton was Europe's top senior golfer between 1996 and 1999, winning the John Jacobs Trophy four years in succession. He had won seven titles on the European Tour, played in two Ryder Cup teams and joined the European Senior Tour in 1992. The small Lancastrian's best year was in 1997 when he won no less than six events and recordedthree runner-up spots. Chairman of the Seniors Tour Committee, Horton was awarded the MBE in 2000.

2000 SEASON. Horton finally relinquished his leadership status, finishing fourth on the Order of Merit. Although he won the season-opening Royal Westmoreland Barbados Open, beating Jerry Bruner by two strokes, he did not have another victory. His next-best placing was T2 at the Tui Golf Championship. He became the first European Senior player to pass $1 million at the British Senior Open, finishing sixth.

Garry Houston
European Tour

Born 12 May 1971
Place of Birth St Asaph, Wales
Year turned Professional 1995
Tour Ranking 18th (Qualifying School)

Houston a 6 foot 2 inch, 17 stone Welshman, won the Welsh Amateur Championship in 1995 and turned professional later that year.

His highest finish on the 2000 European Challenge Tour was forth at the NW Ireland Open. Houston qualified for the 2001 European Tour by finishing in 18th place at Qualifying School, his first successful qualification in six attempts

David Howell
European Tour

Born 23 June 1975
Place of Birth Swindon, England
Year turned Professional 1995
Tour Ranking 40th

BEST FINISH IN MAJORS
Tied 42nd **BRITISH OPEN 1998**

TOUR VICTORIES
EUROPEAN: 1
1999 Dubai Desert Classic
AUSTRALASIAN: 1
1998 Australian PGA Championship

DUNHILL CUP 1999

Managed by the same company as Darren Clarke and Lee Westwood, Howell's amateur career includes the British Amateur Championship in 1993 and the 1995 Walker Cup. He has won once on Tour – at the lucrative Dubai Desert Classic in 1998. That season he finished 22nd on the Order of Merit.

2000 SEASON. Howell slipped to 40th place on the Order of Merit.

2001 STOP PRESS. Howell narrowly missed out on his second Tour win when he lost a four-way play-off at the British Masters.

Brian Huggett
European Senior Tour

Born 18 November 1936
Place of Birth Porthcawl, Wales
Year turned Professional 1951
Tour Ranking 19th

TOUR VICTORIES
SENIOR TOUR: 9
- 1992 Anvil Senior Classic, Northern Electric Seniors
- 1993 Forte PGA Seniors, Northern Electric Seniors
- 1994 Spanish Seniors Open
- 1995 Scottish Seniors Open, Windsor Senior Masters
- 1998 Schroeder Senior Masters, Senior British Open

A small but highly competitive Welshman, Huggett joined the European Tour in 1962 and he had won 16 events in as many years by 1978. He has also competed in six Ryder Cups, and captained the side in the 1977 match. He has also represented Wales in nine World Cups. A tenacious competitor in the mould of Ian Woosnam, Huggett joined the European Senior Tour in 1992 and started off the second part of his career in inspired form, winning two tournaments in his rookie year. In total, he has nine victories on Tour, including back-to-back wins in 1998, his second coming at the Senior British Open.

2000 SEASON. After a shaky start, Huggett finally came good towards the end of the year, claiming the runner-up spot at the Monte Carlo Invitational, five strokes behind John Grace. He finished the year in 19th place on the Order of Merit.

Bradley Hughes
US Tour

Born 10 February 1967
Place of Birth Melbourne, Australia
Year turned Professional 1988
Tour Ranking 103rd

BEST FINISH IN MAJORS
Tied 16th US OPEN 1997

TOUR VICTORIES
AUSTRALASIAN: 5
- 1991 South Australian PGA
- 1993 Australian Masters
- 1996 Australian Players Championship
- 1998 Australian Masters, Western Australian Open

PRESIDENTS CUP 1994
WORLD CUP 1996, 1997

A n ex-professional Australian Rules footballer, Hughes joined the US Tour in 1997 having won three Australasian Tour titles. He has not yet won a US tournament although he was T2 in the 1998 CVS Charity Classic and finished in the same place at the 1999 Kemper Open.

2000 SEASON. Hughes had a very disappointing season, missing 17 out of his first 20 cuts and dropping from 83rd to 103rd in the Money List in the process. However, he managed to secure his 2001 card by finishing T5 at the Michelob Tournament, where he shot an 8 under par 63 in the second round and actually led the field after the third round. Sadly, he had only three other top-20 finishes during the rest of the year.

Jean Hugo
European Tour

Born 3 December 1975
Place of Birth Stellenbosch, South Africa
Year turned Professional 1999
Tour Ranking 13th (Challenge Tour)

TOUR VICTORIES
SOUTH AFRICA: 1
1999 Zimbabwe Open

Hugo won the South African Amateur Championship in 1999 and his first game as a pro was at the 1999 British Open at Carnoustie, where he narrowly failed to make the cut. He won the Zimbabwe Open on the South African Tour in 1999 and qualified for the 2001 European Tour by finishing 13th on the Challenge Tour. He won the Finnish Open and had three other top-5s.

David Huish
European Senior Tour

Born 23 April 1944
Place of Birth Edinburgh, Scotland
Year turned Professional 1959
Tour Ranking 7th

TOUR VICTORIES
SENIOR TOUR: 4
1996 Collingtree Seniors Classic
1998 Scottish Seniors Open
2000 Lawrence Batley Seniors, PGA Seniors Open

This tall (6 foot 3 inch) Scotsman has been club pro at the North Berwick club for more than 30 years. He has had two wins on the European Senior Tour, and three second-place finishes in 1999 took him to his then-highest placing of 11th on the Order of Merit.

2000 SEASON. Huish had two victories. He defeated Neil Coles and John Fourie at the first sudden-death play-off hole at the Lawrence Batley Seniors to claim the title. He won again in Switzerland at the Bad Ragaz PGA Seniors Open, beating Jim Rhodes by four shots and equalling the Senior Tour record of 62 for a round. He ended in seventh place on the Order of Merit, his highest-ever ranking.

Pat Hurst
US Ladies Tour

Born 23 May 1969
Place of Birth San Leandro, California, USA
Year turned Professional 1993
Tour Ranking 6th

MAJORS VICTORIES
DINAH SHORE 1998

TOUR VICTORIES
US: 2
1997 Oldsmobile Classic
2000 Electrolux USA Championship

SOLHEIM CUP 1998, 2000

The 1986 US Junior Champion and 1990 US Women's Amateur Champion, long-hitting Hurst joined the LPGA Tour in 1994 and was Rookie of the Year with four top-10 finishes. She won the Oldsmobile Classic in 1997 and took her first and only Major, the Dinah Shore, the following year. With 11 other top-10 finishes that season Hurst was eighth on the Money List.

2000 SEASON. Hurst won her third LPGA tournament when she led wire-to-wire at the Electrolux USA Championship, scoring a 13 under par 275 to beat Julie Inkster by four strokes. That victory, plus her four other second places, saw her pass the $2 million career earnings mark. A consistent player, Hurst did not miss a cut throughout the whole season. She also made her second appearance in the Solheim Cup where, playing alongside Kelly Robbins, she made a tearful Annika Sorenstam replay her holed chip shot after discovering that the Swede had played out of turn. Sorenstam missed and Europe lost the game. Accusations of gamesmanship were rife.

John Huston

US Tour

Born 1 June 1961
Place of Birth Mt Vernon, Illinois, USA
Year turned Professional 1983
Tour Ranking 25th

BEST FINISH IN MAJORS
Tied 3rd US MASTERS 1990

TOUR VICTORIES
US: 6
1990 Honda Classic
1992 Walt Disney World/Oldsmobile Classic
1994 Doral-Ryder Open
1998 National Car Rental Golf Classic, United Airlines Hawaiian Open
2000 Tampa Bay Classic

PRESIDENTS CUP 1994, 1998

S ix-time winner on the US Tour, Huston has been a regular since 1988. His putting and short game have kept him in contention for well over a decade. His best year was in 1998 when he won the Hawaiian Open with a then PGA record 28 under par 260 and the Walt Disney Clasic when he beat Davis Love by one shot in a final round 6 under par 66. His consistency has made him one of the top-50 career money winners on the US Tour.

2000 SEASON. Another good year for Huston. He made four top-5 finishes, including a fourth at the US Open, and he won the Tampa Bay Classic, scoring 30 on the back nine and beating Carl Paulson by three strokes. He was T14 in the Masters, making his 11th successive cut in the tournament.

Amateur Championship and the US Junior Championship, although he did go on to win the South African Amateur Championship in 1998. With the confidence of a sparkling and impressive amateur career to spur him on, he turned pro in 1999 and almost immediately won the Vodacom Players Championship on the South African Tour. He qualified for the 2001 European Tour by finishing 10th on the Challenge Tour in 2000, where he also won the Tusker Kenya Open.

Juli Inkster
US Ladies Tour

Born 24 June 1960
Place of Birth Santa Cruz, California, USA
Year turned Professional 1983
Tour Ranking 4th

Trevor Immelman
European Tour

Born 16 December 1979
Place of Birth Cape Town, South Africa
Year turned Professional 1999
Tour Ranking 10th (Challenge Tour)

MAJORS VICTORIES
US OPEN 1999
LPGA 1999, 2000
DINAH SHORE 1984, 1989
DU MAURIER CLASSIC 1984

TOUR VICTORIES
SOUTH AFRICA: 1
  2000 Vodacom Players Championship

TOUR VICTORIES
US: 19
  1983 SAFECO Classic
  1985 Lady Keystone Open
  1986 Atlantic City Classic, Kemper Open, Lady Keystone Open, McDonald's Championship
  1988 Atlantic City Classic, Crestor Classic, SAFECO Classic
  1989 Crestor Classic
  1991 Bay State Classic
  1992 JAL Big Apple Classic
  1997 Samsung World of Women's Golf
  1998 Samsung World of Women's Golf
  1999 Longs Drugs Challenge, Safeway Golf Championship, Welch's Circle K Championship
  2000 Longs Drugs Challenge, Samsung World Championship of Women's Golf

The talented young South African Immelman played off a scratch handicap by the age of 12, and by the age of 17 he was playing for the South African amateur team. In 1997 he lost narrowly in the finals of the British Amateur Championship, the New Zealand

EUROPEAN: 1
   2000 Compaq Open

SOLHEIM CUP 1992, 1998

Between 1980 and 1982 Inkster won the US Women's Amateur Championship three years in succession and joined the LPGA Tour in 1984. In her first full season she won two Majors – the Dinah Shore and the du Maurier – and was the Rookie of the Year. Two years later she won four events and finished third on the Money List.

In 1999 she became only the second woman, after Pat Bradley, to achieve the career Grand Slam of winning every Major Championship. She won the US Women's Open with a 16 under par 272, the lowest ever score in the tournament, and at 38 she was the oldest champion for 45 years. She then won the McDonald's LPGA Championship. On the European Tour she won the Compaq Open, in spite of shooting a final round 76. She beat Sweden's Sophie Gustafson by one stroke. She was elected to the LPGA Hall of Fame.

2000 SEASON. Inkster successfully defended her Longs Drugs Challenge title, five shots ahead of Brandie Burton, and also retained her LPGA title, defeating Stefania Croce on the second hole play-off. She has now won 25 times on the LPGA Tour.

Joe Inman
US Seniors Tour

Born 29 November 1947
Place of Birth Indianapolis, Indiana, USA
Year turned Professional 1972
Tour Ranking 16th

TOUR VICTORIES
SENIOR TOUR: 3
   1998 Pacific Bell Senior Classic
   1999 Pacific Bell Senior Classic
   2000 SBC Senior Classic

Finishing T5 at 1997 Qualifying School, Inman joined the US Senior Tour in 1998 and was Rookie of the Year, beating Lee Trevino to lift the Pacific Bell Senior Classic title. The following year he successfully defended his title, shooting a closing 6 under par 65 for a total 14 under par 199 to ease past Dave Stockton and Bruce Summerhays by two strokes.

2000 SEASON. Inman claimed the Bell Pacific title (now called the SBC Senior Classic) for the third time, defeating Larry Nelson by three strokes and exceeding the $1.2 million mark in Tour earnings.

Hale Irwin
US Seniors Tour

Born 3 June 1945
Place of Birth Joplin, Missouri, USA
Year turned Professional 1968
Tour Ranking 3rd

MAJORS VICTORIES
   PGA SENIORS CHAMPIONSHIP 1996, 1997, 1998
   SENIOR PLAYERS CHAMPIONSHIP 1999
   US SENIORS OPEN 1998, 2000

TOUR VICTORIES
SENIOR TOUR: 24
   1995 Ameritech Senior Open, Vantage Championship
   1996 American Express Invitational

1997 BankBoston Classic, Boone Valley Classic, Burnet Senior Classic, Las Vegas Seniors Classic, LG Championship, MasterCard Championship, Maui Kaanapali Classic, Vantage Championship

1998 Ameritech Senior Open, BankBoston Classic, Las Vegas Senior Classic, Senior Tour Championship, Toshiba Senior Classic

1999 Ameritech Senior Open, Boone Valley Classic, Coldwell Banker Burnet Classic, Nationwide Championship

2000 BellSouth Senior Classic, EMC Kaanapali Classic, Nationwide Championship

2001 Siebel Classic, Bruno Memorial

Three-time US Open winner – in 1974, 1979 and 1990 _ four-time Ryder Cup contestant and holder of 17 other USPGA titles, Hale Irwin's arrival on the US Senior Tour in 1995 was greeted with trepidation by some of the leading players. A dour, strong-minded perfectionist with an impressive talent, work ethic and technique, he started as he intended to continue. In his first season he was Rookie of the Year and was tenth on the Money List, and in 1996 he rose to second place on the List.

In 1997, his nine wins on Tour equalled Peter Thomson's record set in 1985 and Irwin earned a record $2.3 million that season. He won the Senior PGA Championship by an astonishing 12 shots, won four titles in seven starts, led the Money List and was Player of the Year. In 1998, his elegant swing, accurate driving and iron play and superb putting skills brought him seven wins, including his third consecutive Senior PGA Championship, and he led the Money List again. He also won the Senior Open, beating Vicente Fernandez on the last hole with a birdie. In 1999 he became the first Senior Tour player to win five or more events three years in succession and he passed $9 million in Senior Tour career earnings.

2000 SEASON. Irwin continued his relentless winning streak with four tournament victories and earned over $2 million for the fourth consecutive season. He won the Senior Open again, beating Bruce Fleisher by three strokes and shooting a 17 under par 267, the lowest score in the history of the tournament. His remarkable six-year performance on Tour had netted him 29 victories and drew him level with Lee Trevino on the all-time victory list. He became the first player to pass $11 million in earnings on the Senior Tour.

2001 STOP PRESS. Irwin overtook Lee Trevino by winning his 30th tournament, the Siebel Classic, a comfortable five shots ahead of Tom Watson and Allen Doyle. He also won the Bruno Memorial Classic the following month.

Tripp Isenhour
US Tour

Born 6 April 1968
Place of Birth Salisbury, North Carolina, USA
Year turned Professional 1990
Tour Ranking 8th (Buy.Com Tour)

A member of the Buy.Com Tour from 1998 till 2000, Isenhour had six top-10 finishes, including one tournament victory, on the 2000 Tour to finish eighth in the Money List. He is a rookie on the 2001 US Tour.

Becky Iverson
US Ladies Tour

Born 12 October 1967
Place of Birth Escanaba, Michigan, USA
Year turned Professional 1993
Tour Ranking 29th

TOUR VICTORIES
US: 1
　　1995 Friendly's Classic

SOLHEIM CUP 2000

The well-built Iverson joined the US Ladies Tour in 1994 and won her only victory, the Friendly's Classic, in 1995. In 1999 she had four top-10s.
　　2000 SEASON. Iverson rose up the rankings with seven top-10s, including a T2 at the Weetabix Women's British Open and a T7 at the du Maurier.

Toshimitsu Izawa
Japanese Tour

Born 2 March 1968
Place of Birth Kanagawa, Japan
Year turned Professional 1989
Tour Ranking 4th

BEST FINISH IN MAJORS
Tied 4th **US MASTERS 2001**

TOUR VICTORIES
OTHER: 6
　　1998 Tokai Cup
　　1999 Aiful Cup, NST Niigata Open
　　2000 Hisamitsu-KBC Augusta, Sumitomo Visa Taiheiyo Masters, TPC Liyama Cup

Izawa won three times on the 2000 Japanese Tour. First, he beat Kaname Yokoo by three strokes to claim the Tour Players Championship. He then won the Hisamitsu-KBC Augusta by four shots, and picked up his third title in November at the Taiheiyo Masters. He also had two second and two third places. He played in the USPGA Championship where he finished tied for 39th place with Colin Montgomerie.
　　2001 STOP PRESS. Izawa finished T4th at The Masters.

John Jacobs

US Seniors Tour

Born 18 March 1945
Place of Birth Los Angeles, California, USA
Year turned Professional 1967
Tour Ranking 14th

TOUR VICTORIES
SENIOR TOUR: 3
  1998 Nationwide Championship
  1999 MasterCard Championship
  2000 Bruno's Memorial Clasic

Jacobs played on the USPGA Tour between 1968 and 1980 but did not win a single tournament. He then played in Europe and Asia, where the tall, cigar-chewing Californian was the first American golfer to win the Asian Order of Merit, in 1984. He joined the US Senior Tour in 1995, T2 from Qualifying School, and by 1997 he had risen to 12th place on the Money List. He captured his first tournament in 1998 when he defeated Hale Irwin by one stroke to win the Nationwide Championship, and followed this up in 1999 by lifting the season-opening MasterCard Championship, three shots clear of Jim Colbert and Raymond Floyd. He was top of the driving distance statistics in 1997, 1998 and 1999. The cheerful Jacobs relaxes by listening to opera and classical music.

2000 SEASON. Jacobs picked up his third tournament win by beating Gil Morgan on the first play-off hole at Bruno's Memorial Classic and he also had seven other top-10 finishes. At the same time, he passed $4 million in Senior career earnings.

Fredrik Jacobson

European Tour

Born 26 September 1974
Place of Birth Molndal, Sweden
Year turned Professional 1994
Tour Ranking 25th

BEST FINISH IN MAJORS
73rd **BRITISH OPEN 1998**

Jacobson had to go to Qualifying School in 1999 to retain his European Tour playing rights, after finishing 127th on the Order of Merit. He finished in seventh place and was back on Tour in 2000. His best performance had been in 1998 when he was narrowly relegated into second place by Lee Westwood in the Belgacom Open. He is ranked ninth in putting on the Tour statistics, but his driving tends to the wayward.

2000 SEASON. The fast improving Jacobson hit a hot streak in the summer. In May, he finished T4 in the French Open. Then, in three successive tournaments, he tied for third place with Ian Woosnam in the Wales Open, was second to Lee Westwood at the European Grand Prix and lost by two strokes to Patrik Sjoland at the Irish Open, his challenge not helped by sixes at the last two holes. He also claimed a respectable T10 at the Volvo Masters later in the year.

Mark James

European Tour

Born 28 October 1953
Place of Birth Manchester, England
Year turned Professional 1976
Tour Ranking 90th

BEST FINISH IN MAJORS
Tied 3rd **BRITISH OPEN 1981**

TOUR VICTORIES
EUROPEAN: 18
1978 Sun Alliance Match Play
 Championship
1979 Carrolls Irish Open, Welsh Classic
1980 Carrolls Irish Open
1982 Italian Open
1983 Tunisian Open
1985 GSI Open
1986 Benson & Hedges International Open
1988 Peugeot Open de Espana
1989 AGF Open, Karl Litten Desert Classic,
 NM English Open
1990 Dunhill British Masters, NM English
 Open
1993 Maderia Island Open, Turespana
 Iberia-Open de Canarias
1995 Moroccan Open
1997 Peugeot Open de Espana
SOUTH AFRICA: 1
1988 South African TPC

RYDER CUP 1977, 1979, 1981, 1989, 1991, 1993,
1995, 1999
DUNHILL CUP 1988, 1989, 1990, 1993, 1995,
1997, 1999
WORLD CUP 1978, 1979, 1982, 1984, 1987, 1988,
1990, 1993, 1997, 1999

One of the most successful players on the
European Tour, and a veteran of nearly
25 years standing, Mark 'Jesse' James is a
highly respected figure in the European game.
The English Amateur Champion in 1975, he
joined the Tour two years later and has since
been ever-present, winning a total of 18 tournaments and accumulating nearly £3.5 million in prize money over his career. He has
played in seven Ryder Cups. In his first
appearance – in 1979 – his silly antics almost
resulted in him being sent home in disgrace,
but 20 years later he was appointed captain of
the European team which lost at Brookline.

He is also a member of the PGA European
Tour Board of Directors.

2000 SEASON. Unfortunately James' writing
skills grabbed more headlines than his golf.
He published a controversial book about the
1999 Ryder Cup match in Boston and was
dogged by criticism throughout the season,
particularly from Nick Faldo, about its tone
and content. Eventually he was forced to
resign as assistant to Sam Torrance for the
2001 Ryder Cup. Not surprisingly, on the
course, James had an average season, finishing a lowly 90th on the Order of Merit. However he tied for second place at the English
Open alongside Michael Campbell and one
stroke behind Darren Clarke, having shot a
65 in the third round, and was T8 in the
Wales Open.

Jeong Jang
                                            US Ladies Tour

Born 11 June 1980
Place of Birth Taejeon, South Korea
Year turned Professional 1999
Tour Ranking 44th

Following in Se Ri Pak's illustrious footsteps,
Jang is one of a group of promising young
Koreans on the LPGA Tour. She was Korean
Amateur Champion in 1999 and then qualified
for the 2000 Tour. Her best finish of the season
was second place behind fellow Korean Mi
Hyun Kim in a play-off at the Safeway LPGA,
but she also had four top-10 spots. Although
she played in only 19 events, she still amassed
enough prize-money to finish 44th on the
Money List.

Lee Janzen
                                            US Tour

Born 28 August 1964
Place of Birth Austin, Minnesota, USA
Year turned Professional 1986
Tour Ranking 62nd

MAJORS VICTORIES
US OPEN 1993, 1998

TOUR VICTORIES
US: 6
1992 Northern Telecom Open
1993 Phoenix Open
1994 Buick Classic
1995 Kemper Open, Sprint International,
The Players Championship

RYDER CUP 1993, 1997
DUNHILL CUP 1995
PRESIDENTS CUP 1998

Minnesotan Janzen won the first of his six US Tour wins – the Northern Telecom Open – in 1992. The following year he began the season by capturing the Phoenix Open and winning his first Major, the US Open, when he beat Payne Stewart by two strokes. His aggregate score of 272 tied Jack Nicklaus' record for the lowest score in the history of the US Open. He lifted three further trophies – including the Players Championship – in 1995 and rose to third in the Money List, his best-ever placing. In 1998, he won the US Open again with another victory over Payne Stewart. Five strokes behind at the beginning of the final round, Janzen shot 68 at the Olympic Club to beat Stewart by one shot (he is known as 'Terminator' for his ability

to finish strongly on Sunday). Having said that, he has not won a tournament since. He has played twice in the Ryder Cup, coming back from one hole down with two to play to beat Jose Maria Olázàbal in their 1997 singles match at Valderrama, in Spain.

2000 SEASON. This was another barren year for Janzen, with nine top-20 places and his highest placing T6 in the Tampa Bay Classic. He slipped from 48th to 62nd in the Money List, his lowest rating since 1991.

2001 STOP PRESS. Janzen finished T2 at the Shell Houston Open.

Raphael Jaquelin
European Tour

Born 8 May 1974
Place of Birth Lyons, France
Year turned Professional 1995
Tour Ranking 80th

BEST FINISH IN MAJORS
Missed Cut BRITISH OPEN 1997

DUNHILL CUP 2000

Ex-French Amateur Champion, Jaquelin joined the European Tour proper in 1988, the year after he won three Challenge Tour victories. In 1999 he was third in the Turespana Masters, still his best performance.

2000 SEASON. Jaquelin moved up the Order of Merit from 104th to 80th, helped by his third-place finish at the Scottish PGA when he broke the course record by shooting a 64 in his first round. He also had five top-25 finishes, including a T13 at the Volvo PGA.

Tom Jenkins
US Seniors Tour

Born 14 December 1947
Place of Birth Houston Texas, USA
Year turned Professional 1971
Tour Ranking 10th

TOUR VICTORIES
SENIOR TOUR: 2
- **1999** Bell Atlantic Classic
- **2000** AT&T Canada Senior Open

Jenkins joined the US Senior Tour in 1998, having finished T10 at Qualifying School. In 1999 he was voted Comeback Player of the Year and won his first tournament when he beat Jim Thorpe on the first play-off hole at the Bell Atlantic Classic. That win, along with his 17 other top-10s, saw him end the year third on the Money List.

2000 SEASON. Jenkins won his second tournament when, shortly after having become a father at the age of 52, he held off Kermit Zarley to claim the AT&T Canada Senior Open by one stroke. A further ten top-10 finishes helped him beyond the $2 million Senior Tour career mark. He was ranked sixth in putting.

2001 STOP PRESS. Jenkins finished T3 at the Royal Caribbean Classic.

Miguel Angel Jimenez
European Tour

Born 5 January 1964
Place of Birth Malaga, Spain
Year turned Professional 1982
Tour Ranking 11th

BEST FINISH IN MAJORS
Tied 2nd **US OPEN 2000**

TOUR VICTORIES
EUROPEAN: 6
- **1992** Piaget Open
- **1994** Heineken Dutch Open
- **1998** Trophee Lancome, Turespana Masters
- **1999** Turespana Masters, Volvo Masters

RYDER CUP 1999
DUNHILL CUP 1990, 1992, 1993, 1994, 1995, 1996, 1997, 1998, 1999, 2000
WORLD CUP 1990, 1992, 1993, 1994

One of the straightest and most accurate players on the European Tour, ex-caddie Jimenez has been a major force on the Tour since the early 1990s. Winner of six Tour victories, the moustachioed Jimenez has accumulated over £4 million in prize money, and he intends to broaden his career by playing on the US Tour. In 1998 and 1999 he finished fourth on the Order of Merit, winning four tournaments and becoming the first Spanish golfer to win the Volvo Masters. In November 1999 he lost to a Tiger Woods birdie on the first hole of a sudden death play-off in the WGC-American Express Championship. Two months before that he had represented Europe at the Ryder Cup, winning one and halving two matches, although he lost to Steve Pate in the singles. He was a member of the Spanish team which won the Dunhill Cup in 1999.

2000 SEASON. Jimenez did not win a title and slipped to 11th in the Order of Merit, partly because he missed the start of the season due to illness. However, he had four top-10 finishes – his highest being sixth in the German Masters – and he also notched up a T19 in the Buick Classic on the US Tour. He tied with Ernie Els for second place in the US Open at Pebble Beach (albeit 15 strokes behind Woods) and was T26 at the British Open. He again represented Spain in the Dunhill Cup as they retained the trophy, with Jimenez winning three out of his five games.

Nick Job
European Senior Tour

Born 27 July 1949
Place of Birth Haslemere, England
Year turned Professional 1965
Tour Ranking 16th

TOUR VICTORIES
SENIOR TOUR: 1
2000 Total Fina Elf Seniors Open

Job, the club professional at Richmond Golf Club, in Surrey, England, remained winless throughout his PGA European Tour career despite several near misses and joined the European Senior Tour through the Qualifying School. In 2000, he had his first career win, beating Seiji Ebihara by two shots at the Total Fina Elf Seniors Open. He had three other top-4 finishes to end the season in 16th place on the Order of Merit.

Brandt Jobe
US Tour

Born 1 August 1965
Place of Birth Oklahoma City, Oklahoma, USA
Year turned Professional 1988
Tour Ranking 120th

BEST FINISH IN MAJORS
Tied 16th USPGA 1999

TOUR VICTORIES
OTHER: 9
1990 British Columbia Open
1991 Payless Classic
1994 Thailand Open
1995 Mitsubishi Galant
1997 Golf Digest, Tokai Classic
1998 Mizuno Open, Japan PGA
Championship, KBE Kosan Open

Jobe was Order of Merit winner on the Canadian Tour in 1990 and he has also won six Japanese tournaments since 1995. His T17

at the 1999 WGC-Andersen Consulting Match Play gave him exempt status on the US Tour and he made T16 at the USPGA Championships that year. His best finish was T4 at the Reno-Tahoe Open.

2000 SEASON. Jobe came in T4 at the Phoenix Open and had three other top-20 finishes. He retained his card for 2001 by virtue of his 120th place on the Money List.

Per-Ulrik Johansson
European Tour

Born 6 December 1966
Place of Birth Uppsala, Sweden
Year turned Professional 1990
Tour Ranking 22nd

BEST FINISH IN MAJORS
Tied 8th USPGA 1996

TOUR VICTORIES
EUROPEAN: 5
1991 Renault Belgian Open
1994 Chemapol Trophy Czech Open
1996 Smurfit European Open
1997 Alamo English Open, Smurfit
European Open

RYDER CUP 1995, 1997
DUNHILL CUP 1991, 1992, 1995, 1997, 1998
WORLD CUP 1991, 1992, 1997

Recognizable by his trademark back-to-front cap, Johansson is a relatively short (5 foot 8 inch) but powerful player. He represented Sweden at amateur level and received a golf scholarship from Arizona State University where he played alongside Phil Mickelson. He turned pro in 1990 and gained his card the European Tour through Qualifying School for 1991 when, in his first season, he was awarded Rookie of the Year, winning the Belgian Open in a play-off and shooting 62 in the Dutch Open.

His best season was in 1997 when he won the English Open and secured his place in the Valderrama Ryder Cup with an emphatic six-shot victory over Peter Baker to claim his second European Open title in succession. He finished T12 in The Masters that year and 11th in the Volvo Order of Merit, but had to return home from the World Cup with a virus which laid him low for several months. In 1999 he had four top-5 finishes.

2000 SEASON. Johansson again posted four top-5 finishes, including a second place in the British Masters. He won all his games in the Dunhill Cup. His all-round ability is demonstrated by his European Tour rankings for accuracy, driving and putting – all in the top 30. He gained his card for the 2001 US Tour through Qualifying School.

Chris Johnson
US Ladies Tour

Born 25 April 1958
Place of Birth Arcata, California, USA
Year turned Professional 1980
Tour Ranking 65th

MAJOR VICTORIES
MCDONALD'S LPGA CHAMPIONSHIP 1997

TOUR VICTORIES
US: 8
1984 Tucson Open, Turquoise Classic
1986 GNA/Glendale Federal Classic

1987 LPGA National Pro-Am
1990 Atlantic City Classic
1991 Ping/Welch's Championship
1995 Star Bank LPGA Classic
1997 Safeway LPGA Golf Championship

SOLHEIM CUP 1998

Tall (5 foot 11 inch) Californian Johnson is a veteran of the LPGA Tour, having joined in 1980. The first of her eight wins was in 1984 when she took the Turquoise Classic and the Tucson Open back-to-back. She won her last title, the Safeway LPGA Golf Championship, in 1997. She played in the Solheim Cup in 1998.

2000 SEASON. Johnson posted four top-10s, the highest being T5 at the Welch's/Circle K Championship, to finish 65th on the Money List.

Kevin Johnson
US Tour

Born 25 April 1967
Place of Birth Plymouth, Maine, USA
Year turned Professional 1990
Tour Ranking Tied 5th (Qualifying School)

BEST FINISH IN MAJORS
Missed Cut US OPEN 2000

Johnson had a fine amateur career, playing in the 1989 US Walker Cup Team and winning the 1987 Amateur Public Links Championship. He played on the Nike Tour between 1996 and 2000, winning three tournaments. His T5 place at Qualifying School granted him his rookie year on the US Tour in 2001.

Richard S. Johnson
European Tour

Born 15 October 1976
Place of Birth Stockholm, Sweden
Year turned Professional 1997
Tour Ranking 96th

Another very promising player from the Swedish school of excellence, Johnson joined the European Tour from the Qualifying School in 2000, having won once on the 1999 Challenge Tour. In his first tournament, the Portugese Open, at Penina, he did well to finish T6, and the following month he did even better at the Madeira Island Open, finishing T2 alongside Mark Davis and Ross Drummond, two shots behind the winner fellow Swede, Niclas Fasth. He then picked up two T11s, at the Sao Paulo Open and the British Masters. A very promising rookie year saw Johnson finish 96th in the Order of Merit and comfortably retain his playing privileges for the following season.

2001 STOP PRESS. Johnson finished T2 at the Sao Paulo Open behind Darren Fitchardt.

Trish Johnson

US Ladies Tour

Born 17 January 1966
Place of Birth Bristol, England
Year turned Professional 1987
Tour Ranking 106th

TOUR VICTORIES

US: 3
- 1993 Atlanta Championship, Las Vegas Canyon Gate
- 1996 Fieldcrest Canon Classic

EUROPEAN: 13
- 1987 Eastleigh Classic, McEwan's Wirral Classic, Woolmark Match Play Championship
- 1990 Eastleigh Classic, European Open, Hennessy Cup, Longines Classic
- 1992 La Manga Club Classic
- 1996 European Open, French Open
- 1999 French Open, Marrakech Palmeraie Open
- 2000 British Women's Masters

SOLHEIM CUP 1990, 1992, 1994, 1996, 1998, 2000

Johnson had a distinguished amateur career, including an appearance at the 1986 Curtis Cup when she was top points earner. She joined the European Ladies Tour in 1987, won three tournaments and was Rookie of the Year. In 1990, she won four more titles and topped the European Money List. Her first LPGA win came in 1993, at the Las Vegas LPGA, and she won again the following week, claiming the Atlanta Championship. She collected her third LPGA title in 1996, winning the Fieldcrest Canon Classic, and won twice more, at the European Open and the French Open, on the European Tour. Two more European victories – the French Open and the Marrakech Palmaraie Open – followed in 1999.

2000 SEASON. Johnson won the British Women's Masters and was T10 at the British Women's Open. In the US she recorded two top-20 finishes. She also played in the Solheim Cup.

Cathy Johnston-Forbes

US Ladies Tour

Born 10 December 1963
Place of Birth High Point, North Carolina, USA
Year turned Professional 1985
Tour Ranking 85th

MAJORS VICTORIES

DU MAURIER CLASSIC 1990

Johnston-Forbes joined the US Ladies Tour in 1986 and her only win to date on Tour was in 1990 when she claimed the prestigious du Maurier Classic in Canada. Since then she has achieved three runner-up positions.

2000 SEASON. A steady, but ultimately frustrating, season. Her highest finish was T4 at the ShopRite LPGA Classic and she ended the season in 85th place on the Money List.

Tony Johnstone
European Tour

Born 2 May 1956
Place of Birth Bulawayo, Zimbabwe
Year turned Professional 1979
Tour Ranking 74th

BEST FINISH IN MAJORS
Tied 34th **BRITISH OPEN 1992**

TOUR VICTORIES
EUROPEAN: 6
- 1984 Quinto do Lago Portuguese Open
- 1990 Murphy's Cup
- 1991 Murphy's Cup
- 1992 Volvo PGA Championship
- 1998 South African PGA Championship
- 2001 Qatar Masters

SOUTH AFRICA: 16
- 1984 Charity Classic, South African Masters, South African Open
- 1986 Goodyear Classic
- 1987 ICL International, Minolta Copiers Match Play, Wild Coast Classic
- 1988 ICL International, Bloemfontein Classic, Minolta Copiers Match Play
- 1989 Lexington PGA
- 1990 Palabora Classic
- 1993 South African Masters, South African Open, Zimbabwe Open
- 1994 Bell's Cup

DUNHILL CUP 1993, 1994, 1995, 1996, 1997, 1998, 2000
WORLD CUP 1994, 1995, 1996, 1997, 1998, 1999

Wisecracking, Zimbabwe-born Johnstone, a long-time friend of Mark McNulty and Nick Price, is one of the characters on the European Tour. He also has an impressive record, having won six tournaments in Europe and 16 in southern Africa. His peak was winning the Volvo PGA in 1992 which gave him a ten-year exemption in Europe and propelled him to seventh place in the Order of Merit, but his game suffered for several years until he won the South African PGA in 1998. He was seventh in the 1999 individual World Cup ranking. A relatively small man, he does not have much length. However, he has a masterful short game and has come top in the sand saves statistics for the past three years. He has written an instructional book on this aspect of the game.

2000 SEASON. Johnstone was T3 in the Portugese Open and had three other top-20 finishes. In the Dunhill Cup he won two out of his three games. He moved from 128th to 74th in the Order of Merit.

2001 STOP PRESS. Johnstone won his first European Tour event for three years when he captured the Qatar Masters in early March. He birdied two of the last three holes to beat Robert Karlsson by two strokes.

David Jones
European Senior Tour

Born 22 June 1947
Place of Birth Newcastle, Northern Ireland
Year turned Professional 1966
Tour Ranking 21st

TOUR VICTORIES
SENIOR TOUR: 1
- 1999 Jersey Seniors Open

An imposing, 6 foot 5 inch golfer from Northern Ireland, Jones played on the European Tour for over 20 years, his best finish being T3 at the 1981 Irish Open. He joined the European Senior Tour in 1997, his only tournament win coming at the Jersey Seniors Open in 1999. He is a member of the Board of Directors of the European Tour.

2000 SEASON. Although Jones led Noel Ratcliffe by seven strokes at the beginning of the final round of the Scotsman Seniors Open, a Ratcliffe surge up the leaderboard resulted in Jones filling the third spot. Jones came second behind John Grace at the Ordina Legends of Golf. He was 21st on the Order of Merit.

Kent Jones
US Tour

Born 8 January 1967
Place of Birth Portales, New Mexico, USA
Year turned Professional 1992
Tour Ranking 7th

BEST FINISH IN MAJORS
Tied 82nd **US OPEN 1996**

Jones played on the Canadian and Hooters Tours before joining the Nike Tour in 1996. He qualified for the US Tour in 1997 and 1998, his highest place being T12 at the Buick Open. In 2000 he claimed two Buy.Com Tour victories and ended the season in seventh place on the Money List. He was a teammate of Tim Herron at the University of New Mexico.

Rosie Jones
US Ladies Tour

Born 13 November 1959
Place of Birth Santa Ana, California, USA
Year turned Professional 1981
Tour Ranking 9th

TOUR VICTORIES
US: 11
1987 Rail Charity Golf Classic
1988 Nestle World Championship, Santa Barbera Open, USX Golf Classic
1991 Rochester International

1995 Pinewild Women's Championship
1996 Corning Classic
1997 Corning Classic
1998 Rochester International
1999 Firstar Classic
2001 Kathy Ireland Championship

SOLHEIM CUP 1990, 1996, 1998, 2000

Veteran Jones ran up ten LPGA tournament wins before 2001, the last being the Firstar Classic in 1999 when she beat Becky Iverson and Jan Stephenson in a play-off. The slim redhead's best year was 1988, when she recorded three victories and was third on the Money List. She has played in four Solheim Cups, in 1990, 1996, 1998 and 2000.

2000 SEASON. Jones had an excellent year, picking up eight top-10 places, including runner-up spots at the JAL Big Apple Classic and the du Maurier. She was also T4 at the US Women's Open and finished ninth on the Money List.

2001 STOP PRESS. Jones became the first American in the season to win on Tour when she collected the Kathy Ireland Championship after a play-off against Mi Hyun Kim.

Steve Jones
US Tour

Born 27 December 1958
Place of Birth Artesia, New Mexico, USA
Year turned Professional 1981
Tour Ranking 87th

MAJORS VICTORIES
US OPEN 1996

TOUR VICTORIES
US: 7
1988 AT&T Pebble Beach National Pro-Am
1989 Bob Hope Chrysler Classic, Canadian Open, MONY Tournament of Champions

1997 Bell Canadian Open, Phoenix Open
1998 Quad City Classic

WORLD CUP 1996

The tall (6 foot 4 inches), powerful Jones played his first full season on the US Tour in 1985. By 1989 he was eighth on the Money List, winning three tournaments, two of them – the Tournament of Champions and the Bob Hope Classic – back-to-back. A dirt-bike accident in 1991 removed him from Tour for three years, but he made an emphatic comeback in 1996. He pre-qualified for the US Open at Oakland Hills and made a par on the last hole to defeat his good friend Tom Lehman and Davis Love III by one stroke. In doing so, he gained an invaluable ten-year exemption on Tour. Capitalizing on his success, he won two more tournaments in 1997, including the Phoenix Open where his 26 under par 258 gave him an 11 shot margin of victory ahead of the field. His last victory was in the Quad City Classic when four rounds in the 60s were sufficient to beat Fred Funk by one stroke.

2000 SEASON. Jones had two T5 finishes, at the Tucson Open and BellSouth Classic. He also made the cut in all four Majors, his lowest placing being T31 in the British Open. He moved up in the Money List from 116th to 87th.

Pete Jordan
US Tour

Born 10 June 1964
Place of Birth Elmhurst, Illinois, USA
Year turned Professional 1996
Tour Ranking 107th

BEST FINISH IN MAJORS
Tied 21st **US OPEN 1995**

Jordan joined the US Tour in 1994, but has never broken into the top-100 on the Money List. His best placing is second in the rain-shortened 1996 BC Open when he lost a play-off against Fred Funk. He ranks in the top-10 in the Tour statistics for driving accuracy, but is relatively short off the tee. He qualified for the 2000 Tour with 15th in Qualifying School.

2000 SEASON. Jordan retained his card with two T4 finishes – at the Fedex St Jude Classic and the Southern Farm Bureau Classic. He moved up to 107 on the Money List.

Jeff Julian
US Tour

Born 29 July 1961
Place of Birth Portland, Maine, USA
Year turned Professional 1986
Tour Ranking Tied 27th (Qualifying School)

Julian played one season – 1996 – on the US Tour, recorded his career best finish of T16 at the Buick Classic, and finished 193rd on the Money List. He spent the next three years on the Nike Tour where he won two tournaments. He qualified for the 2001 US Tour by finishing T27 at Qualifying School.

Craig Kanada
US Tour

Born 2 October 1968
Place of Birth Portland, Oregon, USA
Year turned Professional 1991
Tour Ranking Tied 27th (Qualifying School)

Kanada qualified for the USPGA Tour in 1997, and finished the season in a very lowly 234th place on the Money List. With the exception of 1997, when he recorded his best Tour placing of T28 at the BellSouth Classic, he was a member of the Nike Tour from 1994 until 2000 and was runner-up in four tournaments. He qualified once again for the 2001 US Tour by finishing T27 at the Qualifying School.

Lorie Kane
US Ladies Tour

Born 19 December 1964
Place of Birth Charlottetown, Canada
Year turned Professional 1993
Tour Ranking 5th

TOUR VICTORIES

US: 4

2000 Michelob Light Classic, New Albany Golf Classic, Mizuno Classic
2001 LPGA TakeFuji Classic

A leading Canadian amateur, Kane joined the LPGA Tour in 1996. By 1999 she had accumulated nine runner-up spots, including three in 1999 when she passed $1 million in career earnings, but without actually winning a tournament.

2000 SEASON. Kane's winless streak ended dramatically in 2000. First she won the Michelob Light Classic, three shots ahead of Kristi Albers, and then the New Albany Golf Classic, birdieing the first play-off hole against Mi Hyun Kim. Her effortless swing took her to her third tournament triumph at the Mizuno Classic when she beat Sophie Gustafson on the first hole of a play-off.

2001 STOP PRESS. Kane won the TakeFuji Classic by two shots from Annika Sorenstam.

Olle Karlsson
European Tour

Born 9 April 1969
Place of Birth Falkenburg, Sweden
Year turned Professional 1989
Tour Ranking 22nd (Qualifying School)

An injury-prone Swede, Karlsson's best finish on the European Tour was T2 at the 1998 English Open. The following year he missed the first four months of the season due to a shoulder injury. In 2000, injury again limited his appearances, although he was fifth at the Scottish PGA Championship and had three other top-20s. He kept his card for 2001 by finishing 22nd at Qualifying School.

Robert Karlsson
European Tour

Born 3 September 1969
Place of Birth St Malm, Sweden
Year turned Professional 1989
Tour Ranking 114th

BEST FINISH IN MAJORS
Tied 5th **BRITISH OPEN 1992**

TOUR VICTORIES
EUROPEAN: 4
1995 Turespana Open
1997 BMW International Open
1999 Belgacom Open
2001 Spanish Open

DUNHILL CUP 1992

A Swedish amateur at the age of 16, the massive (6 foot 5 inch) Karlsson joined the European Tour in 1991. He won his first tournament – the Turespana Open – in 1995, and from 1997 to 1999 he was in the top-20 of the Order of Merit, winning two more titles. In 1999, he finished 11th in the Ryder Cup qualifying table, but he missed out on the chance of making his debut appearance in the event after Mark James surprisingly gave a wild card to Andrew Coltart, who was one place behind Karlsson on qualifying points.

2000 SEASON. In a disappointing season, He dropped from 19th to 114th in the Order of Merit. Karlsson played the early part of the year in the US and re-joined the Tour for the Rio De Janeiro and Sao Paolo Opens. His top finish for the year was T13 in the Volvo PGA.

2001 STOP PRESS. Karlsson finished second behind Tony Johnstone at the Qatar Masters, but collected his fourth European title when he won the Spanish Open.

Shingo Katayama
Japanese Tour

Born 31 January 1973
Place of Birth Ibaragi, Japan
Year turned Professional 1995
Tour Ranking 1st

TOUR VICTORIES
OTHER: 7
1998 Sanko Grand Summer Championship
1999 JCB Classic Sendai
2000 Dunlop Phoenix, Fanci Okinawa Open, Kirin Cup, Munsingwear Open KSB Cup, Nippon Series JT Cup

Katayama was the leading money-earner on the Japanese Tour in 2000, the youngest since Jumbo Ozaki more than 25 years before, and he won five tournaments. He won the Kirin Open and the Munsingwear Open KSB Cup in the Spring. In November, he collected the Dunlop Phoenix, two strokes ahead of Bob May and five ahead of Darren Clarke. He ended the season with back-to-back victories, at the Nippon Series JT Cup and the Okinawa Open. He also had two top-3 finishes.

Jonathan Kaye
US Tour

Born 2 August 1970
Place of Birth Denver, Colorado, USA
Year turned Professional 1993
Tour Ranking 40th

BEST FINISH IN MAJORS
Tied 51st **USPGA 2000**

In his first year on Tour – 1995 – Kaye nearly won a tournament, but his bogie on the final hole of the Quad City Classic handed victory to DA Weibring. He qualified again for the US Tour in 1998 by finishing second at Qualifying School. He made sure of retaining his 2000 card with five top-10 finishes and a second place behind Jim Furyk at the Las Vegas Invitational, and a 49th spot on the Money List.

2000 SEASON. An aggressive, all-round player, he is high up in the Tour putting and driving statistics. He had seven top-25 finishes and three top-5s, including T2 at the Pennsylvania Classic, to finish 40th on the Money List.

Laurel Kean

US Ladies Tour

Born 14 June 1963
Place of Birth Portland, Maine, USA
Year turned Professional 1986
Tour Ranking 61st

TOUR VICTORIES

US: 1

2000 State Farm Rail Classic

Nine-times winner on the Future Tour, Kean joined the LPGA Tour in 1987. Her best finish before 2000 was T2 at the 1997 Sara Lee Classic.

2000 SEASON. A surprised Kean became the first Monday qualifier to win a tournament in the history of the LPGA Tour. She won the State Farm Classic by six strokes, shooting three rounds of 66 in the process. That win took her to 61st place in the Money List.

Jerry Kelly

US Tour

Born 23 November 1966
Place of Birth Madison, Wisconsin, USA
Year turned Professional 1989
Tour Ranking 59th

BEST FINISH IN MAJORS

Tied 26th USPGA 1999

The 1995 Nike Tour Player of the Year, Kelly joined the USPGA Tour in 1996. He nearly won in his rookie year but, in spite of his last round 64, he was pipped in a play-

off by Loren Roberts at the Greater Milwaukee Open. Since then, in spite of playing as many tournaments as he can manage, this remains his career-best placing.

2000 SEASON. Kelly had two top-5 finishes and a consistent season, finishing 59th – his highest ranking to date – on the end of season Money List.

Skip Kendall

US Tour

Born 9 September 1964
Place of Birth Milwaukee, Wisconsin, USA
Year turned Professional 1987
Tour Ranking 50th

BEST FINISH IN MAJORS

Tied 10th USPGA 1998

Jules 'Skip' Kendall finally established himself on the US Tour in 1997 after alternating between it and the Nike Tour for some years. He finished runner-up twice – firstly at the 1998 Buick Invitational, losing a play-off to Scott Simpson, and then in 1999 at the Greater Hartford Open, three strokes behind Brent Geiberger. The slight Kendall is one of the best and most consistent putters on Tour.

2000 SEASON. His best finish was second in the Southern Farm Bureau Classic, when he was beaten by Steve Lowery at the first play-off hole, and he was third at the Bay Hill Invitational. He also had five other top-25 finishes during the season.

Christie Kerr
US Ladies Tour

Born 12 October 1977
Place of Birth Miami, Florida, USA
Year turned Professional 1996
Tour Ranking 15th

Low amateur at the 1996 US Women's Open, and member of the 1996 Curtis Cup team, Kerr joined the LPGA Tour in 1997 straight from high school. A teenage golfing phenomenon, she found it difficult to replicate her amateur brilliance on the professional circuit, and to date she is without a victory.

2000 SEASON. Kerr was T2 at the Firstar LPGA Classic and the US Women's Open, and finished 15th on the Money List. She had eight top-10s and missed only one cut in 24 starts.

Mi Hyun Kim
US Ladies Tour

Born 13 January 1977
Place of Birth Inchon, South Korea
Year turned Professional 1996
Tour Ranking 7th

TOUR VICTORIES
US: 3
1999 First Union Betsy King Classic, State Farm Rail Classic
2000 Safeway LPGA Golf Championship

Tiny (5 foot 1 inch) South Korean Kim won nine times on the Korean Ladies Tour in 1997 and she gained her card for the 1999 LPGA Tour through Qualifying School. She was an immediate success on Tour, winning the State Farm Rail Classic and the First

Union Betsy King Classic, and landed ten top-10 spots. She was unquestionably the Rookie of the Year.

2000 SEASON. Kim defeated her fellow South Korean Jeong Jang on the second hole of a play-off at the Safeway LPGA Golf Championship and posted 13 top-10s. She was T4 at the US Women's Open and missed only one cut. She finished seventh on the Money List.

2001 STOP PRESS. Kim was defeated by Annika Sorenstam in a play-off at the Office Depot and by Rosie Jones in a play-off at the Kathy Ireland Championship.

Betsy King
US Ladies Tour

Born 13 August 1955
Place of Birth Reading, Philadelphia, USA
Year turned Professional 1976
Tour Ranking 21st

MAJORS VICTORIES
US OPEN 1989, 1990
LPGA 1992
DINAH SHORE 1987, 1990, 1997

TOUR VICTORIES
US: 28
1984 Columbia Savings Classic, Freedom Orlando Classic, Kemper Open
1985 Rail Charity Classic, Turquoise Classic
1986 Henredon Classic, Rail Charity Classic
1987 Atlantic City Classic, Circle K Tucson Open, McDonald's Championship
1988 Cellular One-Ping Golf Championship, Kemper Open, Rail Charity Classic
1989 Jamaica Classic, Kemper Open, McDonald's Championship, Nestle World Championship, USX Golf Classic
1990 JAL Big Apple Classic
1991 Corning Classic, JAL Big Apple Classic
1992 Mazda Japan Classic, The Pharmor in Youngstown
1993 Toray Japan Queen's Cup

1995 ShopRite Classic
1997 Nabisco Dinah Shore
2000 Hawaiian Open, Corning
  L P G A Classic

SOLHEIM CUP 1990, 1992, 1994, 1996, 1998

One of the veterans of the LPGA Tour, King is a cool and totally undemonstrative perfectionist who has won 28 times on Tour. She first played on Tour in 1977, but did not win until 1984, when her career took off. She won three events that season and was Player of the Year, and in 1987 she won four tournaments, including the Dinah Shore, her first Major. In 1989 she was again Player of the Year, winning six titles, and she received the award for a third time in 1993. She became the first player to pass the $5 million mark in 1995, the same year she qualified for the LPGA Tour's highest accolade, the Hall of Fame. In 1996 the Betsy King LPGA Classic, hosted by King herself, was added to the Tour schedule. She has also played in five Solheim Cups.

2000 SEASON. King still showed no visible signs of allowing age to slow her down, winning the Cup Noodle Hawaiian Open and the Corning LPGA Classic and finishing twice in the top-10. She went on to finish the season in a highly respectable 21st place on the Money List.

Tom Kite

US Seniors Tour

Born 9 December 1949
Place of Birth Austin, Texas, USA
Year turned Professional 1972
Tour Ranking 11th

MAJORS VICTORIES
  THE TRADITION 2000

TOUR VICTORIES
SENIOR TOUR: 1
  2000 SBC Senior Open

Tom Kite arrived on the US Senior Tour in 2000. This unfailingly consistent, determined player, with a superb short game, has won 18 times on the USPGA Tour, had competed on the Ryder Cup on no less than seven occasions and had captained the US team in 1997. His memorable rounds in the competition include a 10-under par win over Sandy Lyle in 1981 and an 8&7 crushing of Howard Clarke in 1985. He had also won the US Open in 1992 after Jack Nicklaus had congratulated Colin Montgomerie on victory with Kite still out on a windy Pebble Beach. Kite battled through the unfavourable conditions to win the tournament by two shots. It is unwise to underestimate Kite's dogged tenacity.

2000 SEASON. Kite had two wins in his rookie year. Firstly he won the Tradition in a play-off against Larry Nelson and Tom Watson, and then he claimed the SBC Senior Open, beating Bruce Fleisher by two strokes. He was also T2 in the PGA Senior Championship and third in the Senior Open. He made over $1 million in his debut year on the Senior Tour.

2001 STOP PRESS. Following laser surgery to improve his eyesight, Kite finished T3 at the Las Vegas Senior Classic.

Soren Kjeldsen
European Tour

Born 17 May 1975
Place of Birth Aarhus, Denmark
Year turned Professional 1995
Tour Ranking 66th

WORLD CUP 1998, 1999

The small Dane Kjeldsen qualified for the 1998 European Tour, and retained his card by the skin of his teeth after finishing in 115th place in the Order of Merit at the end of the season. The next season, however, he finished T2 in the Qatar Masters, as well as T14 in the Belgacom Open, and managed to propel himself up the Order of Merit, eventually finishing the season in 56th place.

2000 SEASON. An accurate driver of the ball, he made four top-25 finishes and two top-10s. His best result was again in the Qatar Masters when he took joint seventh place.

Emilee Klein
US Ladies Tour

Born 11 July 1974
Place of Birth Santa Monica, California, USA
Year turned Professional 1995
Tour Ranking 60th

TOUR VICTORIES
US: 2
1996 British Women's Open, Ping Welch's Championship

After an impressive amateur career, which included playing in the 1994 Curtis Cup at the age of 19, Klein joined the LPGA Tour in 1995. In 1996 she won her first title, the Ping Welch's Championship, and a week later she claimed the Weetabix British Women's Open.

2000 SEASON. Klein fell to 60th slot on the Money List, scoring only two top-10s.

Carin Koch
US Ladies Tour

Born 23 February 1971
Place of Birth Kungalv, Sweden
Year turned Professional 1992
Tour Ranking 28th

TOUR VICTORIES
EUROPEAN: 1
2000 Chrysler Open
US: 1
2001 LPGA Corning Classic

SOLHEIM CUP 2000

Koch arrived on the LPGA Tour in 1995, having spent the previous three years on the European and Asian Tours. In 1996 she recorded seven top-20s including losing in a play-off to Liselotte Neumann at the Edina Realty Classic, and she ran up four other second places between then and 1999.

2000 SEASON. The competitive Koch was second once more at the Los Angeles Women's Championship and had three other top-10 finishes. However, she won all three of her matches at the Solheim Cup and she recorded her first victory at the Chrysler Open on the European Tour, when she shot a last round 69 to edge out the challenge of Samantha Head.

2001 STOP PRESS. Koch claimed her first US title at the LPGA Corning Classic.

Greg Kraft

US Tour

Born 4 April 1964
Place of Birth Detroit, Michigan, USA
Year turned Professional 1986
Tour Ranking 81st

BEST FINISH IN MAJORS
Tied 23rd USPGA 1998

Kraft has been on the US Tour since 1992 and has been placed second in four tournaments. However, he has yet to claim a victory. He did win the Deposit Guaranty Golf Classic in 1993, but at that time it was not an official PGA Tour event. Nonetheless, he has pocketed over $2.5 million in his career. He is a consistent player, although short on distance.

2000 SEASON. His highest finishes were T3 in the Advil Western Open and T6 in the Colonial. He finished 81st on the Money List, down from 1999's 52nd.

Cliff Kresge

US Tour

Born 3 October 1968
Place of Birth Lakewood, New Jersey, USA
Year turned Professional 1991
Tour Ranking Tied 21st (Qualifying School)

Kresge was a member of the Nike Tour in 1997 and 1998. He only made the cut once on the US Tour – at the 1999 Greater Milwaukee Open where he had his career highest finish of T62 – and he went to Qualifying School in 2000 to attempt to qualify for the 2001 US Tour. At Qualifying School, while concentrating on a putt he walked backwards into a pond with nine holes to go. He sheepishly climbed out, finished his round in wet clothing and qualified at T21.

Kelli Kuehne

US Ladies Tour

Born 11 May 1977
Place of Birth Dallas, Texas, USA
Year turned Professional 1996
Tour Ranking 26th

TOUR VICTORIES
US: 1
1999 Corning Classic

A precocious and gifted youngster, Kuehne was US Junior Champion in 1994 and US Women's Amateur Champion in 1995. She followed this up by successfully defending her US Amateur title in 1996 and also claiming the British Amateur title that year, becoming the first player to hold both titles simultaneously. She joined the LPGA Tour in 1997 and won her only title to date, the LPGA Corning Classic, in 1999, one stroke ahead of Rosie Jones. She was also 3third in the US Women's Open in 1999.

2000 SEASON. Kuehne's best finish was T2 at the Corning Classic, where she was beaten by Betsy King. She had two other top-10s.

Martin Lafeber
European Tour

Born 11 December 1973
Place of Birth Eindhoven, Holland
Year turned Professional 1997
Tour Ranking 85th

WORLD CUP 1999

The tall, powerful, long-hitting Dutchman Lafeber had an outstanding amateur career, winning the Dutch, Swiss and Spanish championships before turning pro in 1997. He gained his European Tour card in 1997, but lost it at the end of 1998. He entered the Tour again in 2000 via the Challenge Tour. Demonstrating an entrepreneurial nature, he funded his golf in 1998 by selling shares in himself to Dutch businessmen. His best finish is T5 at the 1999 Dutch Open.

2000 SEASON. Lafeber made two top-20s and also top-10, when he came in T6 in the Scandinavian Masters.

Neal Lancaster
US Tour

Born 13 September 1962
Place of Birth Smithfield, North Carolina, USA
Year turned Professional 1985
Tour Ranking 105th

BEST FINISH IN MAJORS
Tied 4th **US OPEN 1995**

TOUR VICTORIES
US: 1
  1994 GTE Byron Nelson Classic

Lancaster joined the US Tour from the Qualifying School in 1990 and won the only title of his career – the rain-shortened GTE Byron Nelson Classic – in a play-off in 1994. In 1995 he came T4 in the US Open, shooting the first 29 in the history of the competition. He lost his card in 1999, but regained it for 2000.

2000 SEASON. He made sure of his 2001 card when he finished T4 in the Bay Hill Invitational, and four rounds in the 60s later saw him claim T8 at the John Deere Classic.

Barry Lane
European Tour

Born 21 June 1960
Place of Birth Hayes, England
Year turned Professional 1976
Tour Ranking 103rd

BEST FINISH IN MAJORS
13th **BRITISH OPEN 1993**

TOUR VICTORIES
EUROPEAN: 6
  1987 Equity and Law Challenge
  1988 Bell's Scottish Open
  1992 Mercedes German Masters
  1993 Canon European Masters
  1994 Turespana Open de Baleares
  1995 Andersen Consulting World
       Championship of Golf
OTHER: 1
  1983 Jamaica Open

RYDER CUP 1993
DUNHILL CUP 1988, 1994, 1995, 1996
WORLD CUP 1988, 1994

A magnificent iron player, Lane's biggest payday came in 1995 when he won the Andersen Consulting World Championship of Golf, pocketing $1 million. He had won four European Tour titles prior to this bonanza, but has subsequently drawn a blank on Tour. With the exception of 1998, Lane was never out of the Order of Merit top-100 from 1986 till 1999. He played in the 1993 Ryder Cup and, although three up against Chip Beck with five to play in the singles, he lost by one hole.

2000 SEASON. He posted two T11s in the Scandinavian Masters and in the BMW International. He dipped out of the Order of Merit top-100 for the second time in his career

Bernhard Langer

European Tour

Born 27 August 1957
Place of Birth Anhausen, Germany
Year turned Professional 1972
Tour Ranking 19th

MAJORS VICTORIES
US MASTERS 1985, 1993

TOUR VICTORIES
US: 1
  1985 Sea Pines Heritage Classic
EUROPEAN: 37
  1980 Dunlop Masters
  1981 Bob Hope British Classic, German Open
  1982 German Open
  1983 Glasgow Golf Classic, Italian Open, St Mellion Timeshare TPC
  1984 Benson & Hedges Spanish Open, Carrolls Irish Open, KLM Dutch Open, Peugeot French Open
  1985 German Open, Panasonic European Open
  1986 German Open, Lancome Trophy
  1987 Carrolls Irish Open, Whyte and Mackay PGA Championship
  1988 Epson Grand Prix
  1989 German Masters, Peugeot Open de Espana
  1990 Austrian Open, Cepsa Madrid Open
  1991 Benson & Hedges International Open, Mercedes German Masters
  1992 Heineken Dutch Open, Honda Open
  1993 Volvo German Open, Volvo PGA Championship
  1994 Murphy's Irish Open, Volvo Masters
  1995 Deutsche Bank Open-TPC of Europe, Smurfit European Open, Volvo PGA Championship
  1997 Benson & Hedges International Open, Chemapol Trophy Czech Open, Conte of Florence Italian Open, Linde German Masters
AUSTRALASIAN: 1
  1985 Australian Masters
OTHER: 2
  1983 Casio World Open
  1997 Argentinian Masters

RYDER CUP 1981, 1983, 1985, 1987, 1989, 1991, 1993, 1995, 1997
DUNHILL CUP 1992, 1994
WORLD CUP 1976, 1977, 1978, 1979, 1980, 1990, 1991, 1992, 1993, 1994, 1996

With the remarkable total of 37 European Tour wins in 17 years, Langer is one of the living legends of golf. This supremely consistent, single-minded German achieved all these victories in spite of twice suffering the dreaded putting 'yips', which threatened to end his golfing career.

Langer began as a caddy, and the young prodigy turned pro at the age of 15. He joined the Tour in 1976 and won his first title – the Dunlop Masters – in 1980 and, with the exception of 1996, he won at least one tournament every year since 1980 until 1997. He has also been in the top-30 of the Order of Merit every season since 1980, again with the exception of 1996. His superb iron play, tough mental attitude and dedication to the game have brought Langer success across the world, including Japan, South Africa, Australia and South Africa. He has twice – in 1985 and 1993 – won The Masters, the first time shooting 68 in his final round to win by two strokes and in 1993 defeating second-placed Chip Beck by four strokes. He has never won the British Open although he has finished in the top-3 on five occasions.

He was a regular in the European Ryder Cup team from 1981 until 1997, and narrowly failed to qualify in 1999. He has helped Europe to win the trophy three times, but is probably best remembered for missing a 5-foot putt on the last green in 1991 at Kiawah Island to hand victory to the USA. However as captain Seve Ballesteros remarked 'No one could have holed that putt'. To compensate for this miss, Langer scored the winning point in the 1997 Ryder Cup, beating Brad Faxon 2&1. He has also made 11 appearances in the World Cup and was named individual winner in 1993. He has not won on Tour since his victory in the Linde German Masters in 1997, although he ended the 1999 season 15th on the Order of Merit. Langer is a practising Christian who is involved with the Tour Bible Study Group.

2000 SEASON. Langer collected 11 top-20 places, including runner-up in the Dutch Open and the BMW International. He tied for 11th place in the British Open, shooting a 6 under par 66 on his third round, and finished in 19th place on the Order of Merit.

2001 STOP PRESS. Langer finished third in the prestigious Players Championship at the famous TPC of Sawgrass course, in Florida, behind Vijay Singh and Tiger Woods.

Franklin Langham
US Tour

Born 8 May 1968
Place of Birth Augusta, Georgia, USA
Year turned Professional 1992
Tour Ranking 26th

BEST FINISH IN MAJORS
7th USPGA 2000

Born in Augusta, Georgia, just down the road from the famous Augusta National golf course, Langham used to man the scoreboards as a youngster at The Masters Tournament. He graduated to the Nike Tour in 1992 after playing alongside Phil Mickelson and David Duval in the winning 1991 US Walker Cup team, and joined the USPGA Tour in 1998, having previously lost his playing privileges in 1996. He has never won a tournament and his best placing up until 2000 was T2 at the Deposit Guaranty Classic in 1998. He is known as an excellent putter and is 13th in the putting statistics on Tour.

2000 SEASON. Langham had a consistent and lucrative season. He came agonizingly close to winning his maiden event when he was six shots ahead of Jim Furyk with six to play in the Doral-Ryder Open, but he eventually had to settle for second place, due partly to Furyk shooting a remarkable back-nine of 30. He also finished second in two other tournaments – the Kemper Open and the Greater Milwaukee Open – and had three other top-10 places. He finished the season 26th on the Money List, his highest position so far.

Jose Manuel Lara
European Tour

Born 21 May 1977
Place of Birth Valencia, Spain
Year turned Professional 1997
Tour Ranking 11th (Challenge Tour)

A good friend of Spanish superstar Sergio Garcia, the tall Spaniard Lara twice narrowly failed to graduate from the Challenge Tour to the European Tour, finishing 18th in 1998 and 19th in 1999. He did, however, secure his card in 2000 by taking 11th place on the Challenge Tour, helped by two third spots and one top-4.

Paul Lawrie
_____ European Tour

Born 1 January 1969
Place of Birth Aberdeen, Scotland
Year turned Professional 1986
Tour Ranking 26th

MAJORS VICTORIES
BRITISH OPEN 1999

TOUR VICTORIES
EUROPEAN: 2
  1996 Open Catalonia
  1999 Qatar Masters

RYDER CUP 1999
DUNHILL CUP 1999
WORLD CUP 1999

Lawrie had been regarded as something of a journeyman professional on the European Tour since he joined in 1992, with just one win – the Open Catalonia – in six years. However, that all changed in 1999. First he won the Qatar Masters by seven strokes – shooting 68, 65, 67, 68. Then in that year's British Open, after Jean Van De Velde memorably threw away victory on the final hole at Carnoustie, Lawrie won the four-hole play-off which also included the 1997 champion Justin Leonard, with two birdies on the last two holes and lifted the claret jug. His blister-ing last round 67 had taken him into con-tention, and he kept his nerve to become the first Scotsman in nearly 70 years to win the Open on Scottish soil. He was awarded the MBE for his triumph. He made his Ryder Cup debut in 1999 and scored 3½ points out of a possible 4, beating Jeff Maggert in the singles. Lawrie drives the ball a long way (he is 25th on the driving distance statistics) and he is ranked seventh in putting.

2000 SEASON. Lawrie had an injury-hit year, but he managed to claim 26th spot in the Order of Merit. He finished T4 in the Dubai Desert Classic and T5 in the British Masters and had six other top-20 finishes. He played in three US Tour events, and had a T8 at the Mercedes and T5 in the World Match Play. Unfortunately, he missed the cut at the British Open.

Scott Laycock
_____ Australasian Tour

Born 15 September 1971
Place of Birth Brisbane, Australia
Year turned Professional 1992
Tour Ranking 11th

TOUR VICTORIES
AUSTRALASIAN: 1
  2001 Victoria Open

Laycock played on the Asian Tour for three years, winning the Hugo Boss Foursome in 1997. Before 2000–01, his highest finish was third at the Dunhill Masters. He won his first tournament on the Australasian Tour in 2001, the Victoria Open, and was fourth in the Australian Open.

Stephen Leaney
_____ European Tour

Born 10 March 1969
Place of Birth Busselton, Western Australia
Year turned Professional 1992
Tour Ranking 28th

BEST FINISH IN MAJORS
68th USPGA 1998

TOUR VICTORIES
EUROPEAN: 3
  1998 Moroccan Open, TNT Dutch Open
  2000 TNT Dutch Open
AUSTRALASIAN: 7
  1991 Western Australian Open
  1994 Western Australian Open
  1995 Victorian Open
  1997 Victorian Open, Western Australian
       Open, Western Australian PGA
  1998 ANZ Players Championship

DUNHILL CUP 1999, 2000

Amateur Leaney won the Western Australian Open in 1991 and turned professional the following year. He was out of action for nearly two years between 1993 and 1995 after an operation to remove a blood clot in his shoulder, and he graduated from the Challenge Tour to join the European Tour in 1998. He won two tournaments – the Moroccan Open and the Dutch Open – in his first season to finish in 11th place on the Order of Merit. In 1999, he made four top-3 finishes. Leaney is not a particularly long hitter but he is accurate (30th for shot accuracy on the Tour statistics).

2000 SEASON. He began the season in fifth place at the Greg Norman Holden International, but injured a finger and was out of action until March. He collected his third European title in July when he turned in a virtually faultless 19 under par 269 to win the Dutch Open ahead of Bernhard Langer.

Darren Lee
European Tour

Born 10 January 1965
Place of Birth Harlow, England
Year turned Professional 1992
Tour Ranking 115th

BEST FINISH IN MAJORS
Tied 68th BRITISH OPEN 1992

Essex-born Lee first came to public prominence at the 1992 British Open when he tied for 68th place and won the silver medal for the leading amateur. Since then, he played the Challenge Tour with occasional forays into the European Tour. He graduated from Qualifying School in 1999 and received his 2000 card by finishing in tenth place. He does not drive the ball very far but, at 20th in the statistics, he is accurate.

2000 SEASON. Lee's best finish was T5 in the BMW International and he also recorded a couple of top-25s. He finished 115th on the Order of Merit so just retained his 2001 card.

Ian Leggatt
US Tour

Born 23 September 1965
Place of Birth Cambridge, Ontario, USA
Year turned Professional 1990
Tour Ranking 5th (Buy.Com Tour)

WORLD CUP 1998

Ex-Canadian speed skating champion Leggatt was a rookie on the 2000 Buy.Com Tour and won one tournament. He briefly led the Money List and ended the season in fifth place. His highest finish on the US Tour is T56 at the 1998 Greater Vancouver Open. He was T8 in the individual rankings in the 1998 World Cup.

Tom Lehman
US Tour

Born 7 March 1959
Place of Birth Austin, Minnesota, USA
Year turned Professional 1982
Tour Ranking 12th

MAJORS VICTORIES
  BRITISH OPEN 1996

TOUR VICTORIES

US: 4

1994 Memorial Tournament
1995 Colonial National Invitation
1996 The Tour Championship
2000 Phoenix Open

EUROPEAN: 1

1997 Loch Lomond Invitational

OTHER: 1

1993 Casio World Open

RYDER CUP 1993, 1997, 1999
DUNHILL CUP 1999, 2000
PRESIDENTS CUP 1994, 1996, 2000
WORLD CUP 1996

The story of Lehman's rise from the unfashionable mini tours to become British Open champion and the USA's top golfer is one of hard work and determination. Having played on the US Tour in the early 1980s, he came back to the main Tour via the Nike Tour where he was Player of the Year in 1991. In 1994, he won his first tournament, The Memorial, gained second place in the Masters and he was fourth in the Money List. He won again in 1995, but 1996 was the finest season of his career. At Royal Lytham St Anne's, he won the British Open. Taking a six-shot lead over Nick Faldo into the last round he held on to win by two strokes from Ernie Els and Mark McCumber. That year he also finished

T2 at the US Open at Oakland Hills, one shot behind Steve Jones, and crowned his season by winning the Tour Championship and finishing top of the Money List. In 1997 he clinched the Loch Lomond Invitational on the European Tour and he finished runner-up four times in 1999 on the US Tour. He is a committed Christian, although his antics on the 17th hole on the Sunday at the 1999 Ryder Cup provoked an angry Sam Torrance into questioning his Christian charity. He is a fine iron player and in the top-10 for greens in regulation.

2000 SEASON. Lehman was back on a winning streak in 2000. He beat David Duval by three shots to win the (unofficial) inaugural Williams World Challenge and take home $1 million. He also claimed the Phoenix Open – his first title in 68 starts – with a one shot margin over Robert Allenby and Rocco Mediate. He also performed well in the Majors, finishing sixth at the Masters and T4 in the British Open.

Justin Leonard

US Tour

Born 15 June 1972
Place of Birth Dallas, Texas, USA
Year turned Professional 1994
Tour Ranking 14th

MAJORS VICTORIES

BRITISH OPEN 1997

TOUR VICTORIES

US: 4

1996 Buick Open
1997 Kemper Open
1998 The Players Championship
2000 Westlin Texas Open

RYDER CUP 1997, 1999
DUNHILL CUP 1997
PRESIDENTS CUP 1996, 1998
WORLD CUP 1997

A calculating, methodical player, with a low, baseball-like swing, Leonard was US Amateur Champion in 1992 and turned professional at the 1994 Greater Hartford Open. He won his first US Tour tournament, the Buick Open, in 1996 by five strokes, shooting four rounds in the 60s. That year, he was described by *Cosmopolitan* magazine as one of the world's most eligible bachelors. In 1997, Leonard won the Kemper Open and followed this up with victory in the British Open when, trailing Jesper Parnevik by six strokes at the beginning of the final round at Troon, the competitive Texan shot a first nine 31 and beat the Swede by three shots. He finished second to Davis Love in the USPGA a month later. In 1998 he won the Players Championship and in 1999 was defeated by Paul Lawrie in a four-hole play-off at the British Open at Carnoustie. In his 1999 Ryder Cup singles match against Jose Maria Olázabal at Brookline, Leonard came back from four-down to sink the massive 45-foot putt at the 17th for the half point which gave victory to the USA and sparked off the enthusiastic celebrations on the green.

2000 SEASON. Leonard was remodelling his swing during 2000 season in an attempt to get more distance off the tee, but he still managed two runner-up places in consecutive weeks – T2 at the Memorial and Kemper Open – and

he won the Westin Texas Open, beating Mark Wiebe by five strokes. He also finished T2 at the WGC NEC Invitational, 11 strokes behind the Tiger.

Thomas Levet
European Tour

Born 5 September 1968
Place of Birth Paris, France
Year turned Professional 1988
Tour Ranking 88th

BEST FINISH IN MAJORS
Tied 49th **BRITISH OPEN 1999**

TOUR VICTORIES
EUROPEAN: 2
1998 Cannes Open
2001 Victor Chandler British Masters

DUNHILL CUP 1992, 1998, 2000
WORLD CUP 1998

L evet played on the US Tour in the early 1990s. He was on the Challenge Tour in 1998, but received a sponsor's exemption for the Cannes Open that year and duly won the competition. It is his only European Tour victory.

2000 SEASON. Levet had three top-25 finishes, and his best performance came in the Moroccan Open when he was T2, four strokes behind winner Jamie Spence. In the Dunhill Cup, however, he lost all three of his matches.

JL Lewis
US Tour

Born 18 July 1960
Place of Birth Emporia, Kansas, USA
Year turned Professional 1984
Tour Ranking 78th

BEST FINISH IN MAJORS
Tied 21st **USPGA 1999**

TOUR VICTORIES

US: 1

1999 John Deere Classic

Six foot three inch, long-hitting Lewis played on the US Tour in 1989 and 1995, and returned again in 1998, having finished in seventh position in the Nike Tour Money List. He won his only tournament – the John Deere Classic – in 1999, posting rounds of 66-65-65-65 and beating USPGA Tour veteran Mike Brisky with a winning birdie at the fifth play-off hole at Oakwood.

2000 SEASON. His best finish was T3 at the Bob Hope Classic with three other top-20s.

Frank Lickliter

US Tour

Born 28 July 1969

Place of Birth Middletown, Ihio, USA

Year turned Professional 1991

Tour Ranking 53rd

BEST FINISH IN MAJORS

Tied 4th USPGA 1998

TOUR VICTORIES

US: 1

2001 Kemper Insurance Open

Lickliter gratuated from the Qualifying School in 1995 after playing on the Nike Tour and he has been on the US Tour since then. An accurate but short driver, he came a narrow second to Payne Stewart in the rain-shortened 1999 AT&T Pebble Beach Pro-Am at Pebble Beach, in California.

2000 SEASON. Lickliter had three top-5 finishes, his best being third in the Michelob. In the Phoenix Open he was leading for three rounds, but threw it away on the third hole of the last round when he triple-bogeyed the par 5 and ended the tournament T10.

2001 STOP PRESS. Lickliter won his first PGA Tour title – the Kemper Insurance Open.

Jenny Lidback

US Ladies Tour

Born 30 March 1962

Place of Birth Lima, Peru

Year turned Professional 1987

Tour Ranking 36th

TOUR VICTORIES

US: 1

1995 du Maurier Classic

Peruvian-born Lidback was voted Junior Player of the Year in 1981 by *Golf Digest* and played on the Futures Tour until 1988 when she joined the LPGA Tour. In 1995 she had her only victory at the prestigious du Maurier Classic, and in 1997 she achieved the incredible, and altogether more notable, feat of shooting a hole-in-one in successive rounds of the Chrysler-Plymouth Tournament of Champions.

2000 SEASON. Lidback's 11 top-20 finishes, with her highest being T9 at the Cup Noodles Hawaian Open, helped her to 36th place on the Money List.

Fredrik Lindgren

European Tour

Born 28 March 1966

Place of Birth Malmo, Sweden

Year turned Professional 1989

Tour Ranking 131st

BEST FINISH IN MAJORS

Missed Cut BRITISH OPEN 1991 AND 1994

Swede Lindgren joined the European Tour in 1991 and played on Tour until 1996, his best performance being T2 at the Murphy's English Open in 1992. A friendly and amiable man, he rejoined the Tour in 1999 from the Challenge Tour.

2000 SEASON. His best position was only T12 at the Turespana Masters and he lost his fully exempt status.

Leta Lindley
US Ladies Tour

Born 1 June 1972
Place of Birth Phoenix, Arizona, USA
Year turned Professional 1994
Tour Ranking 24th

US Women's Amateur in 1994 and a room-mate and teammate of Annika Sorenstam at the University of Arizona, Lindley joined the LPGA Tour in 1995 but has not managed to match the Swede's massive success. Her best finish was runner-up in the 1997 McDonald's LPGA Championship, when she lost on the second hole of a play-off.

2000 SEASON. Lindley had a respectable season, finishing T3 at the Arch Wireless Championship and recording six top-10s.

Jonathan Lomas
European Tour

Born 7 May 1968
Place of Birth Chesterfield, England
Year turned Professional 1988
Tour Ranking 59th

BEST FINISH IN MAJORS
Tied 11th BRITISH OPEN 1994

TOUR VICTORIES
EUROPEAN: 1
1996 Chemapol Trophy Czech Open

DUNHILL CUP 1996

Lomas was touted as one of the UK's stars of the future when he won three tournaments on the Challenge Tour in 1992 and 1993. He joined the European Tour in 1994, finished the season as Rookie of the Year with four top-10 finishes and ended a very creditable 32nd on the Order of Merit. Since then, his only tournament victory came in 1996, when he claimed the Chemapol Trophy Czech Open.

2000 SEASON. Lomas's best performance came in the French Open when he took on Colin Montgomerie in a head-to-head struggle in the final round. His birdie putt on the 17th cut Monty's lead to one stroke, but the big Scot's eagle on the last hole meant that Lomas eventually had to settle for second place. He also did well to finish T9 in the Benson & Hedges

Peter Lonard
European Tour

Born 17 July 1967
Place of Birth Sydney, Australia
Year turned Professional 1989
Tour Ranking 94th

BEST FINISH IN MAJORS
Tied 49th BRITISH OPEN 1999

TOUR VICTORIES
AUSTRALASIAN: 1
1997 Ericsson Australian Masters

The beefy, popular Australian Lonard has played regularly on the European Tour since 1997. Identifiable by his wrap-around sunglasses and his broomhandle putter, he has still to post a victory in Europe although he has managed two second-place finishes – at the 1997 Johnnie Walker Classic and the Heineken Classic in 1999. Also a member of the Australasian Tour, he won the Order of Merit in the southern hemisphere in 1997 after winning the Australian Masters. He was taken ill in Australia in 1992 and spent the next three years working as a club pro in Sydney.

2000 SEASON. Early in the season Lonard had three top-25s, and his highest placing was fifth in the Irish Open. At the Rio De Janeiro 500 Years Open, he shot an opening round 62, with 29 on the back nine, but some mediocre play over the following three days meant that he could only finish T17.

Nancy Lopez

US Ladies Tour

Born 6 January 1957
Place of Birth Torrance, California, USA
Year turned Professional 1977
Tour Ranking 126th

MAJORS VICTORIES

LPGA 1978, 1985, 1989
DINAH SHORE 1981

TOUR VICTORIES

US: 45

- **1978** Bankers Trust Classic, Bent Tree Ladies Classic, Coca Cola Classic, Colgate European Open, Colgate Far East Open, Golden Light Classic, Greater Baltimore Classic , Sunstar Classic
- **1979** Coca Cola Classic, Colgate European Open, Golden Lights Championship, Lady Keystone Open, Mary Kay Classic, Sahara National Pro-Am, Sunstar Classic, Women's International
- **1980** Kemper Open, Rail Charity Classic, Sarah Coventry
- **1981** Arizona Copper Classic, Sarah Coventry
- **1982** J&B Pro-Am, Mazda Japanese Classic
- **1983** Elizabeth Arden Classic, J&B Pro-Am
- **1984** Chevrolet World Championship of Women's Golf, Uniden LPGA Invitational
- **1985** Chrysler-Plymouth Charity Classic, Henredon Classic, Mazda Hall of Fame Championship, Portland Ping Championship
- **1987** Cellular One-Ping Golf Championship, Sarasota Classic
- **1988** Centinela Hospital Classic, Chrysler-Plymouth Classic, Mazda Classic
- **1989** Atlantic City Classic, Nippon-Travel MBS Classic
- **1990** MBS LPGA Classic

- **1991** Sara Lee Classic
- **1992** Ping-Cellular One Golf Championship, Rail Charity Golf Classic
- **1993** Youngstown-Warren LPGA Championship
- **1997** Chick-fil-A Charity Championship

SOLHEIM CUP 2000

The smiling, charismatic figure of Nancy Lopez set US Women's golf alight in the late 1970s. She announced her arrival at the 1975 US Women's Open when, as an 18-year-old amateur, she tied for second place in the competition. In her rookie year on Tour in 1978, she won no fewer than nine events, five of them back-to-back, and not surprisingly was awarded both Rookie and Player of the Year. The following season she won eight further tournaments and was once again voted Player of the Year. Although her swing was hardly a thing of beauty, her sensational record, dashing and uninhibited stroke play and good looks helped to bring women's golf into the mainstream of US sporting life, in a similar way to which Arnold Palmer had massively widened the appeal of men's golf nearly two decades previously.

By 1983 her unorthodox but effective swing and her putting ability helped her to pass $1 million in career earnings, and in 1985 she picked up her third Player of the Year award with her fourth award coming in 1988. She has won the LPGA Championship three times in her career but has never won the US Women's Open, although she has been runner-up in the championship on no less than four occasions. Her last attempt to gain the trophy was in 1997 when, at age 40, she shot an impressive four rounds in the 60s but was pipped to the post by the diminutive Alison Nicholas.

2000 SEASON. She had surgery in May which limited the number of events she could play. Her best finish was T9 at the Office Depot and she ended 126th on the Money List.

Davis Love III

US Tour

Born 13 April 1964
Place of Birth Charlotte, North Carolina, USA
Year turned Professional 1985
Tour Ranking 9th

MAJORS VICTORIES
USPGA 1997

TOUR VICTORIES
US: 12

- 1987 MCI Heritage Classic
- 1990 The International
- 1991 MCI Heritage Classic
- 1992 Kmart Greater Greensboro Open, MCI Heritage Classic, The Players Championship
- 1993 Infiniti Tournament of Champions, Las Vegas Invitational
- 1995 Freeport-McMoran Classic
- 1996 Buick Invitational
- 1997 Buick Challenge
- 1998 MCI Classic
- 2001 AT&T Pebble Beach National Pro-Am

OTHER: 1
- 1998 Chunichi Crowns

RYDER CUP 1993, 1995, 1997, 1999
DUNHILL CUP 1992
PRESIDENTS CUP 1994, 1996, 1998, 2000
WORLD CUP 1992, 1993, 1994, 1995, 1997

Love is a tall, powerful golfer and, courtesy of his wide and steep swing arc, is perenially one of the longest hitters on the US Tour. He joined the Tour in 1986 and won his first title – the MCI Heritage Classic – the following year. before the 2001 season he had won in total 12 Tour events and these successes, coupled with his consistency, have brought him nearly $15 million in winnings. Previously regarded as perhaps not having the mental toughness to win a Major, he silenced his critics in 1997 when, in a superb display of long hitting and precise iron play, he won the USPGA Championship at Winged Foot. With three rounds of 66 and one of 71, he finished 11 under par, five strokes ahead of Justin Leonard. He also beat Glen Day by seven strokes in the MCI Classic in 1998. Despite not winning a title in 1999, he won nearly $2.5 million, a PGA record for a season without a victory, and he was runner-up to Jose Maria Olázàbal in The Masters.

He has played in four Ryder Cups and, with his partner Fred Couples, he helped the USA to four World Cups in successsion from 1992 to 1995, a record which still stands in the competition. Love received the World Cup individual winner's award in 1995. Despite suffering from back problems, and as a result having to flatten his wide swing, Love still hits the ball a long way with effortless style.

2000 SEASON. Love had a good season although he didn't win. He had five top-5 finishes, his best being runner-up to Tiger Woods at the Bay Hill Invitational, and a further five top-20 placings. In the WGC Matchplay he disposed of Olin Browne, Jeff Sluman, Jim Furyk and Miguel Jimenez before losing 5&4 to Woods in the semi-final. He beat Ernie Els 4&3 in the President's Cup singles and shared the tournament top scoring position with Stewart Cink. He also finished T7 in The Masters, T11th in the British Open and T9 in the USPGA.

2001 STOP PRESS. Seven shots behind at the beginning of the last round, Love shot a 9 under par 63 to win the AT&T Pebble Beach Pro-Am. He came in third at the following tournament, the Buick Invitational.

Steve Lowery

US Tour

Born 12 October 1960
Place of Birth Birmingham, Alabama, USA
Year turned Professional 1983
Tour Ranking 31st

BEST FINISH IN MAJORS
Tied 8th **USPGA 1995**

TOUR VICTORIES
US: 2
1994 Sprint International
2000 Southern Farm Bureau Classic

A big Southerner, Lowery is affectionately known on the US Tour as 'Yogi Bear'. He has played consistently on Tour since 1993, only once (1999) dropping out of the top-100. He won once on Tour in the 1990s, at the 1994 Sprint International after a play-off with Rick Fehr. He is an aggressive and competitive player with a good all-round game.

2000 SEASON. Lowery secured his second tournament victory after a play-off against Skip Kendall in the Southern Farm Bureau Classic, sinking a 45-foot birdie putt to win on the first extra hole. He also achieved nine other top-10 finishes in his career-best season. He was ranked eighth in total driving for the season.

Santiago Luna
European Tour

Born 29 November 1962
Place of Birth Madrid, Spain
Year turned Professional 1982
Tour Ranking 79th

BEST FINISH IN MAJORS
Tied 38th **BRITISH OPEN 1998**

TOUR VICTORIES
EUROPEAN: 1
1995 Madeira Island Open

DUNHILL CUP 1991, 1998
WORLD CUP 1995, 1998, 1999

S paniard Luna is a 15-year veteran of the European Tour although in that time he has only managed to notch up one tournament victory – the 1995 Madeira Island Open. He is widely regarded by his peers on Tour as one of the most under rated golfers in Europe who has yet to fulfil his enormous potential. Since 1990 he has not been out of the top-100 on the Order of Merit. In the 1998 Dunhill Cup he achieved a monumental victory, taking on and beating Tiger Woods in a head-to-head semi-final over the Old Course at St Andrews.

2000 SEASON. Luna recorded three top-10 finishes, his best being T6 in the Rio De Janeiro 500 Years Open. However, he slipped from 45th to 79th in the Order of Merit. He was 17th in the driving statistics, but performed poorly with his broomstick putter.

Mikael Lundberg
European Tour

Born 13 August 1973
Place of Birth Helsinborg, Sweden
Year turned Professional 1995
Tour Ranking 4th (Challenge Tour)

L undberg played as an amateur for Sweden before attempting to join the European Tour through the Qualifying School in 1996, 1997 and 1998. He qualified for the 2001 Tour by finishing fourth on the 2000 Challenge Tour, making two runner-up places – at the NW Ireland Open and the Cuba Challenge – and four other top-10 finishes.

David Lundstrom

US Seniors Tour

Born 7 May 1947
Place of Birth Galesburg, Illinois, USA
Year turned Professional 1970
Tour Ranking 31st

An American with a Swedish sounding surname, Lundstrom was the Medallist at the 1997 US Senior Tour Qualifying School, Lundstrom finished 1998 in 38th place on the Money List, his best finish being second behind Jim Colbert at the Transamerica. The following year he earned $500,000 thanks to four impressive top-10 finishes.

2000 SEASON. Lundstrom ended the season just inside the top-31 players on the Money List, carding five top-10s with his best placing being T3 at the Home Depot Invitational. He earned $600,000.

Mardi Lunn

US Ladies Tour

Born 9 January 1968
Place of Birth Liverpool, Australia
Year turned Professional 1988
Tour Ranking 147th

TOUR VICTORIES
US: 1
  1999 AreaWEB.Com Challenge
EUROPEAN: 1
  1993 The European Classic

Australian Lunn was the Junior Amateur Champion of Australia in 1986, 1987 and 1988 and joined the European Tour in 1988. She won the European Classic in 1993 and made her debut on the LPGA Tour in 1994. She won her only US title in 1999 when she beat fellow Australian Jan Stephenson by one shot at the Area WEB.COM Challenge. That year she also finished T3 at the McDonald's LPGA Championship and finished 13th on the Money List.

2000 SEASON. Lunn had a poor season, her highest finish being T18. She retained her card for 2001 because of her 1999 victory.

David Lynn

European Tour

Born 20 October 1973
Place of Birth Billinge, England
Year turned Professional 1995
Tour Ranking 63rd

Six foot three inch Lynn won his European Tour card through the Challenge Tour in 1997, but lost it again in 1998. He qualified at the 1999 Qualifying School with sixth place. His highest placing on Tour was in the Hohe Brucke Open in 1996 when he finished runner-up to Paul McGinley.

2000 SEASON. Lynn had a consistent and relatively successful year. He made the cut in his first 17 tournaments and posted three top-10s, the highest being T5 in the Alfred Dunhill.

2001 STOP PRESS. Lynn was runner-up to Ian Poulter at the Moroccan Open.

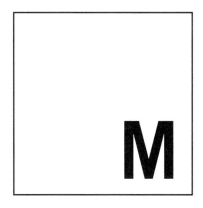

he went out in the first round of that year's competition to Tom Lehman. He hits the ball a long way, but he is only 144th for driving accuracy.

Jeff Maggert
US Tour

Born 20 February 1964
Place of Birth Columbia, Missouri, USA
Year turned Professional 1986
Tour Ranking 39th

BEST FINISH IN MAJORS
3rd USPGA 1997

TOUR VICTORIES
US: 2
   1993 Walt Disney World/Oldsmobile Classic
   1999 WGC-Andersen Consulting Match
      Play Championship
AUSTRALASIAN: 1
   1990 Vines Classic
OTHER: 1
   1989 Malaysian Open

RYDER CUP 1995, 1997, 1999

Andrew Magee
US Tour

Born 22 May 1962
Place of Birth Paris, France
Year turned Professional 1984
Tour Ranking 55th

BEST FINISH IN MAJORS
Tied 5th BRITISH OPEN 1992

TOUR VICTORIES
US: 4
   1988 Pensacola Open
   1991 Las Vegas Invitational, Nestle
      Invitational
   1994 Northern Telecom Open

A popular player on the US Tour, Magee has been a regular since 1985, winning four tournaments. His last victory was at the 1994 Northern Telecom Open when he beat Loren Roberts, Vijay Singh and Steve Stricker by two strokes. From 1994 until 1999 he recorded six second-place finishes, including runner-up to Jeff Maggert after a play-off for the WGC-Andersen Consulting Match Play in 1999.

2000 SEASON. Magee chalked up the seventh second-place finish of his career in the Greater Greensboro Classic and had three other top-10 finishes. He could not replicate the form he showed in the 1999 Andersen Match Play and

In 1999 Maggert secured a three-year exemption on the US Tour and a cheque for $1 million when he chipped in for a birdie on the 38th hole of the inaugural WGC-Andersen

Consulting Match Play Championship. Prior to this, his nine years on Tour had brought him victory in only one tournament, when he beat Greg Kraft by three strokes to win the 1993 Walt Disney World/Oldsmobile Classic. However, he was runner-up no less than 13 times in the 1990s which goes a long way to explaining his consistently high position on the Money List. Maggert is ranked 15th in driving accuracy but 105th in driving distance. He represented his country in the first Presidents Cup in 1994 and in the last three Ryder Cups.

2000 SEASON. He slipped from ninth to 39th in the Money List, but finished T2 in the Buick Challenge and T3 in the prestigious and lucrative Players Championship. He also had four other top-10 finishes.

John Mahaffey
US Seniors Tour

Born 9 May 1948
Place of Birth Kerrville, Texas, USA
Year turned Professional 1971
Tour Ranking 28th

TOUR VICTORIES
SENIOR TOUR: 1
1999 Southwestern Bell Dominion

An accurate striker of the ball, Mahaffey picked up ten USPGA tournament victories between 1973 and 1989, including a second play-off hole win over Tom Watson to secure the 1978 USPGA Championship. He joined the US Senior Tour in 1998, and in 1999 won his only Tour victory, sinking a birdie putt on the second play-off hole of the Southwestern Bell Dominion to see off the challenge of Bruce Fleisher and Jose Maria Canizares.

2000 SEASON. Mahaffey fought his way to nine top-10 placings, the best being a T3 at the Kroger Senior Classic. His Senior career earnings passed $2 million. He hit 75 percent of greens in regulation.

Meg Mallon
US Ladies Tour

Born 14 April 1963
Place of Birth Natcik, Massachussets, USA
Year turned Professional 1987
Tour Ranking 3rd

MAJORS VICTORIES
US OPEN 1991
LPGA 1991
DU MAURIER CLASSIC 2000

TOUR VICTORIES
US: 10
1991 Daikyo World Championship, Oldsmobile Classic
1993 Ping Welch's Championship, Sara Lee Classic
1996 Hawaiian Open, Sara Lee Classic
1998 Star Bank Classic
1999 Sara Lee Classic, Subaru Memorial of Naples
2000 Rochester Invitational

SOLHEIM CUP 1992, 1994, 1996, 1998, 2000

Mallon joined the LPGA Tour in 1987 and won nothing until 1991. That year she claimed the Mazda LPGA Championship, with a 15-foot birdie putt on the last hole, and three weeks later won the US Women's Open. With two other victories that year she finished second on the Money List. Throughout the 1990s the calm and composed Mallon has been a consistent winner on Tour, picking up a further eight tournament victories and proving herself to be one of the world's top women golfers. In 1999 she won two titles and passed the $4 million mark in career earnings. She played in the Solheim Cup in 1992, 1994, 1996, 1998 and 2000.

2000 SEASON. Mallon had two more wins, including the du Maurier Classic, and posted 14 top-10s. She also finished runner-up in three consecutive events, including the US Women's Open, and ended the season third on the Money List. She earned over $1 million in 2000.

Laurette Maritz
European Ladies Tour

Born 13 January 1964
Place of Birth Johannesburg, South Africa
Year turned Professional 1987
Tour Ranking 18th

TOUR VICTORIES
EUROPEAN: 3
    1988 EMS Masters, Marbella Open
    1990 Laing Charity Classic
SOUTH AFRICA: 3
    1989 South African Open
    1996 South African Open
    1998 South African Masters

Blonde-haired South African Maritz was 1988 Rookie of the Year on the European Ladies Tour, winning the Marbella Open on her debut and then claiming the EMS Masters. She won her third and last Tour title in 1990. She has also won the South African Open twice, in 1989 and 1996, and the South African Masters in 1998.

2000 SEASON. Her best finish of the year was T3 at the Marrakesh Palmaeraie, and she had three other top-10s to end 18th on the Money List.

Graham Marsh
US Seniors Tour

Born 14 January 1944
Place of Birth Kalgoorlie, Australia
Year turned Professional 1969
Tour Ranking 32nd

MAJORS VICTORIES
    THE TRADITION 1999
    US SENIOR OPEN 1997

TOUR VICTORIES
SENIOR TOUR: 4
    1995 Bruno's Memorial Classic
    1996 Franklin Quest Championship, World Senior Invitational
    1997 Nationwide Championship

Nomadic Australian Marsh is one of the most experienced golfers on the US Senior Tour, with 58 international victories to his credit, including 15 on the European PGA Tour. Brother of the legendary Australian wicket keeper Rodney, he is a cool, collected player and one of the most accurate drivers on Tour. He finished second at the Senior Qualifying School in 1993 and the following season seven top-10s and a T2 at the US Senior Open helped him reach $500,000 in prize-money. He won his first tournament in 1995, taking the Bruno's Memorial Classic by five strokes ahead of JC Snead, and had two more wins in 1996. He won his first Major in 1997, beating John Bland by one stroke to lift the US Senior Open and move to seventh on the Money List. He collected a second Major in 1999 at the rain-shortened Tradition and that year reached $5 million in Senior career earnings. His nickname on Tour is 'Swampy'. Marsh also runs a successful golf course design company.

2000 SEASON. Marsh fell out of the top-31 for the first time in six years, his best finish being a T2 at the season-opening Mastercard Championship, but his Senior career earnings rose to over $6 million.

Kathryn Marshall

US Ladies Tour

Born 8 June 1967
Place of Birth Dundee, Scotland
Year turned Professional 1990
Tour Ranking 68th

TOUR VICTORIES
US: 1
  1995 Jamie Farr Toledo Classic

Scottish Junior Champion in 1985, 1986 and 1987, Marshall joined the European Tour in 1990. She has finished T2 three times on the European Tour but has not won a tournament. She qualified for the LPGA Tour in 1993 and won the Jamie Farr Toledo Classic in 1995, becoming the first Scot to win on the US Tour. She played in the Solheim Cup in 1996.

2000 SEASON. In the US, Marshall had three top-20 finishes and was placed T10 at the Weetabix Women's British Open. Her best European finish was T3 at the British Ladies Masters. In Europe she ended 31st on the Order of Merit and in the US she was 68th on the Money List.

Miguel Angel Martin

European Tour

Born 2 May 1962
Place of Birth Huelva, Spain
Year turned Professional 1981
Tour Ranking 52nd

BEST FINISH IN MAJORS
Tied 24th **BRITISH OPEN 1999**

TOUR VICTORIES
EUROPEAN: 3
  1992 Peugeot Open de France
  1997 Heineken Classic
  1999 Moroccan Open

DUNHILL CUP 1991, 1994, 1997, 2000
WORLD CUP 1997, 1998

A relatively short (5 foot 6 inches) Spanish ex-caddie, Martin has been a permanent presence on the European Tour since 1983. He has won three tournaments in that period, his last being the Moroccan Open in 1999 when he beat David Park at the sixth play-off hole. He has also scored a 59 in the 1987 South Argentine Open. He qualified to play in the 1997 Ryder Cup but was controversially ruled out as unfit. Martin, who chews on a tee when playing to aid concentration, is accurate off the tee, but is not a long hitter.

2000 SEASON. He made the cut in his first 11 starts and had eight top-20 finishes. His best placing, however, was T5, at the Qatar Masters and the BMW International, in Germany. Replacing Sergio Garcia, Martin's three wins out of four games at the Dunhill Cup at St Andrews helped Spain to the final against South Africa. In the final, his 50-foot putt from the Valley of Sin at the 18th took his crucial match against David Frost into a play-off hole, where his par was enough to win the competition for Spain.

Shigeki Maruyama

US Tour

Born 12 September 1969
Place of Birth Chiba, Japan
Year turned Professional 1992
Tour Ranking 37th

BEST FINISH IN MAJORS
Tied 10th **BRITISH OPEN 1997**

TOUR VICTORIES
OTHER: 9
   1993 Pepsi Ubekousan
   1995 Bridestone Open
   1996 Bridestone Open
   1997 Golf Nippon Hitachi Cup, Japan PGA
         Championship, PGA Match Play
         Promise Cup, Pocari Sweat Yomiuri
   1998 PGA Philanthropy Open
   1999 Bridgestone Open

PRESIDENTS CUP 1998, 2000

Asmall, Japanese golfer with a seemingly permanent grin, Maruyama first attracted attention in the 1998 Presidents Cup when he won all five of his matches in impressive style. A nine-time winner on the lucrative Japanese Tour, including four tournament wins in 1997, his performances in the Andersen Consulting Match Play (T5) and the NEC Invitational (sixth) secured him a card on the 2000 US Tour. He hits the ball a long way off the tee but can also be erratic.

2000 SEASON. Maruyama had an excellent rookie year on the USPGA Tour, posting three top-4 finishes, including a T2 behind Tiger Woods at the Buick Invitational, and four other top-10 placings. He also shot a 58 in a pre-qualifying round for the US Open, where he missed the cut. He ended the season 37th on the Money List.

Catriona Matthew

US Ladies Tour

Born 25 August 1969
Place of Birth Edinburgh, Scotland
Year turned Professional 1994
Tour Ranking 32nd

TOUR VICTORIES
US: 1
   2001 Hawaiian Ladies Open
EUROPEAN: 1
   1998 WPGA Championship of Europe
AUSTRALASIAN: 1
   1996 Australian Ladies Open

SOLHEIM CUP 1998

Matthew joined the European Tour in 1994 after an impressive amateur career when she won the Scottish Amateur Championship in 1991, 1993 and 1994 and made three consecutive Curtis Cup appearances. She won the

Australian Ladies Open in 1996 and qualified for the 1995 LPGA Tour. In 1998 she had eight top-20 appearances and won the McDonald's WPGA Championship of Europe on the European Tour. The following year she achieved her then career-best LPGA placing with a runner-up spot at the Safeco Classic. Matthew is unusual in that she uses the same grip for putting as she does for her full swing.

2000 SEASON. Matthew had seven top-10 finishes on the LPGA Tour, her highest being fifth at the Office Depot Classic and the Australian Ladies Masters.

2001 STOP PRESS. Matthew finally won her first tournament on the US Tour, beating Annika Sorenstam by three shots at the Cup Noodle Hawaiian Ladies Open,

Len Mattiace

US Tour

Born 15 October 1967
Place of Birth Mineola, New York, USA
Year turned Professional 1990
Tour Ranking 61st

BEST FINISH IN MAJORS
Tied 24th US OPEN 1997

Mattiace has played regularly on the US Tour since 1996 but has yet to win a tournament. His best finish is T2 at the 1996 Buick Challenge – and again in the 1999 Sony Open in Hawaii – but he is particularly remembered for his performance in the 1998 Players Championship. At the famous TPC of Sawgrass, in Florida, Mattiace was leading with two holes to go when he hit the water on the par-3 17th hole and took an 8. He finished T5 in the tournament. He is naturally left handed but plays right handed. He was World Putting Champion in 1996.

2000 SEASON. He ended the year in his best ever placing – 61st – on the Money List thanks to four top-10 finishes and a T3 in the Tampa Bay Classic.

Bob May

US Tour

Born 6 October 1968
Place of Birth Lynwood, California, USA
Year turned Professional 1991
Tour Ranking 29th

BEST FINISH IN MAJORS
2nd USPGA 2000

TOUR VICTORIES
EUROPEAN: 1
1999 Victor Chandler British Masters

The much-travelled May had 22 second places in various world tours until he joined the European Tour in 1996. Known as 'Top-10 Bob' for his continual presence at the top of the leaderboard, he finally won a tournament at the 1999 British Masters, shooting a front nine 30 on the last round and beating Montgomerie by one stroke. He also shot an albatross 2 on the par-five 10th in his second round. In 1999 he qualified for the US Tour by finishing 13th in Qualifying School. A small, stocky player, his accurate iron play has led to his position of 12th in greens in regulation.

2000 SEASON. May had a successful rookie year on Tour, tieing for second place with Chris DiMarco in the Fedex St Jude Classic one stroke behind Notah Begay, and third in the Reno-Tahoe Open. He had a memorable battle with Tiger Woods in the USPGA Championship when he lost by one stroke on the third play-off hole, having shot 66 in each of his last three rounds. He defended his British Masters title and finished T5, and he had a T11 placing in the British Open.

Billy Mayfair

US Tour

Born 6 August 1966
Place of Birth Phoenix, Arizona, USA
Year turned Professional 1988
Tour Ranking 106th

BEST FINISH IN MAJORS
Tied 5th USPGA 1990

TOUR VICTORIES
US: 5
1993 Greater Milwaukee Open
1995 Motorola Western Open, The Tour
Championship
1998 Buick Open, Nissan Open

White-haired Mayfair was US Amateur Champion in 1987. He won his very first tournament – the Greater Milwaukee Open – in 1993, five years after joining the US Tour. His best year was 1995 when he won two tournaments, claimed the runner-up spot three times and finished second on the Money List. He came back to form in 1998 when his 5-under-par 67 was sufficient to beat Scott Verplank by two strokes in the Buick Open, and is one of the few players to have triumphed over Tiger Woods in a play-off, beating the world number one in the Nissan Open, in California. He is a short but accurate driver, but is famously known for his unorthodox putting stroke, where he cuts across the ball at impact.

2000 SEASON. A poor season for Mayfair, with only two top-10 finishes, although he did eliminate Phil Mickelson in the first round of the WGC Andersen Match Play. He slumped from 41st to 106th in the Money List.

2001 STOP PRESS. Mayfair lost on the fifth hole of a play-off to Jose Coceres at the Worldcom Classic.

Blaine McCallister
US Tour

Born 17 October 1958
Place of Birth Fort Stockton, Texas, USA
Year turned Professional 1981
Tour Ranking 49th

BEST FINISH IN MAJORS
Tied 17th USPGA 1989

TOUR VICTORIES
US: 5
1988 Hardee's Golf Classic
1989 Bank of Boston Classic, Honda Classic
1991 HEB Texas Open
1993 BC Open

Panama hat-wearing McCallister has been on the US Tour since 1986. Between 1997 and 1999, however, he had to gain his card through Qualifying School, on the latter occasion finishing in first place. A left hander who plays right handed but putts left handed, he has won five tournaments in his career, the last in 1993. He was distracted in the mid-1990s by family illness and his wife's fading eyesight.

2000 SEASON. He finished second to Carlos Franco after a play-off in the Compaq Classic and made further strides toward retaining his card with a T3 in the Texas Open, he had five other top-25 finishes.

Scott McCarron
US Tour

Born 10 July 1965
Place of Birth Sacramento, California, USA
Year turned Professional 1992
Tour Ranking 97th

BEST FINISH IN MAJORS
Tied 10th MASTERS 1996, US OPEN 1997, USPGA 1997

TOUR VICTORIES
US: 3
1996 Freeport-McDermott Classic
1997 BellSouth Classic
2001 BellSouth Classic

Long-hitting Californian McCarron won his first tournament in 1996, the year after he joined the US Tour, with a four-shot victory in the Freeport-McDermott Classic. The following year he won again, this time by three strokes over David Duval and Lee

Janzen in the BellSouth Classic. His best year was 1997 when he also recorded seven top-10 placings and he ended the season in 25th place on the Money List. He has a good record in The Masters, finishing in the top-30 four years running between 1996 and 1999.

2000 SEASON. He was T4 in the Reno-Tahoe and T5 in the Invensys Classic in Las Vegas. However, he was only placed in the top-25 on a further two occasions.

2001 STOP PRESS. McCarron won the Bell-South Classic again, with a three-stroke victory over Mike Weir.

Gary McCord
US Seniors Tour

Born 23 May 1948
Place of Birth San Gabriel, California, USA
Year turned Professional 1971
Tour Ranking 33rd

MAJORS VICTORIES
SENIOR PLAYERS CHAMPIONSHIP 1999

TOUR VICTORIES
SENIOR TOUR: 1
1999 Toshiba Senior Classic

An irreverent and entertaining golf analyst for CBS TV, McCord is probably known more now for his commentary than his play. Although McCord remained winless on the regular USPGA Tour, he won twice in his first season on the US Senior Tour even though his broadcasting commitments permitted him to play in only 17 tournaments. His first victory was at the Toshiba Senior Classic when, playing on a sponsor's exemption, he beat John Jacobs on the fifth play-off hole. He won again at the prestigious, season-ending Senior Players Championship, one stroke ahead of Bruce Fleisher, and collected nearly $350,000. As well as being a regular columnist for the magazine *Golf Digest*, McCord has written three books – *Golf For Dummies* (1 & 2) and *Just a Range*

Ball in a Box of Titleists – a biography of his life as a Tournament professional. He also made a cameo appearance in the movie *Tin Cup*.

2000 SEASON. McCord recorded nine top-10s, including a T2 at the LiquidGolf.com Invitational, and earned almost $500,000. He finished just outside the top-31, at 33rd.

2001 STOP PRESS. McCord tied for third place at the SBC Senior Classic.

Mike McCullough
US Seniors Tour

Born 21st March 1945
Place of Birth Coshocton, Ohio, USA
Year turned Professional 1970
Tour Ranking 18th

TOUR VICTORIES
SENIOR TOUR: 1
2001 Emerald Gold Coast Classic

In 1996 'iron man' McCullough played on the USPGA, Nike and US Senior Tours, and qualified for the 1997 Seniors by finishing third at Qualifying School. He had to return to Qualifying School the following year and made seven top-10 appearances in 1998 in the 37 tournaments in which he played, ending within the crucial top-31 on the Money List.

2000 SEASON. He still did not manage to win on Tour, but he did pick up eight top-10s, earning just under $1 million in prize-money and securing 18th place on the Money List. His highest place was T3 at the Cadillac NFL and the Senior Tour Championship. By the end of the season he had played in 147 consecutive career tournaments for which he had been eligible, a US Senior Tour record.

2001 STOP PRESS. McCullough eventually won his first tournament when he overcame Andy North on the first sudden-death play-off hole at the Emerald Gold Coast Classic. It was his first win in a PGA event since joining the Tour in 1973. McCullough also came second at The Tradition, nine strokes behind Doug Tewell.

Michelle McGann

US Ladies Tour

Born 30 December 1969
Place of Birth West Palm Beach, Florida, USA
Year turned Professional 1988
Tour Ranking 31st

TOUR VICTORIES
US: 7
- 1995 Sara Lee Classic, Youngstown-Warren LPGA Championship
- 1996 Oldsmobile Classic, State Farm Classic, Youngstown-Warren LPGA Championship
- 1997 Healthsouth Inaugural, ShopRite Classic

SOLHEIM CUP 1994, 1996

A tall, long-hitting player with a penchant for gold jewellery and colourful, wide-brimmed hats, the glamorous McGann cuts a stylish figure on the golf course. She joined the LPGA Tour straight from high school in 1989, but did not win her first event until 1995. Between 1995 and 1997, however, McGann more than made up for her seven-year absence from the winners' list by claiming seven victories. In her last win – the 1997 ShopRite Classic – she overcame Sweden's Annika Sorenstam by three strokes, having beaten world number one Karrie Webb earlier that year in a play-off at the Healthsouth Inaugural, and passed $2 million in career earnings.

2000 SEASON. A consistent year with 12 top-20 placings, including a T3 at the Electrolux USA Championship.

Jerry McGee

US Seniors Tour

Born 21 July 1943
Place of Birth New Lexington, Ohio, USA
Year turned Professional 1966
Tour Ranking 63rd

McGee won four times on the USPGA Tour between 1975 and 1979 and also represented his country in the 1977 Ryder Cup. Known on Tour as 'Magoo', he joined the US Seniors in 1993, but to date has not yet managed to win a tournament. The volatile McGee ended his rookie season of 1994 with seven top-10s and finished the 25th on the Money List. He equalled this ranking in 1997, earning $500,000. He was diagnosed with neck cancer in 1999, but came back to compete in the last four tournaments.

2000 SEASON. McGee struggled throughout the year. He played in 33 events, but could only finish once in the top-10.

Jill McGill

US Ladies Tour

Born 30 January 1972
Place of Birth Denver, Colorado, USA
Year turned Professional 1994
Tour Ranking 59th

Six foot tall McGill was 1993 US Women's Amateur Champion and Public Links Champion in 1994. She turned pro in 1994 and joined the European Tour, finishing the season tenth on the Order of Merit and coming second in the Weetabix Women's British Open. She qualified for the LPGA Tour at her second attempt in 1995, but could not repeat her amateur success on the professional circuit and had to go back to Qualifying School in 1998. The following year she posted her career-best finish with a T4 at the Firstar LPGA Classic.

2000 SEASON. McGill had seven top-20s, her best being T10 at the Takefuji Classic.

Paul McGinley

European Tour

Born 16 December 1966
Place of Birth Dublin, Ireland
Year turned Professional 1991
Tour Ranking 18th

BEST FINISH IN MAJORS
Tied 14th BRITISH OPEN 1996

TOUR VICTORIES
EUROPEAN: 2
1996 Hohe Brucke Open
1997 Oki Pro-Am

DUNHILL CUP 1993, 1994, 1996, 1997, 1998,
1999, 2000
WORLD CUP 1993, 1994, 1997, 1998, 1999

Irish Amateur Champion in 1989, McGinley graduated from the Qualifying School
School in 1991 and has played on the European Tour ever since, his best placing on the
Order of Merit being 15th in 1996 when he
won his first tournament, the Hohe Brucke
Open. Playing alongside Padraig Harrington,
he helped Ireland to win the World Cup at
Kiawah Island in 1997 for only the second
time in the country's history. A good player
in windy conditions, he is only average off
the tee. However, he is a strong and accurate
iron player and an excellent putter. He is also
managed by the same company as Darren
Clarke and Lee Westwood.
2000 SEASON. Yet another consistent season.
He had five top-5 finishes, his highest being T2
in the Dubai Desert Classic, two strokes behind
winner Jose Coceres. He also finished T3 in the
Portuguese Open and the Irish Open.

Tom McGinnis
US Seniors Tour

Born 27 November 1947
Place of Birth Memphis, Tennessee, USA
Year turned Professional 1969
Tour Ranking 48th

TOUR VICTORIES
SENIOR TOUR: 1
1999 Bank Boston Classic

McGinnis joined the US Senior Tour in
1998 by finishing T3 at Qualifying
School. In 1999 he surprised the golf world
when, as a virtual unknown, he defeated Hale
Irwin on the second play-off hole to win the
Bank Boston Classic.
2000 SEASON. McGinnis could only pick up
three top-10s and finished 48th on the Money
List.

Jim McGovern
US Tour

Born 5 February 1965
Place of Birth Teaneck, New Jersey, USA
Year turned Professional 1988
Tour Ranking 143rd

TOUR VICTORIES
US: 1
1993 Shell Houston Open

Known as 'The Governor' on Tour for his
aggressive play, McGovern joined the US
Tour in 1991 and had his best year in 1993,
winning the Houston Open and finishing 27th
on the Money List. At this time in his career,
he was tipped to become the next American
superstar, but his form dramatically dipped
over the next couple of seasons.
2000 SEASON. McGovern played on both the
Buy.Com Tour and the US Tour in 2000, and
his best finish on the main Tour was T10, at
the John Deere Classic and the Bell Canadian
Open.

Mhairi McKay
US Ladies Tour

Born 18 April 1975
Place of Birth Glasgow, Scotland
Year turned Professional 1997
Tour Ranking 91st

Mhairi first picked up a club at the tender age of four, and by 18 she had won back-to-back British Girls Championships. In 1992 she set the 18-hole record of 67 at the Old Course of St Andrews. McKay attended Stanford University in California at the same time as Tiger Woods and she earned All-American honours for all four years (1994–97) and featured in the Curtis Cup matches of 1994 and 1996.

Entering the US Tour in 1997 McKay's career really took off in 1998 when she finished tied seventh in the US Open and posted a 66 during the second round of the State Farm Rail Classic. The following year saw her post four top-20 finishes.

2000 SEASON. In 2000 the young Scot grew in confidence, again recording four top-20 finishes, pocketing $94,678 dollars during the season and twice scoring under 68.

2001 STOP PRESS. McKay is now considered a serious contender on the LPGA circuit after a blistering start to 2001. Her highest finish was at the LPGA Corning Classic where she finished tied second after leading through rounds two and three. The previous month Mhairi recorded top-eight finishes at the Kathy Ireland Championship Honoring Harvey Penick and The Champions Classic. Her efforts during the first half of 2001 netted her over $170,000 and boosted her up the rankings to 26th.

Malcolm MacKenzie
European Tour

Born 30 September 1961
Place of Birth Sheffield, England
Year turned Professional 1980
Tour Ranking 6th (Qualifying School)

BEST FINISH IN MAJORS
Tied 5th BRITISH OPEN 1992

TOUR VICTORIES
SOUTH AFRICA: 1
1995 Zimbabwe Open

MacKenzie qualified for his 19th successive year on the European Tour by finishing 6th at the 2000 Qualifying School. He has never won a tournament on Tour and his highest finish is second at the 1990 Murphy's Cup. His best year was 1990 when he finished 25th on the Order of Merit, and two years later he tied with six other players for fifth place at the 1992 British Open.

Andrew McLardy
European Tour

Born 20 January 1974
Place of Birth Triangle, Zimbabwe
Year turned Professional 1997
Tour Ranking 91st

Born in Zimbabwe to Scottish parents, McLardy joined the European Tour from the Qualifying School in 1998. In his rookie year he started impressively making the cut in more than half the events he entered and notching up three top-10 finishes, the best of which was a fifth place at the Volvo Scandinavian Masters, in Sweden. He hits the ball a long way, but tends to be inaccurate.

2000 SEASON. This was not a good year for McLardy, who slipped from 84th to 91st in the Order of Merit. He posted four top-25s, his best being T13 in the Sao Paolo Open, in Brazil. He did, however, gain his USPGA Tour card.

Mark McNulty

European Tour

Born 25 October 1953
Place of Birth Bindwa, Zimbabwe
Year turned Professional 1977
Tour Ranking 49th

BEST FINISH IN MAJORS
Tied 2nd BRITISH OPEN 1990

TOUR VICTORIES
EUROPEAN: 16
  1979 Greater Manchester Open
  1980 German Open
  1986 Quinto de Lagos Portuguese Open
  1987 Dunhill British Masters, German Open, London Standard 4-Stars Pro-Celebrity, Tournament of Champions
  1988 Cannes Open
  1989 Torras Monte Carlo Open
  1990 Credit Lyonnais Cannes Open, Volvo German Open
  1991 Volvo German Open
  1994 BMW International Open
  1996 Dimension Data Pro-Am, Sun Dutch Open, Volvo Masters
  2001 South African Open
SOUTH AFRICA: 22
  1980 Holiday Inns Invitational
  1981 Sigma Series
  1982 SAB Masters, Sharp Classic, SISA Classic

  1984 Wild Coast Pan Am Tournament
  1985 Palabora Classic, Swazi Sun Pro-Am
  1986 Barclays Classic, Gemiston Centenary Tournament, Helix Wild Coast Sun Classic, Safmarine Masters, Swazi Sun International, Tournament of Champions, Wild Coast Classic
  1987 AECI Charity Classic, South African Open, Swazi Sun Pro-Am, Tournament of Champions
  1993 Lexington PGA Championship, Players Championship
  1998 Players Championship
OTHER: 4
  1980 Malaysian Open
  1987 Sun City Million Dollar Challenge
  1992 Zimbabwe Open
  1996 Zimbabwe Open

DUNHILL CUP 1993, 1994, 1995, 1996, 1997, 1998, 1999, 2000
PRESIDENTS CUP 1994, 1996
WORLD CUP 1993, 1994, 1995, 1996, 1997, 1998

The experienced McNulty has had a consistent and highly successful career on the European and South African Tours over the last two decades. He has collected 23 South African titles (13 of which he won in the two years 1986 and 1987) and f15 European titles, his last being the 1996 Volvo Masters which he claimed by the margin of seven shots. He has won more money than any other non-European on the European Tour. Unlike his friend and fellow Zimbabwean Nick Price, he has never won a Major although he came close in the 1990 British Open when he finished T2 with Payne Stewart, five strokes behind winner Nick Faldo. He has a smooth and elegant swing and is very accurate, if not very long, off the tee (eighth for driving accuracy and 176th for driving distance on the Tour statistics). However, his skill with the putter and the precision of his short game have been the keys to his success.

2000 SEASON. He was ill in the early part of the season and rejoined the Tour in May. The following month he was T5 in the Wales Open, and later in the year he shot two opening rounds of 65 in the British Masters, but could only finish in fourth place, his highest position of the season. He finished T11 in the British Open and had two other top-20 placings. He won two out of his three matches in the Dunhill Cup.

2001 STOP PRESS. McNulty won the South African Open, beating Justin Rose by a shot.

Spike McRoy
US Tour

Born 20 May 1968
Place of Birth Huntsville, Alabama, USA
Year turned Professional 1991
Tour Ranking 1st (Buy.Com Tour)

BEST FINISH IN MAJORS
Tied 53rd US OPEN 1999

Robert 'Spike' McRoy played on the US Tour in 1997 and 1998, when he had his best finish, T6 at the Buick Invitational, and on the Buy.Com Tour in 1999 and 2000. In 2000 he won two tournaments – including the Buy.Com Tour Championship – and claimed top spot on the Money List. He earned over $300,000, a record for the Tour.

Rocco Mediate
US Tour

Born 17 December 1962
Place of Birth Greensburg, Pennsylvania, USA
Year turned Professional 1985
Tour Ranking 34th

BEST FINISH IN MAJORS
4th US OPEN 2001

TOUR VICTORIES
US: 4
1991 Doral-Ryder Open
1993 Kmart Greater Greensboro Open
1999 Phoenix Open
2000 Buick Open

Mediate has played on the US Tour since 1986 and has won four tournaments. He won his first title at the Doral-Ryder Open in 1991 after a play-off with Curtis Strange and he beat Steve Elkington to win the Greater Greensboro Open in 1995. In 1999 he finished ahead of Leonard and Woods to win the Phoenix Open. He is accurate off the tee (20th in driving accuracy statistics) but does not achieve huge distance. He uses a broomstick putter.

2000 SEASON. Mediate moved up the Money List with a second at the Phoenix Open and a T4 at the Colonial. He also won his fourth tournament when he birdied the last hole with a 12-foot putt to defeat Chris Perry in the Buick Open.

Sandrine Mendiburu
European Ladies Tour

Born 15 October 1972
Place of Birth Bayonne, France
Year turned Professional 1991
Tour Ranking 15th

TOUR VICTORIES
EUROPEAN: 3
1994 Costa Azul
1999 Hannover Expo 2000 Open, Irish Open

US Junior Champion in 1990, Mendiburu was European Ladies Tour Rookie of the Year in 1994. She won her first tournament in 1992 and also had back-to-back wins in 1999, as well as three top-10s that year.
2000 SEASON. A consistent year where she missed only one out of 15 cuts and recorded three top-10s to end the year 15th on the Money List.

Ross Metherell
European Senior Tour

Born 30 September 1948
Place of Birth Perth, Australia
Year turned Professional 1968
Tour Ranking 24th

TOUR VICTORIES
SENIOR TOUR: 2
1999 Belfry PGA Seniors Championship, De Vere Hotels Seniors Classic

A renowned coach in Australia, whose pupils have included Stephen Leaney, Greg Chalmers and Jarrod Moseley, Metherell joined the European Senior Tour in 1999 through Qualifying School. He won twice in his rookie year.

2000 SEASON. Metherell hit form towards the end of the year, tieing with Maurice Bembridge for second behind Denis O'Sullivan at the Dan Technology Senior Tournament of Champions and securing two other third places. He was 24th on the Order of Merit.

Patricia Meunier Lebouc
European Ladies Tour

Born 16 November 1972
Place of Birth Dijon, France
Year turned Professional 1993
Tour Ranking 8th

TOUR VICTORIES
EUROPEAN: 5
1994 English Open
1997 *Guardian* Irish Open
1998 Air France Madame Open
2000 Austrian Open, French Open

Lebouc joined the European Ladies Tour and won the English Open in her rookie year of 1994. She won again in 1997 at the *Guardian* Irish Open and collected her third title the following year at the Air France Open.
2000 SEASON. Lebouc had her best season so far, finishing eighth on the Money List. She won twice – at the French and Austrian Opens – and became the first French player to compete in the Solheim Cup.
2001 STOP PRESS. She came T6th at the Kathy Ireland Championship on only her second start on the US Ladies Tour.

Shaun Micheel
US Tour

Born 5 January 1969
Place of Birth Orlando, Florida, USA
Year turned Professional 1992
Tour Ranking 104th

BEST FINISH IN MAJORS
Tied 40th US OPEN 2001

icheel entered the 2000 US Tour by finishing ninth on the Buy.Com Money List. His first top-20 placing was in July, but thereafter he finished T5 at the John Deere Classic, shooting a final round 65, and again T5 in the Invensys Classic, securing his card for 2001. On the European Tour he finished T4 in the 1998 Malayasian Open.

Phil Mickelson

US Tour

Born 16 June 1970
Place of Birth San Diego, California, USA
Year turned Professional 1992
Tour Ranking 2nd

BEST FINISH IN MAJORS
2nd US OPEN 1999

TOUR VICTORIES
US: 17
- 1991 Northern Telecom Open
- 1993 Buick Invitational of California, The International
- 1994 Mercedes Championships
- 1995 Northern Telecom Open
- 1996 GTE Byron Nelson Open, NEC World Series of Golf, Nortel Open, Phoenix Open
- 1997 Bay Hill Invitational, Sprint International
- 1998 AT&T Pebble Beach National Pro-Am, Mercedes Championships
- 2000 BellSouth Classic, Buick Invitational, MasterCard Colonial, The Tour Championship
- 2001 Buick Invitational
RYDER CUP 1995, 1997, 1999

DUNHILL CUP 1996
PRESIDENTS CUP 1994, 1996, 1998, 2000

ickelson, like Colin Montgomerie, is 'one of the best players never to have won a Major'. A tall, left-handed golfer (although right-handed in everything else) he is long off the tee, with an exceptionally smooth and precise short game and is an excellent putter. In short, he should by now have won one of golf's greatest prizes, although 17 victories in under ten years is a more than significant achievement.

He was a distinguished amateur, playing in the 1989 and 1991 Walker Cups and winning the US Amateur Championship in 1990, the first left-hander to claim the trophy. He also won his first USPGA event, the 1991 Northern Telecom Open, as an amateur – the first amateur to win on Tour since Scott Verplank in 1985. He won four events on Tour in 1996 and was second on the Money List, and in 1997 and 1998 again won twice each season. The closest he has come to a Major win was in 1999 when Payne Stewart beat him by one stroke at the US Open. Mickelson has played in three Ryder Cups – 1995, 1997 and 1999 – and at the time of writing was publicly critical of the European's 'slow play' at Brookline. The Europeans disagree.

2000 SEASON. Mickelson had his best season since 1996, again collecting four Tour wins. He beat Tiger Woods at the Buick Invitational by four strokes; won the BellSouth Classic in a play-off; took the MasterCard Colonial by two strokes ahead of Stewart Cink and Davis Love III; and won the Tour Championship, shooting a last round 4 under par 69. He was also a three-time runner-up. He earned over $4.7 million and again occupied second place on the Money List.

2001 STOP PRESS. Mickelson contended in the AT&T Pebble Beach Pro Am until the 72nd hole, when he hit a fairway wood into the Pacific and had to settle for T3. He won his next event – the Buick Invitational – at the third extra hole when Frank Lickliter three-putted from six feet. He was defeated by a Tiger Woods birdie putt on the final hole of the Bay Hill Invitational and took second place. He finished third at the Masters and was also in contention to win the US Open

Peter Mitchell
European Tour

Born 6 April 1958
Place of Birth Ruckinge, England
Year turned Professional 1974
Tour Ranking 72nd

BEST FINISH IN MAJORS
Tied 20th **BRITISH OPEN 1995**

TOUR VICTORIES
EUROPEAN: 3
   1992 Mitsubishi Austrian Open
   1997 Madeira Island Open
   1998 Portuguese Open

WORLD CUP 1996

Veteran Mitchell has played regularly on the European Tour since 1987. Something in the warm Portuguese air seems to suit Mitchell as he won the Madeira Open and the Portuguese Open in successive seasons, to go with his only other title, the Austrian Open. In 1996, his 11 top-10 finishes elevated him to his highest-ever position in the Order of Merit –12th – and he has not finished outside the top-100 since 1988. A keen martial arts fan, he is one of the fittest players on Tour, despite being now one of the oldest.

2000 SEASON. All things considered, a disappointing season for Mitchell who fell from 52nd place on the Order of Merit to 72nd. His highest placing was T17 at the Deutsche Bank Open.

Larry Mize
US Tour

Born 2 September 1958
Place of Birth Augusta, Georgia, USA
Year turned Professional 1980
Tour Ranking 111th

MAJORS VICTORIES
US MASTERS 1987

TOUR VICTORIES
US: 3
   1988 Danny Thomas-Memphis Classic
   1993 Buick Open, Northern Telecom Open
OTHER: 4
   1988 Casio World Open
   1989 Dunlop Phoenix
   1990 Dunlop Phoenix
   1993 Johnnie Walker World Championship

RYDER CUP 1987
DUNHILL CUP 2000

Mize will be forever remembered in golf history for his remarkable performance in The Masters, at Augusta National, in 1987. He birdied the last hole to force a play-off with Seve Ballesteros and Greg Norman. Ballesteros was eliminated at the first extra hole. At the second hole Mize pitched the ball straight into the hole from 40 yards to the right of the 11th green. Norman missed his putt and delighted local boy Mize had won The Masters. That year he had his best ever finish – sixth – on the Money List. He has had three other Tour wins in his career, the last in 1993, as well as winning the Japanese Dunlop Phoenix twice and, in 1993, the money-spinning Johnnie Walker World Championship, in Jamaica, at the end of the season. He lacks distance off the tee, but his silky smooth swing consistently puts him in the top-10 statistics for accurate driving. He has cut back his schedule to spend time with his family,

2000 SEASON. He finished T3 in the MCI Classic and had four other top-25 placings. He finished 111th in the Money List, his lowest ranking since his rookie year of 1982.

Marine Monnet
European Ladies Tour

Born 14 July 1978
Place of Birth Paris, France
Year turned Professional 1999
Tour Ranking 8th

The young Frenchwoman qualified for the European Ladies Tour by finishing third at Qualifying School.

2000 SEASON. Monnet had an excellent rookie year with nine top-10 places. She finished second in the Waterford Crystal Irish Open, shooting a final round 74 to lose by one stroke to Sophie Gustafson. She was sixth on the Money List.

Colin Montgomerie
European Tour

Born 23 June 1963
Place of Birth Glasgow, Scotland
Year turned Professional 1987
Tour Ranking 6th

BEST FINISH IN MAJORS
2nd US OPEN 1997 AND 1994, USPGA 1995

TOUR VICTORIES
EUROPEAN: 24
1989 Portuguese Open
1991 Scandinavian Masters
1993 Heineken Dutch Open, Volvo Masters
1994 Murphy's English Open, Peugeot Open de Espana, Volvo German Open
1995 Trophee Lancome, Volvo German Open
1996 Canon European Masters, Dubai Desert Classic, Murphy's Irish Open

1997 Compaq European Grand Prix, Murphy's Irish Open
1998 Linde German Masters, One2One British Masters, Volvo PGA Championship
1999 Benson & Hedges International Open, BMW International Open, Standard Life Loch Lomond, Volvo PGA Championship, Volvo Scandinavian Masters
2000 Novotel Perrier Open de France, Volvo PGA Championship
OTHER: 5
1996 Nedbank Million Dollar Challenge
1997 Andersen Consulting World Championship of Golf, King Hassan II Trophy, World Cup of Golf (indiv)
1999 Cisco World Match Play Championship

RYDER CUP 1991, 1993, 1995, 1997, 1999
DUNHILL CUP 1988, 1991, 1992, 1993, 1994, 1995, 1996, 1997, 1998, 2000
WORLD CUP 1988, 1991, 1992, 1993, 1997, 1998, 1999

A long-hitting, accurate driver with a smooth, classical swing, Monty was the top European golfer in the 1990s, and won the Order of Merit seven years in succession, from 1993 until 2000. His hair-trigger temper and often irascible nature have not always endeared him to the press and spectators, but in victory he can be gracious and charming. Strangely for a player of his talents he has resisted the blandishments of the US Tour and, although he has collected 24 European titles, he is winless in the US. Equally surprisingly, he has never won a Major title and, as with Phil Mickelson, he is regarded as one of the 'best players never to have won a Major'. He has only been placed once in the top-10 at the British Open, although his US record is more impressive. At the 1992 US Open, having been congratulated on his victory by Jack Nicklaus, Mongomerie was overtaken by a battling Tom Kite. In 1994 and 1997 he came second, both times to Ernie Els, and at the 1995 USPGA Championship he shot birdies on the last three holes but lost a play-off to Steve Elkington.

He has played in five Ryder Cups, his most memorable display coming in 1991 when he was four down with four to play against Mark Calcavecchia and drew the match. In 1999 he and Paul Lawrie beat David Duval and Phil Mickelson 3&2 in the opening match of the tournament, giving an important psychological boost to the European team.

Monty's best year on the European Tour was in 1999 when he won five events, including the Standard Life Loch Lomond, his first victory on his native Scottish soil, and the Volvo PGA Championship for the second year in succession. He set a record for the highest earnings in one season, over $1.3 million. Montgomerie was awarded the MBE in 1998.

2000 SEASON. Montgomerie became the first player in history to win the Volvo PGA for three successive years and he also won the French Open. However, he lost his Order of Merit leadership to Lee Westwood. He had his first US victory at the unofficial Skins Game late in the season.

Janice Moodie
US Ladies Tour

Born 31 May 1972
Place of Birth Glasgow, Scotland
Year turned Professional 1996
Tour Ranking 14th

TOUR VICTORIES
US: 1
    2000 Shoprite LPGA Classic

SOLHEIM CUP 2000

Scottish Ladies Champion in 1992, and Curtis Cup member in 1994 and 1996, Glasgow-born Moodie attended San Jose State University and qualified for the LPGA Tour in 1997. In 1998 her eight top-20 finishes helped her to the runner-up spot as Rookie of the Year behind (a long way behind) Se Ri Pak, and in 1999 she twice finished runner-up.

2000 SEASON. Moodie, who lives in the same exclsuive community as Tiger Woods in Orlando, Florida, won her first LPGA title when she beat Pat Hurst and Grace Park by two strokes to lift the ShopRite LPGA Classic. She also represented Europe in the Solheim Cup.

Orville Moodie
US Seniors Tour

Born 9 December 1933
Place of Birth Chickasha, Ohio, USA
Year turned Professional 1967
Tour Ranking 89th

MAJORS VICTORIES
    SENIOR US OPEN 1989

TOUR VICTORIES
SENIOR TOUR: 10
    1984 Daytona Beach Senior Golf Classic, MONY Senior Tournament of Champions
    1987 Kaanapali Classic, Rancho Murieta Senior Gold Rush

1988 Greater Grand Rapids Classic, Senior Players Reunion Pro-Am, Vintage Chrysler Invitational
1989 Senior Tournament Players Championship,
1991 PaineWebber Invitational
1992 Franklin Quest Showdown Classic

Part Choctaw Indian, Moody spent 14 years in the US Army, becoming Army golf champion, before joining the US Tour. His only victory on Tour was in 1969 when he won the US Open. He joined the US Senior Tour in 1984 and his best season was in 1989 when he won the Senior TPC and the US Senior Open. His last official win was in 1992 when he defeated Bob Betley at the eighth play-off hole at the Franklin Quest Showdown Classic. He is known as 'Sarge' on Tour.

2000 SEASON. Moody's best finish was T27 at the GTE Classic and the Gold Rush Classic.

Gil Morgan

US Seniors Tour

Born 25 September 1946
Place of Birth Wewoka, Oklahoma, USA
Year turned Professional 1972
Tour Ranking 4th

MAJORS VICTORIES
SENIOR PLAYERS CHAMPIONSHIP 1997, 1998
THE TRADITION 1997, 1998

TOUR VICTORIES
SENIOR TOUR: 16
1996 Ralphs Senior Classic
1997 Ameritech Senior Open, BellSouth Senior Classic, First of America Classic, Ralphs Senior Classic, Senior Tour Championship
1998 LG Championship, MasterCard Championship, Utah Showdown, Vantage Championship
1999 Comfort Classic, Kroger Senior Classic

2000 Comfort Classic, Emerald Coast Classic, The Instinet Classic
2001 ACE Group Classic

A qualified optometrist who has never practised, the quiet 'Doc' Morgan joined the US Senior Tour in 1996, having won seven times on the USPGA Tour and played in two Ryder Cups. He won his first tournament – Ralphs Senior Classic – 11 days after his 50th birthday, and in 1997 his five victories and 19 top-10s helped him to Rookie of the Year award. The following year he won another six titles and made over $2 million for the second year in succession. By the end of the 1999 season he had recorded 16 victories in his four years on the Senior Tour. Morgan is yet another example of a steady if not spectacular career on the PGA Tour flourishing in the Seniors.

2000 SEASON. Although Morgan did not play on Tour until May owing to a rib injury, he still managed to win three tournaments and post 15 top-5s. He beat close rival Larry Nelson by four strokes at the Emerald Coast Classic, set a record 17 under par 199 when winning the Instinet Classic and claimed the rain-shortened Comfort Classic. He also put together 31 consecutive sub-par rounds. He ended the season in fourth position on the Money List.

2001 STOP PRESS. Morgan claimed his 20th Senior Tour title by winning the ACE Group Classic, two strokes ahead of Dana Quigley. He also lost a marathon nine-hole play-off to Spaniard Jose Canizares at the Toshiba Senior Classic.

John Morgan

US Seniors Tour

Born 3 September 1943
Place of Birth Oxford, England
Year turned Professional 1968
Tour Ranking 54th

TOUR VICTORIES

SENIOR TOUR: 8

- **1994** Forte PGA Seniors, Lawrence Batley Seniors, Northern Electric Seniors
- **1995** Forte PGA Seniors
- **1996** Motor City Seniors Classic, Scottish Seniors Open
- **1998** West of Ireland Seniors Championship
- **1999** AIB Irish Seniors Open

Long-hitting Englishman Morgan won six times on the European Seniors Tour between 1994 and 1996, finishing with one first and two second places on the Order of Merit. He joined the US Seniors Tour in 1997, but despite his success in Europe has yet to win a title on American soil.

Walter Morgan

US Seniors Tour

Born 31 May 1941
Place of Birth Haddock, Georgia, USA
Year turned Professional 1991
Tour Ranking 55th

TOUR VICTORIES

SENIOR TOUR: 3

- **1995** GTE Northwestern Classic
- **1996** Ameritech Senior Open, FHP Health Care Classic

Morgan, a self-taught player who took up golf at the late age of 29, spent 20 years in the US Army before becoming a club pro in Texas. After turning pro in 1991, he played on the US Senior Tour as partially exempt and through open qualification, but he gained full exemption in 1994, by finishing second at Qualifying School. He won the GTE Northwestern Classic in 1995 and was voted Comeback Player of the Year. He won two more events in 1996, earned $850,000 and was tenth on the Money List, but by 1998 he had fallen out of the top-31. Morgan has seven grandchildren and enjoys fishing and working in his garden when not competing on Tour.

2000 SEASON. Morgan played at least 35 events for the sixth consecutive year and had three top-10s to finish in 55th place.

David Morland IV

US Tour

Born 3 April 1969
Place of Birth North Bay, Ontario
Year turned Professional 1991
Tour Ranking Tied 2nd (Qualifying School)

Morland was a member of the Canadian Tour from 1992 until 1999, finishing sixth on the Order of Merit in 1999. He qualified for the US Tour through Qualifying School and played in the 2000 Tour, taking the 156th position, and qualified for the 2001 season tied for second place at Qualifying School. His best finish on Tour is T10 at the NCR Disney Classic. He is one of only four Canadians on the US Tour.

Joanne Morley

US Ladies Tour

Born 30 December 1966
Place of Birth Sale, England
Year turned Professional 1993
Tour Ranking 40th

TOUR VICTORIES
EUROPEAN: 2
    1996 German Ladies Open
    2000 German Ladies Open

SOLHEIM CUP 1996

Englishe Strokeplay Champion in 1992, Morley joined the European Tour the following year. In 1996 she won the German Open and qualified at T15 through the LPGA Qualifying School. In 1999 she had her then-best finish, T7, at the First Union Betsy King Classic. She played in the 1996 Solheim Cup.

2000 SEASON. Morley was third at the Cup Noodles Hawaiian Open, her LPGA career-best finish and she posted eight top-20s. On the European Tour she won her second German Open, leading wire-to-wire and beating Raquel Carriedo by two strokes.

Jarrod Moseley
European Tour

Born 6 October 1972
Place of Birth Perth, Australia
Year turned Professional 1997
Tour Ranking 77th

BEST FINISH IN MAJORS
Tied 42nd BRITISH OPEN 2000

TOUR VICTORIES
EUROPEAN: 1
    1999 Heineken Classic

Western Australian Moseley won the 1998 Australasian Qualifying school and topped the Order of Merit that season. He made an immediate impact on the European Tour in his first season, 1999. Benefiting from a sponsor's exemption, he came from behind to win the Heineken Classic, overtaking Ernie Els on the last round, and he achieved three other top-3 finishes. He ended the season a remarkable 16th on the Order of Merit.

2000 SEASON. Almost inevitably, Moseley could not match his electrifying first season on Tour and he ended the year 77th on the Order of Merit. He had only three top-20 finishes, his best being T8 in the Canon European Masters.

Mark Mouland
European Tour

Born 23 April 1961
Place of Birth St Athan, Wales
Year turned Professional 1981
Tour Ranking 26th (Qualifying School)

TOUR VICTORIES
EUROPEAN: 2
    1986 Car Care Plan International
    1988 KLM Dutch Open

Mouland turned professional in 1981, five years after he had won the British Boys Championship. He won his first European Tour event, the Car Care Plan International, in 1986 and had a bad car crash later that year, breaking a foot and ankle. Having recovered from the accident, he won again – at the Dutch Open – in 1988. He lost his European Tour card in 1999 and retained it at Qualifying School, going on to finish 11th at the 2000 Dutch Open. He went back to Qualifying School in 2000 and his 26th-finish ensured his Tour status in 2001.

Barb Mucha
US Ladies Tour

Born 1 December 1961
Place of Birth Parma Heights, Ohio, USA
Year turned Professional 1985
Tour Ranking 62nd

TOUR VICTORIES
US: 5
    1990 Boston Five Classic
    1992 Oldsmobile Classic

1994 State Farm Rail Classic
1996 Chick-fil-A Championship
1998 Sara Lee Classic

Mucha played on the Futures Tour, winning six titles, and arrived on the LPGA Tour in 1986. She won five titles in the 1990s, her last being the Sara Lee Classic in 1998 which she claimed after a play-off. In 1999 she shot 62 at the Chick-fil-A Charity Championship.

2000 SEASON. Mucha passed the $2 million career earnings mark, recording five top-20 finishes.

Michael Muehr

US Tour

Born 18 December 1971
Place of Birth Livingston, New Jersey, USA
Year turned Professional 1994
Tour Ranking Tied 21st (Qualifying School)

BEST FINISH IN MAJORS
Missed Cut US OPEN 1995

Muehr played only six tournaments on the US Tour and spent 1997 until 2000 competing on the Nike/Buy.Com Tour. He qualified for the 2001 US Tour season by finishing in 21st place at the Qualifying School. His highest finish to date is T42 at the 1998 Kemper Open.

Alison Munt

European Ladies Tour

Born 21 October 1965
Place of Birth Cairns, Australia
Year turned Professional 1988
Tour Ranking 7th

TOUR VICTORIES
EUROPEAN: 2
2000 Hanover Ladies Open, Marrakesh Palmeraie Open

Australian Munt joined the European Ladies Tour in 1991, but it took her a while to find her feet. Her best finish to date came in 1999, where she finsihed third in the Air France Open. An experienced and well-travelled golfer, she has also played on the US and Asian Ladies Tours.

2000 SEASON. Munt enjoyed her best season since turning pro when she won her first tournament, at the Hanover Ladies Open, beating Valerie Van Ryckeghem by one stroke in gale-force conditions. She followed this up with another impressive victory at the Marrakesh Palmaeraie Open, in Morrocco. She had three other top-20s and finished the season in seventh place on the Money List.

Rolf Muntz

European Tour

Born 26 March 1969
Place of Birth Voorschoten, Holland
Year turned Professional 1993
Tour Ranking 55th

BEST FINISH IN MAJORS
Missed Cut BRITISH OPEN 1990,1991

TOUR VICTORIES
EUROPEAN: 1
2000 Qatar Masters

WORLD CUP 1999

Tall and powerful, Dutch-born Muntz was British Amateur Champion in 1990. He left law school in Holland and turned professional in 1993 and has played consistently on the European Tour since 1994. His best finish prior to 2000 was second in the 1999 Scottish PGA Championship after a sudden-death play-off.

2000 SEASON. This was Muntz's best season to date. He claimed the Qatar Masters by an impressive five strokes ahead of former Masters champion Ian Woosnam and, in doing so, became the first Dutchman to win a title on the modern PGA Tour. He then suffered a backlash, missing six successive cuts until he bounced back to top form again, finishing in third place in the Irish Open. His winnings moved him from 100th to 58th in the Order of Merit.

Bob Murphy
US Seniors Tour

Born 14 February 1943
Place of Birth Brooklyn, New York, USA
Year turned Professional 1967
Tour Ranking 30th

TOUR VICTORIES
SENIOR TOUR: 11
- 1993 Bruno's Memorial Classic, GTE Northwest Classic
- 1994 Maui Kaanapali Classic, Rayley's Gold Rush Classic
- 1995 IntelliNet Challenge, Nationwide Championship, PaineWebber Invitational, Senior Championship
- 1996 Cadillac NFL Golf Classic, Royal Caribbean Golf Classic
- 1997 Toshiba Senior Classic

After winning five times on the USPGA Tour and enjoying a spell as an ESPN broadcaster, the jovial, Brooklyn-born Murphy joined the US Senior Tour in 1993. His fine short game and excellent putting brought him two wins on his debut season and eighth spot on the Money List. That year he became the first player to be voted Rookie of the Year on both the USPGA (1969) and US Senior Tour. The following two years saw him collect $2 million and six more victories. He won his last competition in 1997 when, at the Toshiba Senior Classic, he and Jay Sigel ground out the longest play-off in Senior history, Murphy finally prevailing with an 85-foot birdie putt at the ninth extra hole. Thereafter, Murphy's game fell away and in 1999 he was out of the

top-31 for the first time in his career. He can be easily identified by the curious pause at the top of his backswing.

2000 SEASON. Murphy's NBC commentary commitments cut the number of events he played to 26, but he still enjoyed his best season since 1997. Six top-10s and a T2 at the Instinet Classic, and his fourth position on the Putting statistics, helped him move to 30th in the Money List.

Gary Murphy
European Tour

Born 15 October 1972
Place of Birth Kilkenny, Ireland
Year turned Professional 1995
Tour Ranking 136th

Big Irishman Murphy won the Irish Amateur Championship in 1992 at the age of 19 and played on the Asian Tour from 1997 to 1999. He qualified for the 2000 European Tour through Qualifying School.

2000 SEASON. His best finish was T7 at the North West of Ireland Open and he ended the year in 136th place on the Order of Merit.

Sean Murphy
US Tour

Born 17 August 1965
Place of Birth Des Moines, Iowa, USA
Year turned Professional 1988
Tour Ranking Tied 18th (Qualifying School)

Murphy spent the 1990s alternating between the USPGA Tour and the Nike Tour, where he won four events in 1993.

2000 SEASON. Murphy's highest-ever finish of T5 at the Michelob Championship helped him to his best-ever position – 130th – on the Money List. He qualified for 2001 by finishing T18 at Qualifying School.

and 1987. In his US Senior debut year of 1998 the Vietnam vet was unstoppable, finding enough time to win three events and lose two sudden-death play-offs, depsite being absent for two months in the summer with a neck injury. The following year saw him pick up two more tournament wins.

Larry Nelson

US Seniors Tour

Born 10 September 1947
Place of Birth Fort Payne, Alabama, USA
Year turned Professional 1971
Tour Ranking 1st

TOUR VICTORIES

SENIOR TOUR: 13

1998 Amex Invitational, Boone Valley Classic, Pittsburgh Senior Classic
1999 Bruno's Memorial Classic, GTE Classic
2000 Bank One Senior Championship, Boone Valley Classic, FleetBoston Classic, Foremost Insurance Championship, Las Vegas Senior Classic, Vantage Championship
2001 MasterCard Championship, Royal Caribbean Classic

A slight, balding figure, Nelson is one of the most successful players in the history of the US Senior Tour with a reputation for ruthlessly closing out tournaments when he has a chance to win. The holder of seven USPGA titles and a successful competitor in three Ryder Cups (where he won all nine of the matches he played), he has also won three Majors. In the 1983 US Open he shot a third round 65 to overhaul Tom Watson and he also won the USPGA Championship in 1981

2000 SEASON. Nelson swept all before him, ending the season as Player of the Year and collecting a cool $2.7 million. He won six times, with four of those victories coming in the last eight events. He was also runner-up an amazing seven times. He began his winning streak with a record 19 under par 197 at the Las Vegas Senior Classic, five ahead of Bruce Fleisher and Hale Irwin, and ended with a sixth-hole sudden-death play-off win over fellow Senior Tour star Gil Morgan and the big-hitting Jim Dent at the Vantage Championship. He also set a Senior Tour record of 32 consecutive par or better rounds. Unsurprisingly, Nelson, who first hit a golf ball at the age of 21, finished top of the Money List.

2001 STOP PRESS. Nelson once again began the season in unstoppable form, winning the first two tournaments on the schedule. He took the MasterCard Championship, beating Jim Thorpe by one stroke, and then the Royal Caribbean Classic, one shot ahead of Japan's Isao Aoki.

Liselotte Neumann
US Ladies Tour

Born 20 May 1966
Place of Birth Finspang, Sweden
Year turned Professional 1984
Tour Ranking 48th

MAJORS VICTORIES
US OPEN 1988

TOUR VICTORIES
US: 8
- 1991 Mazda Japan Classic
- 1994 Heartland Classic, Minnesota Classic
- 1996 Chrysler-Plymouth Tournament of Champions, Edina Realty LPGA Classic, Ping Welch's Championship
- 1998 Chick-fil-A Charity Championship, Standard Register Ping

EUROPEAN: 11
- 1985 Hoganas Open, IBM European Open
- 1986 BMW German Open
- 1987 Letting French Open
- 1988 BMW German Open
- 1991 IBM Open
- 1993 Hennessy Cup
- 1994 British Women's Open, Hennessy Cup, Trygg Hansa Open
- 1995 Trygg Hansa Open

AUSTRALASIAN: 1
- 1995 Australian Open

OTHER: 4
- 1987 Singapore Open
- 1992 World Team Championship
- 1997 Takara World Invitational, Toray Japan Queen's Cup

SOLHEIM CUP 1990, 1992, 1994, 1996, 1998, 2000

A supremely composed and consistent player, 'Lotta' Neumann has won 25 tournaments worldwide during her 15-year career. A role model to a generation of Swedish players, Neumann enjoyed a successful amateur career and joined the Euro-pean Tour in 1985. She was second on the Order of Merit in 1986. She joined the LPGA Tour in 1988 and won the US Women's Open, defeating Patty Sheehan, to become Rookie of the Year. She has won nine times on the US Tour, lifting three titles in 1996 alone, and her 11 wins on the European Tour include the Weetabix Women's British Open in 1994. Neumann has played in every Solheim Cup.

2000 SEASON. Neumann had four top-20s in the US and finished T2 at the Weetabix British Women's Open. She passed $4 million in career earnings.

Alison Nicholas
US Ladies Tour

Born 6 March 1962
Place of Birth Gibraltar
Year turned Professional 1984
Tour Ranking 43rd

MAJORS VICTORIES
US OPEN 1997

TOUR VICTORIES
US: 3
- 1995 Corning Classic, Ping AT&T LPGA Golf Championship
- 1999 Hawaiian Open

EUROPEAN: 12

1987 British Women's Open, Laing Charity Classic

1988 British Olivetti Tournament, Guernsey Open, Variety Club Celebrity Classic

1989 German Open, Gislaved Open, Qualitair Classic

1990 Variety Club Celebrity Classic

1992 AGF Open de Paris

1995 Scottish Women's Open

1996 Guardian Irish Open

AUSTRALASIAN: 2

1992 Malaysian Open, Western Australia Open

SOLHEIM CUP 1990, 1992, 1994, 1996, 1998, 2000

At five foot nothing the smallest player on the European and LPGA Tours, Gibraltar-born Nicholas has compensated for her lack of inches by winning 16 tournaments, including the US Open. A noted amateur player, she joined the European Tour in 1984 and in 1987 won her first event, the Weetabix Women's British Open by one stroke from Laura Davies. By the time she arrived on the LPGA Tour in 1989 she had collected a further seven titles, and in 1995 she won twice on the US circuit. She picked up her first Majors victory at the US Women's Open in 1997 when she shot a record 10 under par 274, and headed the European Order of Merit. In 1999 she had her fourth US win, the Hawaiian Open. Nicholas has played in every Solheim Cup team, and famously beat Patty Sheehan in the 1994 singles match. The tough little Nicholas is an expert putter.

2000 SEASON. Nicholas' highest finish was T3 at the Philips Invitational. She led the LPGA Tour statistics for sand saves. On the European Ladies Tour, Nicholas played in eight tournaments and finished in the top-10 six times. Her highest place was T3 at the British Masters.

Gary Nicklaus

US Tour

Born 15 January 1969
Place of Birth West Palm Beach, Florida, USA
Year turned Professional 1991
Tour Ranking 119th

BEST FINISH IN MAJORS
Missed Cut **US OPEN 1997**

Having as your dad one of the most illustrious figures in the history of golf must give rise to unrealistic expectations. Gary, however, finally came closer to making his own name in the sport when he qualified for the 2000 US Tour on his ninth attempt, finishing T12 at the Qualifying School. He did not particularly shine on Tour, however, making the cut in his first tournament as an exempt player at the Sony Open, but shooting a 12 on one hole on the last round. However, he managed to retain his card after losing a sudden-death play-off with Phil Mickelson, in the rain-shortened Bell-South Classic and winning over $300,000 in the process. He was also placed T25 in his father's tournament, the Memorial at Muirfield Village, Ohio, and was 119th on the Money List. He played on the European Tour in 1998.

Jack Nicklaus

US Seniors Tour

Born 21 January 1940
Place of Birth Columbus, Ohio, USA
Year turned Professional 1961
Tour Ranking 55th

MAJORS VICTORIES

PGA SENIORS CHAMPIONSHIP 1991
SENIOR PLAYERS CHAMPIONSHIP 1990
THE TRADITION 1990, 1991, 1995, 1996
US SENIOR OPEN 1991, 1993

TOUR VICTORIES

SENIOR TOUR: 2
1994 Mercedes Championship
1996 GTE Suncoast Classic

Nicklaus, 'the Golden Bear', is regarded as the finest golfer ever to have played the game, and along with Arnold Palmer and Gary Player, he was one of the 'Big Three' in the sport in the 1960s. His long, accurate iron play, his ability to hit the precisely-judged percentage shot and his peerless putting have won him 18 professional majors – more than anyone else in the history of golf. Since reducing his playing commitments in the past 15 years or so, Nicklaus has also developed a reputation as one of the world's best golf course designers.

Twice US Amateur Champion, he burst onto the pro golfing scene with a play-off victory over Arnold Palmer in the 1962 US Open. In 1963, after Nicklaus had won the USPGA and The Masters, the legendary Bobby Jones was prompted to remark that 'he plays a game with which I am not familiar'.

In 1965, he won The Masters again, beating Ben Hogan's record score by three strokes, and his period of dominance in world golf began. His supremacy was virtually unchallenged until the arrival of a young Tom Watson in the late 1970s, although he did win his fourth US Open and his fifth USPGA titles in 1980. Perhaps his most magnificent achievement was in 1986 when, as a 46-year-old, he came

from behind to reclaim The Masters title at Augusta, shooting a last round 65 to defeat Tom Kite and Greg Norman by one stroke. Nicklaus was voted USPGA Player of the Year on five occasions, and played five times in the Ryder Cup.

He joined the US Senior Tour in 1990, entering only four events but winning two, and shot a record 27 under par 261 at the Tournament Senior Players Championship. The following year he won three Majors, beating Bruce Crampton by six strokes in the PGA and overcoming Chi Chi Rodriguez in an 18-hole play-off at the Senior Open. Throughout the 1990s he continued to play only a few events each year, but he won the Senior Open again in 1993, and in 1996 he won the Tradition for the fourth time. He underwent hip replacement surgery in 1999 and played only three tournaments. He has won ten times on the US Senior Tour.

2000 SEASON. He played three tournaments and his best finish was T9 at the Tradition. He continues to host the Memorial tournament on the USPGA Tour and he runs a global golf design and architecture business.

2001 STOP PRESS. Nicklaus finished fourth at the Siebel Classic, his highest finish since his T2 at the 1997 PGA Senior Championship.

Catrin Nilsmark

US Ladies Tour

Born 30 August 1967
Place of Birth Gothenburg, Sweden
Year turned Professional 1987
Tour Ranking 88th

TOUR VICTORIES

US: 1
1999 Valley of the Stars Championship
EUROPEAN: 2
1994 Ford Golf Classic
1999 Evian Masters

SOLHEIM CUP 1992, 1994, 1996, 1998, 2000

The tall and stylish Swede joined the European Tour in 1989 after a successful amateur career. She qualified for the LPGA Tour in 1994 through the Qualifying School, having won her first European title, the Ford Golf Classic. In 1999 Nilsmark won her first US tournament – the Valley of the Stars Championship – beating fellow Swede Annika Sorenstam on the first sudden-death play-off hole, and followed this up with her second win on the European Tour, the Evian Masters. She also finished second on the European Order of Merit that season. Nilsmark has played on every Solheim Cup since 1992 and she sunk the putt that year which won the trophy for Europe.

2000 SEASON. Her best finish on the LPGA Tour was T3 at the Subaru Memorial of Naples. On the European Tour Nilsmark played only three tournaments but finished in the top-5 in all three. She won all three of her matches in the Solheim Cup.

Frank Nobilo

US Tour

Born 14 May 1960
Place of Birth Auckland, New Zealand
Year turned Professional 1979
Tour Ranking T18th (Qualifying School)

BEST FINISH IN MAJORS
4th US MASTERS 1996

TOUR VICTORIES
US: 1
1997 Greater Greensboro Classic
EUROPEAN: 7
1988 PLM Open
1991 Trophee Lancome
1993 Turespana Open Mediterrania
1995 BMW International Open, Sarazen World Open
1996 Deutsche Bank Open – TPC, Sarazen World Open
AUSTRALASIAN: 3
1982 NSW PGA Championship
1985 New Zealand PGA Championship
1987 New Zealand PGA Championship
OTHER: 3
1994 Indonesian Open
1997 Hong Kong Open, Mexican Open

DUNHILL CUP 1985, 1986, 1987, 1989, 1990, 1992, 1993, 1994, 1995, 1996, 1997, 1998
PRESIDENTS CUP 1998
WORLD CUP 1982, 1987, 1988, 1990, 1991, 1992, 1993, 1994, 1995, 1998, 1999

The direct descendant of an Italian pirate, bearded New Zealander Nobilo is easily identifiable on the golf course. He joined the European Tour in 1986 and his elegant swing brought him seven Tour victories between 1988 and 1996, his last regular season on the European Tour. In that period he was never out of the Order of Merit top-40 and was a regular contender in the Majors. After qualifying for the US Tour in 1995, he moved to Orlando, Florida, where he lives next door to Ernie Els at the exclusive Lake Nona Golf Club. He played eight events on the US Tour in 1996, and claimed fourth place at the Masters, and in 1997 he won the Greater Greensboro Classic, beating Brad Faxon on the first play-off hole. He reached his highest-ever US placing – 23rd – that season. In the following two years, however, he could not break into the top-100.

2000 SEASON. Nobilo made 20 out of his 28 cuts, but could only finish in 152nd place on the Money List. He regained his US Tour card with a T18th spot at Qualifying School.

Greg Norman

US Tour

Born 10 February 1955
Place of Birth Mt Isa, Australia
Year turned Professional 1976
Tour Ranking 84th

MAJORS VICTORIES
BRITISH OPEN 1986, 1993

TOUR VICTORIES

US: 19

1982 State Express Classic
1984 Canadian Open, Kemper Open
1986 Kemper Open, Las Vegas Invitational
1988 MCI Heritage Classic
1989 Greater Milwaukee Open,
The International
1990 Doral-Ryder Open, The Memorial
Tournament
1992 Canadian Open
1993 Doral-Ryder Open
1994 The Players Championship
1995 Canon Greater Hartford Open,
NEC World Series of Golf,
The Memorial Tournament
1996 Doral-Ryder Open
1997 FedEx St Jude Classic, NEC World
Series of Golf

EUROPEAN: 16

1977 Martini International
1979 Martini International
1980 French Open, Scandinavian
Open, Suntory World Match Play
Championship
1981 Dunlop Masters, Martini International
1982 Benson & Hedges International,
Dunlop Masters, State Express Classic
1983 Cannes Invitational, Suntory World
Match Play Championship
1986 European Open, Suntory World
Match Play Championship
1988 Lancia Italian Open
1994 Johnnie Walker Asian Classic

AUSTRALASIAN: 32

1976 West Lakes Classic
1978 New South Wales Open, Sydney
Open, Traralgon Classic
1979 Traralgon Classic
1980 Australian Open
1981 Australian Masters
1983 Australian Masters,
New South Wales Open,
Queensland Open
1984 Australian Masters, Australian PGA
Championship, Victorian Open
1985 Australian Open, Australian PGA
Championship
1986 New South Wales Open,
Queensland Open, South Australian
Open, Western Australian Open
1987 Australian Masters, Australian Open
1988 Australian Players Championship,
ESP Open, New South Wales Open,
Palm Meadows Cup
1989 Australian Masters, Australian
Players Championship
1990 Australian Masters
1995 Australian Open
1996 Australian Open, South Australian
Open
1998 Greg Norman Holden International

OTHER: 6

1977 Kuzuhz International
1978 South Seas Classic
1979 Hong Kong Open
1983 Hong Kong Open
1989 Chunichi Crowns
1993 Taiheyo Masters

DUNHILL CUP 1985, 1986, 1987, 1988, 1989,
1990, 1992, 1994, 1995, 1996
PRESIDENTS CUP 1994, 1996, 1998, 2000

The 'Great White Shark' has been one of golf's dominant players over the last 20 years. The tall, powerful Queenslander has won over 70 tournaments worldwide and has three times topped the US Tour Money List, but he has only managed to collect two Major titles. Through a combination of bad luck and an apparent tendency to struggle under pressure, Norman has lost his lead in a number of Majors and should have won substantially more than a brace. He won his first title in dreadful conditions at the British Open at Turnberry in 1986 when he shot a magnificent final round 63 to beat Gordon Brand by five strokes. At the USPGA Championship the following month, Norman lost at the final hole when Bob Tway chipped in from a bunker. He was third round leader at all four Majors in 1986.

In 1987 he came second in The Masters, defeated at the second play-off hole by Larry Mize's fluke chip-in from 40 yards off the green. He picked up his second British Open title in 1993 at Royal St George, shooting a last round 64 for the lowest score in the history of the Open. His capacity to throw away a seemingly impregnable lead was graphically and sensationally demonstrated at The Masters in 1996. Having equalled the course record of 63 in the first round, and six shots ahead at the beginning of the final round, Norman collapsed in the face of Nick Faldo's relentless and accurate shot-making and eventually lost to the Englishman by five strokes.

Norman's tournament victories have made him a millionaire many times over, and he was the first player to pass $10 million in earnings. He has many outside commercial interests, including golf course design, golf club manufacture, turf growing and clothing, and he was the principal exponent in the mid-1990s of a World Tour. He continues to compete regularly on the Australasian and US Tours, and hosts his own Australasian Tour event, the Greg Norman Holden International, which he won in 1998. He also hosts the Franklin Templeton Shootout, an unofficial PGA event which raises money for charity.

2000 SEASON. After recovering from surgery, he only made 12 starts on the US Tour and came fourth at the Buick Classic and The International. He was one of the torch bearers in Sydney at the Olympic games, and he received honorary life membership of the European Tour.

Andy North
US Seniors Tour

Born 9 March 1950
Place of Birth Thorpe, Wisconsin, USA
Year turned Professional 1972
Tour Ranking 57th

The 6 foot 4 inch North had only one win on the USPGA Tour but he won the US Open twice. In 1978 he outpaced JC Snead and Dave Stockton by one stroke, and in 1985 he defeated Dave Barr and TC Chen by the same margin. He also played in the 1985 Ryder Cup. An analyst with ESPN TV, he joined the US Senior Tour in 2000, carding three top-10s with his best finish T6 at The Tradition and Bruno's Memorial Classic.

2001 STOP PRESS. North lost at the first play-off hole to Mike McCullough at the Emerald Gold Coast Classic.

Per Nyman
European Tour

Born 14 February 1968
Place of Birth Kristianstad, Sweden
Year turned Professional 1993
Tour Ranking 150th

BEST FINISH IN MAJORS
Missed Cut **BRITISH OPEN 1999**

Nyman joined the 1999 European Tour by virtue of his second spot on the Challenge Tour. He retained his card for 2000, achieving his highest finish, fifth at the Scottish PGA Championship.

2000 SEASON. With his top placing of T19 at the Qatar Masters, Nyman finished in 150th spot on the Order of Merit.

Henrik Nystrom
European Tour

Born 23 April 1969
Place of Birth Stockholm, Sweden
Year turned Professional 1994
Tour Ranking 108th

Nystrom had to return to Qualifying School twice, in 1998 and 1999, his first two years on the European Tour. He had an unremarkable and unprofitable two years.

2000 SEASON. His form showed a significant turn for the better in 2000. He had three top-20 finishes and achieved his highest-ever placing when he finished in second place behind fellow Swede Pierre Fulke at the Scottish PGA. He is ranked high (22nd) in driving accuracy.

Christy O'Connor Jr

US Seniors Tour

Born 19 August 1948
Place of Birth Galway, Ireland
Year turned Professional 1967
Tour Ranking 50th

TOUR VICTORIES

SENIOR TOUR: 4

1999 Foremost Insurance Championship, Senior British Open, State Farm Senior Classic
2000 Senior British Open

Chrisy O'Connor Jr joined the US Senior Tour from the Senior European Tour in 1999. He has won four times on the European PGA Tour and played on two Ryder Cups, and many still remember his courageous 2-iron shot to the 18th at the Belfry in 1989. Fred Couples had laid up short of the treacherous par-4 closing hole and O'Connor's strike ended four foot from the pin. The win was decisive for Europe. He won twice in his debut season, beating Bruce Fleisher by one shot at the State Farm Senior Classic, and picked up the Foremost Insurance Classic by a four-stroke margin. He also won the Senior British Open, dedicating the victory to his 17-year-old son Darren who had died in a car accident the previous year.

2000 SEASON. He successfully defended the Senior British Open, beating John Bland by two strokes. He was T8 in the US Senior Open and 50th on the Money List. O'Connor Jr was also 13th on the European Senior Order of Merit.

Nick O'Hern

European Tour

Born 18 October 1971
Place of Birth Perth, Australia
Year turned Professional 1994
Tour Ranking 42nd

BEST FINISH IN MAJORS

Tied 41st **BRITISH OPEN 2000**

TOUR VICTORIES

AUSTRALASIAN: 1

2000 Coolum Classic

DUNHILL CUP 2000

Naturally right handed, Australian O'Hern plays golf left handed (somewhat similar to Phil Mickelson). He is a consistent, accurate player who made his name in the 1997 Australasian Open – his rookie year – when he came fifth. He won the Coolum Classic on the Australasian Tour in 2000 and joined the European Tour. He had three top-10 finishes, his best being T5 in the Wales Open, and ended the season 42nd on the Order of Merit. He is 16th on the Tour for driving accuracy, but only 173rd for distance. He is a solid putter and is clearly going to win a tournament soon. He made his debut in the Dunhill Cup, winning all his matches.

but 153rd for distance. On the Australasian Tour he finished in the top-10 of the Order of Merit for the sixth successive season, his best placing being T3 at the Ericsson Masters.

2001 STOP PRESS. O'Malley won the Compass Group English Open coming from five shots off the pace to finish with a 66.

Peter O'Malley
European Tour

Born 23 June 1965
Place of Birth Bathurst, Australia
Year turned Professional 1987
Tour Ranking 47th

BEST FINISH IN MAJORS
Tied 7th **BRITISH OPEN 1997**

TOUR VICTORIES
EUROPEAN: 2
1992 Bell's Scottish Open
1995 Benson &Hedges International Open
AUSTRALASIAN: 2
1995 New Zealand Open
1998 Canon Challenge

DUNHILL CUP 1999, 2000
WORLD CUP 1992, 1998

An accurate player but short off the tee, Australian O'Malley joined the European Tour in 1989. A former Australian Rookie of the Year, he won his first tournament in 1992, overtaking Colin Montgomerie on the last five holes to win the Scottish PGA. In 1995 he claimed the Benson & Hedges International Open, and ended the season tenth on the Order of Merit, but he has not won on the European Tour since. He played in the 1999 Dunhill Cup when Australia were defeated by Spain in the final.

2000 SEASON. O'Malley posted four European Tour top-10s, his highest being T7 in the French Open and the Volvo PGA, and a further five top-20s. He was seventh for driving accuracy

Mark O'Meara
US Tour

Born 13 January 1957
Place of Birth Goldsboro, North Carolina, USA
Year turned Professional 1980
Tour Ranking 112th

MAJORS VICTORIES
US MASTERS 1998
BRITISH OPEN 1998

TOUR VICTORIES
US: 14
1984 Greater Milwaukee Open
1985 Bing Crosby Pro-Am, Hawaiian Open
1989 AT&T Pebble Beach National Pro-Am
1990 AT&T Pebble Beach National Pro-Am, H-E-B Texas Open
1991 Walt Disney World/Oldsmobile Classic
1992 AT&T Pebble Beach National Pro-Am
1995 Bell Canadian Open, Honda Classic
1996 Greater Greensboro Chrysler Classic, Mercedes Championships
1997 AT&T Pebble Beach National Pro-Am, Buick Invitational
EUROPEAN: 2
1987 Lawrence Batley International
1997 Trophee Lancome
AUSTRALASIAN: 1
1986 Australian Masters
OTHER: 4
1985 Fuji Sankei Classic
1992 Tokai Classic
1994 Argentine World Open
1998 Cisco World Match Play

RYDER CUP 1985, 1989, 1991, 1997, 1999
DUNHILL CUP 1985, 1986, 1987, 1996, 1997, 1998, 1999
PRESIDENTS CUP 1996, 1998
WORLD CUP 1999

O'Meara is a veteran of the US Tour and one of the most successful golfers currently playing. In his 20 years on Tour he has claimed 14 victories, as well as tournament wins in Europe, Japan and Australia, and is the proud owner of two Majors titles. US Amateur Champion in 1979, he was voted Rookie of the Year in 1981 and won his first event – the Greater Milwaukee Open – in 1984. Between then and 1999 he was consistently in the top-50 on the Money List (with the exception of 1994). His greatest season was 1998. First he won The Masters, scoring birdies on the last two holes, including a winning 20-foot putt on the 72nd, to avoid a play-off with Fred Couples and David Duval. Next he claimed the British Open, beating Brian Watts in a four-hole play-off and became the first player to win two Majors in the same year since Nick Faldo in 1990. He rounded off that remarkable year with a one-hole win over his friend and neighbour Tiger Woods in the Cisco World Match Play Championship. With nine other top-10 finishes, he was voted PGA Tour Player of the Year. The following year was something of an anti-climax, and he slipped from seventh to 45th on the Money List.

2000 SEASON. O'Meara's highest finish was T9 in the Players Championship. He dropped out of the Money List top-100 for the first time since 1982.

Denis O'Sullivan
European Senior Tour

Born 11 March 1948
Place of Birth Cork, Ireland
Year turned Professional 1997
Tour Ranking 3rd

TOUR VICTORIES
SENIOR TOUR: 2
    2000 Abu Dhabi Championship, Senior Tournament of Champions

Irish Amateur Champion in 1985, and seven times a member of the Irish team, O'Sullivan turned professional in 1997 and joined the European Senior Tour in 1998. He was runner-up three times and ended ninth on the Order of Merit in his rookie year.

2000 SEASON. The big Irishman shot three consecutive birdies on his last three holes at the Dan Technology Senior Tournament of Champions to win the event, one stroke ahead of Ross Metherell and Maurice Bembridge. He had his second win in succession at the Abu Dhabi Championship, shooting a 7 under par 65. He finished third on the Order of Merit.

David Oakley
European Senior Tour

Born 27 April 1945
Place of Birth Hemstead, New York, USA
Year turned Professional 1970
Tour Ranking 8th

TOUR VICTORIES
SENIOR TOUR: 2
    1999 MDIS&Partners Festival of Golf
    2000 De Vere Hotels Seniors Classic

American Oakley first came to prominence in the European Senior Tour when he was joint second to Brian Barnes in the 1998 Senior British Open. He ended the season fifth on the Order of Merit. He played again in 1998 and 1999, winning the MDIS&Partners Festival of Golf in the latter season wire-to-wire by six strokes. He was tenth on the Order of Merit.

2000 SEASON. Oakley won one event – the De Vere Hotels Senior Classic – shooting a new Senior Tour record 17 under par 196 to defeat Noel Ratcliffe by two shots. He finished eighth on the Order of Merit.

Vickie Odegard

US Ladies Tour

Born 13 February 1965
Place of Birth Fairmont, West Virginia, USA
Year turned Professional 1988
Tour Ranking 86th

Odegard was three-time winner and Player of the Year on the 1996 Futures Tour, and she qualified for the LPGA Tour as medallist at the Qualifying School. Her highest career finish is fourth at the ShopRite LPGA Classic.

2000 SEASON. Her best placing was T4 at the ShopRite LPGA Classic and she was 86th on the Money List.

Joe Ogilvie

US Tour

Born 8 April 1974
Place of Birth Lancaster, Ohio, USA
Year turned Professional 1996
Tour Ranking 92nd

BEST FINISH IN MAJORS
Tied 58th USPGA 2000

Ogilvie joined the US Tour from the Nike Tour in 1999 and, although he had two top-10 finishes, he ended the season 137th on the Money List. He qualified for 2000 by securing 24th place at Qualifying School.

2000 SEASON. It was a good year for Ogilvie. He retained his card by coming T4 at the Fedex St Jude Classic, two strokes behind Notah Begay and T6 in The International. He also had five other top-25 finishes.

Geoff Ogilvy

European Tour

Born 11 June 1977
Place of Birth Adelaide, Australia
Year turned Professional 1998
Tour Ranking 48th

BEST FINISH IN MAJORS
Missed Cut **BRITISH OPEN 2000**

Something of a temperamental player, the young Ogilvy was Rookie of the Year in 1998–9 on the Australasian Tour and joined the European Tour in 1999, where his best finish by far was T3 with American Bob May (runner-up to Tiger Woods in the 2000 USPGA Championship) at the popular Volvo Scandinavian Masters, when Ogilvy shot a 62 in the second round. The tall, powerfully-built Australian is a long hitter, but can be erratic off the tee.

2000 SEASON. He finished second in the season-opening Johnnie Walker Classic, in Thailand, one stroke behind Michael Campbell, and produced another top-10 finish when he was T6 at the Deutsche Bank Open, in Germany. He lost to Tiger Woods in the Johnnie Walker Classic at the beginning of the 2001 season (although the event actually took place in December 2000) despite shooting a 6 under par 30 on the back nine on the last round. He qualified for the 2001 US Tour from Qualifying School.

2001 STOP PRESS. Ogilvy had an impressive beginning to his rookie year on the US Tour. He finished runner-up to Jesper Parnevik at the Honda Classic and achieved two other top-3 appearances in his first five starts.

Jose Maria Olázàbal
European and US Tour

Born 5 February 1966
Place of Birth Fuenterrabia, Spain
Year turned Professional 1985
Tour Ranking 9th

MAJORS VICTORIES
US MASTERS 1994, 1999

TOUR VICTORIES
US: 3
- **1990** NEC World Series of Golf
- **1991** The International
- **1994** NEC World Series of Golf

EUROPEAN: 19
- **1986** European Masters, Sanyo Open, Swiss Open
- **1988** German Masters, Volvo Belgian Open
- **1989** KLM Dutch Open, Tenerife Open
- **1990** Benson & Hedges International Open, Carrolls Irish Open, Trophee Lancome
- **1991** Grand Prix of Europe, Open Catalonia
- **1992** Open Mediterrania, Turespana Open de Tenerife
- **1994** Turespana Open de Mediterrania, Volvo PGA Championship
- **1997** Turespana Masters
- **1998** Dubai Desert Classic
- **2000** Benson & Hedges International Open
- **2001** Novotel Perrier Open de France

OTHER: 2
- **1989** Visa Taiheiyo Masters
- **1990** Visa Taiheiyo Masters

RYDER CUP 1987, 1989, 1991, 1993, 1997, 1999
DUNHILL CUP 1986, 1987, 1988, 1989, 1992, 1993, 1998, 1999, 2000
WORLD CUP 1989, 2000

With a brilliant short game to match that of his friend Seve Ballesteros, and an exceptional iron player and putter, Olázàbal is one of Spain's finest ever golfers. British Boys, Youth and Amateur Champion (beating Colin Montogomerie in the 1984 competition), he turned pro in 1985 and was a three-time winner in his second year on the European Tour, claiming second place on the Order of Merit. Since then he has won 19 times on the European Tour. He has also won three events on the US Tour – the World Series of Golf in 1990 and 1999 and the 1991 International. In 1994, he won The Masters – beating Tom Lehman by two strokes. In 1995 Olázàbal was sidelined with an apparently degenerative rheumatoid condition in his feet and was virtually bed-ridden for 18 months before the condition was rectified. On his return to the European Tour he won a tournament – the Turespana Open – on his third start. In 1999, he won The Masters again. Olázàbal has played in six Ryder Cups and has had a highly successful partnership with Ballesteros in the competition, their pairing winning 11 out of their 15 matches.

2000 SEASON. Taking advantage of the disqualification of leader Padraig Harrington, Olázàbal shot a final round 66 to win the Benson & Hedges International. His best placing on the US Tour was T4 at the USPGA Championship and 12th at the US Open.

2001 STOP PRESS. Olázàbal shot a 12-under-par 268 to win the French Open

Andrew Oldcorn
European Tour

Born 31 March 1960
Place of Birth Bolton, England
Year turned Professional 1983
Tour Ranking 92nd

BEST FINISH IN MAJORS
Tied 63rd **BRITISH OPEN 1991**

TOUR VICTORIES
EUROPEAN: 3
- **1993** Turespana Masters
- **1995** DHL Jersey Open
- **2001** Volvo PGA Championship

Although Oldcorn won the English Amateur Championship in 1982, he has lived in Scotland virtually all his life. For golfing purposes he is regarded as a Scot. He is accurate but short off the tee, and before 2001 won two European Tour titles. He joined the Tour in 1984 and between 1993 and 1998 was consistently in the top-100 on the Order of Merit. He had a four-year struggle with ME in the early 1990s. In 1999 he had his worst season since 1992, finishing 110th.

2000 SEASON. Oldcorn's highest placing was fifth at the European Grand Prix, but he had only four other top-20 finishes. He was sixth for driving accuracy in the Tour statistics.

2001 STOP PRESS. Oldcorn turned in the performance of his career, winning the illustrious Volvo PGA Championship, holding off a resurgent Nick Faldo on the final day. Although the cheque for £330,000 was very welcome, the five-year exemption onto the Tour was even more valuable

Gary Orr

European Tour

Born 11 May 1967
Place of Birth Helensburgh, Scotland
Year turned Professional 1988
Tour Ranking 10th

BEST FINISH IN MAJORS
41st BRITISH OPEN 2000

TOUR VICTORIES
EUROPEAN: 2
  2000 Portuguese Open, Victor Chandler British Masters

DUNHILL CUP 1998, 1999, 2000

Ex-Scottish Boys Champion, Orr joined the European Tour from the Qualifying School in 1993 and won the Rookie of the Year award, finishing 30th in the Order of Merit. From 1993 through 1999 he failed to win a tournament but was runner-up twice – in 1998 he came second to Colin Montgomerie in the Volvo PGA and in 1999 he was beaten by one stroke by Lee Westwood in the Dutch Open. He ended 1999 in 21st place on the Order of Merit. He does not have a lot of length off the tee, but is one of the most accurate players on Tour and known as a solid ball-striker.

2000 SEASON. After working with renowned golf psychologist David Norman for several months, Orr's victory drought came to an abrupt end when he won two tournaments. At the Portuguese Open, his 12-foot eagle putt at the last hole after an errant tee shot was enough to relegate Welshman Philip Price into second place, and then he captured the British Masters title, shooting a course record 62 on the Friday at Woburn and beating Per Ulrik Johansson by two strokes. He rounded off his season by coming second to Padraig Harrington at the Turespana Masters. The tall Scot ended the season in tenth place on the Order of Merit, his highest-ever placing.

Hennie Otto

European Tour

Born 25 June 1976
Place of Birth Boksburg, South Africa
Year turned Professional 1997
Tour Ranking 28 (Qualifying School)

TOUR VICTORIES
SOUTH AFRICA: 2
  1999 Pieterburg Classic, Vodacom Series: Kwazul-Natal

Holder of two South African Tour titles, Otto won the Philips Challenge on the Challenge Tour in 1999, as well as achieving two runner-up places. He played on the European Tour in 2000, with his highest position being sixth at the Scottish PGA, and retained his 2001 card by coming through the end of season Qualifying School.

Greg Owen
European Tour

Born 19 February 1972
Place of Birth Mansfield, England
Year turned Professional 1992
Tour Ranking 39th

BEST FINISH IN MAJORS
Tied 55th **BRITISH OPEN 2000**

Owen is a towering, powerful golfer with a long and accurate drive but a less than reliable short game. He played on the European Tour in 1996 and 1998 and, in 1999 he retained his card with a fourth place at the Victor Chandler British Masters at Woburn (Chandler is also one of Owen's sponsors). He followed this up a week later with T3 at the Trophee Lancome, an event won by Pierre Fulke. He holds the course record at Royal Zoute, having shot 62 in the Belgacom Open in 1998.

2000 SEASON. Owen had ten top-20 finishes, his highest being T3 in the Sao Paulo Open. He moved from 64th to 39th in the Order of Merit. He finished the year in the top-20 for both driving distance and driving accuracy, but was 142nd for putting.

won 31 Japanese Tour events in his 20 years on the tour, he has yet to win in the US. He is short off the tee and is a wayward putter.

2000 SEASON. He just managed to retain his card, finishing 123rd on the Money List. His highest finish was a T6 in the Buick Open, some six strokes behind winner Rocco Mediate.

Naomichi 'Joe' Ozaki
US Tour

Born 18 May 1956
Place of Birth Tokushima, Japan
Year turned Professional 1977
Tour Ranking 123rd

BEST FINISH IN MAJORS
Tied 25th **US OPEN 1994**

PRESIDENTS CUP 1998

Younger brother of Japanese Tour superstar Jumbo, Joe entered the US Tour by virtue of a T6 at the Players Championship in 1993 and has played on Tour since. Although he has

at 20-years-old, to have won the Open, and equalled Juli Inkster's 1984 record of winning two Majors in a rookie year. She also claimed the Jamie Farr Kroger Classic (by nine clear strokes and shooting a then-record low round of 61) and then the Giant Eagle LPGA Classic that year. She romped away with the 1998 Rookie of the Year award and finished second on the Money List. She ran up another four victories in 1999 to confirm her status as one of the brightest stars of world golf.

Se Ri Pak

US Ladies Tour

Born 28 September 1977
Place of Birth Daejeon, South Korea
Year turned Professional 1996
Tour Ranking 12th

MAJORS VICTORIES
US OPEN 1998
LPGA 1998

TOUR VICTORIES
US: 7
1998 Giant Eagle Classic, Jamie Farr Kroger Classic
1999 Jamie Farr Kroger Classic, Page Net Championship, Samsung Western Championship, ShopRite LPGA Classic
2001 Longs Drugs Challenge, Your Life Vitamins LPGA Classic

2000 SEASON. Pak was without a win for the first season in her US career, but was T3 at the McDonald's LPGA Championship. Another ten top-10 finishes put her 12th on the Money List.
2001 STOP PRESS. Pak won the Longs Drugs Challenge and the Your Life Vitamins LPGA Classic.

A sporting superstar in South Korea, and hailed in the US as the female equivalent to Tiger Woods, 24-year-old Pak has enjoyed phenomenal success since arriving on the LPGA Tour in 1998. A seemingly nerveless, steely competitor, Pak qualified T1 at 1997 Qualifying School and won the LPGA Championship and then the US Women's Open, beating Jenny Chuasiriporn on a sudden death play-off. She became the youngest-ever player,

Arnold Palmer

US Seniors Tour

Born 10 September 1929
Place of Birth Latrobe Pennsylvania, USA
Year turned Professional 1954
Tour Ranking 122nd

MAJORS VICTORIES
PGA SENIORS CHAMPIONSHIP 1980, 1984
SENIOR PLAYERS CHAMPIONSHIP 1984, 1985
US SENIORS OPEN 1981

TOUR VICTORIES

SENIOR TOUR: 5

1982 Denver Post Champions of Golf,
Marlboro Classic
1983 Boca Grove Classic
1984 Quadel Senior Classic
1988 Crestar Classic

The aggressive, swashbuckling Palmer transformed the game of golf in the early 1960s. His arrival coincided with the dawn of the TV age and Palmer's exploits on the golf course made him a hero to millions of viewers and led to an explosion of interest in the sport. His swing was not a thing of beauty, but his swift takeaway and powerful follow-through made him the best driver of the age. He won 61 US Tour events in his career, and in his golden period between 1958 and 1964 he collected no fewer than seven Major titles, including the British Open twice in succession. He also won four Masters and the US Open in 1960 when, six shots behind at the beginning of the final round, he went out in 30 to see off the challenge of the amateur Jack Nicklaus. Adored by his legion of fans –'Arnie's Army' – Palmer was part of the legendary Triumvirate, along with Gary Player and Nicklaus, who ruled the game in the 1960s. Palmer played in six Ryder Cup competitions and was captain of the winning US team in 1975.

Palmer joined the US Senior Tour in 1980 and won his first tournament, the PGA Senior Championship. He followed this up the next year with his second Major, the US Senior Open. In 1984 he won two further Majors, beating Don January by two strokes in the PGA and finishing three ahead of Peter Thomson in the Senior Players Championship. His best year on Tour was in 1986 when he had six top-10 finishes and he picked up his last trophy in 1988. In 1994 he played his last US Open and in 1995 he made an emotional appearance at St Andrews for his 35th consecutive entry into the British Open. **2000 SEASON.** Palmer played in 14 events, his highest finish being T53 at the Vantage. He shot his age (70) for the second time in his career at the Novell Utah Showdown and shot one stroke below his age the following week at the FleetBoston Classic. Palmer hosts the Bay Hill Invitational on the USPGA Tour and is involved in golf course design and construction.

Rod Pampling
US Tour

Born 23 September, 1969
Place of Birth Queensland, Australia
Year turned Professional 1994
Tour Ranking 11th (Buy.Com Tour)

Pampling gained his PGA Tour card after finishing in the crucial 40th position in the Qualifying School. Consequently, he spends his time flitting back and forth between the Buy.Com Tour and the PGA Tour. His finest performance to date came at the 1999 British Open at Carnoustie, in Scotland, where he led the field after an opening round of 71. Between 1996 and 2000, Pampling competed on the Australasian Tour, where he performed consistently, making 37 out of 40 cuts. On the PGA Tour, in 1999, he posted his best finishes to date – 39th in both the Reno-Tahoe and the American Express WGC.

2000 SEASON. Pampling did not compete on the PGA Tour and played on the Buy.Com Tour instead. His best finishes were T20 in the Richmond Open and the Virginia Beach Open.

David Park
European Tour

Born 25 June 1974
Place of Birth London, England
Year turned Professional 1997
Tour Ranking 68th

BEST FINISH IN MAJORS
Missed Cut **BRITISH OPEN 1999**

TOUR VICTORIES
EUROPEAN: 1
  1999 Compaq European Grand Prix

DUNHILL CUP 2000
WORLD CUP 1999

Leading money winner on the 1998 Challenge Tour, Park had a sensational start to his rookie year on the 1999 European Tour. Two shots ahead of Miguel Angel Martin with three to play in the last round of the Moroccan Open, he shot two bogies and went to a play-off. After playing the 18th six times, Park finished in second place. The following week at the European Grand Prix, his par at the last hole ensured him victory over David Carter and his first trophy. He only made 15 starts that season but finished 40th in the Order of Merit.

2000 SEASON. This year was something of an anti-climax for Park. His best finish was fifth in the Greg Norman Holden International and he recorded four other top-20 placings. In his Dunhill Cup debut for Wales, he won two of his three matches to help Wales reach the semi-final, but he lost to Ernie Els by eight strokes and Wales were eliminated.

Champion in 1998 and was voted *Golf Week*'s and *Golf Digest*'s Player of the Year. After a season on the Futures Tour, where she won five out of her ten tournaments, Park joined the LPGA Tour in 2000.

2000 SEASON. Park confirmed her enormous potential by winning the inaugural Kathy Ireland Greens.com Classic, beating Tour veteran Juli Inkster by one stroke, and collecting four other top-10 places.

2001 STOP PRESS. Park won her second LPGA title, collecting the Office Depot Classic, one shot ahead of Australia's Karrie Webb, the world number one.

Grace Park
US Ladies Tour

Born 6 March 1979
Place of Birth Seoul, South Korea
Year turned Professional 1999
Tour Ranking 19th

TOUR VICTORIES
US: 2
  2000 Kathy Ireland Greens.com Classic
  2001 Office Depot Classic

Although only 5 feet 6 inches tall, Park is one of the LPGA Tour's longest drivers. Korean-born, she was US Women's Amateur

Kristal Parker
US Ladies Tour

Born 7 February 1965
Place of Birth Columbus, Ohio, USA
Year turned Professional 1987
Tour Ranking 84th

The 1982 Junior World Champion, Parker played on the Australasian and European Tours between 1991 and 1994. She joined the LPGA Tour in 1995 and her best finish is second at the 1996 Standard Register Ping.

2000 SEASON. She was fourth at the Kathy Ireland and had three other top-20s to finish 84th on the Money List.

Jesper Parnevik

US Tour

Born 3 July 1965
Place of Birth Stockholm, Sweden
Year turned Professional 1986
Tour Ranking 8th

BEST FINISH IN MAJORS
2nd BRITISH OPEN 1994, 1997

TOUR VICTORIES
US: 5
- 1998 Phoenix Open
- 1999 Greater Greensboro Classic
- 2000 Bob Hope Chrysler Classic, GTE Byron Nelson Classic
- 2001 Honda Classic

EUROPEAN: 4
- 1993 Bell's Scottish Open
- 1995 Volvo Scandinavian Masters
- 1996 Trophee Lancome
- 1998 Volvo Scandinavian Masters

RYDER CUP 1997, 1999
DUNHILL CUP 1993, 1994, 1995, 1997
WORLD CUP 1994, 1995

With his upturned cap, lean angular frame and often garish dress sense, the eccentric Parnevik is hard to miss on the golf course. He joined the European Tour in 1987 and became the first Swede to win on tour in his own country when he picked up the Scandinavian Masters in 1995. He has won three other tournaments on the European Tour. In 1995 he decided to play on the US Tour and came fourth in Qualifying School that year. He won his first US Tour event – the Phoenix Open – in 1998 and followed that up by winning the Greater Greensboro Classic in 1999. In the latter, he set a new course record of 23 under par at Forest Oaks, even though he only hit 12 fairways from the tee in the last two rounds. He had been disqualified from the previous event – the MCI Classic – for brushing away dirt on his putting line with his gloves. A conjurer and magician, he swears by the health-giving properties of volcanic dust.

He has twice been runner-up in the British Open. The first was in 1994 when Nick Price sunk a 65-foot putt at the 71st and Parnevik dropped a shot on the last hole. In 1997 he finished behind Justin Leonard at Troon, losing his lead on the last round to a scorching 65 from the Texan. In the 1999 Ryder Cup he teamed up with young rookie Sergio Garcia to beat Tiger Woods and Steve Pate 2&1 but was outplayed by David Duval 5&4 in the singles.

2000 SEASON. Parnevik had an excellent year on Tour. He posted seven top-10 finishes and won two more tournaments. In the first – the Bob Hope Classic – he birdied the final hole to beat Rory Sabbatini by one stroke. Later in the year, the pink pants-wearing Swede defeated Davis Love and Phil Mickelson on the third sudden-death hole at the Byron Nelson Classic. Despite losing ten weeks to surgery and recuperation, Parnevik finished in eighth place in the Money List and earned $2.5 million.

2001 STOP PRESS. Parnevik picked up his fifth US Tour tournament title of his career when he shot an 18 under par total to win the Honda Classic, near his home in Florida.

Craig Parry

US Tour

Born 12 January 1966
Place of Birth Sunshine, Victoria, Australia
Year turned Professional 1985
Tour Ranking 95th

BEST FINISH IN MAJORS
Tied 3rd US OPEN 1993

TOUR VICTORIES
EUROPEAN: 4
- 1989 German Open, Wang Four Stars Pro-Celebrity
- 1991 Italian Open, Scottish Open

AUSTRALASIAN: 10
1987 New South Wales Open
1992 Australian Masters, Australian PGA Championship, New South Wales Open
1994 Australian Masters
1995 Canon Challenge, Greg Norman's Holden Classic
1996 Australian Masters
1997 Coolum Classic
1999 Ford Open
OTHER: 4
1987 Canadian TPC
1989 Bridgestone ASO
1997 Indonesian Open, Japan Open

DUNHILL CUP 1993, 1995, 1996, 1998, 1999
PRESIDENTS CUP 1994, 1996, 1998
WORLD CUP 1989, 1990, 1991

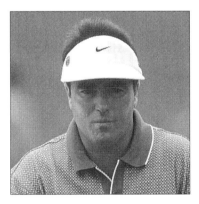

Known on the US Tour as 'Popeye' for his thick forearms, the small (5 foot 6 inch) Parry has an outstanding international record although he has yet to win on Tour. He played on the European and Australaian Tours before joining the US Tour in 1993. Despite performing well in several Major championships, including some very impressive performances in the British Open, he has so far been unable to replicate his international winning form in America although he has finished runner-up on three occasions. In 1991 he won twice on

the European Tour and the following year he won three Australian tournaments. He is one of the most accurate drivers on Tour, but is ranked over 131st for putting.

2000 SEASON. Parry had a disappointing season and he dropped down from 39th to 95th on the Money List. His highest placing was T7 in the Fedex St Jude Classic and he could only manage four more top-25s the whole year. He did, however, make three T3s on the Australasian Tour.

Lucas Parsons
European Tour

Born 4 October 1969
Place of Birth Sydney, Australia
Year turned Professional 1992
Tour Ranking 37th

BEST FINISH IN MAJORS
Tied 41st BRITISH OPEN 2000

TOUR VICTORIES
EUROPEAN: 1
2000 Greg Norman Holden International
AUSTRALASIAN: 3
1993 Victorian Open
1994 New Zealand Open, Queensland Open

Former Australian and New Zealand Amateur Champion, the ebullient and confident Parsons played in Australia – winning three tournaments – but failed to qualify for the European Tour in 1998. He gained his card in 1999, having won two events on the Challenge Tour. He is very long off the tee, but ranks 160th for driving accuracy.

2000 SEASON. Parsons won the Greg Norman International in February in his home town of Sydney, four strokes ahead of fellow Aussie Peter Senior. However, that was his only top-25 finish of the year. He made his debut in the British Open at St Andrews, in Scotland, and finished T41.

Steve Pate

US Tour

Born 26 May 1961
Place of Birth Ventura, California, USA
Year turned Professional 1983
Tour Ranking 72nd

BEST FINISH IN MAJORS
Tied 3rd US OPEN 1988, MASTERS 1991

TOUR VICTORIES
US: 6
- **1987** Southwest Classic
- **1988** MONY Tournament of Champions, Shearson Lehman Hutton-Andy Williams Open
- **1991** Honda Classic
- **1992** Buick Invitational of California
- **1998** CVS Charity Classic

RYDER CUP 1991, 1999
DUNHILL CUP 1991

Winner of six events, Pate has been on the US Tour since 1985, his best year being 1991 when he won the Honda Classic by three strokes and was sixth on the Money List. He was consistently in the top-90 on Tour until early 1996 when a car crash injured his wrist and he was out for the rest of the season. He recorded his sixth tournament success in 1998, with a one stroke win over Scott Hoch and Bradley Hughes in the CVS Charity Classic. The following year he did not win a tournament but was still placed 13th on the Money List and also named PGA Comeback Player of the Year. He also played in that year's winning Ryder Cup team, partnering Tiger Woods in the opening fourballs and winning two out of his three matches, and he set a record at The Masters when he birdied seven consecutive holes. He was known on Tour as 'Volcano' for his occasionally explosive temperament.

2000 SEASON. Continuing his rich vein of form, Pate had no less than seven top-10 finishes, his highest being T3 in the Greater Milwaukee Open. He also finished T20 in the British Open.

Jesse Patino

US Seniors Tour

Born 27 February 1948
Place of Birth Del Rio, Texas, USA
Year turned Professional 1984
Tour Ranking 46th

A comparatively late starter, Patino did not even pick up a golf club until he was 25 years old. He had to go through US Senior Tour Qualifying School in 1998 and 1999.

2000 SEASON. With four top-10s, his highest being a fourth place at the Vantage Championship, Patino made the top-50 on the Money List. An eighth place at Qualifying School gave him full exemption for 2001.

Carl Paulson

US Tour

Born 29 December 1970
Place of Birth Quantico, Virginia, USA
Year turned Professional 1991
Tour Ranking 64th

BEST FINISH IN MAJORS
Missed Cut US OPEN 1996

Paulson played on the US Tour in 1995 and 1996 and spent the following three years on the Nike Tour, where he was leading money-winner in 1999, winning two tournaments and gaining his Tour card.

2000 SEASON. A massive hitter of the ball (14th for driving distance), he had four high placings in the second half of the season, of which his best was second in the Tampa Bay Classic, in Florida, when he led on the last day until he was beaten by a John Huston 65. He wrote a book – *Rookie on Tour* – about his first season. He is no relation to fellow PGA Tour professional Dennis Paulson.

Dennis Paulson

US Tour

Born 27 September 1962
Place of Birth Vista, California, USA
Year turned Professional 1988
Tour Ranking 51st

BEST FINISH IN MAJORS
Tied 11th **BRITISH OPEN 2000**

TOUR VICTORIES
US: 1
  2000 Buick Classic
OTHER: 1
  1990 Philippines Open

As one would expect from the 1996 National Long Driving Champion, Paulson is one of the longest hitters off the tee on the US Tour, although he is often far from accurate. An ex-member of the Asian Tour, where he won the Philippines Open in 1990, he tried eight times to gain his full US Tour card and finally did so in 1993. He lost it in 1997, but regained his full playing privileges for the Tour in 1999 and he was twice runner-up, at the Buick Classic, when he lost a play-off to his good friend Duffy Waldorf at the Bell Canadian Open. He is no relation to Carl Paulson.

2000 SEASON. He won his first tournament when he beat David Duval on the fourth play-off hole of the Buick Classic, but the rest of his season was largely uneventful by comparison. Ironically, his best performances in general came in the Major championships, where he finsihed T14 at The Masters after leading the field after the first round, and a T11 at the British Open at St Andrews.

Corey Pavin

US Tour

Born 16 November 1959
Place of Birth Oxnard, California, USA
Year turned Professional 1982
Tour Ranking 160th

MAJORS VICTORIES
  US OPEN 1995

TOUR VICTORIES
US: 13
  1984 Houston Open
  1985 Colonial National Invitational
  1986 Greater Milwaukee Open, Hawaiian Open
  1987 Bob Hope Chrysler Classic, Hawaiian Open
  1988 Texas Open
  1991 BellSouth Atlanta Classic, Bob Hope Chrysler Classic
  1992 Honda Classic
  1994 Nissan Los Angeles Open
  1995 Nissan Los Angeles Open
  1996 MasterCard Colonial
EUROPEAN: 3
  1983 Calberson Classic, German Open
  1993 Toyota World Match Play Championship
AUSTRALASIAN: 2
  1984 New Zealand Open
  1985 New Zealand Open
SOUTH AFRICA: 2
  1983 South African PGA Championship
  1995 Sun City Million Dollar Challenge

OTHER: 3
- **1994** Tokai Classic
- **1995** Asian Masters
- **1996** Ssang Yong International Challenge

RYDER CUP 1991, 1993, 1995
PRESIDENTS CUP 1994, 1996

Known for his short but accurate drive, Pavin is a fine exponent of the short game. He has been a successful member of the US Tour since 1984. He has won 13 tournaments in the US as well as one Major – the US Open – when his second shot, a four wood, to the 72nd landed four feet from the pin and ensured his victory over Greg Norman. He has also won in Europe, Japan, Australia and South Africa, and his last win was at the 1996 MasterCard Colonial, when he ended the season 18th on the US Money List. Since then, he has plummeted in the List and ended the 2000 season in 160th place. His US Open victory, however, gives him exempt status until 2005.

2000 SEASON. He had three top-25 placings in 25 starts, his highest being T9 at the Westlin Texas Open.

Karen Pearce
European Ladies Tour

Born 19th September 1968
Place of Birth Toowoomba, Australia
Year turned Professional 1990
Tour Ranking 17th

Pearce joined the European Ladies Tour in 1992 and her highest finish during the 1990s was T4 at the 1998 McDonald's WPGA Championship of Europe. In 1999 she gained her LPGA card at Qualifying School.

2000 SEASON. She played in only six European events, posting a career-best T3 at the Waterford Crystal Irish Ladies Open and finishing 17th on the Money List. She was also 116th on the LPGA Tour.

David Peoples
US Tour

Born 9 January 1960
Place of Birth Augusta, Maine, USA
Year turned Professional 1981
Tour Ranking 110th

BEST FINISH IN MAJORS
Tied 52nd **US MASTERS 1993**

TOUR VICTORIES
US: 2
- **1991** Buick Southern Open
- **1992** Anheuser-Busch Golf Classic

After joining the US Tour in 1983, Peoples was in and out of the notoriously stressful Qualifying School several times during the 1980s. He had two highly lucrative years on Tour in 1991 and 1992, where he won two tournaments. However, he has won nothing since then and a barren run of form meant that he had to go back to Qualifying School again to regain his Tour Card. He finished in second place. He is a particularly effective iron player.

2000 SEASON. Peoples retained his card for 2001 with five top-25 finishes and also had a T7 at the Kemper Open, his highest placing of the year.

Dottie Pepper
US Ladies Tour

Born 17 August 1965
Place of Birth: Saratoga Springs, New York
Year turned Professional 1987
Tour Ranking 8th

MAJORS VICTORIES
DINAH SHORE 1992, 1999

TOUR VICTORIES
US: 15
- **1989** Oldsmobile Classic
- **1990** Crestor Classic

1992 SEGA Women's Championship, Sun-Times Challenge, Welch's Classic
1993 World Championship of Women's Golf
1994 Chrysler-Plymouth Tournament of Champions
1995 McCall's Classic, Ping Welch's Championship
1996 Friendly's Classic, Rochester International, Safeway Golf Championship, ShopRite Classic
1999 Oldsmobile Classic
2000 Arch Wireless Championship

SOLHEIM CUP 1990, 1992, 1994, 1996, 1998, 2000

The volatile and unpredictable Pepper has been a major figure in US women's golf over the last ten years. Winner of 17 events on the LPGA Tour, this tough, determined and gritty player won four tournaments in 1992 alone, bringing her the Golf Writers Player of the Year award as well as Player of the Year. She has also won two Majors, collecting the Dinah Shore in 1992 and 1999. The aggressive, perhaps over-competitive side of her nature has been most evident in the Solheim Cup, where she is the only American to have played in all six competitions. In 1994 she controversially refused to shake hands with some of the European team, while in 1998 she was accused by some Europeans of inciting

the crowd while the European players were attempting to concentrate. Pepper refused, however, to concede that her behaviour was unsporting, although there was a noticeable difference in her demeanour at the Solheim Cup in 2000.

2000 SEASON. Another solid year. Pepper won the Arch Wireless Championship, beating Australian Rachel Hetherington by three strokes, and collected ten top-10 finishes, including three runner-up spots. On the European Tour she came third behind Annika Sorenstam and Karrie Webb at the lucrative Evian Masters, in France

Craig Perks
US Tour

Born 6 January 1967
Place of Birth Palmerston North, New Zealand
Year turned Professional 1993
Tour Ranking T8th (Qualifying School)

New Zealander Perks played on the Nike Tour between 1996 and 1999 and joined the US Tour in 2000 from the Qualifying School. His best finish was T4 at the Bell Canadian Open, and he regained his Tour card for 2001 by finishing T8 at the Qualifying School again. In 2000 he lost a play-off to Michael Campbell at the New Zealand Open.

Tom Pernice Jr
US Tour

Born 5th September 1959
Place of Birth Kansas City, Missouri, USA
Year turned Professional 1983
Tour Ranking 127th

BEST FINISH IN MAJORS
Tied 13th US OPEN 1989

TOUR VICTORIES
US: 1
1999 Buick Open

After over 200 starts on the US Tour Pernice finally claimed a tournament win in 1999 at the Buick Open when Tom Lehman's missed birdie putt on the 72nd hole handed victory to journeyman Pernice. Prior to this, he had played on the European, Asian and Nike Tours, rejoining the US Tour from Qualifying School in 1997.

2000 SEASON. His highest finish was T5 in the BellSouth Classic, and he finished 127th on the Money List.

Chris Perry

US Tour

Born 27 September 1961
Place of Birth Edenton, North Carolina, USA
Year turned Professional 1984
Tour Ranking 28th

BEST FINISH IN MAJORS
Tied 10th USPGA 1999

TOUR VICTORIES
US: 1
  1998 BC Open
OTHER: 1
  1994 Mexican Open

Perry joined the US Tour in 1985, but had to wait 13 years before winning his first tournament in 1998, when his last-round 5 under par 67 in the BC Open was enough to see off Peter Jacobsen by three strokes. Accurate off the tee and fairway, and with a reliable putting stroke, he has put in a number of high finishes over his career but the B.C. Open remains his only tournament win. His best year was in 1999 when he posted a remarkable 14 top-10 placings, including T2 in the Sony Open and the Reno-Tahoe Open, and he was fifth in the Money List. He played the Nike Tour in 1993 and 1994, topping the Money List the latter year. His father and uncle both played in the baseball major leagues.

2000 SEASON. The consistent Perry continued with his practice of finishing high on the leaderboards but without actually winning. He had four top-5 placings, his best being runner-up by one shot to Rocco Mediate in the Buick Open and three top-10s. He was consistent in the Majors as well, finishing T32 in the US Open and posting a T14 in The Masters. Perry finished the season 28th on the Money List.

Kenny Perry

US Tour

Born 10 August 1960
Place of Birth Elizabethtown, Kentucky, USA
Year turned Professional 1982
Tour Ranking 52nd

BEST FINISH IN MAJORS
2nd USPGA 1996

TOUR VICTORIES
US: 3
  1991 Memorial Tournament
  1994 New England Classic
  1995 Bob Hope Chrysler Classic

PRESIDENTS CUP 1996

A tall Kentuckian, Perry will probably never forget the 1996 USPGA Championship. Two shots ahead of Mark Brooks with just one hole to play, a confident Perry acknowledged the gallery. Brooks, however managed a birdied at the last, while Perry took a costly bogey, and Brooks won the sudden-death play-off. Prior to that stunning reversal, Perry, a US Tour member since 1987, had won three tournaments on the PGA Tour, but he has won nothing since 1995 although he has never dropped out of the top -100. Perry is a long driver and an excellent iron player.

2000 SEASON. Perry climbed from 94th to 52nd in the Money List largely due to three top-3 finishes – T3 at the Bell South Classic, T3 at the Greater Milwaukee Open and third at the Southern Farm Bureau Classic.

Carl Petterson
European Tour

Born 29 August 1977
Place of Birth Gothenburg, Sweden
Year turned Professional 2000
Tour Ranking 18th (Qualifying School)

Pettersson was European Amateur Champion in 2000 and graduated through the Qualifying School for his place on the 2001 European Tour.

2001 STOP PRESS. Pettersson immediately made his mark in Europe's premier league of golf when he claimed a solid second place at the inaugural Open De Argentina early on in the season.

Van Phillips
European Tour

Born 27 March 1972
Place of Birth Southall, England
Year turned Professional 1993
Tour Ranking 75th

BEST FINISH IN MAJORS
Missed Cut **BRITISH OPEN 1997**

TOUR VICTORIES
EUROPEAN: 1
1999 Algarve Portuguese Open

Philips joined the European Tour in 1997 and had to wait two years for his first tournament win, when he beat John Bickerton in a play-off at the 1999 Portugese Open.
2000 SEASON. Philips had an average season, with only five top-25s, until he finished T5 at the Italian Open. Short off the tee, he has a delicate and effective short game. He relaxes by playing blues guitar.

Fiona Pike
US Ladies Tour

Born 4 November 1964
Place of Birth Adelaide, Australia
Year turned Professional 1995
Tour Ranking 83rd

Adelaide-born Pike played regularly on the European Tour between 1995 and 1998, with her best placing T2 at the 1996 Italian Open. She qualified for the LPGA Tour on her second attempt in 1998. However, she continues to play her best golf on European soil. Her best finish is T3 at the 1999 Weetabix Women's British Open, and she was 15th on the European Order of Merit that year.

2000 SEASON. Her highest placing was T11 at the Giant Eagle LPGA Classic and she also had two other top-25s to finish 83rd on the end of season Money List.

Mark Pilkington

Born 17 March 1978
Place of Birth Bangor, Wales
Year turned Professional 1998
Tour Ranking 27th (Qualifying School)

Winner of two major amateur titles – the Spanish Amateur Championship in 1996, and the Welsh Amateur Championship in 1998 – Pilkington's best finish in the 2000 Challenge Tour was fifth in the Costa Branca Challenge. He qualified for the 2001 European Tour with a 27th place at the 2000 Qualifying School.

Gary Player
US Seniors Tour

Born 1 November 1935
Place of Birth Johannesburg, South Africa
Year turned Professional 1953
Tour Ranking 70th

MAJORS VICTORIES

PGA SENIORS CHAMPIONSHIP 1986, 1988, 1990
US SENIOR OPEN 1987 and 1988

TOUR VICTORIES

SENIOR TOUR: 13

- **1985** Quadel Senior Classic
- **1986** Champions of Golf, General Foods Senior Golf Championship
- **1987** Paine Webber World Series Invitational, Senior Tournament Players Championship
- **1988** Aetna Challenge, Southwestern Bell Classic
- **1989** GTE North Classic, RJR Championship
- **1991** Royal Caribbean Classic
- **1993** Bank One Classic
- **1995** Bank One Classic
- **1998** Northville Long Island Classic

A small, dapper South African, Player moved to Britain in the mid-1950s. By 1959 he had won his first Major – the British Open – and by 1961 he had collected The Masters, the first non-American to lift the trophy. By 1965 he had also won the US Open and USPGA Championship. Although his slight stature limited his distance off the tee, Player's devastatingly effective short game, and in particular his bunker technique, more than compensated for his lack of length. A dedicated practiser (he once remarked 'the more I practise, the luckier I get') and obsessive about physical fitness, he won the British Open again in 1968, two strokes ahead of Bob Charles and Jack Nicklaus, and won the claret jug again six years later in the winds of Royal Lytham. He also won The Masters that year. His most remarkable Majors triumph, however, was in the 1978 Masters when, seven shots behind leader Hubert Green at the beginning of the last round, the 42-year-old Player shot a magnificent back-nine 30, including six birdies, to seize victory.

Player has long played on the international circuit and he has won more than 100 titles worldwide, including seven Australian Opens and five World Matchplay Championships, as well as 21 USPGA Tour titles. He joined the US Senior Tour in 1985, winning the Quad City Classic in his first year, and defeated Lee Elder in 1986 to win the PGA Championship. The following year he won the Senior Open by six strokes, and in 1988 his five wins included a successful defence of the Senior Open as well as another Senior PGA title. He collected his third PGA Championship in 1990 and won another four tournaments during the 1990s, his last being the Northville Long Island Classic in 1998. He has also won the Senior British Open three times and has two other victories on the European Seniors Tour.

2000 SEASON. Player entered 21 events with his highest finish being T11 at the Royal Caribbean Cruise Classic, in Key Biscayne, Florida. However, he became the youngest player to shoot his age, with an 8 under par 64 at the Bell South Classic. This seemingly ageless South African competed in his 43rd Masters and his 45th British Open. Player currently runs a number of international businesses, including a stud farm and a golf course architecture company. He also set up The Gary Player Foundation to promote education in South Africa.

Eddie Polland
European Senior Tour

Born 10 June 1947
Place of Birth Newcastle, Northern Ireland
Year turned Professional 1968
Tour Ranking 22nd

TOUR VICTORIES
SENIOR TOUR: 2
   1999 Lawrence Batley Seniors, Senior
        Tournament of Champions

Irishman Polland won four tournaments in his 20-year career on the European Tour. He joined the European Senior Tour in 1997 and claimed three runner-up positions, including losing two play-offs, the following year. In 1999, he won twice at the Lawrence Batley Seniors and the Senior Tournament of Champions to take second place in the Order of Merit.

   2000 SEASON. The highest position Polland could manage was fifth at the Energis Senior Masters, but he also achieved a further seven top-10s to finish the year 22nd on the final Order of Merit.

Lee Porter
US Tour

Born 26 March 1966
Place of Birth Greensboro, North Carolina, USA
Year turned Professional 1989
Tour Ranking Tied 21th (Qualifying School)

BEST FINISH IN MAJORS
Tied 32nd US OPEN 2000

TOUR VICTORIES
OTHER: 1
   1991 Venezuelan Open

Something of a peripatetic golfer, Porter has played on the Japanese, Asian, Canadian and European Tours as well as on the Nike Tour. He qualified for the 1997 US Tour from the Nike Tour and the following year he finished 95th on the Money List. His best finish is third at the 1998 Greater Vancouver Open. He spent season 2000 on the Buy.Com Tour and qualified for the 2001 US Tour finishing T21 at Qualifying school.

Ian Poulter
European Tour

Born 10 January 1976
Place of Birth Hitchin, England
Year turned Professional 1994
Tour Ranking 31st

BEST FINISH IN MAJORS
64th BRITISH OPEN 2000

TOUR VICTORIES
EUROPEAN: 2
   2000 Italian Open
   2001 Moroccan Open

A powerful, attacking player, Poulter joined the European Tour in 2000 after spending a year on the Challenge Tour. He made a fine start to his rookie year, making four out of his first five cuts and finishing T3 in the Sao Paolo 500 Years Open and T2 in the Moroccan Open. He had by this point already secured his card for 2001. In the Italian Open in Sardinia in October, Poulter shot three birdies on the last six holes and edged out Gordon Brand Jr on the last hole to claim victory and his first Tour title. He was named Rookie of the Year and received a Porsche for his good play. Poulter is sponsored by *The Sun* newspaper and is regarded by many as the best of the up-and-coming British golfers. He is definitely a talent to look out for in the near future

   2001 STOP PRESS. Poulter came third behind Aaron Baddeley and Sergio Garcia at the Greg Norman Holden International. He then shot 15 under par 277 to beat David Lynn by two strokes at the Moroccan Open.

Nick Price

_____ US Tour

Born 28 January 1957
Place of Birth Durban, South Africa
Year turned Professional 1977
Tour Ranking 21st

MAJORS VICTORIES

BRITISH OPEN 1994
USPGA 1992, 1994

TOUR VICTORIES

US: 14
1983 World Series of Golf
1991 Canadian Open, GTE Bryon Nelson Classic
1992 H-E-B Texas Open
1993 Canon Greater Hartford Open, Federal Express St Jude Classic, Sprint Western Open, The Players Championship
1994 Bell Canadian Open, Honda Classic, Motorola Western Open, Southwestern Bell Colonial
1997 MCI Classic
1998 Federal Express St Jude Classic
EUROPEAN: 4
1980 Canon European Masters
1985 Trophee Lancome
1997 Dimension Data Pro-Am, South African PGA Championship
AUSTRALASIAN: 2
1989 South Australian Open
1992 New Zealand Open
SOUTH AFRICA: 15
1979 Asseng Invitational
1981 South African Masters
1982 Vaals Reef Open
1985 ICL International
1993 ICL International, Sun City Million Dollar Challenge
1994 ICL International
1995 Alfred Dunhill Challenge, Zimbabwe Open
1997 South African PGA Championship, Sun City Million Dollar Challenge, Zimbabwe Open
1998 Dimension Data Pro-Am, Sun City Million Dollar Challenge, Zimbabwe Open
OTHER: 1
1999 Suntory Open

DUNHILL CUP 1993, 1994, 1995, 1996, 1997, 1998, 1999, 2000
PRESIDENTS CUP 1994, 1996, 1998, 2000
WORLD CUP 1993

Jovial, South-African born Zimbabwean Price is one of the genuine nice guys in golf and he has accumulated 40 tournament victories across the world in his 20-year career. Coached by David Leadbetter, he began his career on the European and South African Tours and by the mid-1980s he was a regular on the US Tour, his first win coming at the World Series of Golf in 1983. Since then he has won 13 other US events and three Majors. In 1992 he held off a late charge from Nick Faldo to collect the USPGA Championship by three strokes and was fourth on the Money List, and the following year his four US victories helped him to both top the Money List and win the Player of the Year award. His finest year, however, came in 1994. He holed a 65-foot putt on the 71st hole at the British Open to overtake Jesper Parnevik to the title, and then picked up his second USPGA Championship, beating Corey Pavin by six shots. He became the first golfer since Walter Hagen 70 years previously to win both tournaments in the same year. These Major successes, plus a further four tournament wins, saw him retain the leadership of the Money List and his Player of the Year title. His last US win came at the FedEx St Jude Classic in 1998.

2000 SEASON. Price was runner-up to Robert Allenby at the Advill Western Open, losing in a play-off, and T2 at the Buick Challenge, behind David Duval. He was 21st on the Money List. This consistent player has not fallen out of the top-50 since 1986.

Philip Price
European Tour

Born 21 October 1966
Place of Birth Pontypridd, Wales
Year turned Professional 1989
Tour Ranking 8th

BEST FINISH IN MAJORS
Tied 53rd US OPEN 1999

TOUR VICTORIES
EUROPEAN: 2
   1994 Portuguese Open
   2001 Portuguese Open

DUNHILL CUP 1991, 1996, 2000
WORLD CUP 1991, 1994, 1995, 1997, 1998, 1999

Welshman Price has played the European Tour since 1990 and has only once moved out of the top-100. He led throughout to claim his only tournament victory, the Portugese Open in 1994, and was runner-up four times in the 1990s. In 1991, he and Ian Woosnam took Wales to second place in the World Cup. Price is a consistent, accurate player with a superb putting technique and has developed into a top-class golfer over the past couple of seasons

2000 SEASON. Price played magnificently to tie for second place with Justin Leonard behind Tiger Woods in the WGC NEC Invitational at Firestone in August. He won over $400,000 for his efforts. He was placed second three times on Tour – at the Alfred Dunhill, Portuguese Open and Benson & Hedges International – and he had five other top-10 placings. In the Dunhill Cup he won 3½ points out of a possible four as he helped Wales to the semi-final.

2001 STOP PRESS. Price shot a final round 64 to beat Padraig Harrington by two strokes and win the Portuguese Open for the second time in his career. The round included five birdies in the first six holes.

Dicky Pride
US Tour

Born 15 July 1969
Place of Birth Greensboro, North Carolina, USA
Year turned Professional 1989
Tour Ranking Tied 31st (Qualifying School)

BEST FINISH IN MAJORS
Tied 73rd USPGA 1994

TOUR VICTORIES
US: 1
   1994 FedEx St Jude Classic

Pride claimed his only US Tour tournament in his rookie year of 1994 when he won the FedEx St Jude Classic in a play-off against Hal Sutton and Gene Sauers. He had two other top-10 finishes and finished in his highest-ever spot on the Money List, 57th. In 1999, he had another good year, with two top-5 placings, and ended the season just outside the top-100. He qualified for the 2001 Tour with a T31 at Qualifying School.

Ian Pyman
European Tour

Born 3 March 1973
Place of Birth Whitby, England
Year turned Professional 1994
Tour Ranking 127th

BEST FINISH IN MAJORS
Tied 27th **BRITISH OPEN 1993**

British Amateur Champion in 1993, Pyman played on the European Tour between 1994 and 1998. He won twice on the 1999 Challenge Tour and played on the main Tour in 2000. His best finish is second at the 1997 Oki Pro-Am.

2000 SEASON. The highest placing he could manage was T12 at the Peugeot Open.

Brett Quigley

US Tour

Born 18 August 1969
Place of Birth Fort Devens, Maine, USA
Year turned Professional 1991
Tour Ranking 150th

Nephew of the highly successful Senior Tour player Dana Quigley, Brett's best season on the US Tour so far came in 1998 when he finished 127th on the Money List. His career-best finish is T4 at the 1998 Hawaiian Open.

2000 SEASON. He played on the US Tour and the Buy.Com Tour, and his best finish on the main tour was T5 at the BC Open.

2001 STOP PRESS. Quigley improved his play dramatically and had his best-ever performance when he finished T2 behind Scott Hoch at the Greater Greensboro Classic. He capitalized on that success by finishing tied for fifth in the MasterCard Colonial, in Texas, which was won by Sergio Garcia.

Dana Quigley

US Seniors Tour

Born 14 April 1947
Place of Birth Lynfield Centre, Maine, USA
Year turned Professional 1971
Tour Ranking 5th

TOUR VICTORIES
SENIOR TOUR: 4
   1997 Northville Long Island Classic
   1998 Emerald Coast Classic, Raley's Gold Rush Classic
   2000 TD Waterhouse Championship

Quigley joined the US Senior Tour from club golf in 1997, although he had played intermittently on the USPGA Tour. He open qualified for the 1997 Northville Long Island Classic and beat Jay Sigel in a play-off. As he walked off, he was told that his father had died during his round. In 1998 he played every round of every event, won two tournaments and earned over $1 million. Quigley repeated this schedule in 1999 when he recorded 18 top-10s and collected £1.3 million. His nephew is USPGA Tour player Brett Quigley.

2000 SEASON. Quigley enjoyed his best season on the Senior Tour. Again he played in all 39 events and ended fourth on the Money List, earning $1.8 million. He won the TD Waterhouse Championship, sinking a 12-foot birdie putt on the last hole to beat Tom Watson and had five second-place finishes, including T2 at the rain-shortened PGA Senior Championship. He played his 105th straight tournament and posted career winnings of over $4 million.

2001 STOP PRESS. Quigley finished in second place at the ACE Group Classic, two shots behind Gil Morgan.

Paulo Quirici

European Tour

Born 9 November 1967
Place of Birth Muzzano, Switzerland
Year turned Professional 1988
Tour Ranking 78th

DUNHILL CUP 1991
WORLD CUP 1989, 1990, 1991, 1992, 1995, 1996, 1997, 1998

A tall (6 foot 3 inch), long-hitting Swiss, Quirici made six attempts to join the European Tour through Qualifying School and succeeded in 1988. His only top-3 position was when he finished T2 at the 1999 Sarazen World Open. He was diagnosed diabetic in 1996.

2000 SEASON. Quirici had one top-10 finish – T10 in the Spanish Open – and five other top-20 finishes.

from qualifying for his 2001 European Tour card. He had four top-10s on Tour, including a second place at the Beazer Homes Challenge. He finally secured his Tour status for 2001 by finishing in second place at the Qualifying School.

Noel Ratcliffe
European Senior Tour

Born 17 January 1945
Place of Birth Sydney, Australia
Year turned Professional 1974
Tour Ranking 1st

TOUR VICTORIES
SENIOR TOUR: 5
1997 Manadens Affarer Senior Open, Senior German Open
2000 Scottish Seniors Open, Temes Seniors Open
2001 Beko Classic

Andrew Raitt
European Tour

Born 12 September 1969
Place of Birth London, England
Year turned Professional 1996
Tour Ranking 14th (Challenge Tour)

Six foot 2 inch, long-hitting, English-born Raitt studied for a communications degree at the University of Nevada and turned pro in 1996. He won his 1999 European Tour card at Qualifying School and his best finish that year was T7 at the Moroccan Open. He lost his card at the end of the season. He qualified for the 2001 European Tour by playing well toward the end of the season on the Challenge Tour and picking up two second places and a third.

Graham Rankin
European Tour

Born 18 January 1966
Place of Birth Bellshill, Scotland
Year turned Professional 1999
Tour Ranking 2nd (Qualifying School)

A Three-time Walker Cup veteran, Rankin played in the winning GB & Ireland 1995 Walker Cup team. An ex-bricklayer, he turned pro relatively late in life in 1999. He finished 16th on the Challenge Tour, one place away

A tall Australian, Ratcliffe played on the European Tour between 1977 and 1991 and won two tournaments, the last being the Benson & Hedges International Open in 1987. He joined the European Senior Tour in 1996 and finished in second place on the Order of Merit in 1997, collecting two wins. In his first five years on Tour he was runner-up on eight occasions. In 1999 he played his golf mainly on the US Senior Tour and qualified for 2000 through Qualifying School.

2000 SEASON. Ratcliffe began the European Tour modestly, but came storming into contention at the Scottish Seniors Open, which he won by seven strokes. He then won again at the Temes Senior Open, when he took the lead on the Order of Merit. He had two other second-place finishes, and ended Tommy Horton's four-year domination at the season-ending tournament, the Abu Dhabi European Senior Tour Championship, by narrowly maintaining his lead over John Grace. Ratcliffe won the John Jacobs Trophy by a margin of only £935.

Michele Reale
European Tour

Born 14 June 1971
Place of Birth Biella, Italy
Year turned Professional 1991
Tour Ranking 5th (Challenge Tour)

Italian Reale won the Challenge Tour in 1997, but illness prevented him from finishing the 1998 European Tour season any higher than 120th on the Order of Merit. He gained his card for the 1999 European Tour through Qualifying School and played on both tours that year, with little success on either. He qualified for the 2001 European Tour by finishing fifth on the Challenge Tour, his highest finish a runner-up spot at the Credit Suisse Open.

Michelle Redman
US Ladies Tour

Born 15 April 1965
Place of Birth Zanesville, Ohio, USA
Year turned Professional 1988
Tour Ranking 10th

TOUR VICTORIES
US: 2
1997 JAL Big Apple Classic
2000 First Union Betsy King Classic

SOLHEIM CUP 2000

After spending three years on the Futures Tour, Redman joined the LPGA Tour in 1992. She has one win on Tour, when she led Annika Sorenstam to win the 1997 JAL Big Apple Classic wire-to-wire. She had five top-10s that year. Her sister Susie also plays on Tour.

2000 SEASON. This was a good year for Redman, winning the First Union Betsy King Classic with all her rounds in the 60s. She also had nine top-10s, her highest being T2 at the Los Angeles Women's Championship, and she was T4 at the Nabisco, her best-ever finish in a Major. She was tenth on the Money List.

Susie Redman
US Ladies Tour

Born 17 April 1966
Place of Birth Salem, Ohio, USA
Year turned Professional 1984
Tour Ranking 37th

Michelle's younger sister, the tall (6 foot) Redman joined the LPGA Tour in 1984. She has not yet won an event, however, and her best finish to date is second at the 1995 Dinah Shore.

2000 SEASON. She tied for third at the Philips Invitational and posted two top-10s.

Mike Reid
US Tour

Born 1 July 1954
Place of Birth Bainbridge, Maryland, USA
Year turned Professional 1976
Tour Ranking 135th

TOUR VICTORIES
US: 2
1987 Seiko Tucson Open
1988 NEC World Series of Golf

Reid's first win on the US Tour came back in 1987 when he won the Tucson Open, in Arizona. The following year he secured himself a ten-year exemption by beating Tom Watson in a play-off at the NEC World Series of Golf. He went on to end the 1988 season 15th on the Money List. Reid was the first player to win the driving accuracy statistics, in 1980, and he is known on Tour by the nickname 'Radar' for both his accuracy and his resemblance to the character of the same name in the American comedy show *MASH*.

2000 SEASON. He entered 23 tournaments, but only had one top-5 finish – at the Michelob Championship.

Jean-Francois Remesy
European Tour

Born 5 June 1964
Place of Birth Nimes, France
Year turned Professional 1987
Tour Ranking 89th

BEST FINISH IN MAJORS
MissedCut **BRITISH OPEN1997**

TOUR VICTORIES
EUROPEAN: 1
1999 Estoril Open

DUNHILL CUP 1999, 2000
WORLD CUP 1999

French Amateur Champion in 1985, Remesy joined the European Tour in 1997. He won his only tournament when he defeated Andrew Coltart by two strokes in a wind-swept Estoril Open, in Portugal, in 1999, two weeks after he had won the French PGA Championship. He finished the year in his highest-ever position, 57th, on the Order of Merit.

2000 SEASON. He was placed four times in the top-10, with his highest being T5 in the South African Open, but he slipped down the

Order of Merit to finish the year in 89th spot. He also lost all three of his Dunhill Cup matches.

2001 STOP PRESS. Remesy was runner-up at the Spanish Open, two strokes behind Robert Karlsson.

Jim Rhodes
European Senior Tour

Born 29 January 1946
Place of Birth Cannock, England
Year turned Professional 1963
Tour Ranking 11th

Rhodes has played on the European Senior Tour since 1996, having spent over 30 years as a club professional. He finished fifth on the 1997 Order of Merit, and he has not fallen out of the top-20 although he has still to win an event on Tour.

2000 SEASON. His best finish was second to David Huish at the Bad Ragaz PGA Seniors Open, but he played consistently enough throughout the season to bag 11th place on the Order of Merit.

Steven Richardson
European Tour

Born 24 July 1966
Place of Birth Windsor, England
Year turned Professional 1989
Tour Ranking 33th (Qualifying School)

BEST FINISH IN MAJORS
Tied 31st **US MASTERS 1992**

TOUR VICTORIES
EUROPEAN: 3
1991 Girona Open, Portuguese Open
1993 Mercedes German Masters

RYDER CUP 1991
DUNHILL CUP 1991, 1992
WORLD CUP 1991, 1992

The English Amateur Champion in 1989, Richardson won two European Tour titles, the Portuguese Open and the Girona Open, in 1991. That year he played in the Ryder Cup at Kiawah Island, winning his two matches with Mark James, but losing in the singles to Corey Pavin. He won his third and last event in 1993 at the Mercedes German Open and since then his good form has mysteriously vanished. He has played on the European Tour since 1990, and he retained his card for 2001 with a 33rd place at Qualifying School

John Riegger
US Tour

Born 13 June 1963
Place of Birth Metropolis, Illinois, USA
Year turned Professional 1985
Tour Ranking 10th (Buy.Com Tour)

The tall Riegger played on the US Tour in 1992, 1993 and 1998. His highest finish is T12 at the 1993 Fedex St Jude Classic. In 2000 he made eight top-10 finishes on the Buy.Com Tour, and a T3 in the season-ending tournament ensured his tenth place on the Money List and a US Tour card in 2001.

Chris Riley
US Tour

Born 8 December 1973
Place of Birth San Diego, California, USA
Year turned Professional 1996
Tour Ranking 71st

BEST FINISH IN MAJORS
Missed Cut US OPEN 1996

A Walker Cup teammate of Tiger Woods in 1995, Riley graduated to the US Tour from Qualifying School in 1999. He retained his card with three top-10 placings.

2000 SEASON. Riley had a good year with six top-15 finishes from his last 11 starts, the best being a fourth at the John Deere Classic and a T4 at the Air Canada. He ended the season 71st on the Money List.

Wayne Riley
European Tour

Born 17 September 1962
Place of Birth Sydney, Australia
Year turned Professional 1977
Tour Ranking 95th

BEST FINISH IN MAJORS
Tied 32nd BRITISH OPEN 1985

TOUR VICTORIES
EUROPEAN: 2
    1995 Scottish Open
    1996 Portuguese Open
AUSTRALASIAN: 4
    1984 Victorian PGA Championship
    1986 NSW PGA Championship
    1990 New Zealand Open
    1991 Australian Open Championship

DUNHILL CUP 1996
WORLD CUP 1997

A volatile and unpredictable player, the Australian 'Radar' Riley joined the European Tour in 1985 and has been a regular since then. He did not win a title until 1995, when he held off Nick Faldo and Colin Montgomerie to win the Scottish Open. He had two more third-place finishes that season and ended 11th on the Order of Merit. The following year he won again, this time claiming the Portuguese Open. In recent years his form has been disappointing and, depite being regarded as one of the most naturally talented golfers, he lost his Tour card in 1998. A good start to 1999, however, saw Riley regain his playing privileges. He uses a broomhandle putter.

2000 SEASON. Riley's bad form continued and he could only post four top-20 finishes, his best being T6 at the Portuguese Open.

Jose Rivero
European Tour

Born 20 September 1955
Place of Birth Madrid, Spain
Year turned Professional 1973
Tour Ranking 113th

BEST FINISH IN MAJORS
Tied 3rd BRITISH OPEN 1985

TOUR VICTORIES
EUROPEAN: 4
- 1984 Lawrence Batley International
- 1987 Peugeot French Open
- 1988 Monte Carlo Open
- 1992 Open Catalonia

RYDER CUP 1985, 1987
DUNHILL CUP 1986, 1987, 1988, 1989, 1990, 1991, 1992, 1993, 1994, 1995
WORLD CUP 1984, 1987, 1988, 1990, 1991, 1992, 1993, 1994

tional, and finished 11th on the Order of Merit. Two runner-up spots in 1995 saw him at 16th on the Order of Merit but his form has declined since then. He played in two Ryder Cups – 1985 and 1987 – and was a winner in both. Rivero and Jose Maria Canizares won the World Cup for Spain in 1984.

2000 SEASON. He fell to 113th in the Order of Merit, his lowest-ever career position. He only posted three top-20s, the highest being T7 in the Dutch Open.

Kelly Robbins
US Ladies Tour

Born 29 September 1969
Place of Birth Mt Pleasant, Michigan, USA
Year turned Professional 1991
Tour Ranking 22nd

MAJORS VICTORIES
LPGA 1995

TOUR VICTORIES
US: 9
- 1993 Corning Classic
- 1994 Jamie Farr Toledo Classic
- 1996 Twelve Bridges LPGA Classic
- 1997 Dr Pepper National Pro-Am, Jamie Farr Kroger Classic
- 1998 AFLAC Championship, Healthsouth Inaugural
- 1999 Healthsouth Inaugural

SOLHEIM CUP 1994, 1996, 1998, 2000

A consistent, long-serving member of the European Tour, Rivero was only once, in 1996, outside the top-100 in the Order of Merit from 1983 to 1999. A young golf professional in Madrid, he received a loan of £2,500 from the Spanish Golf Federation in 1983 to allow him to compete in the European Tour. The following year he won the first of his four tournaments, the Lawrence Batley Interna-

A popular player on the LPGA Tour, 'Cool' Kelly is one of the longest hitters. She has won nine times, including a Major when she edged out Laura Davies to take the McDonald's LPGA Championship in 1995. Her two wins in 1997 helped her to reach third place on the Money List. Her last two victories were in 1998, when she passed the $3 million mark in career earnings. She played in the Solheim Cup between 1994 and 2000.

2000 SEASON. Robbins had a T2 at the Chick-fil-A Championship and two other top-10s.

Loren Roberts

US Tour

Born 24 June 1955
Place of Birth San Luis Obispo, California, USA
Year turned Professional 1975
Tour Ranking 18th

BEST FINISH IN MAJORS
Tied 2nd US OPEN 1994

TOUR VICTORIES
US: 7
  1994 Nestle Invitational
  1995 Nestle Invitational
  1996 Greater Milwaukee Open, MCI Classic
  1997 CVS Charity Classic
  1999 GTE Byron Nelson Classic
  2000 Greater Milwaukee Open

RYDER CUP 1995
PRESIDENTS CUP 1994, 2000

Known as the 'Boss of the Moss' for his prowess on the greens, Roberts had to visit Qualifying School five times before gaining his US Tour card. Since then his career has certainly compensated for his efforts. He went from 1983 until 1993 without winning a tournament, and then won five events in the next four years. He added another in 1999 when he beat Steve Pate in a play-off at the Byron Nelson Classic. He has not been out of the top-100 in the Money List since 1988. His finest year was 1994 when he won the Nestlé Invitational and ran up three second-place finishes. That year, he came T5 in The Masters, T9 in the USPGA and T2 in the US Open, which he lost to Ernie Els on the second sudden-death hole after a dramatic 18-hole play-off which went to extra holes.

2000 SEASON. This was another great year for Roberts. He won the Greater Milwaukee Open, beating second-placed Franklin Langham by eight strokes and set the tournament's lowest score with 260. In the Majors, he was T7 in the British Open, T8 in the US Open and T3 in The Masters, and he had eight other top-20 finishes. In the Presidents Cup he beat Stuart Appleby in the singles. As well as being a superb putter he is an extremely accurate driver (fourth in the driving accuracy statistics).

Dean Robertson

European Tour

Born 11 July 1970
Place of Birth Paisley, Scotland
Year turned Professional 1993
Tour Ranking 50th

BEST FINISH IN MAJORS
Tied 26th **BRITISH OPEN 2000**

TOUR VICTORIES
EUROPEAN: 1
 1999 Fiat & Fila Italian Open

WORLD CUP 1999

Robertson was Scottish Amateur Champion in 1993 and turned professional that year. He joined the European Tour in 1995 and was runner-up in the Jersey Open in his first season. In 1998, Robertson led the Volvo PGA with five holes remaining, but finished T5. In 1999, he had missed eight of his previous 11 cuts before the Italian Open. However, after working on his mental game with a leading golf psychologist, his last three round scores of 65, 68 and 68 were enough to give him victory in the event by one stroke ahead of Ireland's Padraig Harrington. He is a fine player in the wind and a reliable putter, although his driving can be inaccurate.

2000 SEASON. Robertson caught a virus at the World Cup at the end of 1999 and was laid low until he returned in late April to contest the Spanish Open. He had five top-20 finishes, his best being T5, with fellow Scot Alastair Forsyth, at the Belgacom Open. He also finished T26 at the British Open.

Jeremy Robinson
European Tour

Born 21 January 1966
Place of Birth Scarborough, England
Year turned Professional 1987
Tour Ranking 129th

BEST FINISH IN MAJORS
Tied 58th **BRITISH OPEN 1999**

Robinson joined the European Tour in 1992, but lost his card in 1995 after three unspectacular years. He played on the Challenge Tour between 1996 and 1998 and regained his card at 1998 Qualifying School, rejoining the main Tour in 1999. His highest finish is T5 at both the 1994 Madeira Island Open and the 1994 BMW International Open.
 2000 SEASON. He was T9 at the Scottish PGA Championship, but fell back to 129th on the Order of Merit.

Costantino Rocca
European Tour

Born 4 December 1956
Place of Birth Bergamo, Italy
Year turned Professional 1981
Tour Ranking 152nd

BEST FINISH IN MAJORS
2nd **BRITISH OPEN 1995**

TOUR VICTORIES
EUROPEAN: 5
 1993 Open V33 Du Grand Lyon, Peugeot Open de France
 1996 Volvo PGA Championship
 1997 Canon European Masters
 1999 West of Ireland Golf Classic

RYDER CUP 1993, 1995, 1997
DUNHILL CUP 1986, 1987, 1989, 1991, 1992, 1996, 1999
WORLD CUP 1988, 1990, 1991, 1992, 1993, 1994, 1995, 1996, 1998, 1999

A cheerful Italian, who worked in a factory in Bergamo to finance his golf, Rocca turned pro at the age of 24. He came off the Challenge Tour to join the European Tour, and won his first tournament in 1993. He is best known for his duffed chip from the Valley of Sin at the 72nd green at St Andrews in the 1995 British Open, which he followed by sinking a 60-foot putt to tie with John Daly. He lost the four-hole play-off. Rocca has played three times in the Ryder Cup, his proudest moment being in 1997 when he beat Tiger Woods to help Europe retain the trophy. His 1996 win at the Volvo PGA Championship gave him a ten-year exemption on Tour.

2000 SEASON. Rocca had a very disappointing season, with his highest finish T28 at the Benson & Hedges Open. He slumped from 35th to 152nd on the Order of Merit.

Carlos Rodiles
European Tour

Born 3 May 1975
Place of Birth Malaga, Spain
Year turned Professional 1997
Tour Ranking 3rd (Challenge Tour)

A self-taught young Spaniard who began his golf career as a caddie, Rodiles qualified through the 1998 European Tour Qualifying

School, but could finish in only 162nd place on the 1999 Tour. On the 2000 Challenge Tour he had three runner-up placings, and a T7 at both the French and Spanish Opens, to end the Tour in third position. Rodiles has lived in the US since the age of 15.

Chi Chi Rodriguez
US Seniors Tour

Born 23 October 1935
Place of Birth Rio Piedras, Puerto Rico
Year turned Professional 1960
Tour Ranking 72nd

MAJORS VICTORIES
PGA SENIORS CHAMPIONSHIP 1987

TOUR VICTORIES
SENIOR TOUR: 21
- 1986 Digital Seniors Classic, Senior Tournament Players Championship, United Virginia Bank Seniors
- 1987 Digital Seniors Classic, GTE Northwest Classic, Senior Golf Championship, Senior Players Reunion Pro-Am, Silver Pages Classic, Vantage at the Dominion
- 1988 Digital Seniors Classic, Doug Sanders Celebrity Classic
- 1989 Crestar Classic
- 1990 Ameritech Senior Open, Las Vegas Senior Classic, Sunwest/Charley Pride Classic
- 1991 GTEWest Classic, Las Vegas Senior Classic, Murata Reunion Pro-Am, Vintage Arco Invitational
- 1992 Ko Olina Senior Invitational
- 1993 Burnet Senior Classic

The impish Puerto Rican Rodriguez, a compulsive showman, wisecracker and coiner of corny golfing aphorisms, dominated the US Senior Tour in the late 1980s, in spite of his whiplash swing and his dancing antics on the green. His talkative manner was not always appreciated by his fellow pros, some of whom described him as 'the four-stroke penalty' for his distracting behaviour.

'Cheech' won 22 tournaments on Tour, to add to the eight he captured on the USPGA Tour between 1963 and 1979. He also represented the US in the 1973 Ryder Cup and played no less than 12 times in the World Cup for Puerto Rico. In his rookie year of 1986 he won three events and the following year he lifted another seven, including three in a row. In 1991 he collected four victories in seven weeks, ending the season in fourth place on the Money List, and he won his last title, the Burnet Senior Classic, in 1993, having earned nearly $5 million in Senior tournaments. He runs a charity – the Chi Chi Rodriguez Foundation – which has raised over $3 mllion for good causes.

2000 SEASON. Rodriguez had two top-10 finishes, his highest being T3 at the Fleet-Boston Classic. He is in the top-31 of the All-Time Money List.

Gustavo Rojas
European Tour

Born 28 September 1967
Place of Birth Buenos Aires, Argentina
Year turned Professional 1984
Tour Ranking 121st

The holder of six South American titles, Argentinian Rojas played on the Challenge Tour in 1999 and secured his Tour card for 2000.

2000 SEASON. He was T7 at the BMW International Open, his only top-10 spot, and ended the season in 121st place on the Order of Merit.

Eduardo Romero
European Tour

Born 17 July 1954
Place of Birth Cordoba, Argentina
Year turned Professional 1982
Tour Ranking 16th

BEST FINISH IN MAJORS
Tied 7th **BRITISH OPEN 1997**

TOUR VICTORIES
EUROPEAN: 7
    1989 Trophee Lancome
    1990 Volvo Open di Firenze
    1991 Peugeot French Open, Peugeot Spanish Open
    1994 Canon European Masters, Tisettanta Italian Open
    2000 Canon European Masters

DUNHILL CUP 1988, 1989, 1990, 1993, 1995, 1997, 1998, 2000
WORLD CUP 1983, 1984, 1987, 1988, 1991, 1993, 1994, 1995, 1998, 1999

A long-standing member of the European Tour, Romero has been in the top-30 of the Order of Merit every year since 1989, except for 1995 when he made only eight starts. Known as 'El Gato' (The Cat) for his stalking skills on the course, he is the best Argentinian player of the last 20 years. A tall, powerful golfer, he won six times on the European Tour from 1989 to 1994, his last victory in that period coming at the Canon European Masters. He sponsored fellow countryman Angel Cabrera on the European Tour (Cabrera finished the 2000 Order of Merit two places higher than Romero) and has won on numerous occasions in South America. He recently took up yoga in order to improve his concentration.

2000 SEASON. He had three T3s – in the Qatar Masters, Sao Paolo Open and the Spanish Open – and a T6 at the Irish Open. He then played brilliantly to win the Canon European Masters in September by ten strokes, posting an opening round 64 and a third round course record 62, containing two eagles and five birdies. He became the oldest winner on Tour for nearly ten years.

Jenny Rosales
US Ladies Tour

Born 17 September 1978
Place of Birth Manila, Philippines
Year turned Professional 1999
Tour Ranking 79th

Five times winner of the Philippine Ladies Open, Rosales joined the 2000 LPGA Tour by finishing T7 at Qualifying School. Her best finish was T12 at the US Women's Open.

2001 STOP PRESS. Rosales finished tied for 3third place at the Office Depot.

Justin Rose
European Tour

Born 30 July 1980
Place of Birth Johannesburg, South Africa
Year turned Professional 1998
Tour Ranking 9th (Qualifying School)

South African born, but raised in England, Rose made international headlines at the 1998 British Open at Royal Birkdale when the 17-year-old chipped in at the last hole to claim fourth place and receive the Silver Medal for the leading amateur. The tall young golfer immediately turned professional, but failed to

make his next 21 cuts and had to return to the Qualifying School in 1999, finishing fourth. His best place on the 2000 European Tour was 11th at the BMW International Open and he returned to Qualifying School in 2000.

2001 STOP PRESS. Rose justified the 1998 hype at the beginning of the season when he was runner-up in successive weeks at the Alfred Dunhill Championship and the Mercedes Benz South African Open.

Scott Rowe
European Tour

Born 10 March 1975
Place of Birth Puerto Rico
Year turned Professional 1997
Tour Ranking 146th

Tall Puerto Rican Rowe, now a US citizen, joined the European Tour in 2000. He made nine cuts in 22 tournaments, his highest finish being T14 at the Morocco Open.

Brett Rumford
European Tour

Born 27 July 1977
Place of Birth Perth, Australia
Year turned Professional 2000
Tour Ranking 8th (Qualifying School)

TOUR VICTORIES
AUSTRALASIAN: 1

1999 Australian Players Championship

Rumford won the 1998 Australian Amateur Championship and he claimed the 1999 Australasian Tour TPC as an amateur. He turned pro in 2000 and was runner-up behind Michael Campbell in the Ericsson Masters, as well as finishing seventh in the Trophee Lancome on the European Tour. He secured his European Tour card by coming through Qualifying School.

2001 STOP PRESS. He finished T2 behind Darren Fitchardt at the Sao Paulo Open.

Raymond Russell
European Tour

Born 26 July 1972
Place of Birth Edinburgh, Scotland
Year turned Professional 1993
Tour Ranking 64th

BEST FINISH IN MAJORS
Tied 4th **BRITISH OPEN 1998**

TOUR VICTORIES
EUROPEAN: 1

1996 Air France Cannes Open

DUNHILL CUP 1996, 1997
WORLD CUP 1997

Edinburgh-born Russell joined the European Tour in 1996 and won the Cannes Open in his first season. In 1998 he contracted hepatitis at the Johnnie Walker Classic and he felt its effects throughout the season. In spite of this, however, he retained his card with a T4 at the British Open. He finished his 1999 season with a second-place finish in the Australian Ford Open and a T3 in the Australian Players Championship. He is a very good wind player, an excellent putter and is coached by Bob Torrance.

2000 SEASON. Russell had four top-20 placings, including a third-place finish in the Scandinavian Masters, shooting four rounds in the 60s and finishing four strokes behind winner Lee Westwood.

Johan Rystrom

Born 13 January 1964
Place of Birth Koping, Sweden
Year turned Professional 1986
Tour Ranking 9th (Challenge Tour)

A tall Swede who joined the European Tour in 1988, Rystrom has never won a tournament, although he has finished runner-up on three occasions.

2000 SEASON. Rystrom had six top-10 finishes on Tour.

Rory Sabbatini
US Tour

Born 2 April 1976
Place of Birth Durban, South Africa
Year turned Professional 1998
Tour Ranking 36th

BEST FINISH IN MAJORS
77th USPGA 2000

TOUR VICTORIES
US: 1
2000 Air Canada Championship

South African Sabbatini joined the US Tour in 1999 straight from the Qualifying School and retained his card thanks to two third-place finishes that season. He was also ranked in fourth place for driving distance at the end of that year.

2000 SEASON. Sabbatini won his first US Tour tournament when he sank a 30-foot birdie putt on the last hole to win the Air Canada Championship. Ironocally, he had missed the cut in three of his previous five tournaments.

2001 STOP PRESS. Sabbatini missed a great chance to notch up his second Tour victory when he missed a 3-foot putt on the last green at the Mercedes Championship to hand the title to Jim Furyk.

Kim Saiki
US Ladies Tour

Born 24 January 1966
Place of Birth Inglewood, California, USA
Year turned Professional 1992
Tour Ranking 82nd

Junior World Champion in 1983, Saiki joined the LPGA Tour in 1992. She has subsequently been runner-up on four occasions.

2000 SEASON. Saiki had three top-20 finishes, her highest being T8 at the Dinah Shore. She was 82nd on the Money List.

Jarmo Sandelin
European Tour

Born 10 May 1967
Place of Birth Imatra, Finland
Year turned Professional 1987
Tour Ranking 38th

BEST FINISH IN MAJORS
Tied 31st BRITISH OPEN 2000

TOUR VICTORIES
EUROPEAN: 4
1995 Turespana Open Canarias
1996 Madeira Island Open
1999 German Open, Peugeot Open de Espana

RYDER CUP 1999
DUNHILL CUP 1995, 1996, 1999
WORLD CUP 1995, 1996, 1999

Finnish by birth, but Swedish by naturalization, Sandelin is one of the more flamboyant golfers on the European Tour. He graduated through the Challenge Tour to join the European Tour in 1995 when, with one Tour victory and two runner-up spots, he was Rookie of the Year. Identifiable by his cowboy boots and see-through shirts, he has won three other events on the Tour and played one match in the 1999 Ryder Cup, losing to Phil Mickelson. He had a public dispute with Mickelson in the 1996 Dunhill Cup when the American complained about his excessive celebrating. He also had a disagreement with Mark O'Meara in the 1997 Trophee Lancome when he accused the 1998 British Open Champion of of improperly replacing his ball. Not surprisingly, he received a hostile welcome from American fans in the Ryder Cup match in Boston in 1999. His last wins also came in 1999, at the Peugeot Open de Espana, which he won by four shots, and at the German Open. Sandelin uses a long, 52-inch driver and hits the ball a very long way.

2000 SEASON. Sandelin had a hole in one at the Loch Lomond and picked up £100,000. His best finish was T5 at the European Open.

Sara Hallock Sanders
US Ladies Tour

Born 14 December 1972
Place of Birth Los Angeles, California, USA
Year turned Professional 1996
Tour Ranking 89th

Californian Sanders played on the Futures Tour in 1997 and joined the LPGA Tour in 1998, when she achieved a career-best third at the Michelob Light Classic.

2000 SEASON. Sanders had three top-15s, the best was T10 at the Jamie Farr Kroeger Classic.

Marcello Santi
European Tour

Born 30 September 1969
Place of Birth Milan, Italy
Year turned Professional 1992
Tour Ranking 17th (Qualifying School)

TOUR VICTORIES
OTHER: 1
1995 Mauritius Open

Winner of the Italian Amateur Championship at the age of 15, 6 foot 3 inch Santi went on to win the trophy a further six times. He won the Mauritius Open in 1995 and, in 1998, won the Audi Quattro Trophy on the Challenge Tour. In 2000 his highest finish was second at the Le Touquet Challenge on the Challenge Tour. He qualified for the 2001 European Tour.

Nobuhito Sato
Japanese Tour

Born 12 March 1970
Place of Birth Chiba, Japan
Year turned Professional 1993
Tour Ranking 3rd

TOUR VICTORIES
OTHER: 6
1997 JCB Classic Sendai
1998 Bridgestone Open
2000 ANA Open, Bridgestone Open, Japan PGA Championship, JCB Classic Sendai

Sato was a four-time winner on the 2000 Japanese Tour and was third on the Money List. He played in two US Tour events, his best finish being T25 at the WGC-American Express Championship.

Stephen Scahill

European Tour

Born 3 October 1969
Place of Birth Featherston, New Zealand
Year turned Professional 1993
Tour Ranking 19th (Qualifying School)

TOUR VICTORIES
OTHER: 1
   1993 Pahang Open

New Zealander Scahill played on the European Tour in 1997 and 1998, with his highest finish being second at the Madeira Island Open. He gained his card for the 2001 Tour through Qualifying School.

Massimo Scarpa

European Tour

Born 5 June 1970
Place of Birth Venice, Italy
Year turned Professional 1993
Tour Ranking 110th

TOUR VICTORIES
EUROPEAN: 1
   2000 North West of Ireland Open

DUNHILL CUP 1999

Scarpa won four times on the Challenge Tour circuit in 1998 and joined the European Tour in 1999 when he made 16 out of 25 cuts. He plays both left and right handed, depending on distance.

2000 SEASON. He won his first tournament, at the North West of Ireland Open.

Tom Scherrer

US Tour

Born 20 July, 1970
Place of Birth Syracuse, New York
Year turned Professional 1992
Tour Ranking 35th

TOUR VICTORIES
US: 1
   2000 Kemper Insurance Open

Runner-up to Justin Leonard in the 1992 US Amateur Championship, Scherrer joined the US Tour from the Nike Tour in 1996. He failed to retain his card and played on the Nike Tour in 1997 and 1998. He rejoined the mainTour in 1999.

2000 SEASON. He began the season well, finishing in second place at the Tucson Open, and then shot four sub-70 rounds to win the Kemper Open. He had two other top-10s and finished 35th on the Money List.

Brent Schwarzrock

US Tour

Born 11 May 1972
Place of Birth Orlando, Florida, USA
Year turned Professional 1995
Tour Ranking Tied 31st (Qualifying School)

Schwarzrock is a tall (6 foot 4 inch) Floridan who joined the Nike Tour in 1998 and qualified for the US Tour the following year. A back injury confined him to only one round that year. In 2000 he received a medical exemption and played in 27 events, finishing 195th. His highest placing is T18 at the 2000 Southern Farm Bureau Classic. He qualified from Qualifying School again in 2000 and received his 2001 Tour card.

Adam Scott

Born 16 July, 1980
Place of Birth Adelaide, Australia
Year turned Professional 2000
Tour Ranking 102nd

TOUR VICTORIES
EUROPEAN: 1
   2001 Alfred Dunhill PGA Championship

TOUR VICTORIES
EUROPEAN: 1
2000 Chart Hill Classic

New Zealander Scott played her European Ladies Tour rookie year in 2000. She won the Chart Hills Classic, in a play-off with Italian Isabelle Maconi, and was also T5 at the French Open and T7 at the German Open.

Nancy Scranton
US Ladies Tour

Born 26 April 1961
Place of Birth Centralia, Illinois, USA
Year turned Professional 1984
Tour Ranking 18th

MAJORS VICTORIES
DU MAURIER CLASSIC 1991

TOUR VICTORIES
US: 2
1992 Los Coyotes LPGA Classic
2000 Subaru Memorial of Naples

SOLHEIM CUP 2000

Scott is one of the bright young stars of Australian and world golf. Coached by Butch Harmon, and possessing a swing uncannily similar to Tiger Woods, Scott (known as 'swivel hips' to his mentor Greg Norman) is a very long and accurate driver with a skilful short game. Immediately after turning professional, he visited Harmon at his golf school in Las Vegas and enjoyed a practice round with Harmon's more famous pupil, Tiger Woods. Woods won the friendly game 5&4. He joined the European Tour from the Australasian Tour in 2000 and was sixth in the Moroccan Open, only his second event on Tour. He collected four top-12s in his first six European tournaments and gained his 2001 Tour card. At the 2000 Greg Norman Holden Invitational Scott shot a course record 63 and finished T37 as an amateur.

2001 STOP PRESS. In windy conditions, Scott birdied the 72nd hole to win an exciting Alfred Dunhill PGA Championship, in South Africa, holding off a resurgent Justin Rose to win the title by just one shot.

Gina Scott
European Ladies Tour

Born 27 September 1972
Place of Birth Auckland, New Zealand
Year turned Professional 1997
Tour Ranking 24th

Scranton is a long-time member of the LPGA Tour, having first joined the circuit way back in 1985, and she has won three tournaments in her career. In 1991, she shot a third round 64 at the du Maurier Classic to help her win her first and only Major Championship title. In 1992, her last round 65 enabled her to overcome a seven-shot deficit at the Los Coyotes LPGA Classic to win the event.

2000 SEASON. Scranton picked up her third LPGA title at the Subaru Memorial of Naples, after a sudden-death play-off with Sweden's Maria Hjorth. She also tied for third place at the McDonalds LPGA Championship and had four other top-10s. She played in the Solheim Cup.

2001 STOP PRESS. Nancy made the cut in 14 of the first 15 events she played in, and finished in the top-10 seven times. She also posted a top-3 finish in the Hawaiian Ladies Open.

John Senden
European Tour

Born 20 April 1971
Place of Birth Brisbane, Australia
Year turned Professional 1992
Tour Ranking 71st

TOUR VICTORIES
OTHER: 1
1996 Indonesian PGA Championship

A tall, powerful Australian, Senden joined the European Tour from the Challenge Tour in 1999 when his best finish was T6 at the European Open.

2000 SEASON. Senden had four top-20 finishes as well as a career-best T4 at the French Open.

Peter Senior
European Tour

Born 31 July, 1959
Place of Birth Singapore
Year turned Professional 1978
Tour Ranking 41st

TOUR VICTORIES
EUROPEAN TOUR: 4
1986 PLM Open

1987 Johnnie Walker Monte Carlo Open
1990 Panasonic European Open
1992 Benson & Hedges International Open
OTHER: 4
1978 Dunhill South Australian Open
1984 Stefan Queensland Open, Honeywell Classic
1987 U-Bix Classic, Rich River Classic, PGA Championship of Queensland
1989 NSW PGA Championship, Australian PGA Championship, Johnnie Walker Classic, Australian Open
1990 Four Tours Championship (Japan)
1991 Pyramid Australian Masters, Johnnie Walker Classic
1992 Bridgestone AS0 Open (Japan)
1993 Heineken Classic, Chunichi Crown (Japan)
1995 Dunlop Open (Japan), Australian Masters
1996 Canon Challenge, Greg Norman's Holden Classic
1997 Canon Challenge

A much-travelled international golfer, Senior has won 18 times on the Australasian Tour and three times on the Japanese Tour. The last of his four victories in Europe came in 1992 at the Benson & Hedges International Open when he won a play-off against Tony Johnstone.

2000 SEASON. His best finish was second at the Greg Norman Holden International.

Bob Shearer
European Senior Tour

Born 28 May 1948
Place of Birth Melbourne, Australia
Year turned Professional 1970
Tour Ranking 12th

TOUR VICTORIES
SENIOR TOUR: 3
1998 Jersey Seniors Open
1999 PGA Seniors Open, Philips PFA Golf Classic

ustralian-born Shearer has won over 25 international tournaments in his career, including the Australian Open in 1982 and the Australian PGA in 1983. He also won twice on the European Tour in 1975. He has represented Australia in two World Cups. He joined the European Senior Tour in 1998 and won the Jersey Seniors Open in his rookie year, and he won two more events in 1999.

2000 SEASON. In his highest finish of the season, Shearer lost the first hole play-off to Brian Huggett at the Beko Classic. He finished 12th on the Order of Merit.

Patty Sheehan

US Ladies Tour

Born 27 October 1956
Place of Birth Middlebury, Vermont, USA
Year turned Professional 1980
Tour Ranking 150th

MAJORS VICTORIES
US OPEN 1992, 1994
LPGA 1983, 1984, 1993
DINAH SHORE 1996

TOUR VICTORIES
US: 29
1981 Mazda Japan Classic
1982 Inamori Classic, Orlando Lady Classic, Safeco Classic
1983 Corning Classic, Henredon Classic, Inamori Classic
1984 Elizabeth Arden Classic, Henredon Classic, McDonald's Kids Classic
1985 J&B Pro-Am, Sarasota Classic
1986 Inamori Classic, San Jose Classic, Sarasota Classic
1988 Mazda Japan Classic, Sarasota Classic
1989 Rochester International
1990 Jamaica Classic, McDonald's Championship, Ping-Cellular One LPGA Championship, Rochester International, Safeco Classic
1991 Hawaiian Ladies Open

1992 Jamie Farr Toledo Classic, Rochester International
1993 Standard Register Ping
1995 Rochester International, Safeco Classic

fter a distinguished amateur career, which included winning all four of her matches at the 1980 Curtis Cup, Sheehan joined the US Ladies Tour and was Rookie of the Year in her first season. A small but determined golfer, Sheehan's enthusiastic approach to the game brought her 20 titles in the 1980s, including two Majors, and she was Player of the Year in 1983 when she won four events. She won four times again in 1990. In 1992 she won the US Women's Open, having been runner-up on three occasions, when she defeated Juli Inkster in a play-off at Oakmont. She won the title again in 1994 and captured her first Dinah Shore in 1996. Sheehan is a member of the LPGA Hall of Fame.

2000 SEASON. She played in only 12 events on Tour and was 150th on the Money List.

Jay Sigel

US Seniors Tour

Born 13 November 1943
Place of Birth Bryn Mawr, Pennsylvania, USA
Year turned Professional 1993
Tour Ranking 52nd

MAJORS VICTORIES
SENIOR PLAYERS CHAMPIONSHIP 1996

TOUR VICTORIES
SENIOR TOUR: 5
1994 GTE Western Classic
1997 Bruno's Memorial Classic, Kroger Senior Classic
1998 Bell Atlantic Classic, Kaanapali Classic

igel, one of the greatest amateurs in the history of golf, won the US Amateur Championship in 1982 and 1983 and the British Amateur Championship in 1979. He was also low amateur in The Masters three times, as well as in the 1980 British Open and the 1984 US Open, and he represented the US in nine Walker Cup competitions. The long-hitting, ex-insurance executive joined the US Senior Tour in 1994 and was Rookie of the Year, beating Jim Colbert in the GTE Western Classic and recording fourteen top-10s and three top-3s. In 1996 he won the Senior Players Championship, two shots ahead of Kermit Zarley, and the following year he won twice more. The following year he shot an incredible front nine 27 in the second round of the Players Championship. In 1999 he fell out of the top-31 for the first time in his Senior career.

2000 SEASON. He played in 30 events, but had a niggling shoulder injury and fell to 52nd on the Money List. He remains fully exempt because of his position in the All Time 31.

Simpson had his first win on the US Tour at the 1980 Western Open. He won his only Major title in 1987 when he shot a 68 in the final round at Olympic to overcome an overnight deficit and beat Tom Watson by one stroke. He also lost in a playoff to Payne Stewart at the 1991 US Open. In 1997 he ended outside the top-125 for the first time since 1979. His last victory came in 1998 in a play-off against Skip Kendall on the first extra hole of the Buick Invitational.

2000 SEASON. Simpson broke an ankle while skiing before the start of the season and did not play on Tour. He received a Major medical exemption for 2001.

2001 STOP PRESS. Simpson had his best finish since 1998 when he was T2 behind Scott Hoch at the Greater Greensboro Classic.

Scott Simpson

US Tour

Born 17 September 1955
Place of Birth San Diego, California, USA
Year turned Professional 1977
Tour Ranking N/A

MAJORS VICTORIES
US OPEN 1987

TOUR VICTORIES
US: 6
    1980 Western Open
    1984 Westchester Classic
    1987 Greater Greensboro Open
    1989 BellSouth Atlanta Golf Classic
    1993 GTE Byron Nelson Golf Classic
    1998 Buick Invitational
EUROPEAN: 1
    1990 Perrier Invitational
OTHER: 3
    1984 Chunichi Crowns, Dunlop Phoenix
    1988 Chunichi Crowns

RYDER CUP 1987

Erol Simsek

European Tour

Born 4 March 1971
Place of Birth Tekirdag, Turkey
Year turned Professional 1989
Tour Ranking 12th (Challenge Tour)

Turkish-born Simsek moved to West Germany in 1981 and turned pro in 1989. He became a German citizen in 1993 and played on the European Tour in 1995.

Joey Sindelar

US Tour

Borns 30 March, 1958
Place of Birth Fort Knox, Kentucky
Year turned Professional 1981
Tour Ranking 126th

TOUR VICTORIES
US: 6
    1985 Greater Greensboro Open, BC Open
    1987 BC Open
    1988 Honda Classic, The International
    1990 Hardee's Golf Classic

Sindelar has played on the US Tour since 1983 and has won six tournaments, the last, Hardee's Golf Classic, in 1990. His best year was 1988 when he won two tournaments and was third on the Money List.

2000 SEASON. He had two T5 finishes – at the BellSouth Classic and the Buick Classic – but just slipped out of the top-125 exemption status, finishing 126th on the Money List.

Jeev Milkha Singh

European Tour

Born 15 December 1971
Place of Birth Chandigarh, India
Year turned Professional 1993
Tour Ranking 145th

DUNHILL CUP 1996, 1999

The first Indian to play on the European Tour, Singh joined the Tour from Qualifying School in 1998. The following season he rose to a highly creditable 50th spot on the Order of Merit, helped by a T2 in the South African Open. He has won several tournaments in the Far East. He played in the Indian team which unexpectedly beat Scotland in the 1996 Dunhill Cup.

2000 SEASON. Singh suffered from an injured wrist and was only fit enough to play in 13 tournaments. His best finish was T5 at the Malaysian Open and he was 145th on the Order of Merit.

Vijay Singh

US Tour

Born 22nd February 1963
Place of Birth Lautoka, Fiji
Year turned Professional 1982
Tour Ranking 5th

MAJORS VICTORIES
US MASTERS 2000
USPGA 1998

TOUR VICTORIES
US: 7
  1993 Buick Classic
  1995 Buick Classic, Phoenix Open
  1997 Buick Open, Memorial Tournament
  1998 Sprint International
  1999 Honda Classic
EUROPEAN: 9
  1989 Volvo Open de Firenze
  1990 El Bosque Open
  1992 German Open, Turespana Masters Open de Andalucia
  1994 Scandinavian Masters, Trophee Lancome
  1997 World Match Play Championship
  2001 Malaysian Open, Singapore Masters
SOUTH AFRICA: 3
  1989 Zimbabwe Open
  1993 Bell's Cup
  1997 South African Open
OTHER: 9
  1984 Malaysian PGA
  1988 Nigerian Open, Swedish PGA
  1989 Ivory Coast Open, Nigerian Open
  1991 King Hassan Trophy
  1992 Malaysian Open
  1995 Passport Open
  2000 Taiwan Open

PRESIDENTS CUP 1994, 1996, 1998, 2000

A tall, long-driving Fijian, Singh (whose first name means 'victory' in Hindi), played on the Asian, European and African Tours before joining the US Tour in 1993. An obsessive practiser and a deadly accurate iron player, he is renowned for remaining on the practice range for hour after hour. As a consequence, he is one of the physically stronger golfers on Tour. He won a tournament, the Buick Classic, in his first season and was also Rookie of the Year. By the end of the 1990s he had won a further seven US tournaments, picking up two trophies in both 1995 and 1997, and in 1996 this remarkably consistent golfer made the cut in all of the 24 events he entered. He won his first Major title in 1998 when he beat Steve Stricker by two strokes at the USPGA Championship and he was also victorious that year in the modified Stableford Sprint International event. He ended the decade by beating Payne Stewart by two shots in the 1999 Honda Classic. He has recently switched to the broomhandle putter in an effort to improve his inconsistent putting.

2000 SEASON. Singh claimed his second Major title when he defeated Ernie Els at The Masters by three shots, and was T11 at the British Open and T8 at the US Open.

2001 STOP PRESS. By the time of The Masters in April, Singh had already posted two runner-up places and tied for third on three occasions on the US Tour. In the European Tour, he was even more impressive and notched up back-to-back victories at the Malaysian Open. He beat Irishman Paidrag Harrington firstly in a play-off, and then at the Singapore Masters a week later.

Pearl Sinn
US Ladies Tour

Born 17 July 1967
Place of Birth Seoul, South Korea
Year turned Professional 1989
Tour Ranking 71st

TOUR VICTORIES
US: 1
  1998 State Farm Rail Classic

One of an increasing number of Korean golfers on the LPGA Tour, the glamorous Sinn's amateur achievements include the US Women's Championship and the Public Links Championship, both in 1988. She joined the LPGA Tour in 1991 and in 1998 she picked up her only victory at the State Farm Rail Classic, where she shot three rounds in the 60s.

2000 SEASON. She had two top-10s, her highest being T6 at the State farm.

Patrick Sjoland
European Tour

Born 13 May 1971
Place of Birth Boras, Sweden
Year turned Professional 1990
Tour Ranking 23rd

BEST FINISH IN MAJORS
Tied 18th **BRITISH OPEN 1999**

TOUR VICTORIES
EUROPEAN: 2
  1998 Fiat & Fila Italian Open
  2000 Murphy's Irish Open

DUNHILL CUP 1996, 1998, 1999
WORLD CUP 1996, 1998, 1999

Sjoland joined the European Tour in 1996 and won his first tournament – the Italian Open – two years later. He had three other runner-up spots that year and ended the season in fifth place on the Order of Merit. In 1999, he beat Ian Woosnam by one shot to win the Hong Kong Open – an unofficial Tour event – scoring a course record 62 in his third round.

2000 SEASON. Sjoland claimed his second European Tour title when he defeated Fredrik Jacobson by two strokes at the Murphy's Irish Open at Ballybunion.

Johan Skold
European Tour

Born 28 February 1975
Place of Birth Balsta, Sweden
Year turned Professional 1996
Tour Ranking 120th

Skold played 14 events on the 1997 European Tour but lost his card and played on the Challenge Tour in 1998 and 1999.

2000 SEASON. He achieved his highest-ever finish on Tour – T7 at the Heineken Classic – but still finished 120th on the Order of Merit.

Jeff Sluman
US Tour

Born 11 September 1957
Place of Birth Rochester, New York, USA
Year turned Professional 1980
Tour Ranking 54th

MAJORS VICTORIES
USPGA 1988

TOUR VICTORIES
US: 3
1997 Tucson Chrysler Classic
1998 Greater Milwaukee Open
1999 Sony Open in Hawaii

An accurate and consistent golfer, Jeff Sluman is one of the most popular players on the circuit and has played continuously on the US Tour since 1985. He is best remembered for the 1988 PGA Championship when he won his first title and his only Major by shooting a 6 under par 65 in the final round to beat Paul Azinger by three strokes. He then remained winless for nearly ten years until he picked up the Tucson Classic, in Arizona, in 1997. He won again the following year at the Greater Milwaukee Open when he shot four rounds in the 60s to beat Steve Stricker by one shot. He won again in 1999, beating Jeff Maggert by two strokes at the Sony Open in Hawaii. He is a relatively long hitter for such a slight figure.

2000 SEASON. His best finish was seventh at the National Car Rental Golf Classic, but he made 25 out of a possible 32 cuts and ended the season in 54th place on the Money List.

2001 STOP PRESS. Sluman tied for second place at the Nissan Open, in California.

David Smail
Australasian Tour

Born 20 May 1970
Place of Birth Hamilton, New Zealand
Year turned Professional 1992
Tour Ranking 4th

TOUR VICTORIES
AUSTRALASIAN: 2
2001 Canon Challenge, New Zealand Open

Prior to the 2000–01 season Smail's highest finish on the Australasian Tour was third at the 1996 Australian Open. In 2000–01, however, he enjoyed his best ever-season, winning twice and coming second in the Heineken Classic behind Michael Campbell. He was also T6 in the Tour Championship and ended the season fourth on the Order of Merit.

Chris Smith
US Tour

Born 15th April 1969
Place of Birth Indiannapolis, Indiana, USA
Year turned Professional 1991
Tour Ranking 6th (Buy.Com Tour)

Player of the Year on the 1997 Nike Tour, Smith won three tournaments that season and achieved 'battlefield promotion', ie promoted to the US Tour for gaining three victories in one season. He remained on the main tour in 1998 and 1999 and joined the Buy.Com Tour in 2000, where he made seven top-10 finishes and claimed sixth place on the Money List. A long hitter, he holds the US Tour record for distance, having driven the ball 427 yards at the 1999 Honda Classic. His highest finish is fourth at the 1997 CVS Charity Classic.

Jerry Smith

US Tour

Born 24 April 1964
Place of Birth Council Bluffs, Iowa, USA
Year turned Professional 1987
Tour Ranking 118th

Smith joined the US Tour in 2000 from Qualifying School and had one top-10 finish – ninth at the GTE Byron Nelson Classic – in the season.

Des Smyth

European Tour

Born 12 February 1953
Place of Birth Drogheda, Ireland
Year turned Professional 1973
Tour Ranking 111th

BEST FINISH IN MAJORS
Tied 4th **BRITISH OPEN 1982**

TOUR VICTORIES
EUROPEAN: 8
 1979 European Match Play Championship
 1980 Greater Manchester Open, Newcastle Brown '900'
 1981 Coral Classic
 1983 Sanyo Open
 1988 Jersey Open
 1993 Madrid Open
 2001 Madeira Island Open

RYDER CUP 1979, 1981
DUNHILL CUP 1985, 1986, 1987, 1988
WORLD CUP 1979, 1980, 1982, 1988, 1989

Veteran Irishman Smyth has played on the European Tour since 1974 and has won eight tournaments, the last before 2001

being the 1993 Madrid Open. His best year was 1988 when he won the Jersey Open, had three runner-up spots and finished seventh on the Order of Merit. He has played in two Ryder Cups.

2000 SEASON. Smyth managed only one top-20, T6 at the Irish Open.

2001 STOP PRESS. Smyth won the Madeira Island Open by two strokes from John Bickerton, becoming at 48 the oldest-ever winner on the European Tour

JC Snead

US Seniors Tour

Born 14 October 1940
Place of Birth Hot Springs, Virginia, USA
Year turned Professional 1964
Tour Ranking 45th

MAJORS VICTORIES
 SENIOR PLAYERS CHAMPIONSHIP 1995

TOUR VICTORIES
SENIOR TOUR: 2
 1993 Vantage at Dominion
 1995 Royal Caribbean Classic

Nephew of the great Sam Snead, Jesse Carlyle won eight times on the USPGA Tour and represented the US in the 1971, 1973 and 1975 Ryder Cups, winning all four of his matches in the first tournament. He joined the US Senior Tour in 1990 and collected his first tournament – the Vantage – in 1993. His long, accurate driving helped him to claim two more events in 1995, when he saw off Ray Floyd in a play-off at the Royal Caribbean Classic, and beat Jack Nicklaus at the first sudden-death hole at the Senior Players Championship. His 1999 season was his most profitable since 1995, securing 11 top-10s and passing $5 million in Senior career earnings.

2000 SEASON. He recorded three top-10 finishes, the best being T2 at the LiquidGolf.com Invitational.

Annika Sorenstam

US Ladies Tour

Born 9 October 1970
Place of Birth Stockholm, Sweden
Year turned Professional 1992
Tour Ranking 2nd

MAJORS VICTORIES

US OPEN 1995, 1996
DINAH SHORE 2001

TOUR VICTORIES

US: 25
- 1995 Heartland Cup, Samsung World Championship of Women's Golf
- 1996 Betsy King Classic, Samsung World Championship of Women's Golf
- 1997 Betsy King Classic, Chrysler-Plymouth Tournament of Champions, Hawaiian Open, ITT LPGA Tour Championship, Longs Drugs Challenge, Michelob Light Classic
- 1998 JAL Big Apple Classic, Michelob Light Classic, SAFECO Classic, ShopRite Classic
- 1999 Michelob Light Classic, New Albany Golf Classic
- 2000 Evian Masters, Firstar Classic, JAL Big Apple Classic, Jamie Farr Kroger Classic, Welch's Circle K Championship
- 2001 Standard Register Ping, Welch's Circle K Classic, Office Depot, Chick-Fil-A Charity Championship

EUROPEAN: 6
- 1995 Hennessy Cup, OVB Damen Open
- 1996 Trygg Hansa Open
- 1997 Compaq Open
- 1998 Compaq Open
- 2000 Evian Masters

SOLHEIM CUP 1994, 1996, 1998, 2000

A graduate from the University of Arizona, the quiet, methodical and very shy Swede nonetheless blazed her way through the LPGA Tour in the 1990s, winning an unequalled 18 titles in that decade alone. The World Amateur Champion in 1992, she was 1993 Rookie of the Year on the European Tour and Rookie of the Year again in 1994 on the LPGA Tour. Her finest year was 1995 when she became the first player to top the Money List in both the US and Europe, capturing five titles in total, including the US Women's Open.

She won the Open again in 1996, and she was LPGA Player of the Year in both 1997 and 1998, picking up ten tournament victories. She also won the Vare Trophy for the lowest scoring average in 1995, 1996 and 1998. Born in Stockholm, Sweden, she is now married to an American and lives in Florida.

2000 SEASON. Sorenstam recorded five more tournament wins on the LPGA Tour, including a record-equalling 19 under par at the Firstar LPGA Classic and back-to-back wins at the JAL Big Apple Classic and the Jamie Farr Kroger Classic. She also claimed two runner-up spots to raise her career earnings above $6 million. At the end of the season she had not missed a cut since failing to progress at the 1999 US Women's Open. She finished in second place on the Money List, behind Karrie Webb. On the European Tour she won the Evian Masters, beating Karrie Webb in a pla-off. She played in the Solheim

Cup and was made to retake a holed chip by the US team of Kelly Robbins and Patty Hurst. The upset Swede missed her second attempt and the US won the match amid accusations of gamesmanship.

2001 STOP PRESS. Sorenstam recorded four wins in succession in the early part of the year. She won the Welch's Circle K and the Standard Register Ping, and then claimed the Nabisco Championship, three strokes ahead of reigning women's champion Karrie Webb. At the Standard Register Ping she also set a new record round of 59, birdieing the first eight holes and beating Se Ri Pak's previous record by two strokes. She won her fourth title when she came from ten strokes behind to win the Office Depot after a play-off with Mi Hyun Kim.

Charlotta Sorenstam
US Ladies Tour

Born 16 April 1973
Place of Birth Stockholm, Sweden
Year turned Professional 1994
Tour Ranking 20th

TOUR VICTORIES
US: 1
  2000 Standard Register Ping

SOLHEIM CUP 1998

Younger sister of Annika, Sorenstam played on the European Tour in 1995 and 1996, ending 11th on the Order of Merit in 1996. She came through Qualifying School for the 1997 LPGA Tour. In 1998, she made 15 appearances in the top-20 and was second in the Philips Invitational in 1999. She played in the 1998 Solheim Cup.

2000 SEASON. Sorenstam won her first LPGA trophy – the Standard Register Ping – beating her sister and Karrie Webb, and had two second places to finish 20th on the Money List.

Craig Spence
US Tour

Born 2 June 1953
Place of Birth Colac, Victoria
Year turned Professional 1996
Tour Ranking 129th

TOUR VICTORIES
AUSTRALASIAN: 1
  1999 Australian Masters

Australian-born Spence joined the US Tour from Qualifying School in 2000 but could not retain his exemption status, finishing the season in 129th place. His highest placing was fifth at the International. Spence finished third on the 1999 Australasian Tour Money List in 1999 and won the Australian Masters.

Jamie Spence
European Tour

Born 26 May 1963
Place of Birth Tunbridge Wells, Engaland
Year turned Professional 1985
Tour Ranking 36th

BEST FINISH IN MAJORS
Tied 12th **BRITISH OPEN 1992**

TOUR VICTORIES
EUROPEAN: 2
  1992 Canon European Masters
  2000 Moroccan Open

DUNHILL CUP 1992

Spence has played regularly on the European Tour since 1989, winning his first event – the Canon European Masters in Switzerland – in 1992. In the tournament he overcame a ten-shot deficit at the beginning of the last round to shoot 60 and force a play-off with Sweden's Anders Forsbrand. Spence is a regular columnist with the *Racing Post* newspaper. He is short off the tee but is an excellent putter.

2000 SEASON. Spence collected the second European tournament victory of his career when he shot a final-round, course-record 64 to win the Moroccan Open.

Mike Sposa

US Tour

Born 5 June 1969
Place of Birth Teaneck, New Jersey, USA
Year turned Professional 1991
Tour Ranking Tied 31st (Qualifying School)

Sposa turned pro after playing in the 1991 Walker Cup and was a member of the Nike Tour in 1994–96 and 1998, when he finished ninth on the Money List. He played on the US Tour in 1999, finishing 147th, and in 2000. That year he had his highest-ever finish, T7 at the Houston Open. He qualified for the 2001 USPGA Tour with a T31 at the Qualifying School.

Craig Stadler

US Tour

Born 2 May 1953
Place of Birth San Diego, California, USA
Year turned Professional 1975
Tour Ranking 74th

MAJORS VICTORIES
US MASTERS 1982

TOUR VICTORIES
US: 11
1980 Bob Hope Desert Classic, Greater Greensboro Open
1981 Kemper Open
1982 Kemper Open, Tucson Open, World Series of Golf
1984 Byron Nelson Golf Classic
1991 Tour Championship
1992 NEC World Series of Golf
1994 Buick Invitational
1996 Nissan Open

EUROPEAN: 2
1985 European Masters
1990 Scandinavian Open
OTHER: 2
1987 Dunlop Phoenix
1992 Argentinian Open

RYDER CUP 1983, 1985

The flamboyant, colourful figure of Craig Stadler ('the Walrus') has been ever-present on the US Tour since 1977. He has won 12 times on Tour, and his best year was 1982 when he won The Masters in a play-off on the first extra hole against Dan Pohl. He won a further three events that year to finish in first place on the Money List. He was disqualified from the Shearson Lehman Open in 1987 for kneeling on a towel to play a shot under a tree ('building a stance' said officialdom). He was asked to cut the tree down in 1995, an invitation he accepted with alacrity. His last victory came in 1996 at the Nissan Open, helped by a front-nine 30 on the last day. He made a cameo appearance in the movie *Tin Cup*.

2000 SEASON. A much slimmed-down Stadler appeared at the start of the season. He lost a play-off with Robert Allenby at the Houston Open and was T10 at the Bell Canadian Open.

Paul Stankowski

US Tour

Born 22 December 1969
Place of Birth Oxnard, California, USA
Year turned Professional 1991
Tour Ranking 70th

BEST FINISH IN MAJORS
Tied 5th US MASTERS 1997

TOUR VICTORIES
US: 2
1996 BellSouth Classic
1997 Hawaiian Open

OTHER: 1

1996 Casio World Open

Stankowski joined the US Tour in 1994 and won his first title in 1996 when, as final alternate at the BellSouth Classic, he won the event at the first play-off hole against Brandell Chamblee. That year he also won the Casio World Open in Japan. The following year he won again, in a play-off against Jim Furyk at the fourth play-off hole at the Hawaiian Open. This win, and his 15 other top-25 finishes, helped him to 21st place on the Money List.

2000 SEASON. He had three top-10 finishes, at the Phoenix Open, Byron Nelson Classic and the Bell Canadian Open.

2001 STOP PRESS. Stankowski finished second at the Bob Hope Chrysler Classic.

Ian Stanley
European Senior Tour

Born 14 November 1948
Place of Birth Melbourne, Australia
Year turned Professional 1970
Tour Ranking 5th

TOUR VICTORIES
SENIOR TOUR: 1

2000 Coca Cola Kaiser Karl European Trophy

Moustachioed Australian Stanley won 25 tournaments in his career, mainly in Australia, but he also tied with Christy O'Connor Jr for first place in the 1975 Martini International on the European Tour. He represented Australia in two World Cups and joined the European Senior Tour in 1999, ending 21st on the Order of Merit.

2000 SEASON. Stanley won his only title of the season – the Coca Cola Kaiser Karl European trophy – four shots ahead of Japanese rookie Seiji Ebihara and Denis Durnian. In the *Daily Telegraph* European Seniors Match Play, he was beaten 3&2 by Brazilian rookie Priscillo Diniz. He was fifth place on the Order of Merit.

Sherri Steinhauer
US Ladies Tour

Born 27 December 1962
Place of Birth Madison, Wisconsin, USA
Year turned Professional 1983
Tour Ranking 16th

MAJORS VICTORIES
DU MAURIER CLASSIC 1992

TOUR VICTORIES
US: 4

1994 Sprint Classic
1998 British Women's Open
1999 British Women's Open, JAL Big Apple Classic

SOLHEIM CUP 1994, 1998, 2000

Steinhauer joined the LPGA Tour in 1985. She won her first title – a major – at the du Maurier Classic in 1992, and in 1998 she came back from a first round 81 to claim the Weetabix British Open, one stroke ahead of Sophie Gustafson. In 1998 she also sunk the putt which gave the US victory in the Solheim Cup. In 1999 she defeated Karrie Webb in a play-off at the JAL Big Apple Classic, and defended her British Open title, beating Annika Sorenstam by one stroke.

2000 SEASON. Steinhauer played in 30 Tour tournaments and her best result was T3 in the Evian masters. She had 11 top-10 finishes and played in the Solheim Cup.

Henrik Stenson
European Tour

Born 5 May 1976
Place of Birth Gothenburg, Sweden
Year turned Professional 1999
Tour Ranking 1st (Challenge Tour)

TOUR VICTORIES
EUROPEAN: 1

2001 Benson & Hedges International Open

A young Swede with a great future ahead of him, Stenson played on the Challenge Tour in 1999, achieving five top-10s in only six starts. The following year, he topped the Challenge Tour Order of Merit, winning three tournaments, and qualified for the main Tour. **2001 STOP PRESS.** Stenson won his first title in his rookie year, capturing the Benson & Hedges International Open by three shots.

Dave Stockton
US Seniors Tour

Born 2 November 1941
Place of Birth San Bernardino, California, USA
Year turned Professional 1964
Tour Ranking 36th

MAJORS VICTORIES
SENIOR PLAYERS CHAMPIONSHIP 1992, 1994
US SENIOR OPEN 1996

TOUR VICTORIES
SENIOR TOUR: 11
1993 Franklin Quest Championship, GTE Northwest Classic, Murata Reunion Pro-Am, Southwestern Bell Classic, The Transamerica
1994 Burnet Senior Classic, Nationwide Championship
1995 GTE Suncoast Classic, Quicksilver Classic
1996 First of America Classic
1997 Franklin Quest Championship

S tockton is a nine-times USPGA Tour winner and he competed in two Ryder Cups. He was also in charge of the US team in the 1991 'War by the Shore' Ryder Cup at Kiawah Island, when the victorious US team threw him into the Atlantic Ocean. He also won two Majors. He claimed the PGA Championship in 1970, ahead of Arnold Palmer and he won again in 1976.

In 1992, his debut year on the US Senior Tour, Stockton was Rookie of the Year and in

1993 he won five titles, including a nine-stroke victory at the Franklin Quest Championship. He topped the Money List that year and again the following year, and was once more Player of the Year. In 1996 he won the Senior US Open, beating Hale Irwin by two shots and earned over $1 million for the fourth year in succession. However, after seven successive years in the top-10, he fell to 45th in 1999, his best finish being T2 at the Pacific Bell Senior Classic. Stockton is a renowned putter.

2000 SEASON. Stockton posted four top-10s and his highest position was second at the Foremost Insurance Championship.

Dave Stockton Jr
US Tour

Born 31 July 1968
Place of Birth Redlands, California, USA
Year turned Professional 1991
Tour Ranking 140th

S on of ex-US Tour player and ex-US Ryder Cup captain, Junior's best finish on the US Tour was T2 at the 1995 Greater Hartford Open.

2000 SEASON. His best finish was T5 at the BC Open and he ended the season 140th on the Money List.

Knud Storgaard

European Tour

Born 10 August 1972
Place of Birth Skive, Denmark
Year turned Professional 1993
Tour Ranking 144th

With an Msc in Maths and Physics, Storgaard relaxes on the European Tour by solving complex maths problems. He played on the European Tour in 1998 and lost his card, but qualified for the 2000 Tour by finishing sixth on the European Challenge Tour Order of Merit.

2000 SEASON. For a mathematician, Storgaard's figures were disappointing and didn't quite add up to good totals. His best finish of the season was T16 at the BMW International Open and he finished the year 144th on the Order of Merit.

Graeme Storm

European Tour

Born 13 March, 1978
Place of Birth Hartlepool, England
Year turned Professional 2000
Tour Ranking 12th (Qualifying School)

BEST FINISH IN MAJORS
90th **US MASTERS 2000**

Storm was touted as one of the UK's most prominent young golfers after he became the English Amateur Champion in 1999. He played in the winning 1999 Walker Cup team and turned professional in 2000 shortly after playing in The Masters, where he finished in 90th place after missing the cut. His highest finish on the Challenge Tour was fourth at the Finnish Masters and he qualified for the 2001 European Tour with a 12th place at Qualifying School.

2001 STOP PRESS. Storm achieved his highest finish on Tour when he was third in the Open de Argentina.

Paul Streeter

European Tour

Born 29 November 1966
Place of Birth Grantham, England
Year turned Professional 1997
Tour Ranking 35th (Qualifying School)

Streeter took the last qualifying place at 2000 Qualifying School. He turned pro in 1997 and in his first season on Tour missed nine out of the first 12 cuts and this was his fourth attempt to qualify for the European Tour.

Steve Stricker

US Tour

Born 23 February 1967
Place of Birth Edgerton, Wisconsin, USA
Year turned Professional 1990
Tour Ranking 113th

BEST FINISH IN MAJORS
2nd **USPGA 1998**

TOUR VICTORIES
US: 3
  1996 Kemper Open, Western Open
  2001 WGC-Accenture Match Play
       Championship

Stricker, whose wife is his regular caddie, was one of the bright young hopes of US golf in 1996 when he won two tournaments – the Kemper Open and the Western Open – and had five other top-3 placings. He ended the season fourth on the Money List. He also won all five of his matches that year at the Dunhill Cup. Since then his game has gone into relative decline, although he did finish runner-up to Vijay Singh at the 1998 USPGA Championship.

2000 SEASON. He had only one top-10 finish – T4 at the Compaq Classic.

2001 STOP PRESS. Stricker won the season-opening WGC-Accenture Match Play Championship, beating Pierre Fulke and collecting $1 million.

Sven Strüver
European Tour

Born 9 August 1967
Place of Birth Bremen, Germany
Year turned Professional 1990
Tour Ranking 99th

BEST FINISH IN MAJORS
Tied 32nd **US OPEN 1999**

TOUR VICTORIES
EUROPEAN: 3
1996 Alfred Dunhill South African PGA Championship
1997 Dutch Open
1998 Canon European Masters

DUNHILL CUP 1994, 1995, 1996, 1997, 1998
WORLD CUP 1993, 1994, 1995, 1997, 1998, 1999

Son of a Hamburg golf pro, the fair-haired Struver has been a regular player on the European Tour since 1993. He has won three times on Tour, his last victory coming at the 1998 Canon European Masters in Switzerland after a play-off with Patrik Sjoland.

2000 SEASON. He only posted three top-25s, but won all three of his matches for Germany in the Dunhill Cup.

2001 STOP PRESS. Struver came third at the Portuguese Open, behind winner Philip Price and Padraig Harrington.

Bruce Summerhays
US Seniors Tour

Born 14 February 1944
Place of Birth St Louis, Missouri, USA
Year turned Professional 1966
Tour Ranking 19th

TOUR VICTORIES
SENIOR TOUR: 2
1997 St Luke's Classic
1998 State Farm Senior Classic

A former club pro and ex-Stanford University golf coach, Summerhays did not play on the USPGA Tour and joined the US Senior Tour in 1984, after a T4 at the Qualifying School. He had 14 top-10s in 1995 and won his first tournament – the St Luke's Classic – in 1997, beating Hugh Baiocchi in a play-off. He won again in 1998, a birdie putt at the last hole seeing off Hale Irwin and Walter Hall at the State Farm Senior Classic. In 1999 he earned $1 million in prize money and was eighth on the Money List for the second year in succession. Summerhays has played in every event for which he has been eligible and is known as one of the 'iron men' of the Tour because of his tiring playing schedule.

2000 SEASON. He played in 38 out of the 39 tournaments for which he was eligible, achieved ten top-10 finishes and climbed past the $5 million Senior earnings mark for his career.

Carl Suneson
European Tour

Born 22 July 1967
Place of Birth Las Palmas, Spain
Year turned Professional 1990
Tour Ranking 60th

BEST FINISH IN MAJORS
Tied 63rd **BRITISH OPEN 1997**

Born to a Swedish father and an English mother, the long-hitting Suneson perhaps surprisingly took Spanish citizenship in 1996. He joined the European Tour in 1994 and discovered in 1995 that he was diabetic. He lost his card in 1998 and joined the Challenge Tour where his three victories brought him the 1999 Order of Merit

2000 SEASON. He achieved his best-ever finish on Tour with an impressive third place at the prestigious BMW International tournament in Germany.

David Sutherland
US Tour

Born 20 January 1966
Place of Birth Roseville, California, USA
Year turned Professional 1989
Tour Ranking 96th

BEST FINISH IN MAJORS
70th **USPGA 1998**

Younger brother of Kevin, Sutherland joined the US Tour in 1997 from Qualifying School. His best finish on Tour was in 1997 when he tied for second place at the Greater Milwaukee Open.

2000 SEASON. Sutherland had two top-10 finishes, his highest being T7 at the Houston Open.

Kevin Sutherland
US Tour

Born 4 July 1964
Place of Birth Sacramento, California, USA
Year turned Professional 1987
Tour Ranking 66th

BEST FINISH IN MAJORS
Tied 44th **USPGA 1998**

Californian Sutherland has played on the US Tour since 1996, with his best season being 1997 when he recorded his highest-ever placing, second at the Houston Open. His brother David also plays on the US Tour. Kevin is an accurate player with a great bunker game.

2000 SEASON. He had three top-10 finishes, his best being T5 at the Buick Invitational.

2001 STOP PRESS. Sutherland was runner-up to Garrett Willis at the first full-field event of the season, the Tucson Open.

Hal Sutton
US Tour

Born 28 April 1958
Place of Birth Shreveport, Louisiana, USA
Year turned Professional 1981
Tour Ranking 4th

MAJORS VICTORIES
USPGA 1983

TOUR VICTORIES
US: 13
- 1982 Walt Disney World Golf Classic
- 1983 Tournament Players Championship
- 1985 Southwest Golf Classic, St Jude Memphis Classic
- 1986 Memorial Tournament, Phoenix Open
- 1995 BC Open
- 1998 Tour Championship, Westin Texas Open
- 1999 Bell Canadian Open
- 2000 Greater Greensboro Chrysler Classic, Players Championship
- 2001 Shell Houston Open

RYDER CUP 1985, 1987, 1999
PRESIDENTS CUP 1998, 2000

Described early in his career as the next Jack Nicklaus – the 'Bear Apparent' – Sutton was a golfing star in the early 1980s. US Amateur Champion in 1980, Sutton joined the US Tour in 1982 and, in his first year, had three runner-up spots and won the Walt Disney World Golf Classic to finish the season as Rookie of the Year and 11th on the Money List. The following season he underlined his enormous potential by winning the Tournament Players Championship and the PGA Championship, beating Jack Nicklaus by one shot in the latter tournament. He topped the Money List, and by 1986 he had won four more events. His form, however, dipped dramatically and it was not until 1995 that he picked up his next victory at the BC Open, where he shot an opening round 61. He forced his way back into the top-10 in 1998 when he won twice, including beating Vijay Singh in a play-off at the Tour Championship, and continued his comeback in 1999 with another win, at the Canadian Open, and occupied sixth place on the Money List. Sutton played in three Ryder Cup teams, the last in 1999 when he was top scorer for the US.

2000 SEASON. The consistent Sutton won another two tournaments. He beat Andrew Magee by three shots to take the Greater Greensboro Classic and he also won the Players Championship, defeating Tiger Woods by one stroke and picking up $1 million. He represented the US in the Presidents Cup and ended the season fourth on the Money List.

2001 STOP PRESS. Sutton shot five birdies in his final round at the Shell Houston Open to win the title, three strokes ahead of Lee Janzen and Joe Durant.

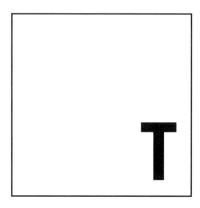

Hidemichi Tanaka
Japanese Tour

Born 29 March 1971
Place of Birth Hiroshima, Japan
Year turned Professional 1991
Tour Ranking 5th

TOUR VICTORIES
OTHER: 2
2000 Dydo-Drinco Shizuoka Open, The
Crowns

Tanaka won twice in his first five starts on the 2000 Japanese Tour. He collected the Shizuoka Open title by two strokes and the following month he beat Mitsutaka Kusakbe by two shots to win The Crowns. He played in the WGC-American Express Championship in Valderrama in November and finished T11.

Toru Taniguchi
Japanese Tour

Born 10 February 1968
Place of Birth Nara, Japan
Year turned Professional 1992
Tour Ranking 2nd

TOUR VICTORIES
OTHER: 3
1998 Mitsubishi Galant Championship

2000 Acom International, Philip Morris
Championship

Taniguchi won two tournaments in 2000 on the Japanese Tour. He collected the Acom International, shooting a final round 64 for a six-stroke victory, and the following month he won the Philip Morris Championship, one shot ahead of Hidemichi Tanaka and Shingo Katayama.

Kirsty Taylor
European Ladies Tour

Born 18 June 1971
Place of Birth Clitheroe, England
Year turned Professional 1994
Tour Ranking 2nd

Taylor's best finishes prior to 2000 on the European Ladies Tour were T8 at the 1995 Dutch Open and the 1996 Sicilian Open.
2000 SEASON. The Englishwoman had the best season of her career. She missed one out of 15 cuts and had five top-10 finishes, including T2 at the British Open and at the Mexx Sport Open. She ended 2000 in second place on the Money List.

Benoit Teilleria
European Tour

Born 12 May 1973
Place of Birth Versailles, France
Year turned Professional 1993
Tour Ranking 140th

BEST FINISH IN MAJORS
Missed Cut **BRITISH OPEN 1993**

Frenchman Teilleria qualified for the 2000 European Tour after a consistent performance on the Challenge Tour.
2000 SEASON. His best finish was T24 at the Portuguese Open

Des Terblanche

European Tour

Born 27 October 1965
Place of Birth Vryburg, South Africa
Year turned Professional 1987
Tour Ranking 100th

TOUR VICTORIES
SOUTH AFRICA: 7
- 1993 Highveld Classic, Leopard Park Classic
- 1994 Royal Swazi Sun Classic
- 1996 Highveld Classic, Pro Series: Botswana
- 1997 Vodacom Series: Eastern Cape
- 2000 Emfulani Classic

Big, beefy South African Terblanche gained his 2001 European Tour card through his performances in 2000 at the Malaysian Open (T2) and the Moroccan Open (5). He secured four other top-20 placings. He is an excellent, smooth putter and he hits the ball a long way, although not always on target.

Rachel Teske

US Ladies Tour

Born 23 April 1972
Place of Birth Port McQuarie, Australia
Year turned Professional 1994
Tour Ranking 17th

TOUR VICTORIES
US: 3
- 1998 First Union Betsy King Classic
- 1999 Chick-fil-A Championship, Myrtle Beach Classic

Teske, who played up till 2000 under her maiden name Hetherington, turned pro in 1994 and played on the European Ladies Tour, winning the German and Spanish Opens. She qualified for the 1997 LPGA Tour, finishing T11 at Qualifying School, and won her first LPGA title in 1998, beating Annika Sorenstam on the first play-off hole at the First Union Betsy King Classic. She won two more titles back-to-back in 1999.

2000 SEASON. Teske had seven top-10 finishes, including two runner-up placings at the Jamie Farr Toledo Classic and the Arch Wireless Championship. She and Karrie Webb also won the first Women's World Cup.

2001 STOP PRESS. Teske was second at the ANZ Ladies Masters on the European Tour, eight shots behind Karrie Webb.

Doug Tewell

US Seniors Tour

Born 27 August 1949
Place of Birth Baton Rouge, Louisiana, USA
Year turned Professional 1971
Tour Ranking 8th

MAJORS VICTORIES
PGA SENIORS CHAMPIONSHIP 2000
THE TRADITION 2001

TOUR VICTORIES
SENIOR TOUR: 2
- 2000 Novell Utah Showdown, SBC Seniors Classic

Tewell had four USPGA victories between 1980 and 1987, including winning the Los Angeles Open by seven strokes. He joined the US Senior Tour in 1999.

2000 SEASON. In his first full season, Tewell had three tournament victories and was voted Rookie of the Year. He won the rain-shortened Senior PGA Championship by seven strokes, sunk a birdie putt for a one-stroke win at the SBC Senior Classic and beat Dr Gil Morgan by two shots to collect the Novell Utah Showdown. He also carded six other top-10 finishes and moved up to eighth place on the Money List.

2001 STOP PRESS. Tewell led The Tradition wire-to-wire, shooting a last round 10 under par 62 to win by nine strokes ahead of Mike McCullough.

Leonard Thompson
US Seniors Tour

Born 1 January 1947
Place of Birth Laurinburg, North Carolina, USA
Year turned Professional 1970
Tour Ranking 15th

TOUR VICTORIES
SENIOR TOUR: 2
1998 Coldwell Banker Burnett Classic
2000 State Farm Senior Classic

A college teammate of fellow US Senior pro Lanny Wadkins, Thompson joined the Seniors in 1998 and won his first tournament – the rain-shortened Coldwell Banker Burnett Classic – in his debut year, beating Isao Aoki on the second hole play-off. He finished 14th on the Money List.

2000 SEASON. Thompson won his second event when he again beat Aoki on a play-off, this time at the State Farm Senior Classic. He had ten other top-10s and was 15th on the Money List.

Rocky Thompson
US Seniors Tour

Born 14 October 1939
Place of Birth Shreveport, Louisiana, USA
Year turned Professional 1964
Tour Ranking 73rd

TOUR VICTORIES
SENIOR TOUR: 3
1991 Digital Senior Classic, MONY Syracuse Senior Classic
1994 GTE Suncoast Classic

Sometime Mayor of the Texas town of Toco, Hugh 'Rocky' Thompson was medalist at US Senior Tour Qualifying School in 1989 and won his first two titles in 1991. He won his last event – the GTE Suncoast Classic – in 1994, shooting a 10 under par 61 on his final round to come back from seven behind.

2000 SEASON. The ever busy Thompson played in 32 tournaments, but could only finish twice inside the top-25. He did, however, beat Bob Charles to collect the Super Seniors Nationwide title.

Jim Thorpe
US Seniors Tour

Born 1 February 1949
Place of Birth Roxboro, North Carolina, USA
Year turned Professional 1972
Tour Ranking 6th

TOUR VICTORIES
SENIOR TOUR: 2
2000 Gold Rush Classic, Transamerica

Qualifying T6 at US Senior Tour Qualifying School, three-time USPGA winner and renowned big-hitter Thorpe played his first season among the seniors in 1999 and his nine top-10 finishes placed him comfortably in the top-20 on the end of season Money List.

2000 SEASON. He won twice on Tour, shooting an 18 under par 198 at the Transamerica to beat Bruce Fleisher by three strokes and also picking up the Gold Rush Classic. He also finished runner-up on three occasions and passed the $2 million barrier in Senior career earnings.

2001 STOP PRESS. Thorpe finished runner-up to Larry Nelson at the season-opening Master Card Championship.

Chris Tidland
US Tour

Born 28 September 1972
Place of Birth Torrance, California, USA
Year turned Professional 1995
Tour Ranking Tied 21st (Qualifying School)

BEST FINISH IN MAJORS
Tied 51st **US OPEN 1999**

While still an amateur, Tidland played in the 1994 and 1995 Nissan Opens and the 1995 US Open. He played on the Nike Tour in 1996 and 1999 and the Canadian Tour in 1998. His highest finish is T36 at the 2000 Tucson Open. Tidland qualified for the 2001 US Tour by finishing T21 at the Qualifying School.

Iben Tinning
European Ladies Tour

Born 4 February 1974
Place of Birth Copenhagen, Denmark
Year turned Professional 1995
Tour Ranking 28th

A cousin of European Tour pro Steen Tinning, the Dane joined the European Ladies Tour in 1996. After a couple of solid years, her best finish to date came in 1998 at the Donegal Irish Ladies Open, when she came second.
2000 SEASON. A more consistent year, in which she had two top-10 finishes and four top-20s to end the year in 28th position on the Money List.

Steen Tinning
European Tour

Born 10 July 1962
Place of Birth Copenhagen, Denmark
Year turned Professional 1985
Tour Ranking 30th

BEST FINISH IN MAJORS
Tied 36th BRITISH OPEN 1998

TOUR VICTORIES
EUROPEAN: 1
   2000 Celtic Manor Resort Wales Open

DUNHILL CUP 1988
WORLD CUP 1987, 1988, 1989, 1990, 1993, 1994, 1995

Tinning has been something of a journeyman on the European Tour since 1986. Until 2000 he had not made a top-10 finish and had not been any higher than 77th on the Order of Merit.
2000 SEASON. Tinning started the season well with a T9 at the Johnnie Walker Classic and a T13 at the South Africa Open. He then won £125,000 for his maiden tournament victory at the Wales Open in June, beating David Howell by one stroke and pushing local boy Ian Woosnam into third place. He also finished T6 at the Scandinavian Masters. In what was a profitable year for the Dane, he moved from 77th to 30th in the Order of Merit.

Esteban Toledo
US Tour

Born 10 September 1962
Place of Birth Mexicali, Mexico
Year turned Professional 1986
Tour Ranking 69th

BEST FINISH IN MAJORS
Tied 34th US OPEN 1999

TOUR VICTORIES
OTHER: 1
   2000 Mexican Open

WORLD CUP 1992, 1994, 1995, 1998

An ex-professional, teenage boxer from Mexico, Toledo escaped from poverty to gratuate through the Qualifying School to the USPGA Tour in 1993. He only lasted one season before losing his card, however, and returned to the Tour in 1998. He ended the 1999 season 107th in the Money List. Toledo's story is well-chronicled in Michael D'Antonio's book *Tin Cup Dreams: A Long Shot Makes It On The PGA Tour.*

2000 SEASON. Toledo retained his card for the 2001 season with a runner-up spot, one stroke behind Brad Faxon, in the BC Open, earning himself over $200,000. He also had seven top-25 finishes.

Tommy Tolles
US Tour

Born 21 October 1966
Place of Birth Fort Myers, Florida, USA
Year turned Professional 1995
Tour Ranking 4th (Qualifying School)

BEST FINISH IN MAJORS
3rd US MASTERS 1997

After five highly successful seasons on the USPGA Tour, Tolles had to return to the Qualifying School in 2000 to retain his card. He played in South Africa and on the Nike Tour until he gained his US Tour card in 1994, and in 1996 he was runner-up in the Players Championship and had two other top-3 finishes to rapidly rise to 16th place on the Money List. The following year, he was third in The Masters, T5 in the US Open, T13 at the USPGA and looked set to go on to become one of the leading players in the world. Since then, however, he has dropped dramatically down the rankings almost as quickly as he rose up through them in the mid-1990s. He had fallen to 180th in the Money List by the end of 2000, his highest finish being T14 in the Tampa Bay Classic, in Florida.

David Toms
US Tour

Born 4 January 1967
Place of Birth Monroe, Louisiana, USA
Year turned Professional 1989
Tour Ranking 15th

BEST FINISH IN MAJORS
Tied 4th BRITISH OPEN 2000

TOUR VICTORIES
US: 4
    1997 Quad City Classic
    1999 Buick Challenge, Sprint International
    2000 Michelob Championship
    2001 Compaq Classic

Straight-shooting Toms has been on the US Tour since 1992. He lost his card in 1994 and played on the Nike Tour in 1995, winning two tournaments and finishing third on the Money List. His first win on the main Tour was the Quad City Classic in 1997 when he shot a last round 65 to win. He made an auspicious debut in The Masters in 1998, when he shot 29 on the back nine on the last round and finished T6. His big year, however, was 1999. He won the Sprint International, beating David Duval into second place and he was also winner of the Buick Challenge, in spite of bad back pain, three strokes ahead of Stuart Appleby. Toms finished tenth on the Money List that year.

2000 SEASON. Toms had yet another very successful year on Tour and is now one of the most consistent performers week in week out. He finished T16 in the US Open at Pebble Beach and then had the best Majors finish of his career, T4 at the British Open at St Andrews. Building on his success, he went on to win another US tournament – the Michelob Championship – in October, defeating Canadian left-hander Mike Weir at the first, sudden-death play-off hole. He also finished in the top-5 at the Bob Hope (T3) and the Colonial (T4).

2001 STOP PRESS. Toms won his fifth tournament at the Compaq Classic.

Sam Torrance
European Tour

Born 24 August 1953
Place of Birth Largs, Scotland
Year turned Professional 1970
Tour Ranking 87th

BEST FINISH IN MAJORS
5th BRITISH OPEN 1981

TOUR VICTORIES
EUROPEAN: 21
- 1976 Martini International, Piccadilly Medal
- 1981 Carrolls Irish Open
- 1982 Benson & Hedges Spanish Open, Portuguese Open
- 1983 Portuguese Open, Scandinavian Open
- 1984 Benson & Hedges International, Sanyo Open, Tunisian Open
- 1985 Johnnie Walker Monte Carlo Open
- 1987 Lancia Italian Open
- 1990 Mercedes German Masters
- 1991 Jersey Open
- 1993 Heineken Open Catalonia, Honda Open, Kronenbourg Open
- 1995 Collingtree British Masters, Italian Open, Murphy's Irish Open
- 1998 Peugeot Open de France

AUSTRALASIAN: 1
- 1980 Australian PGA Championship

SOUTH AFRICA: 1
- 1975 Zambian Open

OTHER: 1
- 1979 Colombian Open

RYDER CUP 1981, 1983, 1985, 1987, 1989, 1991, 1993, 1995
DUNHILL CUP 1985, 1986, 1987, 1989, 1990, 1991, 1993, 1995, 1999
WORLD CUP 1976, 1978, 1982, 1984, 1985, 1987, 1989, 1990, 1991, 1993, 1995

The affable, moustachioed Scot Torrance has been a regular fixture on the European Tour since 1972, and has won 21 Tour events in that period. However, he has rarely ventured outside of Europe to play. Coached from the beginning of his career by his respected father Bob, Torrance has twice – in 1985 and 1995 – finished second on the Order of Merit although he has never won a Major. His highest finish was fifth at the 1981 British Open. Afflicted at one point in his career with the 'yips', he now employs a broomhandle putter.

Torrance is best remembered for his performances in the Ryder Cup, where he represented Europe from 1981–95. His 20-foot birdie putt in the 1985 competition in a singles match against Andy North won the competition, and a tearful but delighted Torrance celebrated his side's first win for 28 years. In 1995 his pairing with Costantino Rocca, and their 6&5 victory over Davis Love III and Jeff Maggert, helped to pave the way for a European victory. He was captain Mark James' assistant in 1999, and in a TV interview he expressed his disgust at the over-exuberant behaviour of the victorious US team, in particular Tom Lehman, on the 17th green. He is captain of the 2001 European team at The Belfry. Torrance was awarded the MBE in 1996.

2000 SEASON. Torrance missed the cut in the British Open and USPGA. His best finish was T6 at the Linde German Masters.

Lee Trevino
US Seniors Tour

Born 1 December 1939
Place of Birth Dallas, Texas, USA
Year turned Professional 1960
Tour Ranking 34th

MAJORS VICTORIES
US SENIORS OPEN 1990
PGA SENIORS CHAMPIONSHIP 1992, 1994
THE TRADITION 1992

TOUR VICTORIES
SENIOR TOUR: 25
- 1990 Aetna Challenge, Doug Sanders Celebrity Classic, NYNEX

Commemorative, Royal Caribbean Classic, Transamerica, Vintage Chrysler Invitational

1991 Aetna Challenge, Charley Pride Classic, Vantage at the Dominion

1992 Bell Atlantic Classic, Las Vegas Senior Classic, Vantage at the Dominion

1993 Cadillac NFL Golf Classic, Nationwide Championship, Vantage Championship

1994 Bell Atlantic Classic, BellSouth Senior Classic, Northville Long Island Classic, Paine Webber Invitational, Royal Caribbean Classic

1995 Northville Long Island Classic, Transamerica

1996 Emerald Coast Classic

1998 Southwestern Bell Dominion

2000 Cadillac NFL Golf Classic

The chatty and ebullient Trevino rose from a desperately poor background in Texan to become a six-time Majors winner and the highest-ever money winner on the US Senior Tour. Rags to riches, indeed, but Trevino did have to struggle in his early years, hustling his way through his teenage years on Texas golf courses, and spending four years in the Marines, until his first USPGA Tour victory at The Hawaiian Open in 1967. He arrived on the national golfing stage when he won the US Open in 1968, becoming the first player to win the event with four rounds in the 60s. His unconventional, self-taught and decidedly non-textbook swing helped to bring him six titles in 1970–71 and he led the Money List, but his best year was 1971 when he won the US Open again, beating Jack Nicklaus in a play-off. He then won the Canadian Open and the British Open that memorable summer. He successfully defended his British Open title in 1972, beating Nicklaus and Tony Jacklin. In 1974, Trevino defeated Nicklaus in another Major, the PGA Championship. Most of 'Super Mex's' 23 USPGA Tour wins came in the 1970s with his last, the Tournament of

Champions, in 1981, although he won his final Major, the PGA, in 1984, where he pushed that other old campaigner Gary Player and Lanny Wadkins into second place.

Trevino joined the US Senior Tour in 1989, and went on to record 29 Tour victories by the end of the century. In 1990 he was Rookie and Player of the Year, topped the Money List and became the first Senior golfer to exceed $1 million in a single season. He picked up Player of the Year again in 1992 and 1994 and collected the 25th win of his Senior career, when he successfully defended the Northville Long Island Classic. In 1997, he failed to win a tournament for the first year in his senior career, and in 1999 he fell out of the top-31 for the first time, although he did pass the $12 million all-time earnings mark.

2000 SEASON. Trevino won his first tournament in over two years when he shot 17 birdies in 54 holes to beat Walter Hall at the Cadillac NFL Golf Classic. He also had two top-5s, including a T2 at the MasterCard Championship, and his Senior career earnings passed $9 million. His record of 29 wins was equalled by the new pretender, Hale Irwin.

Kirk Triplett

US Tour

Born 29 March 1962
Place of Birth Moses Lake, Wichita, USA
Year turned Professional 1985
Tour Ranking 11th

BEST FINISH IN MAJORS
Tied 6th **MASTERS 2001**

TOUR VICTORIES
US: 1
  2000 Nissan Open
OTHER: 1
  1988 Alberta Open

PRESIDENTS CUP 2000

A tall, consistent player with accuracy off boyth the tee and fairway, Triplett has been on the US Tour since 1990, graduating through the Australasian, Asian and Canadian Tours. Until 2000 Triplett had five second-place finishes on Tour but had never won a tournament. His best year was in 1995 when he had two runner-up finishes, one third placing and the 29th spot on the Money List. He wears a trademark bucket-shaped hat.

2000 SEASON. Triplett finally became a winner after 266 attempts. In the Nissan Open at Riviera Country Club he sealed his maiden win with a 4-foot par putt on the last hole to beat Jesper Parnevik by one stroke. He had four other top-5 finishes, including a third place at the Greater Hartford Open where he shot a course record 61, and four other top-10 finishes. He made his Presidents Cup debut partnering Stewart Cink and they won their three matches, although Triplett was beaten in the singles. His excellent form this season took him from 47th to 11th in the Money List.

Ted Tryba
US Tour

Born 15 January 1967
Place of Birth Wilkes-Barre, Pennsylvania, USA
Year turned Professional 1989
Tour Ranking 148th

BEST FINISH IN MAJORS
Tied 31st **USPGA 1999**

TOUR VICTORIES
US: 2
    1995 Anheuser-Busch Golf Classic
    1999 FedEx St Jude Classic

A t 6 foot 4 inches one of the tallest players on the US Tour, Tryba came off the Ben Hogan Tour to join the US Tour in 1993. He won his first tournament – the Anheuser-Busch in 1995 when he beat Scott Simpson by one stroke. His second Tour win was in 1999 at the FedEx St Jude Classic, when he ended two shots in front of Tom Lehman and Tim Herron. He finished the season in 20th place on the Money List.

    2000 SEASON. Tryba plummeted to 148th on the List, with his highest finish T21 at the Doral-Ryder Open. He missed the cut at The Masters.

Greg Turner
European Tour

Born 21 February 1963
Place of Birth Dunedin, New Zealand
Year turned Professional 1984
Tour Ranking 84th

BEST FINISH IN MAJORS
Tied 7th **BRITISH OPEN 1996**

TOUR VICTORIES
EUROPEAN: 4
    1986 Scandinavian Enterprise Open
    1993 Lancia Martini Italian Open
    1995 Turespana Open Baleares
    1997 One2One British Masters
AUSTRALASIAN: 6
    1984 New Zealand PGA
    1989 Johnnie Walker Classic, New Zealand
         Open
    1991 Daikyo Palm Meadows Cup
    1997 Australian PGA, New Zealand Open

DUNHILL CUP 1986, 1987, 1990, 1992, 1994, 1995, 1996, 1998, 1999, 2000
PRESIDENTS CUP 1998
WORLD CUP 1985, 1987, 1988, 1989, 1990, 1991, 1992, 1993, 1994, 1998

New Zealander Turner has been with the European Tour for 15 years. Brother to New Zealand Test cricketer Glenn, Turner has won four times on the European Tour and has six other international titles, including the Johnnie Walker Classic which he won in 1990. His most recent championship victory was at the Australian PGA in 1999. He was Rookie of the Year on the Australasian Tour in 1985.

2000 SEASON. Turner began the year promisingly, with a sixth place at the Heineken Classic. However, he could only manage another five top-20 finishes, his best being the Compaq European Grand Prix (T9).

Sherri Turner
US Ladies Tour

Born 4 October 1956
Place of Birth Grenville, South Carolina, USA
Year turned Professional 1983
Tour Ranking 64th

MAJORS VICTORIES
LPGA 1988

TOUR VICTORIES
US: 2
   1988 Corning Classic
   1989 Hawaiian Open

Turner has three wins on the LPGA Tour. Her best year was 1988 when she won the Mazda LPGA Championship and the Corning Classic back-to-back and was runner-up twice. That year she was *Golf Illustrated's*, *Golf World's* and *Golf Magazine's* Player of the Year. By 1992 she had passed $1 million in career earnings and she had her second-highest

finish in the Majors in 1999, claiming second place at the US Women's Open.

2000 SEASON. Turner recorded two top-10s, her highest being T5 at the Takefuji Classic.

Bob Tway
US Tour

Born 4 May 1959
Place of Birth Oklahoma City, Oklahoma, USA
Year turned Professional 1981
Tour Ranking 114th

MAJORS VICTORIES
USPGA 1986

TOUR VICTORIES
US: 6
   1986 Georgia Pacific Atlanta Classic, Manufacturers Hanover Westchester Classic, Shearson Lehman Bros-Andy Williams Open
   1989 Memorial Tournament
   1990 Las Vegas Invitational
   1995 MCI Classic

The highlight of Bob Tway's 15 years on the USPGA Tour occurred early in his career at the 1986 USPGA Championship at Inverness. Three strokes behind world number one at the time, Greg Norman, with six holes to play, he caught up with the Australian to level at the final hole. Tway chipped in from a bunker, Norman missed, and Tway had won in his second year on Tour. He won three other tournaments in the season, ended second on the Money List and was voted PGA Player of the Year. He won two more events in the late 1980s, but his golf went into decline until 1995 when he had eight top-10 finishes, won the MCI Classic and became PGA Comeback Player of the Year. He has not won on Tour since.

2000 SEASON. Tway posted six top-25 placings, but tumbled from 43rd to 114th in the Money List. 0

2001 STOP PRESS. Tway began the season well, securing third place in the season-opening Tucson Open, T4 in the Bob Hope Chrysler Classic and T2 at the Nissan Open (shared with four other players).

Howard Twitty

Born 15 January 1949
Place of Birth Phoenix, Arizona
Year turned Professional 1974
Tour Ranking 41st

A towering, 6 foot 5 inch Arizonian, Twitty qualified sixth at the 1998 US Senior Q ualifyingSchool and had to qualify again in 1999, finishing in the top-8 and therefore fully exempt for 2000. Following foot surgery, he plays in sandals equipped with spikes.

2000 SEASON. His best finish was T2 at the Toshiba Senior Classic and he ended the year in 41st place on the Money List.

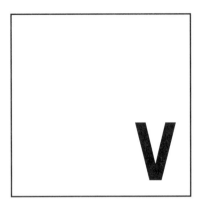

Francis Valera

European Tour

Born 13 July 1974
Place of Birth Stiges, Spain
Year turned Professional 1994
Tour Ranking 25th (Qualifying School)

Spaniard Valera was British Boys Champion in 1991. He played on the Challenge Tour in 2000 with his best performance being third at the Challenge d'Espana. He qualified for the 2001 European Tour through 2000 Qualifying School.

Jean van de Velde

US Tour

Born 29 May 1966
Place of Birth Mont de Marsan, France
Year turned Professional 1987
Tour Ranking 60th

BEST FINISH IN MAJORS
Tied 2nd **BRITISH OPEN 1999**

TOUR VICTORIES
EUROPEAN: 1
    1993 Roma Masters

RYDER CUP 1999
DUNHILL CUP 1990, 1992, 1994, 1997, 1998, 1999

WORLD CUP 1989, 1990, 1991, 1992, 1993, 1994, 1995, 1996, 1997, 1998

No one who witnessed it will ever forget van de Velde's performance at the last hole in the 1999 British Open at Carnoustie, in Scotland. A comfortable three shots clear of the field standing on the 18th tee in the final round, the eccentric Frenchman ran up a triple bogey (famously removing his socks and shoes in the Barry Burn) to let American Justin Leonard and Scotland's Paul Lawrie tie with him. Lawrie eventually won the four-hole play-off with two birdies in virtual darkness, although van de Velde's antics understandably dominated most of the headlines the following day.

Twice French Youth Champion, the amiable Frenchman has been in the top-100 on the European Tour Order of Merit since he joined in 1989. He won the Roma Masters in a play-off in 1993 and that remains his only Tour victory. He made his Ryder Cup debut in 1999, becoming the first Frenchman to play in the competition. However, he did not play until the final day singles match where he was beaten convincingly by Davis Love III. Not particularly long off the tee, he is an excellent putter with 'the touch of a pickpocket on the greens' (David Feherty).

2000 SEASON. Van de Velde put his British-

Open disaster behind him and chose to play mainly on the PGA Tour, in the USA, where he had a T2 finish at the Tucson Open, in Arizona, and another second-place finish after losing a sudden-death play-off with Scott Verplank at the Reno-Tahoe Open. In Europe, he was also very consistent, posting a T3 at the Deutsche Bank Open and a T7 in the French Open, as well as two other top-20s.

Tjaart van der Walt
European Tour

Born 26 September 1964
Place of Birth Pretoria, South Africa
Year turned Professional 1996
Tour Ranking 7th (Qualifying School)

South African van der Walt had two European Tour fifth places in 1999, at the Alfred Dunhill and the South African Open. He finished third in the South African Order of Merit in 1999–00, and qualified for the 2001 European Tour season through Qualifying School.

Valerie van Ryckeghem
European Ladies Tour

Born 21 August 1975
Place of Birth Bruges, Belgium
Year turned Professional 1995
Tour Ranking 9th

TOUR VICTORIES
EUROPEAN: 1
    1997 Sicilian Open

She joined the European Ladies Tour in 1996 and won her only title, the Sicilian Ladies Open, the following year.
    2000 SEASON. Van Ryckeghem had her best season, with second place at the Hanover Ladies Open, T2 at the Italian Open and third at the German Open. She finished the year ninth on the Money List.

Jeff van Wagenen
European Senior Tour

Born 16 July 1948
Place of Birth Phoenix, Arizona, USA
Year turned Professional 1996
Tour Ranking 17th

TOUR VICTORIES
SENIOR TOUR: 1
    2000 Tui Golf Championship

Arizonan van Wagenen, a successful businessman in the US, qualified for the 2000 European Senior Tour through Qualifying School.
    2000 SEASON. He led the Tui Golf Championship wire-to-wire to record his first victory on Tour, finishing one stroke ahead of Tommy Horton and Noel Ratcliffe, and claimed 17th spot on the Order of Merit.

Nicholas Vanhootegem
European Tour

Born 7 October 1972
Place of Birth Knokke, Belgium
Year turned Professional 1994
Tour Ranking 98th

Representing the Royal Zoute, home to the Belgian Open, Vanhootegem joined the European Tour by finishing in third place at Qualifying School in 1999. He had two top-10 finishes in 2000, T6 (with a last round 63) at the Rio de Janeiro Open and eighth at the Compaq European Grand Prix. He ended the season 98th in the Order of Merit.

Steven Veriato
US Seniors Tour

Born 6th May 1946
Place of Birth Hilo, Hawaii
Year turned Professional 1973
Tour Ranking 58th

Ex-USPGA Tour member, Veriato had to open qualify for US Senior Tour events four years in succession between 1996 and 1999. His best finish was third, at the Kaanapali Classic in 1996 and 1999.

2000 SEASON. He had one top-10, but qualified to be fully exempt for 2001.

Scott Verplank

US Tour

Born 9 July 1964
Place of Birth Dallas, Texas, USA
Year turned Professional 1986
Tour Ranking 22nd

BEST FINISH IN MAJORS
Tied 15th BRITISH OPEN 1999, US OPEN 1986

TOUR VICTORIES
US: 3
1985 Western Open
1988 Buick Open
2000 Reno-Tahoe Open

and ten top-10s saw him receive the PGA Comeback Player of the Year and finish 18th on the Money List. He also won the individual title in the 1998 World Cup. He is not long off the tee, but is one of the straightest players on Tour. He is a diabetic.

2000 SEASON. The consistent Texan made 80 per cent of his cuts and had a fine year. He won his third tournament – the Reno-Tahoe Open – beating Jean Van De Velde on the fourth play-off hole. He also had five other top-10 finishes and six top-25s.

US Amateur Champion in 1984, Verplank became the first amateur to win a US Tour tournament – the 1985 Western Open – in over 30 years. As a professional he won the Buick Open in 1988. An elbow injury affected his play in the early 1990s and he struggled until 1998 when two second-place finishes

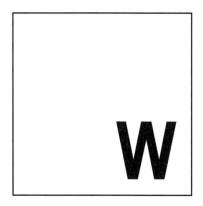

the USPGA – in 1977 at Pebble Beach, beating Gene Littler at the third play-off hole.

Known for his quick-fire swing and his tough, competitive approach to the game, Wadkins joined the US Senior Tour in 2000 and won on his debut event, overcoming Spain's Jose Maria Canizares at the third play-off hole to claim the ACE Group Classic, becoming only the sixth player in Senior Tour history to win his first tournament. It was his first win since the 1992 Greater Hartford Classic on the PGA Tour. He ended the season ranked 44th on the Money List.

Lanny Wadkins

US Seniors Tour

Born 5 December 1949
Place of Birth Richmond, Virginia, USA
Year turned Professional 1971
Tour Ranking 44th

TOUR VICTORIES
SENIOR TOUR: 1
2000 ACE Group Classic

US Amateur Champion in 1970, Wadkins had a distinguished USPGA Tour record, winning 21 tournaments and playing in the Ryder Cup on no less than eight occasions. He also captained his country when they lost the match in 1995. He won his only Major –

Fred Wadsworth

US Tour

Born 17 July 1962
Place of Birth Munich, Germany
Year turned Professional 1984
Tour Ranking Tied 14th (Qualifying School)

TOUR VICTORIES
US: 1
1986 Southern Open

The tall, athletic Wadsworth came out of the pre-tournament qualifying to win the Southern Open on the USPGA Tour in 1986. However, the victory was not a sign of things to come and he played on Tour without much success for a few years before alternating between the main Tour and the Nike Tour in the 1990s. He qualified for the 2001 USPGA Tour, finishing 14th at the Qualifying School.

Grant Waite

US Tour

Born 11 August 1964
Place of Birth Palmerston North, New Zealand
Year turned Professional 1987
Tour Ranking 38th

BEST FINISH IN MAJORS
Tied 36th **US OPEN 1997**

TOUR VICTORIES
US: 1
   1993 Kemper Open
AUSTRALASIAN: 1
   1992 New Zealand Open

DUNHILL CUP 1989, 1992, 1994, 1995, 1996, 2000

New Zealander Waite has been a regular on the US Tour since 1993, the year he won his only tournament, the Kemper Open.

2000 SEASON. Waite had seven top-10 finishes and two runner-up spots. He was second behind Rory Sabbatini in the Air Canada, and the following week he shot a final round 66 in the Bell Canadian Open only to be beaten by Tiger Woods, who hit a 200-yard 6-iron over trees and water from a fairway bunker on the final hole to give him a round of 65. However, Waite went on to win two out of his three matches in the Dunhill Cup and also earned over $1 million in a season for the first time in his career.

Rocky Walcher
_____
                                    US Tour
Born 12 October 1961
Place of Birth Carnegie, Oklahoma, USA
Year turned Professional 1985
Tour Ranking 26th (Qualifying School)

Walcher first played on the US Tour in 1994 and was a member of the Nike Tour between 1996 and 2000, winning one tournament. He gained his US Tour card for 2001 by finishing 26th at Qualifying school.

Duffy Waldorf
_____
                                    US Tour
Born 20 August 1962
Place of Birth Los Angeles, California, USA
Year turned Professional 1985
Tour Ranking 32nd

BEST FINISH IN MAJORS
Tied 5th **US MASTERS 1996**

TOUR VICTORIES
US: 4
   1995 LaCantera Texas Open
   1999 Buick Classic, Westin Texas Open
   2000 NCR Classic at Walt Disney World

James 'Duffy' Waldorf, sporting his colourful hats and shirts, has played on the US Tour since 1987, winning four tournaments. The long-hitting Californian claimed his first title in 1995, when he beat Justin Leonard by six strokes to win the LaCantera Texas Open. His most successful year on Tour came in 1999 when he won the Buick Classic in a play-off with his friend Dennis Paulson and the Texas Open again in another play-off, this time against Ted Tryba. These victories, as well as three top-10 finishes saw Waldorf end the season 28th on the Money List. His children write messages on his golf balls before every tournament.

2000 SEASON. Waldorf had two top-10 finishes and then won his fourth tournament, the NCR Classic at Walt Disney World, shooting a last round 62 to overhaul and beat Steve Flesch by one stroke. He also claimed the T3 spot, alongside Vijay Singh, at the season-ending WGC-American Express Championship. He dipped from 28th to 32nd on the Money List.

Anthony Wall
European Tour

Born 29 May 1975
Place of Birth London, England
Year turned Professional 1995
Tour Ranking 44th

TOUR VICTORIES
EUROPEAN: 1
2000 Alfred Dunhill Championship

Londoner Wall qualified for the European Tour through the Qualifying School in 1997. Coached by his cab-driving father, Wall gained six top-10 places in his first two years to advance up the Order of Merit. A big, powerful player, he has a solid and consistent swing and is known for being particularly effective with his long irons. He is widely regarded as one of the most amiable golfers on the European Tour.

2000 SEASON. 'Wonder Wall' won his first Tour event early in the season at the Alfred Dunhill Championship at Houghton GC, South Africa. In the rain-shortened competition, his 31 on the back nine gave him a 68 for his last round, leaving him two strokes ahead of Wales' Philip Price and Scotland's Gary Orr for the competition. He withdrew from the Dubai Desert Classic and the Dutch Open with glandular fever and struggled with his health for much of the season, but he did secure three other top-20 finishes.

Bobby Walzel
US Seniors Tour

Born 26 September 1949
Place of Birth Houston, Texas, USA
Year turned Professional 1973
Tour Ranking 144th

Walzell, whose best ever season on the regular USPGA Tour event came in 1977 when he finished third in the Bobe Hope Desert Classic and the Tallahassee Open, managed to graduate in the top-8 at the 2000 Qualifying School for the 2001 US Seniors Tour.

2001 STOP PRESS. He ended tied for second place at the 2001 Verizon Classic and finished forth in the Mexico Senior Classic.

Wendy Ward
US Ladies Tour

Born 6 May 1973
Place of Birth San Antonio, Texas, USA
Year turned Professional 1995
Tour Ranking 34th

TOUR VICTORIES
US: 2
1997 Fieldcrest Canon Classic
1998 Hawaiian Ladies Open

The 1994 US Women's Amateur Champion, Ward achieved third place at the Standard Register Ping that year as an amateur. She qualified T3 at Qualifying School for the 1996 LPGA Tour and won her first tournament the following year with a 23 under par 265 at the Fieldcrest Cannon Classic. She won again in 1998 at the Cup Noodles Hawaiian Ladies Open, beating Dana Dormann on the first play-off hole.

2000 SEASON. Ward made four appearances in the top-10, including T3 at both the McDonald's LPGA Championship and the Giant Eagle LPGA Classic. She was 34th on the Money List.

Tom Wargo
US Seniors Tour

Born 16 September 1942
Place of Birth Marlette, Michigan, USA
Year turned Professional 1976
Tour Ranking 22nd

MAJORS VICTORIES
PGA SENIORS CHAMPIONSHIP 1993

TOUR VICTORIES

SENIOR TOUR: 3

> 1994 Doug Sanders Celebrity Classic
> 1995 Dallas Reunion Pro-Am
> 2000 Liquidgolf.com Invitational

A true-life rags to riches story, Wargo taught himself to play golf at the relatively late starting age of 25 and worked as a barman and a car assembly line worker before turning pro in 1976. He joined the US Senior Tour in 1993 and won the Senior PGA Championship in his sixth start on Tour, beating Bruce Crampton on the second play-off hole. Something of an 'iron man', he played 36 events the following season and also won the Doug Sanders Celebrity Classic as well as the *Senior British Open* that year. In 1995, he won the Dallas Reunion Pro-Am by seven strokes. Wargo now owns a golf club in Illinois.

2000 SEASON. It was a good year for Wargo. He won the LiquidGolf.com Invitational, out-playing Gary McCord and JC Snead on the third hole play-off, and had six other top-10s. He passed the $5 million Senior career earnings mark and was 22nd on the Money List.

Tom Watson
US Seniors Tour

Born 4 September 1949
Place of Birth Kansas City, Missouri, USA
Year turned Professional 1971
Tour Ranking 13th

TOUR VICTORIES

SENIOR TOUR: 2

> 1999 Bank One Championship
> 2000 Senior Tour Championship

H older of eight Majors titles and 31 USPGA tournament victories, the slight psychology graduate from Missouri can be ranked as one of golf's finest-ever exponents. His accurate long game, exquisite ball-striking and his confident putting enabled him to dominate the game between the mid-1970s and the mid-1980s, and during this period he took over Jack Nicklaus' mantle as the world's best golfer. Watson joined the USPGA Tour in 1972 and won his first tournament – the Western Open – in 1974. By 1977 he topped the Money List and remained there until 1981. He led the List again in 1984.

A masterful links player, his greatest performances without doubt came in the British Open, which he won five times between 1975 and 1983. His duel at Turnberry with Nicklaus in 1977, when he shot two final rounds of 65 to beat the 'Golden Bear' by one stroke, has already passed into legend, and in 1982 he won both the British Open and the US Open. However, he blew his chance of a sixth Open title in 1984 at St Andrews on the famous 17th Road Hole, when he overhit an iron shot onto the road, and lost to Seve Ballesteros. Many blame his subsequent relative decline on this disappointment, although his well-documented battle with alcohol no doubt contributed to his problems.

On the USPGA Tour, Watson won his first title – the Memorial – for nine years in 1996 and his last victory on the regular Tour came in the MasterCard Colonial in 1998. Watson played in four Ryder Cups and captained the American side for the 1993 competition at The Belfry. Watson played in two events on the 1999 US Senior Tour, and in his second start he shot a course record 10 under par 62 to defeat Bruce Summerhays by five strokes in the Bank One Championship.

2000 SEASON. Watson made only 13 starts but still cleared $1 million, helped by his $365,000 cheque for winning the IR Senior Tour Championship by one stroke over John Jacobs, shooting 66 on the final round. He also carded seven top-5s and made the cut in three Majors. He finished the season 13th on the Senior Money List.

2001 STOP PRESS. Watson finished T2 at the Siebel Classic, five shots behind one of his main rivals, Hale Irwin.

Brian Watts

US Tour

Born 18 March 1966
Place of Birth Montreal, Canada
Year turned Professional 1988
Tour Ranking 133rd

BEST FINISH IN MAJORS
2nd **BRITISH OPEN 1998**

Canadian-born but a naturalized US citizen, Watts has played most of his competitive golf in Japan and has won twice on the Japanese Tour. He is remembered for leading the British Open after three rounds in 1998 before eventually losing in a four-hole play-off to Mark O'Meara. On the back of this success, he joined the US Tour in 1999, and finished the season in 57th place on the Money List to comfortably regain his card.

2000 SEASON. After his promising first season, Watts could manage only one top-10 – T9 at the Texas Open – and he dropped to 133rd on the Money List.

Shani Waugh

US Ladies Tour

Born 2 September 1969
Place of Birth Banbury, Australia
Year turned Professional 1991
Tour Ranking 39th

TOUR VICTORIES
US: 1
1996 Costa Azul Open

Fair-haired Australian Waugh made her debut on the European Tour in 1991 and won her only European title in 1996, the Costa Azul Open. She joined the LPGA Tour in 1997 and had to qualify again in 1999.

2000 SEASON. She recorded a best-ever LPGA finish of third in the New Albany Classic. She had seven top-20s, including a T17 in the US Open, her highest Major finish.

Karrie Webb

US Ladies Tour

Born 21 December 1974
Place of Birth Ayr, Australia
Year turned Professional 1994
Tour Ranking 1st

MAJORS VICTORIES
DINAH SHORE 2000
US OPEN 2000, 2001
DU MAURIER CLASSIC 1999
NABISCO CHAMPIONSHIP 2000
LPGA 2001

TOUR VICTORIES
US: 20
1995 British Women's Open
1996 Healthsouth Inaugural, ITT LPGA Tour Championship, SAFECO Classic
1997 British Women's Open, SAFECO Classic, Susan G Komen International
1998 Australian Ladies Masters, Myrtle Beach Classic
1999 Australian Ladies Masters, Office Depot Classic, Rochester International, Standard Register Ping, Titleholders Championship
2000 AFLAC Championship, Australian Masters, Office Depot Classic, Oldsmobile Classic, Takefuji Classic
EUROPEAN: 2
2000 Australian Women's Open
2001 ANZ Ladies Masters

Webb burst on to the women's golf scene in 1995 when she won the Women's British Open by a six-stroke margin, becoming Rookie of the Year on the European Ladies Tour. In 1996 she played on the US Tour, won four tournaments and became the first woman golfer to earn $1 million in a single season. In 1997 she won the British Women's Open again, and had 21 top-10 finishes and two victories on the US Tour. In 1999, she won a further six events, including her first Major, the du Maurier Classic, and was Player of the Year.

2000 SEASON. She exceeded even this phenomenal record by claiming seven tournaments. She beat Dottie Pepper by ten strokes to win her second Major, the Dinah Shore Championship, and was again Player of the Year. By the end of the season she had passed the $6 million mark in career earnings. On the European Tour she won the Australian Women's Open, playing the last six holes in six under par and beating Australia's Rachel Hetherington (now Teske) in the process by three strokes, and she lost in a play-off with Annika Sorenstam at the Evian Masters.

2001 STOP PRESS. Webb was runner-up on three occasions on the US Tour at the Nabisco, Office Depot and the Subaru Memorial of Naples. She won the ANZ Ladies Masters on the European Tour, eight shots ahead of Rachel Teske, and was second to Sweden's Sophie Gustafson at the Australian Women's Open.

Shaun Webster
European Tour

Born 29 November 1976
Place of Birth Bedford, England
Year turned Professional 1998
Tour Ranking 23rd (Qualifying School)

The long-hitting son of a golf professional, Webster won the English Amateur Championship in 1996. In 1999, he just failed to qualify from the Challenge Tour – finishing in 17th place – and also missed out via the Qualifying School. However, he played on the Challenge Tour in 2000, winning the Beazer Homes Championship and posting three top-20 places on the Tour. He gained his 2001 European Tour card by finishing in 23rd place at the end of season Qualifying School, although his 2001 season has been something of a disappointment to date.

Steve Webster
European Tour

Born 17 November 1975
Place of Birth Nuneaton, England
Year turned Professional 1995
Tour Ranking 69th

BEST FINISH IN MAJORS
Tied 24th **BRITISH OPEN 1995**

Webster won the Amateur medal in the 1995 British Open at St Andrews, finishing T24 in an illustrious group which also included Mark Calcavecchia, Jesper Parnevik and Bernhard Langer. He turned professional the following year, but immediately lost his European Tour card. He qualified again at the end of 1996 and has been on Tour since. He is a long hitter off the tee, accurate with his irons, and his best finish to date is second in the 1999

Turespana Masters. Although Webster shot seven birdies in 14 holes in the last round, he still finished four strokes behind winner Miguel Angel Jimenez.

2000 SEASON. Webster's highest finish was T3 in the Sao Paolo Open and he claimed a further six top-25 places. He also shot a course record 63 in the Australian Open.

Mike Weir

US Tour

Born 12 May 1970
Place of Birth Samia, Ontario
Year turned Professional 1992
Tour Ranking 6th

BEST FINISH IN MAJORS
Tied 10th USPGA 1999

TOUR VICTORIES
US: 2
   1999 Air Canada Championship
   2000 WGC-American Express World
      Championship

PRESIDENTS CUP 2000

A smallish, left-handed Canadian player with a smooth swing, Weir began his career on the Canadian Tour, winning Rookie of the Year in 1993 and the Canadian Order of Merit in

1997. In 1998, he won the USPGA Tour Qualifying School medal and joined the Tour the following year. He had a very successful rookie season, winning the Air Canada Championship by two shots over Fred Funk and becoming the first Canadian to win on the US Tour for seven years and the first to win on home soil since 1954. He also came second in the Motorola Open and had five other top-10 finishes. In the Majors he was T10 in the USPGA and T37 in the British Open.

2000 SEASON. Weir opened his campaign with a T4 at the Mercedes and secured five more top-10 finishes in the season. However, his biggest payday and the most important victory of his career came at the WGC-American Express Championship at Valderrama, when he ended the last day two strokes ahead of runner-up Lee Westwood to collect the trophy and $1 million. He made the cut in all four Majors – his highest placing being T16 in the US Open – and he made his Presidents Cup debut, winning both his paired matches and beating Phil Mickelson in the singles. He was top international points scorer in the competition. With all this success, it was no surprise to see him finish the season in sixth position in the Money List.

Karen Weiss

US Ladies Tour

Born 15 March 1966
Place of Birth St Paul, Minnesota, USA
Year turned Professional 1987
Tour Ranking 80th

A graduate of the Futures and Asian Tours (where she won the Republic of China Open), the small but long-hitting Weiss joined the LPGA Tour in 1994. Her best finish on Tour is T3 at the 1996 Ping/Welch's Championship.

2000 SEASON. Weiss carded five top-20 placings to take 80th spot on the Money List.

Kevin Wentworth
US Tour

Born 17 October 1968
Place of Birth Modesto, California, USA
Year turned Professional 1991
Tour Ranking 131st

Tall, left-handed Californian Wentworth won the Philippines Open in 1997 and joined the US Tour from 1997 Qualifying School. He retained his card in 1998 and 1999 but finished 98th on the Money List.

2000 SEASON. He made the cut in less than one-third of the tournaments he entered, although he did achieve a T2 placing in the Honda classic. He ended 131st on the List.

Roger Wessels
European Tour

Born 4 March 1961
Place of Birth Port Elizabeth, South Africa
Year turned Professional 1987
Tour Ranking 35th

WORLD CUP 1994

Wessels came through the South African mini-Tour and the Canadian Tour, where he won the Canadian Masters in 1994, to join the European Tour in 1995. He has never won a Tour event and his highest finish was T2 at the 1995 South African PGA. He is coached by Sky TV pundit Scott Cranfield.

2000 SEASON. The tall (6 foot 3 inch) South African had his best year to date on Tour although he continued to miss out on a win. He had a good run in the summer with three top-10s – French Open (T4), Irish Open (T10) and Dutch Open (T6). He then picked up three more top-10s in successive weeks at the season's end, at the Turespana Masters (T9), and T7s at the Italian Open and the Volvo Masters. He also shot a first round 8 under par 63 at the Trophee Lancome, but failed to make the cut. He finished 35th on the Order of Merit.

Lee Westwood
European Tour

Born 24 April 1973
Place of Birth Worksop, England
Year turned Professional 1993
Tour Ranking 1st

BEST FINISH IN MAJORS
Tied 5th **US OPEN 2000**

TOUR VICTORIES
US: 1
  1998 Freeport McDermott Classic
EUROPEAN: 14
  1996 Volvo Scandinavian Masters
  1997 Volvo Masters
  1998 Belgacom Open, Deutsche Bank SAP Open, NCR English Open, Standard Life Loch Lomond
  1999 Canon European Masters, Smurfit European Open, TNT Dutch Open
  2000 Belgacom Open, Compaq European Grand Prix, Deutsche Bank SAP Open, Smurfit European Open, Volvo Scandinavian Masters
AUSTRALASIAN: 1
  1997 Holden Australian Open
SOUTH AFRICA: 1
  2000 Dimension Data Pro-Am
OTHER: 7
  1996 Sumitomo Visa Taiheiyo Masters
  1997 Malaysian Masters, Sumitomo Visa Taiheiyo Masters
  1998 Dunlop Phoenix, Sumitomo Visa Taiheiyo Masters
  1999 Macau Open
  2000 Cisco World Match Play

RYDER CUP 1997, 1999
DUNHILL CUP 1996, 1997, 1998, 1999

The man who ended Colin Montgomerie's run of seven successive Volvo Order of Merit wins in 2000, Westwood is a golfer with an impressive list of trophies and an even more promising future. British Youth Champion in 1993, he joined the European Tour in 1994 and has not been out of the top-10 since 1996. A powerful but relaxed player, he has won 14 European Tour tournaments as well as events in Japan, South Africa, USA and Australia. He is married to Andrew Coltart's sister, Laurae.

2000 SEASON. This was the year Westwood broke through into international golf superstardom. After a so-so start to the season, he won the Deutsche Bank Open, shooting a 15 under par 273 to beat Emanuele Canonica by three shots. He then picked up the Compaq European Grand Prix, the Smurfit European Open and the Volvo Scandinavian Masters. He completed his fifth European victory of the year when he beat Eduardo Romero by four shots to collect the Belgacom Open. At the final tournament of the year – the WGC-American Express Championship – he finished in second place to secure the Volvo Order of Merit ahead of his friend and stablemate Darren Clarke. He played ten tournaments on the US Tour with his best finish T5 at the US Open at Pebble Beach. He also won the Cisco World Match Play Championship, beating Colin Montgomerie at the second sudden death play-off hole with an 18-foot birdie putt.

Brett Wetterich
US Tour

Born 6 August 1973
Place of Birth Cincinnati, Ohio, USA
Year turned Professional 1994
Tour Ranking Tied 13th (Qualifying School)

BEST FINISH IN MAJORS
Missed Cut **US OPEN 1998**

Wetterich injured his wrist in his US Tour rookie season of 2000 and was granted a medical extension for 2001. He also finished T31 at Qualifying School in 2000. His highest finish on Tour is T63 at the 2000 Compaq Classic.

Mark Wiebe
US Tour

Born 13 September 1957
Place of Birth Seaside, Oregon, USA
Year turned Professional 1980
Tour Ranking 94th

BEST FINISH IN MAJORS
Tied 12th **USPGA 1989**

TOUR VICTORIES
US: 2
    1985 Anheuser Busch Classic
    1986 Hardee's Golf Classic

An experienced professional on the US Tour, Wiebe has won two tournaments, the last 16 years ago. In 1985 he won the Anheuser-Busch Classic in a play-off with John Mahaffey, and the following year he took the Hardee's Golf Classic. His highest place in the Money List was 25th in 1986.

2000 SEASON. He had three top-25s and made sure of retaining his card for 2001 with a 2nd place in the Texas Open, five strokes behind winner Justin Leonard.

Maggie Will
US Ladies Tour

Born 22 November 1964
Place of Birth Whiteville, North Carolina, USA
Year turned Professional 1988
Tour Ranking 73rd

TOUR VICTORIES
US: 3
    1990 Desert Inn LPGA International
    1992 Sara Lee Classic
    1994 Children's Medical Centre LPGA
    Classic

A three-time winner on the LPGA Tour, the slender, blonde-haired Will won her first title – the Desert Inn LPGA International – in 1990 and her last victory was in 1994. In

1999, she finished T6 at the du Maurier, her highest placing in a Major.

2000 SEASON. Will had two top-10 spots, her best being T7 at the Safeway LPGA Classic, and took 73rd position on the Money List.

Kim Williams

US Ladies Tour

Born 23 March 1963
Place of Birth Bethesdsa, Maryland, USA
Year turned Professional 1986
Tour Ranking 74th

The 6-foot tall, auburn-haired Williams joined the LPGA Tour in 1987, having played in the 1986 Curtis Cup. In 1988 she achieved her best-ever finish, tieing for second place in the Sara Lee Classic. Bizarrely, she was hit in the neck by a bullet in a drugstore in 1994, although she quickly recovered from the incident. In 1998 and 1999 her appearances were limited by injury.

2000 SEASON. Williams had the best season of her career and recorded three top-10s, her highest being T4 at the Oldsmobile Classic. She was fifth on the putting statistics and ended 74th on the Money List.

Jay Williamson

US Tour

Born 7 February 1967
Place of Birth St Louis, Missouri, USA
Year turned Professional 1990
Tour Ranking 109th

BEST FINISH IN MAJORS
Missed Cut **US OPEN 2000**

Williamson was a member of the US Tour in 1995 and 1996 and played in the Nike Tour in 1998. He finished in fourth place in the 1999 Qualifying School. His highest finish on Tour is T4, at the 1995 Ideon Classic and the 1999 AT&T Pebble Beach Pro-Am.

2000 SEASON. Williamson had four top-10s, his best being T7 at the Bay Hill Invitational. He ended the season in 109th position on the Money List.

Garrett Willis

US Tour

Born 21 November 1973
Place of Birth Charlotte, North Carolina, USA
Year turned Professional 1996
Tour Ranking Tied 11th (Qualifying School)

TOUR VICTORIES
US: 1
2001 Tucson Open

Willis played on the Hooters Tour and the Buy.Com Tour, finishing 68th on the Money List in 2000. He qualified for the 2001 Tour with T11 at the Qualifying School.

2001 STOP PRESS. Willis stunned the world of American golf when he won the first full-field event of the 2001 US Tour, the Tucson Open in Arizona, and picked up over $500,000. 'Ain't this a great country', he gleefully remarked afterwards. He became only the third player, after Ben Crenshaw in 1973 and Robert Gamez in 1990, to win his first ever event on Tour.

Brian Wilson

US Tour

Born 26 July 1964
Place of Birth Tyler, Texas, USA
Year turned Professional 1987
Tour Ranking 2th (Qualifying School)

A long-term veteran of the Asian Tour, the tall Texan Wilson joined the Buy.Com Tour in 2000, but finished in a lowly position on the Money List. However, after trying for the US Tour for nearly 15 years, he finally made his card for the 2001 season by taking second place at Qualifying School.

Roger Winchester

European Tour

Born 28 March 1967
Place of Birth Exeter, England
Year turned Professional 1990
Tour Ranking 82nd

English Amateur Champion in 1985, Winchester spent most of the 1990s on the Challenge Tour, winning two tournaments. In 1998 he regained his Tour card and three top-10 finishes, including a T3 in the Scottish PGA, in 1999 left him 82th in the Order of Merit.

2000 SEASON. He posted seven top-25 finishes, his best being T14 at the Moroccan Open, and he ended the season again in 82nd place on the Order of Merit.

Tiger Woods

US Tour

Born 30 December 1975
Place of Birth Cypress, California, USA
Year turned Professional 1996
Tour Ranking 1st

MAJORS VICTORIES
US MASTERS 1997, 2001
BRITISH OPEN 2000
US OPEN 2000
USPGA 1999, 2000

TOUR VICTORIES
US: 22

1996 Las Vegas Invitational, Walt Disney World/Oldsmobile Classic
1997 GTE Byron Nelson Golf Classic, Mercedes Championship, Motorola Western Open
1998 BellSouth Classic
1999 Buick Invitational, Memorial Tournament, Motorola Western Open, National Car Rental Golf Classic /Disney, The Tour Championship, WGC American Express Championship, WGC NEC Invitational

2000 AT&T Pebble Beach National Pro-Am, Bay Hill Invitational, Bell Canadian Open, Memorial Tournament, Mercedes Championships, WGC-NEC Invitational
2001 Bay Hill Invitational, Players Championship, Memorial Tournament

EUROPEAN: 3
1998 Johnnie Walker Classic
1999 Deutsche Bank Open
2000 Johnnie Walker Classic
OTHER: 1
1997 Asian Honda Classic

RYDER CUP 1997, 1999
DUNHILL CUP 1998
PRESIDENTS CUP 1998, 2000
WORLD CUP 1999, 2000

Eldrick 'Tiger' Woods is the golfing phenomenon of the age. Named 'Tiger' after a Vietnamese soldier friend of his father's, his transcendent skills have propelled him at a young age into the position of number one golfer in the world, where he seems likely to remain for the foreseeable future.

His talent has been obvious since, at two years old, he appeared on TV putting with Bob Hope. At three, he shot 48 for nine holes, and by the age of five he had featured in an article in *Golf Digest* magazine. He was the youngest-ever winner of the US Amateur Championship at the age of 15 in 1994, winning the title again the next two years in succession, and he turned professional in 1996. His ability to hit the golf ball a prodigious distance (his first drive on the professional tour at the Greater Milwaukee Classic travelled over 330 yards), his subtle touch around the green and his confident and nerveless putting soon identified him as a star, and he signed long-term and lucrative contracts with Nike and Titleist. He won two tournaments, including the Las Vegas Invitational, in his first year, and was voted Rookie of the Year and *Sports Illustrated* magazine's Sportsman of the Year.

In 1997, he made golfing history by winning The Masters by an astonishing 12-stroke margin, and his final score of 270 was the lowest ever recorded in The Masters. He was also, at the age of 21, the youngest player to have won the prestigious event. He won his first international tournament – the Asian Honda Classic – in 1997 and his second, the Johnnie Walker Classic in Thailand, in 1998. His eight PGA Tour victories in 1999 were the most in one season since Johnny Miller in 1974, and his four wins in succession equalled Ben Hogan's record set in 1953. His earnings in that amazing year were $6.6 million, $3 million more than the second-placed David Duval. The six foot two inch athlete crowned that season with victory in the USPGA Championship, holding on in the face of a late surge from Sergio Garcia to win by one stroke. In 1999, he also represented the USA for the second time in the Ryder Cup.

2000 SEASON. Woods continued on his remarkable winning streak with an astonishing 15-stroke victory in the 2000 US Open, and he followed that up with an eight-stroke win at the British Open. He went on to defeat Bob May by one stroke becoming the youngest golfer ever to win the Career Grand Slam in a dramatic play-off at the USPGA Championship. He also won six other US Tour events, as well as picking up the Johnny Walker Classic again, and ran up 47 consecutive rounds at par or better. He pocketed a record $9 million in Tour earnings alone and topped the Money List by some distance.

2001 STOP PRESS. Woods had his longest spell without winning from the start of the season, sparking press speculation that he was entering a 'slump'. He answered his critics by winning over $2 million in his next three events. In his seventh start of the season, at the Bay Hill Invitational in Orlando, a 15-foot birdie putt on the last hole was enough to beat Phil Mickelson by one stroke. He also won the following week – the Players Championship – by one shot ahead of Vijay Singh, moving to the top

of the Money List. Woods created golfing history yet again when, in his very next event, he held off the challenges of Phil Mickelson and David Duval to win The Masters. At this point he held all four Majors at the same time and the golfing world was split as to whether this constituted a 'Grand Slam', a record never before achieved on the professional circuit.

He picked up his fourth title of the season at the Memorial, seven shots ahead of Sergio Garcia and Paul Azinger, but his Majors streak came to an end when he managed only 12th place at the US Open.

Ian Woosnam

European Tour

Born 2 March 1958
Place of Birth Oswestry, England
Year turned Professional 1976
Tour Ranking 24th

MAJORS VICTORIES
US MASTERS 1991

TOUR VICTORIES
US: 1
  1991 US F&G Classic
EUROPEAN: 28
  1982 Swiss Open
  1983 Silk Cut Masters
  1984 Scandinavian Open
  1986 Lawrence Batley TPC
  1987 Bell's Scottish Open, Jersey Open, Madrid Open, Trophee Lancome
  1988 Carrolls Irish Open, Panasonic European Open, Volvo PGA Championship
  1989 Carrolls Irish Open
  1990 Amex Mediterranean Open, Bell's Scottish Open , Epson Grand Prix, Monte Carlo Open
  1991 Fujitsu Mediterranean Open, Monte Carlo Open
  1992 Monte Carlo Open

1993 Murphy's English Open, Trophee
Lancome
1994 Air France Cannes Open, Dunhill
British Masters
1996 Heineken Classic, Johnnie Walker
Classic, Scottish Open, Volvo
German Open
1997 Volvo PGA Championship
OTHER: 8
1985 Zambian Open
1986 Kenya Open
1987 Hong Kong Open, Suntory World
Match Play Championship, World
Cup (indiv)
1988 Sun City Million Dollar Challenge
1990 Suntory World Match Play
Championship
1991 World Cup (indiv)

RYDER CUP 1983, 1985, 1987, 1989, 1991, 1993
DUNHILL CUP 1985, 1986, 1988, 1989, 1990,
1991, 1993, 1995
WORLD CUP 1980, 1982, 1983, 1984, 1985, 1987,
1990, 1991, 1992, 1993, 1994, 1996, 1997,
1998

A small, stocky, long-hitting Welshman, Woosnam came up the hard way, failing the European Tour Qualifying School twice in the 1970s and living in a camper van to save money. A superb iron player, he won his first tournament – the Swiss Open – in 1982 and to date has collected 28 European titles, and a millionaire residence in Jersey has replaced the van. In 1987, he had four victories, won the World Matchplay Championship and won the individual award at the World Cup, to top the Order of Merit. His most memorable year, however, was 1991 when, in spite of some unsporting behaviour by a section of the US crowd, he sank a 7-foot birdie putt on the final hole of The Masters to beat local favourite Tom Watson and Jose Maria Olázàbal, and don the famous green jacket. He also won the USF&G Classic on the US Tour that year. He was a regular on the European Ryder Cup team from 1983 till 1997. He commutes to Tour events in his own airplane.

2000 SEASON. 'Woosie' posted three top-3s, his best finish being second in the Qatar Masters. He had two other top-10 finishes to end the season 24th on the Order of Merit.

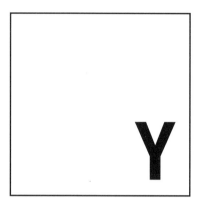

Yokoo came from the Japanese Tour to play in the US Tour in 1999, where he ended the season 193rd on the Money List. In 2000, he played in five Tour tournaments, making the cut three times. He qualified for the 2001 US Tour by finishing T18 at Qualifying School.

Wei-Tze Yeh
European Tour

Born 20 December 1973
Place of Birth Taipei, Taiwan
Year turned Professional 1994
Tour Ranking 101st

TOUR VICTORIES
EUROPEAN: 1
2000 Malaysian Open

Yeh surprised the world of golf when he became the first Asian to win on the European Tour for almost 20 years at the 2000 Malaysian Open in Kuala Lumpur. Coached by Liang Huan Lu ('Mr Lu'), who came second in the 1971 British Open and won the French Open shortly afterwards, the unknown Taiwanese golfer held on to win the title by one stroke over Padraig Harrington, Des Terblanche and Craig Hainline. He gained a three-year Tour exemption, but has not broken 70 on any of his subsequent European events.

Kaname Yokoo
US Tour

Born 24 July 1972
Place of Birth Tokyo, Japan
Year turned Professional 1996
Tour Ranking Tied 18th (Qualifying School)

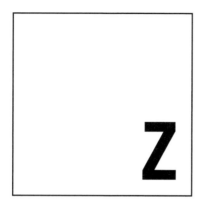

Kermit Zarley

US Seniors Tour

Born 29 September 1941
Place of Birth Seattle, Washington, USA
Year turned Professional 1963
Tour Ranking 47th

TOUR VICTORIES
SENIOR TOUR: 1
1991 Transamerica

Cowboy-hatted Zarley joined the US Senior Tour in 1991 and won in his rookie season, beating Isao Aoki on the first play-off hole at the Transamerica. He has not won since and his best season was 1996 when he was twice runner-up, earned $700,000 and was 13th on the Money List. He is devoutly religious and was co-founder of the PGA Tour Bible Study Group.

2000 SEASON. Zarley had two top-10s and ended 47th on the Money List. He passed the $4 million Senior earnings mark.

Lian-Wei Zhang

European Tour

Born 2 May 1965
Place of Birth Shenzen, China
Year turned Professional 1994
Tour Ranking 139th

DUNHILL CUP 1998, 2000

Chinese Zhang plays most of his golf in Asia, Europe and Canada, where he won the Ontario Open and became the first Asian player to win in Canada. He has won once on the Asian Tour, at the 1996 Volvo Asian Matchplay Championship, but has yet to make any kind of real impact in Europe.

2000 SEASON. Zhang made six cuts in seven starts on the European Tour and ended the season in 139th place on the Order of Merit – not high enough to automatically retain his card. However, the highlight of the year was beating Nick Price at the Dunhill Cup although Zimbabwe defeated China.

Larry Ziegler

US Seniors Tour

Born 12 August 1939
Place of Birth St Louis, Missouri, USA
Year turned Professional 1959
Tour Ranking 71st

TOUR VICTORIES
SENIOR TOUR: 2
1991 Newport Cup
1998 St Luke Classic

An ex-caddie in St Louis, Ziegler played on the USPGA Tour, won three tournaments and was T3 in the 1976 Masters. He has won twice on the US Senior Tour, his first title coming when he won the 1991 Newport Cup by six strokes, his first tournament victory for 25 years. In 1998, he contrived to shoot bogeys on the last three holes of the St Luke Classic, but still won ahead of Bruce Summerhays and Tom Shaw. His two wins created a record for the time between victories on the Senior Tour.

2000 SEASON. Ziegler had a disappointing year, his best finish being T22 at the TD Waterhouse Championship.

APPENDICES

APPENDIX I CUPS

RYDER CUP

1927 USA 9½ GB 2½
Worcester CC, Massachussetts

1929 GB 7 USA 5
Moortown, Yorkshire

1931 USA 9 GB 3
Scioto CC, Columbus, Ohio

1933 GB 6½ USA 5½
Southport and Ainsdale, Lancashire

1935 USA 9 GB 3
Ridgewood CC, New Jersey

1937 GB 4 USA 8
Southport and Ainsdale, Lancashire

1947 USA 11 GB 1
Portland GC, Oregon

1949 GB 5 USA 7
Ganton, Yorkshire

1951 USA 9½ GB 2½
Pinehurst, N Carolina

1953 GB 5½ USA 6½
Wentworth, Surrey

1955 USA 8 GB 4
Thunderbird G&CC, California

1957 GB 7½ USA 4½
Lindrick, Sheffield

1959 USA 8½ GB 3½
Eldorado CC, California

1961 GB 9½ USA 14½
Royal Lytham & St Anne's, Lancashire

1963 USA 23 GB 9
East Lake CC, Georgia

1965 GB 12½ USA 19½
Royal Birkdale, Lancashire

1967 USA 23½ GB 8½
Champions GC, Texas

1969 GB 16 USA 16
Royal Birkdale, Lancashire

1971 USA 18½ GB 13½
Old Warson CC, Missouri

1973 GB 13 USA 19
Muirfield, East Lothian

1975 USA 21 GB 11
Laurel Valley GC, Pennsylvania

1977 GB 7½ USA 12½
Royal Lytham & St Anne's, Lancashire

1979 USA 17 EUROPE 11
The Greenbrier, West Virginia

1981 EUROPE 9½ USA 18½
Walton Heath, Surrey

1983 USA 14½ EUROPE 13½
PGA National GC, Florida

1985 EUROPE 16½ USA 11½
The Belfry G&CC, West Midlands

1987 USA 13 EUROPE 15
Muirfield Village, Ohio

1989 EUROPE 14 USA 14
The Belfry G&CC, West Midlands

1991 USA 14½ EUROPE 13½
Kiawah Island, S. Carolina

1993 EUROPE 13 USA 15
The Belfry G&CC, West Midlands

1995 USA 13½ EUROPE 14½
Oak Hill CC, New York

1997 EUROPE 14½ USA 13½
Valderrama GC, Spain

1999 USA 14½ EUROPE 13½
Brookline GC, Massachussetts

SOLHEIM CUP

1990 USA 11½ EUROPE 4½
Lake Nona Golf Club, Orlando,
Florida

1992 EUROPE 11½ USA 6½
Dalmahoy Hotel Golf and Country
Club, Edinburgh

1994 USA 13 EUROPE 7
The Greenbrier, White Sulphur
Springs, West Virginia

1996 EUROPE 11 USA 17
Marriott, St Pierre Hotel and Country Club, Chepstow

1998 USA 16 EUROPE 12
Muirfield Village Golf Club, Dublin,
Ohio

2000 EUROPE 14½ USA 11½
Loch Lomond Golf Club,
Alexandria

PRESIDENTS CUP

1994 USA **20** INTERNATIONAL **12**
Robert Trent Jones GC, Virginia

1996 USA **16½** INTERNATIONAL **15½**
Robert Trent Jones GC, Virginia

1998 INTERNATIONAL **20½** USA **11½**
Royal Melbourne GC, Victoria, Australia

2000 USA **21½** INTERNATIONAL **10½**
Robert Trent Jones, GC, Virginia

WORLD CUP OF GOLF

1953 ARGENTINA (Cerda, De Vicenzo)
1954 AUSTRALIA (Thomson, Nagle)
1955 USA (Harbert, Furgol)
1956 USA (Hogan, Snead)
1957 JAPAN (Nakamura, Ono)
1958 IRELAND (Bradshaw, O'Connor)
1959 AUSTRALIA (Thomson, Nagle)
1960 USA (Snead, Palmer)
1961 USA (Snead, Demaret)
1962 USA (Snead, Palmer)
1963 USA (Palmer, Nicklaus)
1964 USA (Palmer, Nicklaus)
1965 SOUTH AFRICA (Player, Henning)
1966 USA (Palmer, Nicklaus)
1967 USA (Palmer, Nicklaus)
1968 CANADA (Balding, Knudson)
1969 USA (Moody, Trevino)
1970 AUSTRALIA (Devlin, Graham)
1971 USA (Nicklaus, Trevino)
1972 TAIWAN (Hsieh Min Nan,
     Lu Liang Huan)
1973 USA (Nicklaus, Miller)
1974 SOUTH AFRICA (Cole, Hayes)
1975 USA (Miller, Graham)
1976 SPAIN (Ballesteros, Pinero)
1977 SPAIN (Ballesteros, Garrido)
1978 USA (Mahaffey, North)
1979 USA (Mahaffey, Irwin)
1980 CANADA (Halldorson, Nelford)

1981 *Not played*
1982 SPAIN (Pinero, Canizares)
1983 USA (Caldwell, Cook)
1984 SPAIN (Canizares, Rivero)
1985 CANADA (Halldorson, Barr)
1986 *Not played*
1987 WALES (Woosnam, Llewellyn)
1988 USA (Crenshaw, McCumber)
1989 AUSTRALIA (Grady, Fowler)
1990 GERMANY (Langer, Gideon)
1991 SWEDEN (Forsbrand, Johansson)
1992 USA (Couples, Love III)
1993 USA (Couples, Love III)
1994 USA (Couples, Love III)
1995 USA (Couples, Love III)
1996 SOUTH AFRICA (Els, Westner)
1997 IRELAND (Harrington, McGinley)
1998 ENGLAND (Faldo, Carter)
1999 USA (Woods, O'Meara)
2000 USA (Woods, Duval)

APPENDIX II MAJORS

THE MAJORS (2000)

6–9 April
THE MASTERS
Augusta Golf Club, Georgia, USA
Winner: Vijay Singh

20–23 July
THE OPEN
St Andrews, Fife, Scotland
Winner: Tiger Woods

15–18 June
US OPEN
Pebble Beach Golf Links, California, USA
Winner: Tiger Woods

17–20 August
USPGA CHAMPIONSHIP
Valhalla Golf Club, Louisville, Kentucky, USA
Winner: Tiger Woods

The Open Golf Championship

* After play-off   (AM) Amateur   Names in italics are runners up

1860 Willie Park
Tom Morris, Snr
Prestwick

1861 Tom Morris, Snr
Willie Park
Prestwick

1862 Tom Morris, Snr
Willie Park
Prestwick

1863 Willie Park
Tom Morris, Snr
Prestwick

1864 Tom Morris, Snr
Andrew Strath
Prestwick

1865 Andrew Strath
Willie Park
Prestwick

1866 Willie Park
David Park
Prestwick

1867 Tom Morris, Snr
Willie Park
Prestwick

1868 Tom Morris, Jnr
Tom Morris, Snr
Prestwick

1869 Tom Morris, Jnr
Tom Morris, Snr
Prestwick

1870 Tom Morris, Jnr
David Strath,
Bob Kirk
Prestwick

1871 *No tournament*

1872 Tom Morris, Jnr
David Strath
Prestwick

1873 Tom Kidd
Jamie Anderson
St Andrews

1874 Mungo Park
Tom Morris, Jnr
Musselburgh

1875 Willie Park
Bob Martin
Prestwick

1876 Bob Martin
David Strath
(refused play-off)
St Andrews

1877 Jamie Anderson
Bob Pringle
Musselburgh

1878 Jamie Anderson
Bob Kirk
Prestwick

1879 Jamie Anderson
Andrew Kirkaldy,
James Allan
St Andrews

1880 Bob Ferguson
Peter Paxton
Musselburgh

1881 Bob Ferguson
Jamie Anderson
Prestwick

1882 Bob Ferguson
Willie Fernie
St Andrews

1883 Willie Fernie*
Bob Ferguson
Musselburgh

1884 Jack Simpson
Willie Fernie
Douglas Rolland
Prestwick

1885 Bob Martin
Archie Simpson
St Andrews

1886 David Brown
Willie Campbell
Musselburgh

1887 Willie Park, Jnr
Bob Martin
Prestwick

1888 Jack Burns
Ben Sayers,
David Anderson
St Andrews

1889 Willie Park, Jnr*
Andrew Kirkaldy
Musselburgh

1890 John Ball (AM)
Willie Fernie
Prestwick

1891 Hugh Kirkaldy
Andrew Kirkaldy,
Willie Fernie
St Andrews

1892 Harold H Hilton (AM)
John Ball (AM),
Hugh Kirkaldy,
Alexander Herd
Musselburgh

1893 William Auchterlonie
John E Laidlay (AM)
Prestwick

1894 John H Taylor
Douglas Rolland
Sandwich

1895 John H Taylor
Alexander Herd
St Andrews

1896 Harry Vardon*
John H Taylor
Muirfield

1897 Harold H Hilton (AM)
James Braid
Hoylake

1898 Harry Vardon
Willie Park, Jnr
Prestwick

1899 Harry Vardon
Jack White
Sandwich

1900 John H Taylor
Harry Vardon
St Andrews

1901 James Braid
Harry Vardon
Muirfield

1902 Alexander Herd
Harry Vardon,
James Braid
Hoylake

1903 Harry Vardon
Tom Vardon
Prestwick

1904 Jack White
John H Taylor,
James Braid
Sandwich

1905 James Braid
John H Taylor,
Rowland Jones
St Andrews

1906 James Braid
John H Taylor
Muirfield

1907 Arnaud Massy
John H Taylor
Hoylake

1908 James Braid
Tom Ball
Prestwick

1909 John H Taylor
James Braid,
Tom Ball
Deal

1910 James Braid
Alexander Herd
St Andrews

1911 Harry Vardon*
Arnaud Massy
Sandwich

1912 Edward Ray
Harry Vardon
Muirfield

1913 John H Taylor
Edward Ray
Hoylake

1914 Harry Vardon
John H Taylor
Prestwick

1915-1919 *No tournament*

1920 George Duncan
Alexander Herd
Deal

1921 Jack Hutchison*
Roger Wethered
St Andrews

1922 Walter Hagen
George Duncan,
James Barnes
Sandwich

1923 Arthur Havers
Walter Hagen
Royal Troon

1924 Walter Hagen
Ernest Whitcombe
Hoylake

1925 James Barnes
Archie Compston,
Ted Ray
Prestwick

1926 Robert T Jones Jnr (AM)
Al Watrous
Royal Lytham & St Annes

1927 Robert T Jones, Jnr (AM)
Aubrey Boomer
Fred Robson
St Andrews

1928 Walter Hagen
Gene Sarazen
Sandwich

1929 Walter Hagen
Johnny Farrell
Murfield

1930 Robert T Jones, Jnr (AM)
Macdonald Smith,
Leo Diegel
Hoylake

1931 Tommy Armour
Jose Jurado
Carnoustie

1932 Gene Sarazen
Macdonald Smith
Prince's, Sandwich

1933 Denny Shute*
Craig Wood
St Andrews

1934 Henry Cotton
Sidney F. Brews
Sandwich

1935 Alfred Perry
Alfred Padgham
Murfield

1936 Alfred Padgham
James Adams
Hoylake

1937 Henry Cotton
R A Whitcombe
Carnoustie

1938 R A Whitcombe
James Adams
Sandwich

1939 Richard Burton
Johnny Bulla
St Andrews

1940-1945   *No tournament*

1946 Sam Snead
Bobby Locke, Johnny Bulla
St Andrews

1947 Fred Daly
Reg W Horne,
Frank Stranahan (AM)
Hoylake

1948 Henry Cotton
Fred Daly
Muirfield

1949 Bobby Locke*
Harry Bradshaw
Royal St George's

1950 Bobby Locke
Roberto de Vicenzo
Royal Troon

1951 Max Faulkner
Antonio Cerda
Royal Portrush

1952 Bobby Locke
Peter Thomson
Royal Lytham & St Anne's

1953 Ben Hogan
Frank Stranahan (AM),
Dai Rees, Peter Thomson,
Antonio Cerda
Carnoustie

1954 Peter Thomson
Syd Scott,
Dai Rees,
Bobby Locke
Royal Birkdale

1955 Peter Thomson
John Fallon
Hoylake

1957 Bobby Locke
Peter Thomson
St Andrews

1958 Peter Thomson*
Dave Thomas
Royal Lytham & St Anne's

1959 Gary Player
Fred Bullock,
Flory van Donck
Muirfield

1960 Kel Nagle
Arnold Palmer
St Andrews

1961 Arnold Palmer
Dai Rees
Royal Birkdale

1962 Arnold Palmer
Kel Nagle
Royal Troon

1963 Bob Charles*
Phil Rodgers
Royal Lytham & St Anne's

1964 Tony Lema
Jack Nicklaus
St Andrews

1965 Peter Thomson
Brian Huggett,
Christy O'Connor
Royal Birkdale

1966 Jack Nicklaus
Doug Sanders,
Dave Thomas
Muirfield

1967 Roberto De Vicenzo
Jack Nicklaus
Hoylake

1968 Gary Player
Jack Nicklaus,
Bob Charles
Carnoustie

1969 Tony Jacklin
Bob Charles
Royal Lytham & St Anne's

1970 Jack Nicklaus*
Doug Sanders
St Andrews

1971 Lee Trevino
Liang Huan Lu
Royal Birkdale

1972 Lee Trevino
Jack Nicklaus
Muirfield

1973 Tom Weiskopf
Johnny Miller,
Neil Coles
Royal Troon

1974 Gary Player
Peter Oosterhuis
Royal Lytham & St Anne's

1975 Tom Watson*
Jack Newton
Carnoustie

1976 Johnny Miller
Jack Nicklaus,
Seve Ballesteros
Royal Birkdale

1977 Tom Watson
Jack Nicklaus
Turnberry

1978 Jack Nicklaus
Ben Crenshaw, Tom Kite,
Ray Floyd,Simon Owen
St Andrews

1979 Seve Ballesteros
Ben Crenshaw,
Jack Nicklaus
Royal Lytham & St Anne's

1980 Tom Watson
Lee Trevino
Muirfield

1981 Bill Rogers
Bernhard Langer
Royal St George's

1982 Tom Watson
Nick Price,
Peter Oosterhuis
Royal Troon

1983 Tom Watson
Andy Bean,
Hale Irwin
Royal Birkdale

1984 Seve Ballesteros
Tom Watson,
Bernhard Langer
St Andrews

1985 Sandy Lyle
Payne Stewart
Royal St George's

1986 Greg Norman
Gordon J. Brand
Turnberry

1987 Nick Faldo
Paul Azinger,
Rodger Davis
Muirfield

1988 Seve Ballesteros
Nick Price
Royal Lytham & St Anne's

1989 Mark Calcavecchia*
Wayne Grady,
Greg Norman
Royal Troon

1990 Nick Faldo
Payne Stewart,
Mark McNulty
St Andrews

1991 Ian Baker-Finch
Mike Harwood
Royal Birkdale

1992 Nick Faldo
John Cook
Muirfield

1993 Greg Norman
Nick Faldo
Royal St George's

1994 Nick Price
Jesper Parnevik
Turnberry

1995 John Daly*
Costantino Rocca
St Andrews

1996 Tom Lehman
Mark McCumber,
Ernie Els
Royal Lytham & St Anne's

1997 Justin Leonard
Darren Clarke,
Jesper Parnevik
Royal Troon

1998 Mark O'Meara*
Brian Watts
Royal Birkdale

1999 Paul Lawrie*
Jean Van de Velde,
Justin Leonard
Carnoustie

2000 Tiger Woods
Ernie Els, Thomas Bjorn
St Andrews

The Masters Tournament

Augusta National Golf Club, Augusta, Georgia
* After play-off

(AM) Amateur
Names in italics are runners up

1934 Horton Smith
Craig Wood

1935 Gene Sarazen*
Craig Wood

1936 Horton Smith
Harry Cooper

1937 Byron Nelson
Ralph Guldahl

1938 Henry Picard
Ralph Guldahl,
Harry Cooper

1939 Ralph Guldahl
Sam Snead

1940 Jimmy Demaret
Lloyd Mangrum

1941 Craig Wood
Byron Nelson

1942 Byron Nelson*
Ben Hogan

1943–45 *No tournament*

1946 Herman Keiser
Ben Hogan

1947 Jimmy Demaret
Byron Nelson,
Frank Stranahan(AM)

1948 Claude Harmon
Cary Middlecoff

1949 Sam Snead
Johnny Bulla,
Lloyd Mangrum

1950 Jimmy Demaret
Jim Ferrier

1951 Ben Hogan
Skee Riegel

1952 Sam Snead
Jack Burke, Jnr

1953 Ben Hogan
Ed Oliver, Jnr

1954 Sam Snead*
Ben Hogan

1955 Cary Middlecoff
Ben Hogan

1956 Jack Burke, Jnr
Ken Venturi

1957 Doug Ford
Sam Snead

1958 Arnold Palmer
Doug Ford, Fred Hawkins

1959 Art Wall, Jnr
Cary Middlecoff

1960 Arnold Palmer
Ken Venturi

1961 Gary Player
Charles R. Coe (AM),
Arnold Palmer

1962 Arnold Palmer*
Gary Player,
Dow Finsterwald

1963 Jack Nicklaus
Tony Lema

1964 Arnold Palmer
Dave Marr, Jack Nicklaus

1965 Jack Nicklaus
Arnold Palmer,
Gary Player

1966 Jack Nicklaus*
Tommy Jacobs,
Gay Brewer Jnr

1967 Gay Brewer, Jnr
Bobby Nichols

1968 Bob Goalby
Roberto de Vicenzo

1969 George Archer
Billy Casper, George
Knudson, Tom Weiskopf

1970 Billy Casper*
Gene Littler

1971 Charles Coody
Johnny Miller,
Jack Nicklaus

1972 Jack Nicklaus
Bruce Crampton,
Bobby Mitchell,
Tom Weiskopf

1973 Tommy Aaron
J.C. Snead

1974 Gary Player
Tom Weiskopf,
Dave Stockton

1975 Jack Nicklaus
Johnny Miller,
Tom Weiskopf

1976 Ray Floyd
Ben Crenshaw

1977 Tom Watson
Jack Nicklaus

1978 Gary Player
Hubert Green,
Rod Funseth,
Tom Watson

1979 Fuzzy Zoeller*
Ed Sneed,
Tom Watson

1980 Seve Ballesteros
Gibby Gilbert,
Jack Newton

1981 Tom Watson
Johnny Miller,
Jack Nicklaus

1982 Craig Stadler*
Dan Pohl

1983 Seve Ballesteros
Ben Crenshaw,
Tom Kite

1984 Ben Crenshaw
Tom Watson

1985 Bernhard Langer
Curtis Strange,
Seve Ballesteros,
Ray Floyd

1986 Jack Nicklaus
Greg Norman,
Tom Kite

1987 Larry Mize*
Seve Ballesteros,
Greg Norman

1988 Sandy Lyle
Mark Calcavecchia

1989 Nick Faldo*
Scott Hoch

1990 Nick Faldo*
Ray Floyd

1991 Ian Woosnam
Jose Maria Olázàbal

1992 Fred Couples
Ray Floyd

1993 Bernhard Langer
Chip Beck

1994 Jose Maria Olázàbal
Tom Lehman

1995 Ben Crenshaw
Davis Love III

1996 Nick Faldo
Greg Norman

1997 Tiger Woods
Tom Kite

1998 Mark O'Meara
David Duval,
Fred Couples

1999 Jose Maria Olazabal
Davis Love III

2000 Vijay Singh
Ernie Els

US Open Championship

* After play-off   (AM) Amateur   Names in italics are runners up

1895 Horace Rawlins
Willie Dunn
Newport

1896 James Foulis
Horace Rawlins
Shinnecock Hills

1897 Joe Lloyd
Willie Anderson
Chicago

1898 Fred Herd
Alex Smith
Myopia Hunt Club

1899 Willie Smith
George Low, Val Fitzjohn,
W.H. Way
Baltimore

1900 Harry Vardon
J.H. Taylor
Chicago

1901 Willie Anderson*
Alex Smith
Myopia Hunt Club

1902 Laurie Auchterlonie
Stewart Gardner,
Walter Travis (AM)
Garden City

1903 Willie Anderson*
David Brown
Baltusrol

1904 Willie Anderson
Gil Nicholls
Glen View

1905 Willie Anderson
Alex Smith
Myopia Hunt Club

1906 Alex Smith
Willie Smith
Onwentsia Club

1907 Alex Ross
Gil Nicholls
Philadelphia Cricket Club

1908 Fred McLeod*
Willie Smith
Myopia Hunt Club

1909 George Sargent
Tom McNamara
Englewood

1910 Alex Smith*
John McDermott,
Macdonald Smith
Philadelphia Cricket Club

1911 John McDermott*
Mike Brady,
George Simpson
Chicago

1912 John McDermott
Tom McNamara
CC of Buffalo

1913 Francis Ouimet (AM)*
Harry Vardon, Edward
Ray
The Country Club, Brookline

1914 Walter Hagen
Charles Evans Jnr (AM)
Midlothian

1915 Jerome Travers (AM)
Tom McNamara
Baltusrol

1916 Charles Evans Jnr (AM)
Jock Hutchison
Minikahda Club

1917–18 *No tournament*

1919 Walter Hagen*
Mike Brady
Brae Burn

1920 Edward Ray
Harry Vardon, Jack Burke,
Leo Diegel, Jock Hutchison
Inverness

1921 James M. Barnes
Walter Hagen, Fred
McLeod
Columbia

1922 Gene Sarazen
John L. Black,
Robert T. Jones Jnr (AM)
Skokie

1923 Robert T. Jones Jnr* (AM)
Bobby Cruickshank
Inwood

1924 Cyril Walker
Robert T. Jones Jnr (AM)
Oakland Hills

1925 W. MacFarlane*
Robert T. Jones Jnr
Worcester

1926 Robert T. Jones Jnr (AM)
Joe Turnesa
Scioto

1927 Tommy Armour*
Harry Cooper
Oakmont

1928 Johnny Farrell*
Robert T. Jones Jnr (AM)
Olympia Fields

1929 Robert T. Jones Jnr (AM)*
Al Espinosa
Winged Foot

1930 Robert T. Jones Jnr (AM)
Macdonald Smith
Interlachen

1931 Billy Burke*
George von Elm
Inverness Club

1932 Gene Sarazen
Phil Perkins, Bobby
Cruickshank
Fresh Meadows

1933 Johnny Goodman (AM)
Ralph Guldahl
North Shore

1934 Olin Dutra
Gene Sarazen
Merion Cricket Club

1935 Sam Parks Jnr
Jimmy Thomson
Oakmont

1936 Tony Manero
Harry Cooper
Baltusrol

1937 Ralph Guldahl
Sam Snead
Oakland Hills

1938 Ralph Guldahl
Dick Metz
Cherry Hills

1939 Byron Nelson*
Craig Wood, Denny Shute
Philadelphia

1940 Lawson Little*
Gene Sarazen
Canterbury

1941 Craig Wood
Denny Shute
Colonial Club

1942–45 *No tournament*

1946 Lloyd Mangrum*
Vic Ghezzi,
Byron Nelson
Canterbury

1947 Lew Worsham*
Sam Snead
St Louis

1948 Ben Hogan
Jimmy Demaret
Riviera

1949 Cary Middlecoff
Sam Snead,
Clayton Heafner
Medinah

1950 Ben Hogan*
Lloyd Mangrum, George
Fazio
Merion

1951 Ben Hogan
Clayton Heffner
Oakland Hills

1952 Julius Boros
Ed Oliver
Northwood

1953 Ben Hogan
Sam Snead
Oakmont

1954 Ed Furgol
Gene Littler
Baltusrol

1955 Jack Fleck*
Ben Hogan
Olympic Club

1956 Cary Middlecoff
Ben Hogan, Julius Boros
Oak Hill

1957 Dick Mayer*
Cary Middlecoff
Inverness Club

1958 Tommy Bolt
Gary Player
Southern Hills

1959 Billy Casper
Bob Rosburg
Winged Foot

1960 Arnold Palmer
Jack Nicklaus (AM)
Cherry Hills

1961 Gene Littler
Bob Goalby, Doug Sanders
Oakland Hills

1962 Jack Nicklaus*
Arnold Palmer
Oakmont

1963 Julius Boros*
*Jacky Cupit, Arnold
Palmer*
The County Club, Brookline

1964 Ken Venturi
Tommy Jacobs
Congressional

1965 Gary Player*
Kel Nagle
Bellerive

1966 Billy Casper*
Arnold Palmer
Olympic Club

1967 Jack Nicklaus
Arnold Palmer
Baltusrol

1968 Lee Trevino
Jack Nicklaus
Oak Hill

1969 Orville Moody
*Deane Beman,
Al Geiberger, Bob Rosburg*
Champions GC

1970 Tony Jacklin
Dave Hill
Hazeltine

1971 Lee Trevino*
Jack Nicklaus
Merion

1972 Jack Nicklaus
Bruce Crampton
Pebble Beach

1973 Johnny Miller
John Schlee
Oakmont

1974 Hale Irwin
Forrest Fezler
Winged Foot

1975 Lou Graham*
John Mahaffey
Medinah

1976 Jerry Pate
Tom Weiskopf, Al Geiberger
Atlantic Athletic Club

1977 Hubert Green
Lou Graham
Southern Hills

1978 Andy North
Dave Stockton, J.C. Snead
Cherry Hills

1979 Hale Irwin
*Gary Player,
Jerry Pate*
Inverness Club

1980 Jack Nicklaus
Isao Aoki
Baltusrol

1981 David Graham
George Burns, Bill Rogers
Merion

1982 Tom Watson
Jack Nicklaus
Pebble Beach

1983 Larry Nelson
Tom Watson
Oakmont

1984 Fuzzy Zoeller*
Greg Norman
Winged Foot

1985 Andy North
*Dave Barr, T.C. Chen,
Dennis Watson*
Oakland Hills

1986 Ray Floyd
*Lanny Wadkins,
Chip Beck*
Shinnecock Hills

1987 Scott Simpson
Tom Watson
Olympic Club

1988 Curtis Strange*
Nick Faldo
The Country Club, Brookline

1989 Curtis Strange
*Chip Beck,
Mark McCumber,
Ian Woosnam*
Oak Hill

1990 Hale Irwin*
Mike Donald
Medinah

1991 Payne Stewart*
Scott Simpson
Hazeltine

1992 Tom Kite
Jeff Sluman
Pebble Beach

1993 Lee Janzen
Payne Stewart
Baltusrol

1994 Ernie Els*
Colin Mongomerie,
Loren Roberts
Oakmont

1995 Corey Pavin
Greg Norman
Shinnecock Hills

1996 Steve Jones
Tom Lehman,
Davis Love III
Oakland Hills

1997 Ernie Els
Colin Montgomerie
Congressional

1998 Lee Janzen
Payne Stewart
Olympic Club

1999 Payne Stewart
Phil Mickelson
Pinehurst No.2

2000 Tiger Woods
Ernie Els, Miguel Angel
Jiminez
Pebble Beach

USPGA Championship

* After play-off   (AM) Amateur   Names in italics are runners up

1916 Jim Barnes
Jock Hutchison
Siwanoy

1919 Jim Barnes
Fred McLeod
Engineers

1920 Jock Hutchison
J. Douglas Edgar
Flossmor

1921 Walter Hagen
Jim Barnes
Inwood

1922 Gene Sarazen
Emmett French
Oakmont

1923 Gene Sarazen
Walter Hagen
Pelham

1924 Walter Hagen
James Barnes
French Lick

1925 Walter Hagen
Bill Mehlhorn
Olympia Fields

1926 Walter Hagen
Leo Diegel
Salisbury

1927 Walter Hagen
Joe Turnesa
Cedar Crest

1928 Leo Diegel
Al Espinosa
Five Farms

1929 Leo Diegel
Johnny Farrell
Hillcrest

1930 Tommy Armour
Gene Sarazen
Fresh Meadows

1931 Tom Creavy
Denny Shute
Wannamoisett

1932 Olin Dutra
Frank Walsh
Keller

1933 Gene Sarazen
Willie Goggin
Blue Mound

1934 Paul Runyan
Craig Wood
Park Club

1935 Johnny Revolta
Tommy Armour
Twin Hills

1936 Denny Shute
Jim Thomson
Pinehurst

1937 Denny Shute
Harold McSpaden
Pittsburgh

1938 Paul Runyan
Sam Snead
Shawnee

1939 Henry Picard
Byron Nelson
Pomonock

1940 Byron Nelson
Sam Snead
Hershey

1941 Vic Ghezzi
Byron Nelson
Cherry Hills

1942 Sam Snead
Jim Turnesa
Seaview

1943 *No tournament*

1944 Bob Hamilton
Byron Nelson
Manito

1945 Byron Nelson
Sam Byrd
Morraine

1946 Ben Hogan
Ed Oliver
Portland

1947 Jim Ferrier
Chick Harbert
Plum Hollow

1948 Ben Hogan
Mike Turnesa
Norwood Hills

1949 Sam Snead
Johnny Palmer
Hermitage

1950 Chandler Harper
Henry Williams Jnr
Scioto

1951 Sam Snead
Walter Burkemo
Oakmont

1952 Jim Turnesa
Chick Harbert
Big Spring

1953 Walter Burkemo
Felice Torza
Birmingham

1954 Chick Harbert
Walter Burkemo
Keller

1955 Doug Ford
Cary Middlecoff
Meadowbrook

1956 Jack Burke
Ted Kroll
Blue Hill

1957 Lionel Hebert
Dow Finsterwald
Miami Valley

1958 Dow Finsterwald
Billy Casper
Llanerch

1959 Bob Rosurg
Jerry Barber, Doug Sanders
Minneapolis

1960 Jay Herbert
Jim Ferrier
Firestone

1961 Jerry Barber*
Don January
Olympia Fields

1962 Gary Player
Bob Goalby
Aronimink

1963 Jack Nicklaus
Dave Ragan Jnr
Dallas Athletic Club

1964 Bobby Nichols
*Jack Nicklaus,
Arnold Palmer*
Columbus

1965 Dave Marr
*Billy Casper,
Jack Nicklaus*
Laurel Valley

1966 Al Geiberger
Dudley Wysong
Firestone

1967 Don January*
Don Massingale
Columbine

1968 Juluis Boros
*Bob Charles, Arnold
Palmer*
Pecan Valley

1969 Ray Floyd
Gary Player
NCR

1970 Dave Stockton
*Arnold Palmer,
Bob Murphy*
Southern Hills

1971 Jack Nicklaus
Billy Casper
PGA National

1972 Gary Player
*Tommy Aaron, Jim
Jamieson*
Oakland Hills

1973 Jack Nicklaus
Bruce Crampton
Canterbury

1974 Lee Trevino
Jack Nicklaus
Tanglewood

1975 Jack Nicklaus
Bruce Crampton
Firestone

1976 Dave Stockton
*Ray Floyd,
Don January*
Congressional

1977 Lanny Wadkins*
Gene Littler
Pebble Beach

1978 John Mahaffey*
Jerry Pate, Tom Watson
Oakmont

1979 David Graham*
Ben Crenshaw
Oakland Hills

1980 Jack Nicklaus
Andy Bean
Oak Hill

1981 Larry Nelson
Fuzzy Zoeller
Atlanta Athletic Club

1982 Ray Floyd
Lanny Wadkins
Southern Hills

1983 Hal Sutton
Jack Nicklaus
Riviera

1984 Lee Trevino
*Gary Player,
Lanny Wadkins*
Shoal Creek

1985 Hubert Green
Lee Trevino
Cherry Hills

1986 Bob Tway
Greg Norman
Inverness

1987 Larry Nelson*
Lanny Wadkins
PGA National

1988 Jeff Sluman
Paul Azinger
Oak Tree

1989 Payne Stewart
*Mike Reid,
Andy Bean,
Curtis Strange*
Kemper Lakes

1990 Wayne Grady
Fred Couples
Shoal Creek

1991 John Daly
Bruce Lietzke
Crooked Stick

1992 Nick Price
*John Cook,
Jim Gallahger Jnr,
Gene Sauers,
Nick Faldo*
Bellerive

1993 Paul Azinger*
Greg Norman
Inverness

1994 Nick Price
Corey Pavin
Southern Hills

1995 Steve Elkington*
Colin Montgomerie
Riviera

1996 Mark Brooks*
Kenny Perry
Valhalla

1997 Davis Love III
Justin Leonard
Winged Foot

1998 Vijay Singh
Steve Stricker
Sahalee

1999 Tiger Woods
Sergio Garcia
Medinah

2000 Tiger Woods
Bob May
Valhalla

APPENDIX III USPGA MEN'S TOUR

MONEY LIST 2000 – TOP-50

1	Tiger Woods	20	Notah Begay III	39	Jeff Maggert
2	Phil Mickelson	21	Nick Price	40	Jonathan Kaye
3	Ernie Els	22	Scott Verplank	41	Greg Chalmers
4	Hal Sutton	23	Mark Calcavecchia	42	Sergio Garcia
5	Vijay Singh	24	Stuart Appleby	43	Dudley Hart
6	Mike Weir	25	John Huston	44	Scott Dunlap
7	David Duval	26	Franklin Langham	45	Billy Andrade
8	Jesper Parnevik	27	Paul Azinger	46	Brad Faxon
9	Davis Love III	28	Chris Perry	47	Fred Couples
10	Stewart Cink	29	Bob May	48	Jim Carter
11	Kirk Triplett	30	Carlos Franco	49	Blaine McCallister
12	Tom Lehman	31	Steve Lowery	50	Skip Kendall
13	Steve Flesch	32	Duffy Waldorf		
14	Justin Leonard	33	Scott Hoch		
15	David Toms	34	Rocco Mediate		
16	Robert Allenby	35	Tom Scherrer		
17	Jim Furyk	36	Rory Sabbatini		
18	Loren Roberts	37	Shigeki Maruyama		
19	Chris DiMarco	38	Grant Waite		

US TOUR TOURNAMENTS 2000

6–9 January
Mercedes Championship
The Plantation Course, Kapalua, Maui, Hawaii
Winner: Tiger Woods

13–16 January
Sony Open in Hawaii
Walalae Country Club, Honolulu, Hawaii
Winner: Paul Azinger

19–23 January
Bob Hope Chrysler Classic
Bermuda Dunes Country Club, Bermuda Dunes, California
Winner: Jesper Parnevik

27–30 January
Phoenix Open
Tournament Players Club of Scottsdale
Winner: Tom Lehman

3–7 February
AT&T Pebble Beach National Pro-Am
Pebble Beach Golf Links, Pebble Beach, California
Winner: Tiger Woods

10–13 February
Buick Invitational
Torrey Pines Golf Course, La Jolla, California
Winner: Phil Mickelson

17–20 February
Nissan Open
Riviera Country Club, Pacific Palisades, California
Winner: Kirk Triplett

24–27 February
Touchstone Energy Tucson Open
Omni Tucson National Golf Resort, Tucson, Arizona
Winner: Jim Carter

2–5 March
Doral-Ryder Open
Doral Golf Resort (Blue Course), Miami, Florida
Winner: Jim Furyk

9–12 March
Honda Classic
Tournament Players Club at Heron Bay, Coral Springs, Florida
Winner: Dudley Hart

16–19 March
Bay Hill Invitational Presented by Cooper Tires
Bay Hill Golf Club, Orlando, Florida
Winner: Tiger Woods

23–27 March
The Players Championship
Tournament Players Club at Sawgrass, Ponte Vedra Beach, Florida
Winner: Hal Sutton

30 March–April 2
BellSouth Classic
Tournament Players Club at Sugarloaf, Duluth, Georgia
Winner: Phil Mickelson

13–16 April
MCI Classic
Harbour Town Golf Links, Hilton Head Island, S. Carolina
Winner: Stewart Cink

20–23 April
Greater Greensboro Chrysler Classic
Forest Oaks Country Club, Greensboro, N. Carolina
Winner: Hal Sutton

27–30 April
Shell Houston Open
Tournament Players Course at The Woodlands, Texas
Winner: Robert Allenby

4–7 May
Compaq Classic of New Orleans
English Turn Golf and Country Club, New Orleans, Louisiana
Winner: Carlos Franco

11–14 May
GTE Byron Nelson Classic
Tournament Players Course Four Seasons-Las Colinas, Irving, Texas
Winner: Jesper Parnevik

18–21 May
MasterCard Colonial
Colonial Country Club, Fort Worth, Texas
Winner: Phil Mickelson

25–29 May
Memorial Tournament
Muirfield Village Golf Club
Winner: Tiger Woods

1–4 June
Kemper Insurance Open
Tournament Players Club at Avenel, Potomac, Maryland
Winner: Tom Scherrer

8–11 June
Buick Classic
Westchester Country Club, Harrison, New York
Winner: Dennis Paulson

22–25 June
Fedex St Jude Classic
Tournament Players Club at Southwind, Memphis, Tennessee
Winner: Notah Begay III

29 June–2 July
Canon Greater Hartford Open
Tournament Players Club at River Highlands, Cromwell, Connecticut
Winner: Notah Begay III

6–9 July
Advil Western Open
Cog Hill Golf and Country Club, Lemont, Illinois
Winner: Robert Allenby

13–16 July
Greater Milwaukee Open
Brown Deer Park Golf Course, Milwaukee, Wisconsin
Winner: Loren Roberts

20–23 July
BC Open
En-Joie Golf Club, Endicott, New York
Winner: Brad Faxon

27–30 July
John Deere Classic
Tournament Players Club at Deere Run, Silvis, Illinois
Winner: Michael Clark II

3–6 August
International presented by Qwest
Castle Pines Golf Club. Castle Rock, Colorado
Winner: Ernie Els

10–13 August
Buick Open
Warwick Hills Golf Club, Grand Blanc, Michigan
Winner: Rocco Mediate

24–27 August
Reno-Tahoe Open
Montreux Golf and Country Club, Reno, Nevada
Winner: Scott Verplank

31 August–3 September
Air Canada Championship
Northview Golf Club, Surrey, British Columbia, Canada
Winner: Rory Sabbatini

7–10 September
Bell Canadian Open
Glen Abbey Golf Club, Ontario, Canada
Winner: Tiger Woods

14–17 September
SEI Pennsylvania Classic
Waynesborough Country Club, Paoli, Pennsylvania
Winner: Chris DiMarco

21–24 September
Westin Texas Open
La Cantera Golf Club, San Antonio, Texas
Winner: Justin Leonard

28 September–1 October
Buick Challenge
Callaway Gardens Resort, Pine Mountain, Georgia
Winner: David Duval

5–8 October
Michelob Championship at Kingsmill
Kingsmill Golf Club, Williamsburg, Virginia
Winner: David Toms

11–15 October
Invensys Classic at Las Vegas
Tournament Players Club at Summerlin, Las Vegas, Nevada
Winner: Billy Andrade

19–22 October
Tampa Bay Classic
Westin Innisbrook Resort, Palm Harbor, Florida
Winner: John Huston

26–29 October
National Car Rental Golf Classic at Walt Disney World Resort
Walt Disney World Resort, Lake Buena Vista, Florida
Winner: Duffy Waldorf

2–5 November
Southern Farm Bureau Classic
Annandale Golf Club, Madison, Mississippi
Winner: Steve Lowery

2–5 November
The Tour Championship presented by Southern Company
East Lake Golf Club, Atlanta, Georgia
Winner: Phil Mickelson

Buy.Com Tour 2000 – Top-15

1 Spike McRoy	6	Chris Smith	11	David Berganio Jr
2 Mark Hensby	7	Kent Jones	12	Jeff Gallagher
3 Tim Clarke	8	Tripp Isenhour	13	JJ Henry
4 Briny Baird	9	Paul Gow	14	Kelly Grunewald
5 Ian Leggat	10	John Reigger	15	Jeff Hart

PGA Tour Player of the Year Award

1990	Wayne Levi	1994	Nick Price	1998	Mark O'Meara
1991	Fred Couples	1995	Greg Norman	1999	Tiger Woods
1992	Fred Couples	1996	Tom Lehman	2000	Tiger Woods
1993	Nick Price	1997	Tiger Woods		

Arnold Palmer Award (Leader on Money List)

1990	Greg Norman	1994	Nick Price	1998	David Duval
1991	Corey Pavin	1995	Greg Norman	1999	Tiger Woods
1992	Fred Couples	1996	Tom Lehman	2000	Tiger Woods
1993	Nick Price	1997	Tiger Woods		

Rookie of the Year

1990	Robert Gamez	1994	Ernie Els	1998	Steve Flesch
1991	John Daly	1995	Woody Austin	1999	Carlos Franco
1992	Mark Carnevale	1996	Tiger Woods	2000	Michael Clark II
1993	Vijay Singh	1997	Stewart Cink		

USPGA Tour statistics

DRIVING DISTANCE

John Daly	301.4 YARDS
Tiger Woods	298 YARDS
Davis Love III	288.7 YARDS
Phil Mickelson	288.7 YARDS
Scott McCarron	288 1/2 YARDS

GREENS IN REGULATION

Tiger Woods	75.2%
Joe Durant	72.3%
Kenny Perry	71.9%
Chris Perry	71.2%
Fred Couples	71.1%

SCORING

Tiger Woods	67.79
Phil Mickelson	69.25
Ernie Els	69.31
David Duval	69.41
Paul Azinger	69.68

DRIVING ACCURACY

Fred Funk	79.7%
Joe Durant	79.6%
Scott Verplank	78.8%
Loren Roberts	78.7%
Larry Mize	78%

SAND SAVES

Fred Couples	67%
Peter Jacobsen	64%
Craig Perks	63 1/2%
Kevin Sutherland	63.4%
Stuart Appleby	63.2%

ALL-AROUND

Tiger Woods	113
David Duval	184
Phil Mickelson	216
Steve Flesch	261
Ernie Els	286

TOTAL DRIVING

Tiger Woods	56
David Duval	57
Harrison Frazar	65
Sergio Garcia	65
Robert Allenby	75

PUTTING

Brad Faxon	1.704
Tiger Woods	1.717
Phil Mickelson	1.726
Paul Azinger	1.733
Sergio Garcia	1.733

USPGA Tour 2001 (Previous tournament names over the last 20 years:)

MERCEDES CHAMPIONSHIP: Infiniti Tournament of Champions (1991–93), Mony Tournament of Champions (1975–90)

TOUCHSTONE ENERGY TUCSON OPEN: Tucson Chrysler Classic (1997–98), Nortel Open (1996), Northern Telecom Open (1991–95), Northern Telecom Tucson Open (1988–90), Seiko-Tucson Open (1987), Seiko-Tucson Match Play Championship (1984–86), Joe Garagiola Tucson Open (1977–83)

SONY OPEN IN HAWAII: United Airlines Hawaiian Open (1992–98), United Hawaiian Open, Hawaiian Open (1965–90)

PHOENIX OPEN

AT&T PEBBLE BEACH NATIONAL PRO-AM: Bing Crosby National Professional-Amateur (1964–85)

BUICK INVITATIONAL: Shearson Lehman Brothers Open (1991), Shearson Lehman Hutton Open (1989–90), Shearson Lehman Hutton Andy Williams Open (1988), Shearson lehman Brothers Andy Williams Open (1986–87), Isuzu/Andy Williams San Diego Open (1983–85), Wickes/Andy Williams San Diego Open (1981–82)

BOB HOPE CHRYSLER CLASSIC: Bob Hope Classic (1984–85), Bob Hope Desert Classic (1965–83)

NISSAN OPEN: Nissan Los Angeles Open (1989–94), Los Angeles Open (1984-88), Glen Campbell Los Angeles Open (1971–83)

GENUITY CHAMPIONSHIP: Doral-Ryder Open (1987–2000), Doral-Eastern Open Invitational (1970–86)

HONDA CLASSIC: Honda Inverarry Classic (1982–83), American Motors Inverarry Classic (1981)

BAY HILL INVITATIONAL: Nestle Invitational (1989–95), Hertz Bay Hill Classic (1985–88), Bay Hill Classic (1980–84)

PLAYERS CHAMPIONSHIP: Tournament Players Championship (1974–87)

BELLSOUTH CLASSIC: BellSouth Atlanta Golf Classic (1989–91), Georgia-Pacific Atlanta Golf Classic (1982–88), Atlanta Classic (1967–81)

MASTERS

WORLDCOM CLASSIC: MCI Classic (1995–2000), MCI Heritage Classic (1987–94), Sea Pines Heritage Classic (1971–86)

SHELL HOUSTON OPEN: Independent Insurance Agent Open (1988–91), Big I Houston Open (1987), Houston Open (1985–86), Houston Coca-Cola Open (1983–84), Michelob Houston Open (1980–82)

GREATER GREENSBORO CHRYSLER CLASSIC: Kmart Greater Greensboro Open (1988–95), Greater Greensboro Open (1938–87)

COMPAQ CLASSIC OF NEW ORLEANS: Freeport-McDermott Classic (1996–98), Freeport McMoran Classic (1992–95), USF&G Classic (1982–91), USF&G New Orleans Open (1981), Greater New Orleans Open (1980)

VERIZON BRYON NELSON CLASSIC: GTE Bryon Nelson Golf Classic (1988–2000), Byron Nelson Golf Classic (1968–87)

MASTERCARD COLONIAL: Colonial National Invitation (1995), Southwestern Bell Colonial (1989–94), Colonial National Invitation Tournament (1946–88)

KEMPER INSURANCE OPEN: Kemper Open (1968–99)

THE MEMORIAL TOURNAMENT

FEDEX ST JUDE CLASSIC: Federal Express St Jude Classic (1986–94), St Jude Memphis Classic (1985), Danny Thomas Memphis Classic (1970–84)

US OPEN

BUICK CLASSIC: Manufacturers Hanover Westchester Classic (1979–89)

CANON GREATER HARTFORD OPEN: Canon-Sammy Davis Jr Greater Hartford Open (1985–88), Sammy Davis Jr-Greater Hartford Open (1973–84)

ADVIL WESTERN OPEN: Motorola Western Open (1994–99), Sprint Western Open (1993), Centel Western Open (1990–92), Beatrice Western Open (1987–89), Western Open (1899–86)

GREATER MILWAUKEE OPEN

BC OPEN

JOHN DEERE CLASSIC: Quad City Classic (1995–98), Hardee's Golf Classic (1986–94), Lite Quad Cities Open (1985), Miller High-Life Quad Cities Open (1982–84), Quad Cities Open (1980–81)

THE INTERNATIONAL: Sprint International (1994–99)

BUICK OPEN

PGA CHAMPIONSHIP

WGC-NEC INVITATIONAL: NEC World Series of Golf (1984–98), World Series of Golf (1976–83)

RENO-TAHOE OPEN

AIR CANADA CHAMPIONSHIP: Greater Vancouver Open (1996–98)

BELL CANADIAN OPEN: Canadian Open (1904–93)

MARCONI PENNSYLVANIA CLASSIC: SEI Pennsylvania Classic (2000)

WGC-AMERICAN EXPRESS CHAMPIONSHIP

TAMPA BAY CLASSIC

TEXAS OPEN AT LA CANTERA: Westin Texas Open (1998–2000), LaCantera Texas Open (1995–97), Texas Open (1994), HEB Texas Open (1990–93), Vantage Championship (1986), Texas Open (1981–85)

MICHELOB CHAMPIONSHIP AT KINGSMILL: Anheuser-Busch Golf Classic (1977–95)

INVENSYS CLASSIC AT LAS VEGAS: Las Vegas Invitational (1989–99), Panasonic Las Vegas Invitational (1984–88), Panasonic Las Vegas Pro-Celebrity Classic (1983)

NATIONAL CAR RENTAL GOLF CLASSIC AT WALT DISNEY WORLD RESORT: Walt Disney World/Oldsmobile Classic (1985–97), Walt Disney World Golf Classic (1982–84)

BUICK CHALLENGE: Buick Southern Open (1990–94), Southern Open Invitational (1971–89)

THE TOUR CHAMPIONSHIP: Nabisco Championships (1987–90)

SOUTHERN FARM BUREAU CLASSIC: Deposit Guaranty Golf Classic (1986–98), Magnolia State Classic (1968–85)

APPENDIX IV EUROPEAN MEN'S TOUR

ORDER OF MERIT 2000 – TOP-50

1 Lee Westwood	20 Mathias Gronberg	39 Greg Owen
2 Darren Clarke	21 Sergio Garcia	40 David Howell
3 Ernie Els	22 Per-Ulrik Johansson	41 Peter Senior
4 Michael Campbell	23 Patrik Sjoland	42 Nick O'Hern
5 Thomas Björn	24 Ian Woosnam	43 Ignacio Garrido
6 Colin Montgomerie	25 Fredrik Jacobson	44 Anthony Wall
7 Padraig Harrington	26 Paul Lawrie	45 Niclas Fasth
8 Philip Price	27 Emanuele Canonica	46 Alastair Forsyth
9 Jose Maria Olázàbal	28 Stephen Leaney	47 Peter O'Malley
10 Gary Orr	29 Brian Davis	48 Geoff Ogilvy
11 Miguel Angel Jiminez	30 Steen Tinning	49 Mark McNulty
12 Pierre Fulke	31 Ian Poulter	50 Dean Robertson
13 Jose Coceres	32 Jean van de Velde	
14. Angel Cabrera	33 Roger Chapman	
15 Retief Goosen	34 Ricardo Gonzalez	
16 Eduardo Romero	35 Roger Wessels	
17 Andrew Coltart	36 Jamie Spence	
18 Paul McGinley	37 Lucas Parsons	
19 Bernhard Langer	38 Jarmo Sandelin	

EUROPEAN TOUR TOURNAMENTS 2000

11–14 November
Johnnie Walker Classic
The Westin Resort, Ta Shee, Taiwan
Winner: Michael Campbell

13–16 January
The Alfred Dunhill Championship
Houghton Golf Club, Johannesburg, South Africa
Winner: Anthony Wall

20–23 January
Mercedes-Benz-Vodacom South African Open
Randpark Golf Club, Johannesburg, South Africa
Winner: Mathias Gronberg

27–30 January
Heineken Classic
The Vines Resort, Perth, Australia
Winner: Michael Campbell

3–6 February
Greg Norman Holden International
The Lakes Golf Club, Sydney, Australia
Winner: Lucas Parsons

10–13 February
The Benson & Hedges Malaysian Open
Templer Park Golf and Country Club, Kuala Lumpur, Malaysia
Winner: Wei-tze Yeh

17–20 February
Algarve Portuguese Open
Le Meridien Penina, Algarve, Portugal
Winner: Gary Orr

2–5 March
Dubai Desert Classic
Dubai Creek Golf and Yacht Club
Winner: Jose Coceres

9–12 March
Qatar Masters
Doha Golf Club, Qatar
Winner: Rolf Muntz

16–19 March
Madeira Island Open
Santo Da Serra, Madeira
Winner: Niclas Fasth

23–26 March
Brazil Rio De Janeiro 500 Years Open
Itanhanga, Rio de Janeiro, Brazil
Winner: Roger Chapman

30 March–2 April
Brazil Sao Paulo 500 Years Open
Sao Paulo Golf Club, Sao Paulo, Brazil
Winner: Padraig Harrington

14–16 April
Eurobet Seve Ballesteros Trophy
Sunningdale Golf Club, Berkshire, England
Winner: Continental Europe

20–23 April
Moroccan Open Meditel
Golf D'Amelkis, Marrakech, Morocco
Winner: Jamie Spence

28 April–1 May
Peugeot Open de Espana
PGA Golf de Catalunya, Girona, Spain
Winner: Brian Davis

4–7 May
Novotel Perrier Open de France
Le Golf National, Paris, France
Winner: Colin Montgomerie

11–14 May
Benson & Hedges International Open
De Vere Belfry, Sutton Coldfield, England
Winner: Jose Maria Olázàbal

18–21 May
Deutsche Bank-SAP Open TPC of Europe
Gut Kaden, Hamburg, Germany
Winner: Lee Westwood

26–29 May
Volvo PGA Championship
Wentworth Golf Club, Surrey, England
Winner: Colin Montgomerie

1–4 June
Compass Group English Open
Marriott Forest of Arden Hotel, Warwickshire, England
Winner: Darren Clarke

8–11 June
Celtic Manor Resort Wales Open,
Celtic Manor Resort, Newport, Wales
Winner: Steen Tinning

22–25 June
Compaq European Grand Prix
De Vere Slaley Hall, Northumberland, England
Winner: Lee Westwood

29 June–2 July
Murphy's Irish Open
Ballybunion Golf Club, County Kerry, Ireland
Winner: Patrik Sjoland

6–9 July
Smurfit Irish Open
The K Club, Dublin, Ireland
Winner: Lee Westwood

12–15 July
Standard Life Loch Lomond
Loch Lomond, Glasgow, Scotland
Winner: Ernie Els

27–30 July
TNT Dutch Open
Noordwijkse Golf Club, Noordwijkse, The Netherlands
Winner: Stephen Leaney

3–6 August
Volvo Scandinavian Masters
Kungsangen, Stockholm, Sweden
Winner: Lee Westwood

10–13 August
Victor Chandler British Masters
Woburn Golf and Country Club, Milton Keynes, England
Winner: Gary Orr

17–20 August
Buzzgolf.com North West of Ireland Open
Slieve Russell Hotel Golf Club, Country Cavan, Ireland
Winner: Massimo Scarpa

24–27 August
Scottish PGA Championship
Gleneagles Hotel, Auchterarder, Scotland
Winner: Pierre Fulke

31 August–3 September
BMW International Open
Golfclub Munchen Nord-Eichenried, Munich, Germany
Winner: Thomas Björn

7–10 September
Canon European Masters
Crans-Sur-Sierre, Crans Montana, Switzerland
Winner: Eduardo Romero

14–17 September
Trophee Lancome
Saint-Nom-La-Breteche, Paris, France
Winner: Retief Goosen

21–24 September
Belgacom Open
Royal Zoute, Knokke-Le Zoute, Belgium
Winner: Lee Westwood

28 September–1 October
Linde German Masters
Gut Larchenhof, Cologne, Germany
Winner: Michael Campbell

5–9 October
Cisco World Match Play Championships
Wentworth Golf Club, Surrey, England
Winner: Lee Westwood

19–22 October
BBVA Open Turespana Masters
Communidad de Madrid
Club De Campo, Madrid, Spain
Winner: Padraig Harrington

26–29 October
Italian Open
Is Molas, Sardinia, Italy
Winner: Ian Poulter

2–5 November
Volvo Masters
Montecastillo, Jerez, Spain
Winner: Pierre Fulke

Challenge Tour Order of Merit 2000 – Top-15

1	Henrik Stenson	6	Tobias Dier	11	Jose Manuel Lara
2	David Higgins	7	Fredrik Henge	12	Erol Simsek
3	Carlos Rodiles	8	Christian Cevaer	13	Jean Hugo
4	Mikael Lundberg	9	Johan Rystrom	14	Andrew Rait
5	Michele Reale	10	Trevor Immelman	15	Marco Bernardini

Golfer of the Year (Asprey & Garrard)

1990	Nick Faldo	1994	Ernie Els	1998	Lee Westwood
1991	Seve Ballesteros	1995	Colin Montgomerie	1999	Colin Montgomerie
1992	Nick Faldo	1996	Colin Montgomerie	2000	Lee Westwood
1993	Bernhard Langer	1997	Colin Montgomerie		

Harry Vardon Trophy (Order of Merit Leader)

1990	Ian Woosnam	1994	Colin Montgomerie	1998	Colin Montgomerie
1991	Seve Ballesteros	1995	Colin Montgomerie	1999	Colin Montgomerie
1992	Nick Faldo	1996	Colin Montgomerie	2000	Lee Westwood
1993	Colin Montgomerie	1997	Colin Montgomerie		

Rookie of the Year

1990	Russell Claydon	1994	Jonathan Lomas	1998	Olivier Redmond
1991	Per-Ulrik Johansson	1995	Jarmo Sandelin	1999	Sergio Garcia
1992	Jim Payne	1996	Thomas Björn		
1993	Gary Orr	1997	Scott Henderson		

European Tour 2000 Statistics

DRIVING DISTANCE

Emanuele Canonica	295.3 YARDS
Angel Cabrera	293.5 YARDS
Adam Scott	292.4 YARDS
Ricardo Gonzalez	291.4 YARDS
Stephen Allan	290.5 YARDS

GREENS IN REGULATION

Gary Orr	77.8%
Colin Montgomerie	77.1%
Jose Coceres	76.4%
Ian Garbutt	74.4%
Greg Owen	74.3%

SAND SAVES

Tony Johnstone	78.9%
Ian Hutchings	77.9%
Mark Mouland	77.8%
John Senden	71.2%
Bernhard Langer	70.6%

DRIVING ACCURACY

Richard Green	79.5%
Jose Coceres	78.7%
John Bickerton	78%
Gary Orr	76.3%
Pierre Fulke	75.6%

PUTTING

Lee Westwood	1.718
Michael Campbell	1.719
Pierre Fulke	1.726
Jamie Spence	1.741
Philip Price	1.743

STROKE AVERAGE

Lee Westwood	69.62
Ernie Els	69.67
Michael Campbell	70.25
Colin Montgomerie	70.26
Darren Clarke	70.29

APPENDIX V MISC MEN'S TOUR

OFFICIAL WORLD GOLF RANKING 2000 – TOP-50

1 Tiger Woods	21 Mike Weir	41 Dudley Hart
2 Ernie Els	22 Loren Roberts	42 Greg Norman
3 David Duval	23 David Toms	43 Steve Flesch
4 Phil Mickelson	24 Padraig Harrington	44 Jose Coceres
5 Lee Westwood	25 Carlos Franco	45 Pierre Fulke
6 Colin Montgomerie	26 Bob May	46 Scott Hoch
7 Davis Love III	27 Miguel Angel Jiminez	47 Angel Cabrera
8 Hal Sutton	28 Kirk Triplett	48 Mark Calcavecchia
9 Vijay Singh	29 Chris Perry	49 Shigeki Maruyama
10 Tom Lehman	30 Paul Azinger	50 Scott Verplank
11 Jesper Parnevik	31 Stuart Appleby	
12 Darren Clarke	32 Rocco Mediate	
13 Nick Price	33 Notah Begay III	
14 Michael Campbell	34 Jose Maria Olázàbal	
15 Jim Furyk	35 Robert Allenby	
16 Sergio Garcia	36 Duffy Waldorf	
17 Stewart Cink	37 Jeff Maggert	
18 Justin Leonard	38 Retief Goosen	
19 John Huston	39 Fred Couples	
20 Thomas Björn	40 Eduardo Romero	

WORLD GOLF CHAMPIONSHIPS 2000

23–27 February
WGC-Andersen Consulting Match Play
La Costa Resort, Carlsbad, California, USA
Winner: Darren Clarke

24–27 August
WGC-NEC Invitational
Firestone Country Club, Akron, Ohio, USA
Winner: Tiger Woods

9–12 November
American Express World Golf Championship
Valderrama, Satogrande, Spain
Winner: Mike Weir

7–10 December
WGC-EMC World Cup
Buenos Aires Golf Club, Buenos Aires, Argentina
WINNERS: Tiger Woods and David Duval

APPENDIX VI LADIES TOURS

US LADIES TOUR 2000 – TOP-25

1 Karrie Webb
2 Annika Sorenstam
3 Meg Mallon
4 Juli Inkster
5 Lorie Kane
6 Pat Hurst
7 Mi Hyun Kim
8 Dottie Pepper
9 Rosie Jones
10 Michele Redman
11 Laura Davies
12 Se Ri Pak
13 Sophie Gustafson
14 Janice Moodie
15 Cristie Kerr
16 Sherri Steinhauer
17 Rachel Hetherington
18 Nancy Scranton
19 Grace Park
20 Charlotta Sorenstam
21 Betsy King
22 Kelly Robbins
23 Brandie Burton
24 Leta Lindley
25 Dorothy Delasin

US LADIES TOURNAMENT SCHEDULE 2000

13–16 January
The Office Depot
Ibis G&CC West Palm Beach, Florida
Winner: Karrie Webb

20–23 January
Subaru Memorial of Naples
Club at The Strand, Naples, Florida
Winner: Nancy Scranton

11–13 February
Los Angeles Women's Championship
Wood Ranch GC, Simi Valley, California
Winner: Laura Davies

17–19 February
Cup Noodles Hawaiian Ladies Open
Kapolei GC, Kapolei, Oahu, Hawaii
Winner: Betsy King

24–27 February
Australian Ladies Masters
Royal Pines Resort, Ashmore, Queensland, Australia
Winner: Karrie Webb

2–4 March
LPGA Takefuji Classic
Kona CC, Kailua-Kona, Hawaii
Winner: Karrie Webb

9–12 March
Welch's/Circle K Championship
Randolph North GC, Tucson, Arizona
Winner: Annika Sorenstam

16–19 March
Standard Register PING
Legacy Golf Resort, Phoenix, Arizona
Winner: Charlotta Sorenstam

23–26 March
Nabisco Championship
Mission Hills CC, Rancho Mirage, California
Winner: Karrie Webb

13–16 April
Longs Drugs Challenge
Twelve Bridges GC, Lincoln, California
Winner: Juli Inkster

28–30 April
Chick-fil-A Charity Championship
Eagles Landing CC, Stockbridge, Georgia
Winner: Sophie Gustafson

4–7 May
The Phillips Invitational
Onion Creek Club, Austin, Texas
Winner: Laura Davies

12–14 May
Electrolux USA Championship
The Legends GC, Franklin, Tennessee
Winner: Pat Hurst

19–21 May
Firstar LPGA Classic
CC of the North, Beavercreek, Ohio
Winner: Annika Sorenstam

25–28 May
LPGA Corning Classic
Corning CC, Corning, New York
Winner: Betsy King

1–4 June
Kathy Ireland-Greens.com LPGA Classic
Wachesaw Plantation East GC, Murrells Inlet,
S. Carolina
Winner: Grace Park

8–11 June
Wegmans Rochester International
Locust Hill CC, Pittsford, New York
Winner: Meg Mallon

15–18 June
Evian Masters
Royal Evian Club Course, Evian, France
Winner: Annika Sorenstam

22–25 June
McDonald's LPGA Championship
DuPont CC, Wilmington, Delaware
Winner: Juli Inkster

30 June–2 July
ShopRite LPGA Classic
Marriott Seaview Resort (Bay Course),
Atlantic City, New Jersey
Winner: Janice Moodie

6–9 July
Jamie Farr Kroger Classic
Highland Meadows GC, Sylvania, Ohio
Winner: Annika Sorenstam

13–16 July
Japan Airlines Big Apple Classic
Wykagyl CC, New Rochelle, New York
Winner: Annika Sorenstam

20–23 July
U.S. Women's Open
Merit Club, Libertyville, Illinois
Winner: Karrie Webb

28–30 July
Giant Eagle LPGA Classic
Avalon Lakes, Warren, Ohio
Winner: Dorothy Delasin

4–6 August
Michelob Light Classic
Fox Run GC, St. Louis, Missouri
Winner: Lorie Kane

10–13 August
du Maurier Classic
Royal Ottawa GC, Aylmer, Quebec, Canada
Winner: Meg Mallon

17–20 August
Weetabix Women's British Open
Royal Birkdale GC, Lancashire, England
Winner: Sophie Gustafson

24–27 August
Oldsmobile Classic
Walnut Hills CC, East Lansing, Michigan
Winner: Karrie Webb

1–3 September
State Farm Rail Classic
The Rail GC, Springfield, Illinois
Winner: Laurel Kean

8–10 September
First Union Betsy King Classic
Berkleigh CC, Kutztown, Pennsylvania
Winner: Michele Redman

22–24 September
Safeway LPGA Golf Championship
Columbia Edgewater CC, Portland, Oregon
Winner: Mi Hyun Kim

28 September–1 October
New Albany Golf Classic
New Albany CC, New Albany, Ohio
Winner: Lorie Kane

12–15 October
Samsung World Championship
of Women's Golf
Hidden Brooke Country Club, Vallejo, California
Winner: Juli Inkster

19–22 October
AFLAC Champions
RTJ Trail (Magnolia Groves), Mobile, Alabama
Winner: Karrie Webb

27–29 October
Cisco World Ladies Challenge
Sohsei Country Club Narita, Chiba, Japan
Japan

3–5 November
Mizuno Classic
Otsu, Japan
Winner: Lorie Kane

16–19 November
Arch Wireless Championship
LPGA International Legends Course, Daytona Beach, Florida
Winner: Dottie Pepper

EUROPEAN LADIES TOUR (2000) – TOP-25

1 Sophie Gustafson
2 Kirsty Taylor
3 Alison Nicholas
4 Trish Johnson
5 Raquel Carriedo
6 Marinne Monnet
7 Alison Munt
8 Patricia Meunier Lebouc
9 Valerie Van Ryckegham
10 Joanne Morley
11 Laura Davies
12 Silvia Cavalleri
13 Kathryn Marshall
14 Samantha Head
15 Sandrine Mandiburu
16 Joanna Head
17 Karen Pearce
18 Laurette Moritz
19 Catrina Nilsmark
20 Elizabeth Esterl
21 Sofia Gronberg Whitmore
22 Asa Gottmo
23 Maria Hjorth
24 Gina Marie Scott
25 Vibeke Stensrud

LADIES EUROPEAN TOUR TOURNAMENTS 2000

17–20 February
Women's Australian Open
Yarra Yarra Golf Club, Melbourne, Australia
Winner: Karrie Webb

18–21 May
Ladies Italian Open\
Poggio dei Medici, Tuscany, Italy
Winner: Sophie Gustafson

26–28 May
Hanover Expo 2000 Ladies Open
Rethmar Links, Hannover, Germany
Winner: Alison Munt

1–4 June
Chrysler Open
Halmstad, Sweden
Winner: Carin Koch

8–11 June
Waterford Crystal Ladies Irish Open
Faithlegg, Waterford, Ireland
Winner: Sophie Gustafson

14–17 June
Evian Masters
Evian Les Bains, Switzerland
Winner: Annika Sorenstam

29 June–2 July
Ladies French Open
Arras, Anzin St Aubin, France
Winner: Patricia Meunier Lebouc

6–9 July
Stilwerk Ladies German Open
Treudelberg, Germany
Winner: Joanne Morley

13–15 July
Ladies Austrian Open
Steiermarkischer Murhof, Austria
Winner: Patricia Meunier Lebouc

4–6 August
Daily Telegraph Ladies British Masters
Mottram Hall, Cheshire, England
Winner: Trish Johnson

17–20 August
Weetabix Women's British Open
Royal Birkdale, Lancashire, England
Winner: Sophie Gustafson

24–27 August
Compaq Open
Barseback, Sweden
Winner: Juli Inkster

31 August–2 September
Kronenbourg 1664 Chart Hills Classic
Chart Hills, England
Winner: Gina Scott

15–17 September
TSN Ladies World Cup of Golf
Adare Manor, Ireland
Winner: Sweden

21–23 September
Mexx Sport Open
Kennemer, Holland
Winner: Tina Fischer

13–15 October
Marrakech Palmaraie Open
Marrakech, Morocco
Winner: Alison Munt

APPENDIX VII SENIORS TOURS

US SENIOR TOUR (2000) – TOP-25

1 Larry Nelson	10 Tom Jenkins	19 Bruce Summerhays
2 Bruce Fleisher	11 Tom Kite	20 Walter Hall
3 Hale Irwin	12 Jose Maria Canizares	21 John Bland
4 Gil Morgan	13 Tom Watson	22 Tom Wargo
5 Dana Quigley	14 John Jacobs	23 Vicente Fernandez
6 Jim Thorpe	15 Leonard Thompson	24 Jim Colbert
7 Allen Doyle	16 Joe Inman	25 Jim Dent
8 Doug Tewell	17 Ed Dougherty	
9 Hubert Green	18 Mike McCullough	

US SENIORS TOUR – 2000

20–23 January
MasterCard Championship
Hualalai Golf Club, Kaupulehu-Kona, Hawaii
Winner: George Archer

31 January–6 February
Royal Caribbean Classic
Key Biscayne, Florida
Winner: Bruce Fleisher

7–13 February
ACE Group Classic
Naples, Florida
Winner: Lanny Wadkins

14–20 February
GTE Classic
Lutz, Florida
Winner: Bruce Fleisher

21–27 February
LiquidGolf.com Invitational
Sarasota, Florida
Winner: Tom Wargo

28 February–5 March
Toshiba Senior Classic Club
Newport Beach, California
Winner: Allen Doyle

6–12 March
Audi Senior Classic
Puebla, Mexico
Winner: Hubert Green

13–19 March
Liberty Mutual Legends of Golf
St. Augustine, Florida
Winner: Andy North & Jim Colbert

20–26 March
Emerald Coast Classic
Milton, Florida
Winner: Gil Morgan

March–2 April
The Countrywide Tradition
Desert Mountain (Cochise Course), Scottsdale, Arizona
Winner: Tom Kite

10–16 April
PGA Seniors Championship*
PGA National Golf Club (Champion), Palm Beach Gardens, Florida
Winner: Doug Tewell

17–23 April
Las Vegas Senior Classic by TruGreen-ChemLawn
TPC at Summerlin, Las Vegas, Nevada
Larry Nelson

24–30 April
Bruno's Memorial Classic
Greystone Golf Club, Birmingham, Alabama
Winner: John Jacobs

1–7 May
The Home Depot Invitational
TPC at Piper Glen, Charlotte, N. Carolina
Winner: Bruce Fleisher

8–14 May
Nationwide Championship
The Golf Club of Georgia (Lakeside),
Alpharetta, Georgia
Winner: Hale Irwin

15–21 May
TD Waterhouse Championship
Tiffany Greens Golf Club, Kansas City, Missouri
Winner: Dana Quigley

22–28 May
Boone Valley Classic
Boone Valley Golf Club, Augusta, Missouri
Winner: Larry Nelson

29 May–4 June
BellSouth Senior Classic at Opryland
Springhouse Golf Club, Nashville, Tennessee
Winner: Hale Irwin

5–11 June
SBC Senior Open
Kemper Lakes, Long Grove, Illinois
Winner: Tom Kite

12–18 June
SBC Championship
The Dominion Country Club, San Antonio, Texas
Winner: Doug Tewell

19–25 June
Cadillac NFL Golf Classic
Upper Montclair Country Club,
Clifton, New Jersey
Winner: Lee Trevino

26 June–2 July
U.S. Senior Open *
Saucon Valley Country Club, Bethlehem,
Pennsylvania
Winner: Hale Irwin

3–9 July
State Farm Senior Classic
Hobbit's Glen Golf Club, Columbia, Maryland
Winner: Leonard Thompson

10–16 July
FORD SENIOR PLAYERS Championship
TPC of Michigan, Dearborn, Mississippi
Winner: Ray Floyd

Jul 17–23
Instinet Classic
TPC at Jasna Polana, Princeton, New Jersey
Winner: Gil Morgan

24–30 July
Lightpath Long Island Classic
Meadow Brook Club, Jericho, New York
Winner: Bruce Fleisher

31 July–6 August
Coldwell Banker Burnet Classic
Bunker Hills Golf Club, Coon Rapids, Minnesota
Winner: Ed Dougherty

7–13 August
AT&T Canada Senior Open Championship
St. Charles Golf & Country Club,
Winnipeg, Manitoba, Canada
Winner: Tom Jenkins

14–20 August
Novell Utah Showdown
Park Meadows Country Club, Park City, Utah
Winner: Doug Tewell

21–27 August
FleetBoston Classic
Nashawtuc Country Club,
Concord, Massachussetts
Winner: Larry Nelson

28 August–3 September
Foremost Insurance Championship
Egypt Valley Country Club, Ada, Minnesota
Winner: Larry Nelson

4–10 September
Comfort Classic
Indianapolis, Indiana
Winner: Gil Morgan

11–17 September
Kroger Senior Classic
The Golf Center at Kings Island (Grizzly),
Mason, Ohio
Winner: Hubert Green

18–24 September
One Senior Championship
Dallas, Texas
Winner: Larry Nelson

25 September–1 October
Vantage Championship
Tanglewood Park (Championship), Clemmons, N. Carolina
Winner: Larry Nelson

2–8 October
The Transamerica
Silverado Resort (South), Napa, California
Winner: Jim Thorpe

9–15 October
Gold Rush Classic
Serrano Country Club, El Dorado Hills, Napa, California
Winner: Jim Thorpe

16–22 October
EMC2 Kaanapali Classic
Kaanapali Golf Course (North), Maui, Hawaii
Winner: Hale Irwin

23–29 October
SBC Senior Classic
The Wilshire Country Club, Los Angeles, California
Winner: Joe Inman

30 October–5 November
IR SENIOR TOUR Championship
TPC of Myrtle Beach, Myrtle Beach, S. Carolina
Winner: Tom Watson

EUROPEAN SENIORS TOUR ORDER OF MERIT 2000 – TOP-10

1 Noel Ratcliffe
2 John Grace
3 Denis O'Sullivan
4 Tommy Horton
5 Ian Stanley
6 Priscillo Diniz
7 David Huish
8 David Oakley
9 Neil Coles
10 David Creamer

EUROPEAN SENIOR TOUR TOURNAMENTS 2000

30 March–1 April
Royal Westmoreland Barbados Open
Royal Westmoreland GC, Barbados
Winner: Tommy Horton

5–7 May
Beko Classic
Gloria Golf Resort, Turkey
Winner: Brian Huggett

12–14 May
AIB Irish Seniors Open
Tulfarris, Ireland
Winner: Bruce Fleisher

2–4 June
Microlease Jersey Seniors Open
La Moye, Jersey
Winner: Neil Coles

22–24 June
Lawrence Batley Seniors
Huddersfield, England
Winner: David Huish

30 June–2 July
Coca-Cola Kaiser Karl European Trophy
Haus Kambach, Germany
Winner: Ian Stanley

7–9 July
TotalFina Seniors Open
Le Golf de Joyenval, France
Winner: Nick Job

27–30 July
Senior British Open
Royal County Down, Northern Ireland
Winner: Christy O'Connor Jnr

4–6 August
Energis Senior Masters
Wentworth, England
Winner: David Creamer

11–13 August
Bad Ragaz PGA Seniors Open
Bad Ragaz, Switzerland
Winner: David Huish

18–20 August
De Vere Hotels Seniors Classic
Ferndown, England
Winner: David Oakley

25–28 August
The Belfry PGA Seniors Championship
PGA National, England
Winner: John Grace

1–3 September
The Scotsman Scottish Seniors Open
Dalmahoy, Scotland
Noel Ratcliffe

8–10 September
Ordina Legends in Golf
Crayestein, Holland
John Grace

15–17 September
Tui Golf Championship Fleesensee
Fleesensee, Germany
Jeff van Wagenen

22–24 September
TEMES Seniors Open
Glyfada, Greece
Noel Ratcliffe

6–8 October
Big 3 Records Monte Carlo Invitational
Monte Carlo, France
John Grace

11–14 October
Daily Telegraph European Seniors Match Play
Le Meridien Penina, Portugal
Priscillo Diniz

20–22 October
Dan Technology Senior Tournament of Champions
The Buckinghamshire, England
Denis O'Sullivan

26–28 October
Abu Dhabi European Seniors Tour Championship
Abu Dhabi
Denis O'Sullivan

BIBLIOGRAPHY

I consulted a wide variety of sources in the compilation of this volume, and what follows is a necessarily incomplete but, I hope, helpful reading list.

The indispensable background references for any serious student of the current game are the Media Guides published on an annual basis by the various Tours. These contain an amazing wealth of information – statistical, anecdotal and historical – and provide a level of detail which would be impossible to match in this relatively small volume. As they can be difficult to find in the average bookshop, contact the marketing departments of the Tour headquarters direct.

There is also a number of good general reference books which provide much information on the game's history, development and players, the best by some distance being Derek Lawrenson's lucid and authoritative *Complete Encyclopedia of Golf*. *The Ultimate Encyclopedia of Golf*, by Ted Barrett and Michael Hobbs and Michael Campbell's *The Encyclopedia of Golf* are also useful primers. The European PGA Tour also publishes an annual *European Tour Yearbook*, an illustrated guide to the season which covers all the tournaments of the previous year. A more exhaustive and comprehensive guide to the world game is Mark McCormack's *The World of Professional Golf*, a 700-page annual commentary on the previous season worldwide with tournament reports, statistics, placings, scores and ranking tables. Also valuable, although aimed principally at the betting market, are the annual *Elliot's Golf Form Guide* and *Racing and Football Outlook's Golf*, both of which offer player profiles and form guides to the coming season on the US and European Men's Tours as well as all the results and placings from the season just gone. The annual *Royal and Ancient Golfer's Handbook* is also a useful source book, although it is rather UK-centric and its remit is wider than professional golf.

There are numerous guides to, histories of and reflections on the Majors and a good selection will be found in most bookstores. A useful reference to have to hand is *The Golf Majors Records and Yearbook*, by Alun Evans, which lists the leading scorers and placings in all four Majors since the first British Open teed off in 1860, as does the *Virgin Golf Record File*. If you'd like to find out more about the leading courses worldwide then look no further than the well-illustrated and comprehensive *World Atlas of Golf*, while the USPGA Tour venues are described in *Golf Magazine's Golfwatching* by George Peper. Otherwise, there is a wide selection of course guides, national and regional, in most decent bookstores.

Sports journalists, too, have recently contributed some fine books on the subject of the professional tours, particularly John Feinstein's revealing and award-winning *A Good Walk Spoiled* – on the 1994 USPGA Tour – and his equally impressive sequel, *The Majors*, which concentrates on the four 1998 tournaments. Feinstein well conveys the pressures and tensions faced by the top modern US golfers, as well as the exhilaration and disappointments which the US Tour brings. Also worth reading are *Bud, Sweat and Tees: A Walk on the Wild Side of the PGA Tour*, by Alan Shipnuck, an account of Rich Beem's rookie 1999 season and his unlikely win at the Kemper Open, and Esteban Toledo's biography – *Tin Cup Dreams: A Long Shot Makes It on the PGA Tour*, by Michael D'Antonio – which exposes the less glamorous side of the US Tour. Also of interest is John Streegs's *Tournament Week – Inside the Ropes and Behind the Scenes on the PGA Tour. Diamonds in the Rough*, by Mark Shaw, offers an insider's view on the 1997 US Senior Tour while Jim Burnett's *Tee Times* is a perceptive chronicle of the 1996 US Ladies Tour. The European Tour has not been ignored, particularly with Lawrence Donnegan's amusing *Four Iron in the Soul* (his account of a season caddying for Ross Drummond) and Lauren St John's *Fairway Dreams*. For an insight into the pressures and tensions of the Ryder Cup, read Mark James' controversial *Inside the Bear Pit*, a captain's perspective on the 1999 Brookline tournament. Top players' biographies and autobiographies also keep appearing, some of the more recent being *Zinger* (Paul Azinger), *A Feel for the Game* (Ben Crenshaw), which contains the US captain's reflections on Brookline and Larry Guest's *The Payne Stewart Story*. Tim Rosaforte's *Raising the Bar* is, naturally enough, on Tiger Woods and Gary McCord's *Just a Range Ball in a Box of Titleists* lives up to the promise of its title.

Then there are newspapers – particularly, for my purposes in the UK, The *Daily* and *Sunday Telegraph*, *Racing Post*, *The Times*, *The Guardian* and *Scotland on Sunday* – and a wide selection of magazines, from *Golf Monthly, Women and Golf* and *Golf International* in the UK and *Golf Digest, Golf Illustrated, Golf Magazine, Golf World, Senior Golfer* and *Golf For Women* in the USA.

As for television, a warm hand for SKY's excellent coverage of golf in the UK, without which it would be virtually impossible to keep up with tournaments across the world and with developments on the various Tours. And finally, John Updike's lyrical, affectionate and absorbing collection of essays – *Golf Dreams* – considers the game's perversities, elations and mysteries, and helps explain why we play golf in the first place.

INTERNET GOLF

The worldwide web is the best place to keep up with developments in world professional golf. The leading sites are constantly updated to give the latest news on tournaments, interviews, videos and players, and profiles, statistics and features are freely available.

For an initial taste of the sheer quantity of information on the internet, check out some general sites – for example, **www.golfsight.com** and **www.golf.com** – or links sites such as **www.golfweb.com**, **www.golflinks.com**, **www.golfbytes.com**, **www.piagolf.co.kr/golflinkswww** or **yahoo.com.** For specific tours and tournaments contact the following:

USPGA Tour/US Seniors Tour: **www.pgatour.com**
US Ladies: **www.lpga.com**
European Tour: **www.europeantour.com**
European Ladies: **www.ladieseuropeantour.com**
Australasian Tour: **www.pgatour.com.au**
South African Tour: **www.pgatour.co.za**
Asian Tour: **www.asianpgatour.com**

There are also several online golfing magazines which provide up-to-the-minute news and comment, such as *Golf Illustrated* (**www.golfillustrated.com**), *Golf Digest* (**www.golf.digest.com**), *Golf Week* (**www.golfweek.com**), *Golf Magazine* (**www.golfonline.com**) and *Golf Today* (**www.golftoday.co.uk**). Several TV and media companies also have their own golf-related websites. These include CNN/*Sports Illustrated* (**www.cnnsi.com**), CBS (**www.cbs.sportsline.com**), The Golf Channel (**www.thegolfchannel.com**), ESPN (**espnet.sportszone.com**), Fox (**www.foxsports.com**) and TSN (**www.sportsnetwork.com**).

Many of the individual tournaments and competitions have their own sites, including the Ryder Cup (**www.rydercup.com**), the US Open (**www.usopen.com**), The Masters (**www.masters.org**) and the AT&T Pebble Beach Pro-Am (**www.attpebblebeachproam.com**). Many of the larger newspapers in the USA and the UK have specific sites dedicated to golf. As a sample, try *The New York Times* (**www.nytimes.com**), *USA Today* (**www.usatoday.com**), *The Daily Telegraph* (**www.telegraph.co.uk**) and *The Scotsman* (**www.scotsman.com**).

Several of the leading players have their own websites – John Daly (**www.gripitandripit.com**), Ernie Els (**www.ernieels.com**), Lee Westwood (**www.lee-westwood.co.uk**) and Tiger Woods (**www.tigerwoods.com**) are just a few of these. Type what you want to know into a search engine, such as Google (**www.google.com**) or Ask Jeeves (**www.askjeeves.com**), and the odds are that you'll find it somewhere. Other useful addresses include the Royal and Ancient (**www.randa.org**), the USGA (**www.usga.org**), USPGA (**www.pga.com**) and the World Golf Village and Hall of Fame (**www.wgv.com**). And for fans of US Seniors golf, **www.broadcast.com** contains the last two years' episodes of 'Inside the Senior Tour'.

Acknowledgements in Source Order

Mark Newcombe/ Visions in Golf 15, 16, 35, 41, 43, 53, 122, 128, 133 right, 149, 151, 165, 210 left, 210 right, 212, 217, 219 right, 225, 231, 248.
The Phil Sheldon Golf Picture Library 24, 26, 27, 33, 40, 46 left, 46 right, 54, 55, 62, 65, 68, 77, 78, 79, 82, 84, 86, 88, 93, 95, 99, 103, 106, 107, 111, 112, 113, 114, 115, 116, 117, 121, 123, 125, 129, 131, 133 left, 134, 139, 141, 142, 147, 150, 152, 153, 158, 159, 160, 161, 166, 167, 172, 173, 174, 180, 183, 186, 187, 189, 191, 192, 195, 198, 201, 205, 209, 211, 213, 214, 219 left, 227, 232, 239, 243, 246, 249, 250, 254 left, 254 right, 255.

EXECUTIVE EDITORS: Julian Brown and Trevor Davies
EDITOR: Rachel Lawrence
DESIGNER: Geoff Fennell
PICTURE RESEARCH: Zoë Holtermann
PRODUCTION CONTROLLER: Ian Paton
ADDITIONAL TEXT: Nick Wright
INFORMATION DATABASE COMPILED BY JIM LINDSAY
TEXT PROVIDED BY SPORT AND LEISURE BOOKS LTD